ANSELM WEBER, O.F.M.

Missionary to the Navaho, 1898–1921

Chischilli with visitors at St. Michaels

ANSELM WEBER, O.F.M.

Missionary to the Navaho

1898-1921

ROBERT L. WILKEN

With fondest regards to Ann
R L Wilken

THE BRUCE PUBLISHING COMPANY
MILWAUKEE

Nihil obstat: LAMBERT BROCKMANN, O.F.M., *Censor deputatus*
Imprimi potest: VINCENT KROGER, O.F.M., Provincial, Cincinnati, Ohio
Nihil obstat: MONSIGNOR EDW. J. HICKEY, *Censor deputatus*
Imprimatur: ✠ EDWARD CARDINAL MOONEY, Archbishop of Detroit
September 25, 1953

Copyright, 1955, The Bruce Publishing Company
Made in the United States of America

Dedicated to my Franciscan confreres
who spend themselves so selflessly
in the Navaho mission for the
growth of Christ's Body

Preface

Anselm Weber of the Order of Friars Minor established the first permanent Catholic mission among the Navaho Indians at St. Michaels, Apache County, Arizona. In point of time his life spanned the period from the Civil War to the end of World War I, 1862–1921. While as a missionary he belonged to the first quarter of the twentieth century, he has a rightful place in that long line of Catholic missionaries that ties together the centuries back to apostolic times.

Physical conditions of life and travel facing the "Apostle to the Navaho" in 1898 were scarcely less harsh than in earlier ages. Even though in 1915 he could jolt over Navaho trails and across arroyos in an open Ford car, and could run tap water while resting at St. Michaels, his relationship as missioner to a thoroughly pagan people left his essential service of selflessness unchanged.

In many respects his task was actually harder than in earlier times. Not only were the Navaho utterly pagan: they distrusted and feared whites and generally detested most of what whites represented. Moreover the whites of the area, for the most part, were indifferent to religion; the government workers usually reflected the official government attitude of neutral toleration, which sometimes bordered on opposition, particularly where sectarianism was rife. For Anselm Weber it was definitely a problem of winning the Navaho's confidence before he might expect a favorable hearing for his religious message.

The Navaho language and thought patterns, which defied accurate translation, made harder the problem of the missionary, who could hope for no foreseeable cultural change or rift. Strangeness and intricacy of language and conceptual patterns only drew the Navaho closer under his blanket of group isolation and group self-centeredness. Only a complete upheaval, such as an economic revolution, might have burst the shell of tribal solidarity.

Paradoxically to some, it was in this very area that Anselm Weber provided the Indians with their strongest defense against cultural breakdown. He worked for their group independence by promoting tribal ownership, opposing family allotments on reservation land, and by gaining for the prolific tribe vast new land areas to support their sheep.

To convert a pagan community, the Franciscan missioner realized, meant to create a new soul within a people. Conversion to be genuine could not deal with superficial veneers, mere additions, or name changing. Religion is a core, a cluster of key concepts and values, around which a people's whole way of life, its culture, grows.

Accordingly Anselm Weber projected his plan to Christianize the Navaho toward a future date far beyond his lifetime. Personally he was content to plod along, laying the groundwork and clearing the way until the fullness of time, according to God's good pleasure, when his Franciscan confreres might reap the harvest.

Some of these facts in the life of Father Anselm Weber have been set down in various mission magazine articles. This present study attempts to draw together in one source the outstanding features of his life as an Indian missionary from 1898 to 1921, the time of his death. The author wishes to reconstruct Anselm Weber's larger works, especially the founding of St. Michaels Mission with its system of regional outposts, its thoroughly scientific linguistic and ethnological approach, and its educational and social services.

In the introductory Chapter I, "Navaho Backgrounds," no pretense is made at offering a definitive chapter on Navaho history. However, some résumé of tribal history seemed necessary for an understanding of Navaho ways and traditions; hence the brief sketch based on reputable secondary sources is given.

Rather lengthy treatment has been given to the period 1898–1903, the first five years of the Navaho mission, including the opening of the boarding school, and the fixing of a flexible and experimental mission program. These early chapters also attempt to portray daily life during the cradle days of the Franciscan Navaho mission. A survey is offered which traces the leading role played by Anselm Weber in the taking over again by Franciscans of the Rio Grande missions, and the renewing of work among the Pueblos and Hispanos of New Mexico, a service of Father Anselm frequently overlooked.

Some insights are also offered for evaluating the degree and quality of direction and financial aid given to the missions by Franciscan leadership of the Province of St. John the Baptist of Cincinnati. On this latter point there can be seen the outline of Father Anselm's policy and method of promoting designs and projects within the political framework of an authoritarian community control. He displayed rare success in the technique of volume production of propaganda letters with which he bombarded and wore down those individuals who were in central control in his province of the Franciscan Order.

Interpretation belonging in part more properly to anthropology than to history has been attempted in Chapter XIII in an effort to analyze Anselm Weber's missionological approach to Navaho religious belief.

Anselm Weber maintained a huge correspondence with his Franciscan confreres, with the Bureau of Catholic Indian Missions, with government agencies, and with a host of friends and relatives. These letters and papers, preserved in five principal collections, have furnished the base for research. Fortunately for the historian, the missionary saved practically every letter he received, and made copies of all business letters he wrote, even before be began to use a typewriter in 1903. Moreover, he wrote regularly and on a great variety of subjects for mission and church magazines.

While from a historical stand the author deeply values the completely impersonal tone of these primary sources, it is still regrettable that these documents fail to throw conclusive light on the personal attitudes, reflections, and missionary hopes or regrets of Father Anselm. The letters are rigidly factual and objective. Happily it was not too late to consult contemporaries, friends, and acquaintances among clergy and laity, who were gracious in furnishing added data on the personality of this Navaho missionary.

Deep thanks are due a host of persons who gave generously of time and talent to advance this work. I should like to offer special acknowledgment to all whose names appear in the footnotes in connection with interviews, questionnaires, and letters sent in response to many bothersome appeals for help and information.

Likewise I offer my sincere thanks for the aid and counsel given by Frank D. Reeve, Professor of History, University of New Mexico; to my Franciscan confreres, John Forest McGee, since deceased, Berard Haile, Barnabas Meyer, Robert Kalt, Jerome Hesse, Turibius Christman, Emmanuel Trockur, who read and criticized the manuscript; to Anthony Kroger, Burcard Fisher, Silver Meyer, and Elmer Von Hagel, present superior at St. Michaels; to J. B. Tennelly, Director of the Bureau of Catholic Indian Missions at Washington, who gave critical advice and deeply valuable suggestions; to Jewell Adams, who furnished the "Anna Burbridge Day *Diary*"; and to Mother Philip Neri and the Sisters at Cornwells Heights, who were extremely kind with their archival materials.

For financial aid during my studies at the University of New Mexico and after, while carrying on research, I am deeply indebted to my friends Walter and Ly Werner, John Murray and Gustava Holahan Murray, and to Harry Read. For typing the manuscript I wish to thank Elizabeth Forte and Florence Forte Payne.

ROBERT L. WILKEN, O.F.M.

Detroit, Michigan
March 25, 1953

Contents

Preface vii

List of Abbreviations xiv

I. Navaho Backgrounds 3

II. La Cienega Ranch 22

III. First Friars at St. Michaels 33

IV. Student of the Navaho, 1899 43

V. Experiments Toward a Mission Plan, 1900 . 56

VI. Founding of St. Michaels Boarding School . 73

VII. Teachers and Pupils Arrive 91

VIII. Chin Lee and Lukachukai Missions . . . 109

IX. San Juan and Jémez Missions 125

X. Attempted Hopi Mission 149

XI. Gallup via Zuñi 160

XII. Peacemaker 173

XIII. Missionary Approach to Navaho Culture . 190

XIV. Missionary Support and the Preservation Society 216

XV. Illness and Death 226

Bibliography 235

Index 249

Acknowledgment

All of the illustrations in this volume appear through the courtesy of St. Michaels Mission and *St. Anthony Messenger*.

List of Abbreviations

B.I.A. Bureau of Indian Affairs. The National Archives, Washington, D. C. "Letters Received" is indicated by L.R.; "Special Cases," which includes outgoing correspondence, is indicated by S.C.

C.H.A. Cornwells Heights Archives. Motherhouse of the Sisters of the Blessed Sacrament, Cornwells Heights, Pennsylvania. Letters chronologically filed.

C.I.A. Commissioner of Indian Affairs.

C.I.B.A. Catholic Indian Bureau Archives. Bureau of Catholic Indian Missions, Washington, D. C. Letters and documents filed chronologically, as well as by states and by missions. In designating the bilingual publication of the Bureau, *Indianer Wache* and *The Indian Sentinel,* the initials B.C.I.M. are used.

F.M.S. Magazine, *The Franciscan Missions of the Southwest.*

H.A.C. Houck, Arizona, Collection. Letters and materials collected by Father Emmanuel Trockur, O.F.M., Houck, Arizona.

I.R.A. Indian Rights Association, The.

P.A. Provincial Archives. Provincial headquarters of St. John the Baptist Province, Cincinnati, Ohio. Materials arranged in folders by person and subject matter, and filed in four drawers under name of Anselm Weber. Folders are alphabetically initialed; a typical citation P.A., AY., refers to Provincial Archives and to the folder initialed AY.

Sendbote Magazine, *Der Sendbote des Goettlichen Herzens Jesu.*

S.M.C. St. Michaels Collection. Letter books, letters, papers, and chronicle at St. Michaels Mission, St. Michaels, Arizona. Folders are initialed and numbered.

W.R.C. Window Rock Collection. Letter books, diaries, record books, and documents at Navajo Indian Service headquarters, Window Rock, Arizona.

(When a citation refers to a letter, journal, diary, etc., the footnote will indicate each specifically.)

ANSELM WEBER, O.F.M.

Missionary to the Navaho, 1898–1921

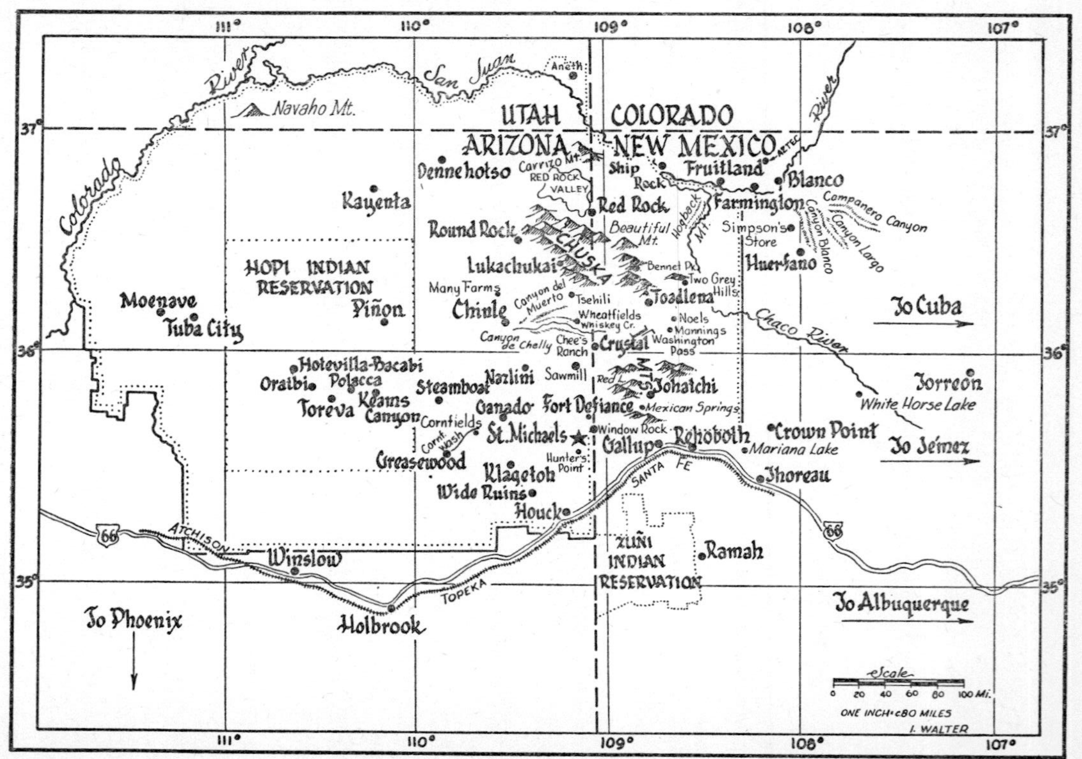
111°
110°
109°
108°
107°
37°
36°
35°
UTAH
COLORADO
ARIZONA
NEW MEXICO
San Juan
River
Colorado
Navaho Mt.
Aneth
Carrizo Mt.
RED ROCK VALLEY
Aztec
River
Dennehotso
Kayenta
Ship Rock
Fruitland
Blanco
Farmington
Red Rock
Round Rock
Beautiful Mt.
Hogback Mt.
Simpson's Store
Campanero Canyon
Canyon Largo
Canyon Blanco
Huerfano
CHUSKA
Lukachukai
Bennet Pk.
Two Grey Hills
HOPI INDIAN RESERVATION
Many Farms
Canyon del Muerto
Tsehili
Toadlena
Moenave
Tuba City
Piñon
Chinle
Wheatfields
Whiskey Cr.
Noels
Mannings
Washington Pass
Chaco River
To Cuba
Canyon de Chelly
Chee's Ranch
Crystal
Hotevilla-Bacabi
Oraibi
Polacca
Steamboat
Nazlini
Sawmill
Red L.
MTS.
Tohatchi
Torreon
Toreva
Keams Canyon
Ganado
Fort Defiance
Mexican Springs
White Horse Lake
Cornfields
Cornf. Wash
St. Michaels
Window Rock
Rehoboth
Crown Point
Gallup
Mariana Lake
To Jémez
Greasewood
Hunter's Point
Klagetoh
Wide Ruins
Santa Fe
Thoreau
Houck
66
Atchison
Winslow
Zuñi Indian Reservation
Ramah
Topeka
Holbrook
To Albuquerque
To Phoenix
Scale
0 20 40 60 80 100 Mi.
ONE INCH=80 MILES
I. WALTER

Chapter I

NAVAHO BACKGROUNDS

VAST stretches of southwestern United States bear no marks oı modern man's power to harness and tame nature. There is a touch of the boundless and the ageless in the magnificent sweep of desert, mountain mass, and turquoise sky. Over it all broods a spirit of grandeur and mystery that seems to cast a defiant spell over things modern and man-made.

Some humans, however, have made close adjustment to this land which is both harsh and mild. Centuries of weathering and of hardening has touched the native Indian inhabitants of the Southwest with something of the independence, the toughness and primitive vitality of the terrain and arid climate. These Indian peoples, such as the Pueblos and the Navaho, appear singularly equipped to withstand the normally eroding friction of contact with foreign and aggressive white peoples. Protected both by relatively impenetrable country, as well as by tight-woven tribal cohesion, the Navaho, perhaps best of all, symbolize the ruggedness and proud freedom of the great Southwest.

Athapascan by language the Navaho tribe forms one of the southernmost roots of the great *Diné* family tree which spreads down along the Rocky Mountains from the far north.[1] Evidence points to migration by the Navaho and related Apache groups from the north along the western slopes of the continental divide. Precisely when

[1] Washington Matthews, *Navaho Legends,* publication of the American Folklore Society (Boston: Houghton Mifflin and Company, 1897), p. 13; A. G. Morice, *The Great Déné Race* (St. Gabriel-Moedling, Vienna: Anthropos Administration, n.d.), pp. 1, 16. "Navaho" rather than "Navajo" is used throughout this dissertation. "Navajo" is the Hispanicized version of an old Tewa Indian name, *Navahu,* meaning "area of large cultivated fields." Government publications and many popular works retain "Navajo"; practically all scientific works use "Navaho." The Indians belonging to this tribe call themselves properly *Diné,* The People. See Berard Haile, "Navaho or Navajo?" *The Americas,* 6:85–90, July, 1949; also Barbara Aitken in *New Mexico Historical Review,* 26:335 (1951).

they arrived in the Southwest is uncertain, though there is evidence to suggest a period around the year A.D. 1000.[2] Rather certain proof, based on tree-ring dating, indicates that by the time Columbus landed the Navaho had already settled in north central New Mexico and were infiltrating the area surrounding Governador, New Mexico, northeast of their present country.[3] Here they probably remained pocketed for some two hundred years between Paiutes, Utes, and Pueblos, and here likely they experienced some physical assimilation with, and borrowed culture traits from, both the Plains Indians to the east and south, and from the Intermontane group to the west.[4]

The facts seem to warrant the conclusion that these invader groups from the north brought in a simple hunting culture. They dwelt in circular or curved stone houses to which they gradually added Pueblo features. Evidence uncovered near the Rosa and Largo areas of New Mexico suggests that the Navaho had slowly pushed out an original group from this area possibly as early as A.D. 1000.[5] At any rate this general area between the upper San Juan and the Chama Rivers belonged to Navaho country. During the period from 1500–1700 evidence indicates that they occupied the triangular section between Horse Lake, Gallina, and Governador. By this time they had already begun to make an adjustment to their environment and to stress agriculture.[6] From this first Navaho center in north central New Mexico all present scattered Navaho bands eventually branched out.[7]

Written history of the early Spanish period in New Mexico seemingly bears out these general findings of archaeology. Padre Gerónimo Zárate Salmerón, a Franciscan friar, writing in 1626, places the Navaho in the grassland valley of the Chama River, northwest of the Pueblo of Santa Clara.[8] Another Franciscan, Benavides, writes in 1629 that

[2] The Franciscan Fathers, *An Ethnologic Dictionary of the Navaho Language* (St. Michaels, Ariz.: The Franciscan Fathers, 1910), pp. 28–30; Clyde Kluckhohn and Dorothea Leighton, *The Navaho* (Cambridge: Harvard University Press, 1947), p. 3.

[3] Edward Twitchell Hall, Jr., "Recent Clues to Athapascan Prehistory in the Southwest," *American Anthropologist,* 46:99–100, January-March, 1944.

[4] Betty H. and Harold A. Huscher, "Athapascan Migration Via the Intermontane Region," *American Antiquity,* 8:81, July, 1942.

[5] Edward Twitchell Hall, Jr., *op. cit.,* p. 103; Berard Haile, *Origin Legend of the Navaho Enemy Way,* Yale University Publications in Anthropology, No. 17 (New Haven: Yale University Press, 1938), p. 38.

[6] Hall, *ibid.,* pp. 98, 105.

[7] Betty H. and Harold A. Huscher, *op. cit.,* p. 81.

[8] Katharine Bartlett, "Why the Navahos Came to Arizona," *Museum Notes* (Museum of Northern Arizona), 5:29, December, 1932; Richard Van Valkenburgh, *A Short History of the Navajo People,* mimeograph (Window Rock, Ariz.: United States Department of Interior, Navajo Indian Service, 1938), p. 3.

he sent a delegation of Indians from Santa Clara Pueblo into Navaho country, a distance of one day's journey, to make peace with the marauding Apache Navaho and to initiate missionary work among them.[9] His peace pledge to the Navaho headmen was a rosary. According to the editors of the Benavides *Memorial,* at least two other friars were sent into Navaho country at this time to convert the pagan nation.[10]

By 1700, as pressure was exerted on the Jicarillas and Utes by the Comanches to the east, the Navaho had begun their shift south and westward from their "old country" between the Chama and the San Juan.[11] Through contact with the Spanish during the 1630–1700 period, and with Pueblo and Ute Indians along the upper Rio Grande Valley, the Navaho agricultural hill people acquired horses and some sheep.[12] Sheep herding, in the true sense of the word, introduced no basic change in their agricultural way of life until the nineteenth century.[13]

Horses, however, radically changed their way of life, for the Spanish horse enabled them to retain tribal community life in a vastly broader land area. And on horseback they soon learned to sweep down on the Pueblo and Spanish settlements and to withdraw before resistance could be planned. Horses, sheep, goats, and women were booty. The Navaho were raiders primarily; they did not develop the trained military horsemanship of the Plains Indians. Neither were they true nomads, as they frequently were — and still are — called, since they held fairly well-defined lands and boundaries, and subsisted principally through agriculture.[14]

From the upland plains region of the Navaho, which by 1750 extended south from the "old country" to the Cabezon area, three main gateways led down to the Rio Grande settlements: the river valleys of the Chama and the Puerco of the east, and the pass

[9] Frederick Webb Hodge, George P. Hammond, and Agapito Rey, editors, *Fray Alonzo de Benavides' Revised Memorial of 1634* (Albuquerque: The University of New Mexico Press, 1945), pp. 85–89.

[10] *Ibid.,* Editorial Notes, p. 306.

[11] Bartlett, *op. cit.,* pp. 30–31; Alfred Barnaby Thomas, *The Plains Indians and New Mexico,* 1751–1778 (Albuquerque: The University of New Mexico Press, 1940), pp. 8–9, 44–46.

[12] Van Valkenburgh, *op. cit.,* p. 4.

[13] W. W. Hill, *The Agricultural and Hunting Methods of the Navaho Indians* (New Haven: Yale University Press, 1938), p. 18.

[14] Kluckhohn and Leighton, *The Navaho,* pp. 5, 7; Cosmos Mindeleff, "Navaho Houses," in Bureau of American Ethnology, *Seventeenth Annual Report,* 1895–1896, Part 2 (Washington, D. C.: Government Printing Office, 1898), p. 482.

leading east below Jémez Pueblo.[15] Already in the seventeenth century the Navaho had raided Pueblo villages; at other times during that early period they would ally with the Pueblo Indians against the Spanish masters. After the Great Rebellion of 1680, Jémez and other Pueblo Indians migrated northwest to live among the Navaho for varying periods during their intermittent warfare with the forces of De Vargas in the period of reconquest. Some of these groups remained to become equal clans within the Navaho nation.[16]

In reprisal, frequent punitive expeditions were sent out by the Spanish and Mexican governments during the eighteenth and early nineteenth centuries to punish the raiding Navaho, and to recapture slaves and herds.[17] As an aftermath of frequent contacts with Pueblo Indians and whites, the Navaho during the two centuries following 1626 adopted many foreign methods, particularly in herding, agriculture, home construction, weaving, and pottery. Navaho blankets and silvercrafts in the nineteenth century were to become distinctive features in both the art and trading economy of this pastoral and farming people.[18]

By 1750 Navaho country extended westward from the Cuba-Cabezon-Cebolleta front across the intervening Chaco Cañon region to Cañon de Chelly, beyond the Chuska Mountains. Recent excavations near this farthest outpost west at the mid-eighteenth-century period indicate that agriculture, seed gathering, hunting, and raiding still formed the base of Navaho economy. No bones of sheep or goats were found.[19] By this time Navaho country ran south to the lands of the Laguna, Ácoma, and Zuñi Indians; northward to Ute country along the San Juan Valley; westward they were approaching the sky villages of the Hopi. Broadly their lands lay within the quadrangle formed by Blanca Peak, twenty miles east of Alamosa, Colorado; the La Plata Mountains in southwestern Colorado; Mount Taylor in Valencia County, New Mexico; and San Francisco Peaks, near Flagstaff, Arizona.[20]

[15] Bartlett, *op. cit.*, p. 29.

[16] Edgar L. Hewett and Reginald G. Fisher, *Mission Monuments of New Mexico* (Albuquerque: The University of New Mexico and the School of American Research, 1943), p. 180; Hall, *op. cit.*, p. 99; Van Valkenburgh, *op. cit.*, p. 5.

[17] Kluckhohn and Leighton, *The Navaho,* pp. 5, 6.

[18] *Ibid.*, p. 6; Franciscan Fathers, *An Ethnologic Dictionary,* pp. 221–223, 257, 271. Hereafter this dictionary will be cited *An Ethnologic Dictionary.*

[19] Wesley R. Hurt, Jr., "Eighteenth Century Navaho Hogans from Canyon De Chelly National Monument," *American Antiquity,* 8:97, July, 1942.

[20] See maps of 1776 and 1846, reproduced in Van Valkenburgh, *op. cit.*, opposite pages 5 and 15 and on page 2; see also Matthews, *Navaho Legends,* p. 221.

One particularly heavy concentration of the tribe, according to a Spanish writer of the mid-eighteenth century, focused in the neighborhood of the Cabezon-Mount Taylor area whither Ute pressure at the time had driven them. Here an organized attempt to establish Christian missions among these heathen raiders was initiated in the middle of the eighteenth century.[21] In 1744 Friars Delgado of Isleta and Yrigoyen of Jémez trudged west through the gap from Jémez Valley into Navaho territory. For six days they traveled from camp to camp in this country of the "Navajoo," passing out beads, ribbons, and tobacco, and instructing the curious natives in the meaning of the Faith. Their military guards and interpreters assured them that the Indians desired conversion. In reporting to his superiors, Delgado explained that these Indians would be even more effectively reduced to Christianity by arms.[22]

Revealing that the governor of the province was about to ask the viceroy for three or four missionaries, Padre Delgado begged the Franciscan Commissary General to send tried religious, forty years and older, who were mild and humble, for the contemplated mission work in the province of Navajoo, west of Jémez.[23]

To further mission work among the Indians the King of Spain requested the Mexican viceroy to send friars and supplies to the Navaho field on the proviso that the report of five thousand conversions was really true.[24]

One year later in the summer of 1746 the *visitator* of the New Mexico Franciscan Custody, Friar Juan Miguel Menchero, was reported to have entered the Navaho mission field personally, with marvelous success both in the province of Navajoo and at La Cebolleta. West of Jémez in the Cabezon region he certified to the five thousand conversions reported earlier by Delgado; near Mount Taylor at Cebolleta, Menchero personally "brought 500 lambs into the fold of the Divine Shepherd."[25]

21 Don Tomás Vélez Gachupín, "Instructions to his successor, 1754," in Alfred Barnaby Thomas, *op. cit.*, p. 138.

22 Fray Carlos Delgado to Fray Pedro Navarrete, Isleta, June 18, 1744, in Charles Wilson Hackett, editor, *Historical Documents Relating to New Mexico, Nueva Vizcaya, and Approaches Thereto, to 1773* (Washington, D. C.: Carnegie Institution of Washington, 1937), Vol. 3, pp. 391–393.

23 Delgado to Navarrete, Isleta, June 18, 1744, in Hackett, *ibid.*, pp. 393–394.

24 The King of Spain to Viceroy of New Spain, November 23, 1745, in Hackett, *ibid.*, p. 416.

25 Juan José Pérez Mirabel to Commissary General, Isleta, July 8, 1746, in Hackett, *ibid.*, pp. 420–421; Delgado, José Yrigoyen, and Juan José Toledo, letter of thanks to Commissary General, Friar Juan Fogueras, Isleta, July 11, 1746, *ibid.*, pp. 421–422.

Accordingly missions were founded at La Cebolleta and at Encinal along the lines of centralized Spanish reductions, agricultural communities with facilities for teaching religion, handcrafts, and farming. Friar Juan Sanz Lezaún was stationed at Encinal and Friar Manuel Vermejo at Cebolleta in 1748. Within five months they had the Navaho "repented" and, obviously they thought, on the way to complete conversion.[26]

Don Tomás Gachupín, governor of New Mexico, hearing complaints in 1750 from the Laguna and Ácoma Indians, particularly over the intended move of the Encinal mission to Cubero, advised Friar Manuel Trigo to accompany Lieutenant General Bernard Bustamente y Tagle, to investigate and settle the issue of the best location for the *reductio* of Encinal.[27]

When he arrived at Laguna, Trigo, the Franciscan Custodial Vicar, learned on April 16 that the expected trouble had already erupted in the form of a revolt of the Navaho at both Encinal and Cebolleta. On that very day they had driven out the two priests and abandoned the two missions.[28] In the *autos* subsequently drawn up officially before Bustamente and Trigo, the *officiales* of Laguna and Ácoma who acted as interpreters, swore that the Navaho at Cebolleta and Encinal had originally fallen in with Menchero's desires to baptize the children only because he had given them hoes and picks in payment, and had promised them "mares, mules, horses, cows, clothing, and many sheep."[29]

As for themselves, the adult Navaho, according to the Pueblo interpreters, frankly admitted, "they were like deer . . . who wandered from place to place." They did not wish to settle down in pueblos, nor did they wish to become Christians, nor had they ever asked for a Father to come among them. It would be all right if he wished to remain with them, they went on, and the poor man would suffer no harm. Perhaps their children, "having received the water of holy baptism, might . . . after they were grown up, become Christians and ask for a pueblo."[30] With the other interpreter-witnesses it was the same story: the adult Navaho did not wish to be Christians and live in one place at a pueblo; moreover, they would not be separated from their

[26] Juan Sanz de Lezaún, "An Account of Lamentable Happenings in New Mexico, 1760," in Hackett, *ibid.*, p. 472.

[27] Gachupén (sic) to Trigo, Santa Fe, March 24, 1750, in Hackett, *ibid.*, pp. 424–425.

[28] Trigo to Bustamente, n.d. [April 17], 1750, in Hackett, *ibid.*, p. 432.

[29] *Auto* of Bustamente y Tagle, April 18, 1750, testimony of the *alcalde major* of Ácoma and Laguna, in Hackett, *ibid.*, p. 434.

[30] *Ibid.*

children. If those who had been baptized wished to live as Christians and in a pueblo when they grew up, that, they made it clear, would be well and good.[31]

Quite different was the account of the Apache-Navaho revolt as drawn up by the Encinal missionary, Friar Juan Sanz de Lezaún, writing ten years later. Later investigations, he complained, convinced him that the very *officiales* of Laguna and Ácoma who testified as witnesses, had themselves incited the revolt. Lezaún accused the governor of the province of having forced the Laguna and Ácoma Indians to tend the governor's personal fields at Cebolleta and Encinal, and of having commanded them also to build the pueblos and churches for the Navaho. This had incensed the Christian Pueblo Indians, especially the Ácomas, when they moreover learned of the contemplated move of the Encinal group to their own well-watered lands around Cubero. Determined to free themselves of these burdens, the friars continued, the Lagunas and Ácomas had urged the Navaho to revolt and to abandon the mission projects.[32]

Thus ended a six-year-long organized effort of the early friars to reduce and Christianize the Navaho. Several pertinent factors characterize the failure, for even though the actual revolt may have been incited by the Pueblos, the testimony of the Navaho as rendered by the three interpreters followed a pattern remarkably identical with Navaho culture traits in reference to later mission work among them. The Navaho in council had alleged as reasons for their defection: their desire to wander about freely, with no fixed village site; their willingness to oblige the white missionaries so long as gifts were forthcoming; and their refusal to turn over their children to strangers for indoctrination away from home.

Cebolleta retained a degree of significance in subsequent Navaho history since the band living in the neighborhood assimilated many customs and culture traits from their more frequent contacts with Hispanos, Pueblo Indians, and Anglos. Many were baptized during the following century so that by 1865 a band of 190 Navaho living in the Cebolleta region were considered Catholic.[33] During forays and

31 *Auto* of Bustamente y Tagle, Ácoma, April 18, 1750, testimony of Lieutenant Pedro Romero of Laguna and Ácoma, and others, in Hackett, *ibid.*, pp. 435–438.

32 Lezaún, "An account of lamentable happenings in New Mexico, 1760," in Hackett, *ibid.*, p. 472.

33 Joint Special Committee, Report of the, *Condition of the Indian Tribes,* 39 Cong., 2 sess., Report No. 156 (Washington, D. C.: Government Printing Office, 1867), pp. 310, 354. Hereafter this work will be cited as Joint Special Committee, *Condition of the Indian Tribes.*

reprisal raids which were frequently undertaken against the Navaho by New Mexicans, these marginal Navaho, and others of their kind, served as guides and interpreters, thus gaining the hatred and the sinister title among the Navaho of "People who are enemies." Descendants of these enemy Navaho now live on allotments at Cañoncito, forty miles west of Albuquerque; others live in the isolated Alamo, or Puertocito region, eighty miles southwest of Albuquerque.[34]

What with offering honorary military titles and bribing of influential Navaho headmen, the Spanish were tolerably successful from 1750–1800 in holding the raiding Indians to their own country west of the Rio Grande settlements and north of the Laguna-Ácoma-Zuni line of the Pueblos. The Utes kept them south of the San Juan Valley. After 1800, and for the next sixty years, during both Mexican and American regimes, guerrilla warfare and raiding between Navaho and the settlements heightened until it again became an accepted pattern.[35] Navaho herds by the middle of the century were heavily on the increase though the marauders lost in women and children who were captured and sold as slaves to the Mexicans and Americans in New Mexico. Between 1850–1860, while the slavery issue drew to a climax in the United States, a group of Mexicans at Cebolleta, the "Cebolleteños," gained notoriety and pesos throughout New Mexico as Navaho slave procurers and sellers.[36]

After 1846, United States army officers, like their Spanish and Mexican predecessors, concluded numerous peace treaties with the Navaho.[37] As the tribe lacked central political or social organization, leaders of regional bands who made peace could exert no direct controls over other Navaho raiding parties, which easily escaped reprisals by reason of their hide-outs in the interior of the wild country.[38] Fort Defiance was established in 1851 in the heart of Navaho country, and numerous expeditions were sent out to track down the outlaw bands. Only once did the Indians retaliate with a full-scale, planned attack at dawn on Fort Defiance. They were repulsed.[39] Organized campaigning by the United States Army got under way in 1858, ostensibly because the Indians refused to turn over the

[34] Van Valkenburgh, *op. cit.*, p. 15; Kluckhohn and Leighton, *The Navaho*, p. 6.

[35] Van Valkenburgh, *op. cit.*, pp. 6–8; Bartlett, *op. cit.*, p. 31.

[36] See Ralph Emerson Twitchell, *The Leading Facts of New Mexican History* (Cedar Rapids, Iowa: The Torch Press, 1912), Vol. 2, pp. 303–304.

[37] Van Valkenburgh, *op. cit.*, pp. 10–19.

[38] Kluckhohn and Leighton, *The Navaho*, p. 73.

[39] Anonymous, "Reminiscences of Fort Defiance, New Mexico, 1860," *Journal of the Military Service Institution of the U. S.*, 4:90–92, 1883.

murderer of a Negro slave belonging to Major Brooks of Fort Defiance. Such excursions as followed accomplished little beyond the destruction of crops and the capture of Indian herds.

With the resultant food shortages, raids on the settlements mounted in tempo, especially after the drawing off of frontier troops at the outbreak of the Civil War. Brigadier General Carleton, in command of the Department of New Mexico, commissioned Kit Carson in 1863 to remove the whole Navaho tribe to a concentration-camp type of reservation at Bosque Redondo on the Pecos River in New Mexico. Colonel Christopher Carson campaigned relentlessly, grinding down the spirit of Navaho resistance by a scorched-earth policy that eventually, in 1864, drove the broken people southeastward on their sad "Big Walk" to Bosque Redondo. Some bands of Navaho managed to slip through the dragnet laid by Carson, hiding out in out-of-the-way corners, like Largo and Grand Canyons. At Bosque under Fort Sumner military control and direction, the Navaho tried to support themselves by farming. Disease, poverty, lack of firewood, repeated crop failure, and closed bounds — all conspired to deepen their degradation. In 1868 they were permitted by treaty with the United States to return to their homeland of deserts and upland sage plains, prairies, canyons, and mountain. Excessive financial upkeep for eight thousand Navaho, plus a new peace policy on the part of the government, had argued strongly against continuing the Bosque Redondo experiment.[40]

Almost destitute except for government rations and the herds of sheep and goats allotted them by treaty, the thoroughly chastened Navaho began what seemed to be a dubious struggle for survival in their barren, arid land. Their wide homeland had been surveyed and narrowed down to 3,328,302 acres, but government Indian agents — and definitely the Indians themselves — seemed little concerned during the first decade after 1868 with exact observance of the boundaries.[41]

Though it lingers as an utterly bad memory for the Navaho, Bosque Redondo did give the Indians their taste for coffee, and the womenfolk a taste for gathered and fluted calico skirts and velveteen blouses patterned after the 1865 fashions of the officers' wives at Fort Sumner.

[40] See Frank D. Reeve, "The Federal Indian Policy in New Mexico, 1858–1880," *New Mexico Historical Review,* 12:218–269; 13:14–62, July, 1937, and January, 1938; Sallie Pierce Brewer, "The 'Long Walk' to Bosque Redondo," as told by Peshlakai Etsidi, *Museum Notes,* 9:55–62, May, 1937; Van Valkenburgh, *op. cit.,* maps opposite pp. 15 and 23.

[41] Reeve, *ibid.,* p. 47; Bartlett, *op. cit.,* p. 32; Van Valkenburgh, *op. cit.,* pp. 33–37.

During the captivity also the men learned new techniques in silversmithing and something of ditch irrigation, an improvement on their native flood irrigation methods. Above all, it instilled into the Navaho a wholesome respect for the power of the Americans. What with the long dependency on government rations, the exile had also helped to develop wheedling and scrounging from the whites into something of a convention.[42]

Sheep, goat, and horse herding now became thoroughly integrated into Navaho culture. Terrain, climate, and social habits based on regional migration and on simple hogan construction lent themselves nicely to a prosperous herding economy. Rainfall, running in broad cycles, averages around six inches annually in altitudes of four thousand feet and increases to twenty inches in the higher mountain regions. Mountain pastures at six to eight thousand feet altitudes in the Chuska-Tunicha Range provide summer range when plains and foothills are parched. This movement of Navaho outfits from summer to winter forage lands, a seasonal changing of pastures, led many people mistakenly to apply the term "nomad" to the Navaho.[43]

The blending of native and hybrid ethnic strains, along with cultural cross fertilization with Pueblo Indian, Mexican, and American traits, may account for the astounding vitality shown by the *Diné* in the period since their rebirth in 1868. From a tribe of perhaps 10,000 paupers, with land and flocks allotted to care for 9000 Indians by official count, The People increased to 20,000 in 1900, and to approximately 60,000 in 1950. This represents for the past fifty years an annual increase rate of 2.2 per cent while the natural increase rate for the rest of the United States averaged 0.96. Navaho births at 35 per 1000 population, as compared with 21 for the United States in 1942, placed the Navaho among the most prolific of ethnic groups within the United States. Future estimated increase hinges on the age grouping within The People which can boast 60 per cent of its population under 20 years of age![44]

The Navaho official 1868 land base of nearly three and one-third

[42] Kluckhohn and Leighton, *The Navaho,* pp. 26, 44, 48; W. W. Hill, *op. cit.,* p. 24; Van Valkenburgh, *op. cit.,* p. 36.

[43] See Cosmos Mindeleff, *op. cit.,* pp. 478, 481–485; *An Ethnologic Dictionary,* pp. 32–33; Herbert E. Gregory, *The Navajo Country,* Department of the Interior, United States Geological Survey (Washington, D. C.: Government Printing Office, 1916), pp. 21, 49–61; W. W. Hill, *op. cit.,* p. 20.

[44] *Ibid.,* pp. 17–19; Kluckhohn and Leighton, *The Navaho,* p. 18; see Paul H. Landis, *Population Problems: A Cultural Interpretation* (New York: American Book Company, 1943), pp. 58, 123, 417. The population rate for the United States in 1952 had increased to 28 births per 1000 population.

million acres has increased to almost 16,000,000 acres, or about 25,000 square miles in 1950. Even though this represents according to country-wide standards a meager density of 2.4 persons per square mile, the land is actually densely overpopulated and perilously overgrazed, because of the worthless condition of large areas.[45]

With a thoroughly pagan population spread thin across a land where mountains and canyons discouraged communication, little or no effort at Christianizing the Navaho had been organized from the mid-eighteenth century until the Americans took possession of the Southwest a hundred years later. A rare note mentions conversions of one or the other Navaho family to Catholicism through contact with the Pueblo missions, as at Zuñi in 1775.[46] In 1804, it is true, the Cebolleta band requested special missionaries but none was sent.[47] Possessed of an unusually tight social and cultural unity, which tied in closely with naturalistic and pragmatic Navaho ceremonial dances and therapeutic songs, The People were seemingly little conditioned to accept voluntarily a "white" faith which stressed deeply spiritual mysteries and offered latreutic worship.[48]

When Lieutenant J. H. Simpson made his expedition through the Navaho country in 1849 he reported of Cañon de Chelly:[49] "I noticed the cross, the usual emblem of the Roman Catholic Faith, stuck up but in one instance in the canon; and this is the only one I have seen in the Navajo country." In itself the presence of the cross would by no means indicate that a missionary had lived in Cañon de Chelly. Some Navaho have claimed positively that a priest did live among them in the Cañon:[50]

> Among all the other Indian races of New Mexico the Navajos glory themselves not to have obeyed the order of Segundo and to have saved the life of the priest who was living in their midst in the Canon de Shay [sic] while in all the pueblos the priests were killed.

45 J. A. Krug, Secretary of the Interior, Report of, *The Navajo: A Long-Range Program for Navajo Rehabilitation* (Washington, D. C.: Government Printing Office, 1948), pp. 2–3; Kluckhohn and Leighton, *The Navaho*, pp. 17–19.

46 Alfred Barnaby Thomas, *op. cit.*, p. 180.

47 Frederick Webb Hodge, Hammond, and Rey, *op. cit.*, p. 309.

48 See *An Ethnologic Dictionary*, pp. 346–347.

49 Lieutenant J. H. Simpson, *Report of an expedition into the Navajo Country in 1849*, 31 Cong., 1 sess., Sen. Ex. Doc. 64 (Washington, D. C.: Union Office, 1850), p. 105.

50 Interpreter Frank Walker to Archbishop of Santa Fe, December 14, 1896, C.H.A. White Hair, an old Navaho warrior, recounted to the first Fathers at St. Michaels, Arizona, in 1900 that Navaho legends recalled *e'nishodis*, "long robes," with rope belts and prayer beads working among The People long ago, and pouring water on their heads. See Frederick Hartung, O.F.M., "Die Franziskaner Mission unter den Navajo-Indianern," *Sendbote*, 27:734, September, 1900.

Folklore and legend alone appear to bolster the possibility that direct mission activity existed in the mid-eighteenth century.

Doubtless, however, some Navaho had come in contact with Franciscan priests in the period when the friars were missioned at the Hopi, Zuñi, Jémez, and Rio Grande pueblos. Even after Mexican secularization went into effect, the secular clergy continued to visit the pueblos and missions on the fringe of Navaho country, baptizing a few Navaho infants, especially in the Cebolleta area.[51]

Moreover, not a few Catholic Hispanos were enslaved during the two centuries of raiding and counterraiding between the Navaho and the Rio Grande settlements.[52] Before and after the emancipation of peons in 1867, some baptized Navaho likely returned to their people.[53] Personal experiences recalled and tales retold in hogan and camp would readily sift and blur in the memory of the *Diné* as group tradition.

In 1852, and for most of the decade, Bishop Lamy pleaded with the St. Louis Jesuits to send De Smet, De Blieck, or any of their men for work among the Navaho. A large parish, he assured them, was waiting for them at Zami (Zuñi), near the Navaho country, and another parish at Santa Fe.[54]

At the close of the Navaho War Bishop Lamy journeyed some three thousand miles on horseback or wagon from November 1, 1864, to May 1, 1865, collecting for the Santa Fe cathedral building, and studying at firsthand conditions in the Arizona area of his diocese. His interest focused especially on the problem of Christianizing the

[51] Zephyrin Engelhardt, O.F.M., *The Franciscans in Arizona* (Harbor Springs, Mich., 1899), p. 208. A. Weber wrote the article on St. Michaels Mission, pp. 208–211. See his diary, *Diary, 1899,* July 6, P.A., AF–2.

[52] Estimates run as high as two and three thousand Navaho slaves held by Hispano and Anglo families even after the Civil War. J. B. Lamy, Bishop of Santa Fe, testimony, Joint Special Committee, *Condition of the Indian Tribes,* p. 357. See C.I.A., *Annual Report,* 1867, p. 325. Major Riordan began the work of freeing the more than three hundred Hispano and Indian slaves held by the Navaho in 1882. C.I.A., *Annual Report,* 1883, p. 179; Herbert Welsh, *Report of a Visit to the Navajo, Pueblo, and Hualpais Indians* (Philadelphia: The Indian Rights Association, 1885), p. 42.

[53] Albert Daeger, later Archbishop of Santa Fe, to A. Weber, April 19, 1913, P.A., NH., bears a request from old Padre Redon to locate his "adopted Navajo son, José Nacaje." He had purchased the Indian for $100 at Cebolleta in 1863, had instructed, baptized, and employed him as sacristan in Antonchico for several years until the Navaho's mother found and claimed her grown son. A. Redon was pastor at Cebolleta 1863–1866 when he moved to Antonchico. Cebolleta Parish Records, in Parish Records, Sacred Heart Cathedral, Gallup, New Mexico.

[54] Lamy to Roothan, July 29, 1852; Murphy to Beckx, September 14, 1854; Machebeuf to Beckx, n.d., 1855, all in Gilbert J. Garraghan, *The Jesuits of the Middle United States* (New York: American Press, 1938), Vol. 2, pp. 490–491.

"uncivilized Indians" whose geographical and cultural isolation had withstood thus far Spanish, Mexican, and American assimilation efforts. The pacification-by-expatriation experiment at Bosque Redondo, where the military was attempting to land-base the semi-nomadic Navaho, he viewed hopefully:[55]

> It appears that the government of Washington is thinking of adopting a plan in regard to them which if carried out with prudence and humanity, would conduce to the conversion of the Indians, or at least of their children. The proposal is to assign them a certain extent of territory and oblige them to live on it. This experiment of colonization has been tried with the Navajos, and has succeeded.

To the Bishop's mind this reservation policy was an open invitation to attempt the plantation approach of earlier Spanish missionaries. Moreover, the army officers who investigated conditions at Bosque Redondo recommended that the Catholic Church be entrusted with the task of educating and Christianizing the Navaho. They pointed out that Sandoval's Cebolleta band was "professedly Catholic" already, and that this Faith was traditionally the prevalent religion in New Mexico.[56] Lamy sent newly ordained Reverend Fleurant and two clerics in minor orders to Fort Sumner late in 1864 to open a mission and school. From his own meager income the Bishop offered $2,000 to begin building operations.[57]

Obviously the Navaho were indifferent to education and Christianity; they insisted that the long-gowned men should pay for the amusement they found in teaching the children.[58] On October 25, 1865, not quite one year later, Father Michael Fleurant died and the Navaho mission failed.[59]

With the inauguration of the Indian Peace Policy a treaty was signed June 1, 1868, between the United States Peace Commissioners and the Navaho tribe, represented respectively by Colonel S. F. Tappan and General W. T. Sherman, and the Navaho headmen. Article III stipulated a school and chapel to be furnished by the government as soon as pupils in sufficient number could be provided.[60]

55 J. B. Lamy to the Society for the Propagation of the Faith, August 25, 1866, in *Annals of the Propagation of the Faith,* 28:222, 1867. He records that at this time there were three priests in Arizona, five in Colorado, and thirty-three in New Mexico. Hereafter these annals will be cited as *Annals of the Propagation.*

56 Joint Special Committee, *Condition of the Indian Tribes,* p. 310.

57 *Ibid.,* p. 358; Lamy, *Annals of the Propagation,* 28:222, 1867.

58 George Gwyther, "An Indian Reservation," *Overland Monthly,* 10:127–128, February, 1873, in Reeve, *op. cit., N.M.H.R.,* 12:266, July, 1937.

59 While still in minor orders Fleurant left France on April 17, 1861. *Annals of the Propagation,* 28:222, 1867.

60 15 U. S. Stats., 667–671.

Bishop Lamy's request again at this period to be entrusted with the education of the Navaho, a petition signed by leading New Mexico military and political figures, was refused.[61] Already religious and educational work had been entrusted to the Presbyterians, who sent Reverend J. M. Roberts to Fort Defiance in 1868.[62] Captain Frank Tracy Bennett, agent at Fort Defiance, fitted out an abandoned adobe house for a school, and Charity A. Gaston, a woman missionary from the Free School at Santa Fe, was sent in October, 1869, to aid Roberts as a teacher. School and mission work made out poorly, and after Reverend John Menaul joined their efforts for some months after 1870, all three transferred to Laguna. Menaul had been sent as missionary because of his skill at practical weaving. Before leaving Fort Defiance Miss Charity had become Mrs. John Menaul, and the Navaho delighted in quipping over the striking contrast between the tall wife and her diminutive "Long Gown with a Short Coat," as they dubbed the Protestant ministers.[63]

After the Presbyterians had temporarily left Fort Defiance, Father Gasparri, S.J., of Albuquerque, opened fruitless negotiations to establish a Navaho mission.[64] Bishop Lamy also repeated his request to have charge of education and mission work among the Navaho:[65]

> The Navajo tribe also have many children baptized in our Church. . . . We are acquainted with their habits, knowing the Spanish and some of their language. We think we might do some good among them if we have a little help from the public funds, applied for the good of the Indians.

Bishop J. B. Salpointe, appointed first Vicar Apostolic of Arizona Territory in 1868 and consecrated bishop June 20, 1869, came to Santa Fe in 1885 as coadjutor with the right of succession. In July of 1885 Archbishop Lamy resigned and Salpointe succeeded in office.[66]

[61] J. B. Lamy in (Santa Fe) *New Mexico Union,* January 9, 1873.

[62] Thomas C. Moffett, *The American Indian on the New Trail* (New York: The New York City Missionary Education Movement, 1914), p. 74.

[63] Captain F. T. Bennett to Major William Clinton, August 19, 1870, and Charity A. Gaston to same, August 23, 1870, in C.I.A., *Annual Report,* 1870, pp. 612–617, and 618 respectively; *ibid.,* 1872, pp. 296, 302, 304; Moffett, *op. cit.,* p. 75; Van Valkenburgh, *op. cit.,* p. 38.

[64] James H. Defouri, *Historical Sketch of the Catholic Church in New Mexico* (San Francisco: McCormick Bros., 1887), p. 126.

[65] July 10, 1873, in General Charles Ewing, *Petition of the Catholic Church in Behalf of the Pueblos and Other Indians of New Mexico* (Washington, D. C., 1874), pp. 10–11.

[66] John Sallepoint (sic) was nominated Bishop of Doryla *in partibus* and charged with the vicariate apostolic newly erected in Arizona Territory by the Consistory of September 21, 1868. *Annals of the Propagation,* 30:51, 1869; Jean Baptiste Salpointe, *Soldiers of the Cross* (Banning, Calif.: St. Boniface Indian Trade School, 1898), p. 272,

Success in the form of contracts whereby the government farmed out Indian education to religious denominational schools was to some extent realized by this successor of Lamy.[67]

Salpointe made a mission trip through Navaho country, striking west from Socorro, "from Sabinal to Colorado Chiquito," during the course of which he met peaceful off-reservation Navaho who were willing to have a council with the Bishop. In February, 1887, he visited Fort Defiance to prospect for a possible school there, but by the following year had decided to locate rather at Zuñi and at Hopi. He was hoping to enlist the Jesuits for these missions.[68] Finally in July, 1889, a planned effort to found a Navaho school and mission was made. Dr. Chapelle, vice-president of the Bureau of Catholic Indian Missions, and the future archbishop of Santa Fe, along with Father Antonio Jouvenceau, Navaho Agent C. E. Vandever, with Frank Walker as interpreter, traveled deep into northern Arizona to select a site.[69] Earlier in the year the Bureau of Catholic Indian Missions had been awarded a government permit to select a site for an industrial boarding school on the Hopi reservation.[70]

After calling a council at which headmen of the various Hopi villages expressed agreement on a location, and willingness to have a school, an application was sent to Washington for a quarter section of land including Wipo Spring, some eight miles north of First Mesa.[71] Close to the Hopi, and still in the heart of Navaho territory, the school and mission, it was thought, could serve both peoples.[72]

In this latter assumption of a combined Navaho-Hopi foundation lay a generous charge of Christian optimism, or possibly a naïve

[67] Salpointe, *ibid.*, pp. 273–274; Sister Blandina Segale, *At the End of the Santa Fe Trail* (Milwaukee: Bruce Publishing Co., 1948), p. 271. The industrial school, blessed by Salpointe in 1886 and dedicated by Lamy in 1887, had been built by Miss Katharine Drexel of Philadelphia at a cost of $14,000. In 1894, a year after the government contract was not renewed — subsequent to a visit of inspection by Commissioner Morgan — the community of (now) Mother Katharine Drexel, called "Sisters of the Blessed Sacrament for Indian and Colored People," took charge. A. Weber in *St. Anthony Messenger,* 8:262–268, January, 1901.

[68] Salpointe, *op. cit.*, p. 267.

[69] A. Weber, *Sendbote,* 33:99, November, 1906; A. Jouvenceau to A. Weber, September 18, 1905, P.A., MO.

[70] On April 4, 1889, Authority 19695, 1889, B.I.A.L.R., Special Cases 143, Miscellaneous Navajo. Special Cases 143, Misc. Nav., contains bundles of correspondence, both received and copies of outgoing, relative to mission foundations, 1880–1915; hereafter these materials will be cited as B.I.A., SC 143.

[71] Agent Vandever to Commissioner of Indian Affairs, July 16, 1889, 20032, B.I.A., SC 143.

[72] *Ibid.;* see also A. Weber to Bishop Granjon (Tucson), November 23, 1908, and A. Weber to Commissioner of Indian Affairs, December 2, 1909, P.A., MO.

disregard for cultural antagonism and for the history of Navaho-Hopi conflict. In any event no actual Catholic educational or mission work developed from this selection at Wipo Spring, notwithstanding Father J. A. Stephan's effort to enlist the Jesuits for this Navaho-Hopi mission.[73]

At the moment, however, signing contracts and filing on mission locations was paramount. There was little time for systematic planning and mission economics at a period when the government was signing educational contracts on a broad policy with the various denominations, mission societies, and the Indian Rights Association in an effort to broaden inadequate government educational facilities. Some contracts had been let as early as 1870, but the denominational competition grew rather keen during the next decade. Mormon traders and missionaries had even earlier lived among the Navaho, whom Mormon tradition regarded as an offshoot of one of the lost tribes of Israel.[74]

Recognizing the inadequacy of government facilities, Commissioner Oberly had stepped up the program which advanced this co-operation in education between the government and religious groups.[75] Denominational schools under contract to the government to educate a specific number of pupils were subsidized by the government on an average-daily-attendance basis, provided they observed governmental regulations.[76]

Something of a crusade among the churches to establish mission schools among the Navaho and receive teaching contracts was touched off in 1887 by Horatio O. Ladd, president of the University of New Mexico at Santa Fe. Apparently he had been nursing along a plan for such missions to be sponsored by the Methodist Episcopal (North) Woman's Home Missionary Society, for on May 6, 1887, he requested permission from Commissioner J. D. Atkins for his Delaware, Ohio, protégés to begin.[77] Under the usual proviso that no right of ownership would accrue to the Methodist Episcopals, Commissioner Lamar authorized his Navaho agent to set aside eighty acres near the "Chinali" trading post, or on any other unoccupied location within the reservation.[78]

[73] J. A. Stephan to Minister General Anderledy, S.J., November 7, 1889, C.I.B.A.; A. Weber to Bishop Granjon, *ibid.*

[74] See Lawrence F. Schmeckebier, *The Office of Indian Affairs . . . Its History, Activities and Organization* (Baltimore: Johns Hopkins Press, 1927), p. 212; Van Valkenburgh, *op. cit.*, p. 43.

[75] Indian Rights Association, *Annual Report,* 1889, p. 8.

[76] Schmeckebier, *op. cit.*, p. 212.

[77] Ladd to Atkins, May 6, 1887, 15697, enclosure 1, B.I.A., SC 143.

[78] Authority of June 29, 1887, 15697, B.I.A., SC 143.

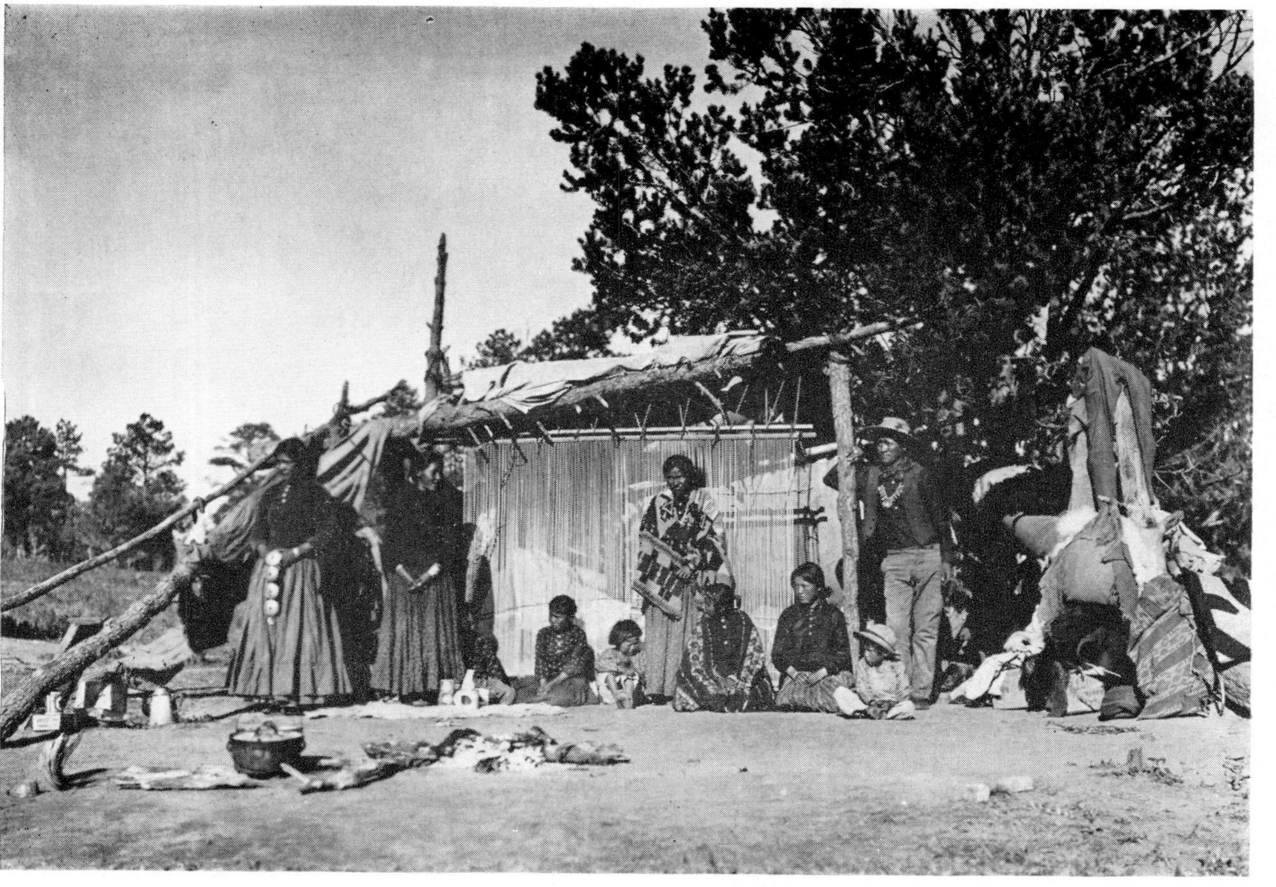

Herdsmen: mutton in the pot; handspun wool on the loom

Joe Wilkin's old homestead serving as first Navaho school and interpreter's home at St. Michaels

Agent Patterson reported later that the Methodist Episcopal Society was sending representatives in a few days, but that by date of September 8, 1887, no mission had been founded.[79] Authority was issued two years later for the same group to make two additional 160-acre selections, one at "Tse a lee" and one at Jewetts, New Mexico.[80] At the latter place (Hogback) the first Methodist Episcopal mission to take root was founded in 1891 by a widow, Mrs. Mary Eldridge, a former matron at Haskell Institute.[81]

Two other quarter sections were granted in 1891 to the Methodist Episcopal Church, one at Pueblo, Colorado, near Cotton's Store, and another at Red Lake.[82] How all these selections could be approved is hard to comprehend since the two latter sites were definitely opposed by the Navaho in council. At Fort Defiance, September 29, 1893, the Navaho headmen, Charley Mitchell, Manuelito, Many Horses, Sam Bogata, Wah-nee-ka, and Gish-in-begay had bluntly and angrily objected to this second council "when we clearly said 'no' last time." They needed the Red Lake site, they insisted, as a salt field for their horses and sheep. They agreed that when Mr. Riggin (Reverend F. A.) could show some results at Fort Defiance they might let him go farther into the reservation.[83]

Separately, also, the Methodists and the Episcopals entered the Navaho mission field. On the San Juan River in 1889 Reverend Howard R. Antes was scouting the country for the Methodist Church, which planned a school and mission among the northern Navaho.[84] He had been escorted to Fort Defiance by Brother Thomas Harwood, superintendent of New Mexico Spanish Missions.[85]

Bishop Kendrick of Albuquerque, Episcopal, was also at Fort Defiance in 1889, conferring with Agent Vandever regarding an industrial school for forty Navaho children at Chin Lee. Eventually the Commissioner approved the plan with modification: the government would build and equip the school, and pay the teachers. Their selection would be "made with a view to harmony and cooperation with the proposed mission. . . . This suggestion is in the line of the Commissioner's policy of making Government Indian Schools

[79] Samuel S. Patterson to Commissioner, September 8, 1887, 24279, B.I.A., SC 143.

[80] Authority of June 5, 1889, 20909, B.I.A., SC 143.

[81] Pauline G. Malehorn, *The Tender Plant,* mimeograph (Farmington, N. Mex., 1948), pp. 2–4.

[82] Authority of April 29, 1892, 30687, and 4532, 1894, B.I.A., SC 143.

[83] Council Proceedings, September 29, 1893, 39007, B.I.A., SC 143.

[84] I.R.A., *Annual Report,* 1889, p. 6.

[85] T. S. Wiltsee to Dr. Dorchester, August 21, 1889, 24268, B.I.A., SC 143.

channels of Christian as well as secular education. . . ."[86] Of this Chin Lee Episcopal mission nothing developed, nor, seemingly, of the Episcopal effort under elderly Miss Helen Dodge who was authorized to select eighty acres for a mission school on the reservation.[87] At Fort Defiance, however, an Episcopal hospital did materialize: a small plot of agency land was allotted and Mrs. Thackara was appointed and paid a salary by the Woman's Auxiliary of New York, which appropriated $1,200 for this work of mercy.[88]

As might be predicted, such pre-emption of certain fields led to interdenominational friction. At Albuquerque, where the Presbyterians from 1884–1886 had conducted a large Indian school north of town, there was chagrin and dismay because Catholic Pueblo children were forbidden by the Catholic Bishop to attend, even though the school was no longer denominational. Herbert Welsh of the Indian Rights Association was deeply disturbed over the somewhat gloomy situation, especially, as he complained, since the Hispano teachers in the Catholic Indian schools could "scarcely speak English."[89]

When the contract system was abandoned, "chiefly owing to the great A.P.A. [American Protective Association] wave which swept over the country in the early nineties,"[90] some measure of sectarianism carried over as an aftermath of earlier contract institutions. Lay missionary teachers frequently continued as government employees even after the mission schools were sold or leased to the government.[91] Both the missionaries who had opened schools and missions under governmental aegis, as well as the former teachers, inclined to regard

86 I.R.A., *Annual Report,* 1889, p. 8.

87 George G. Smith (Presbyterian pastor at Santa Fe, writing from J. B. Block's trading store at Jémez Hot Springs) to T. J. Morgan, Commissioner of Indian Affairs, June 30, 1890, 20522, B.I.A., SC 143.

88 Kendrick to Plummer, July 11, 1894; Plummer to Commissioner, July 18, 1894; Secretary of the Interior to Commissioner, August 10, 1894, in 40841, 1894, with enclosures, B.I.A., SC 143.

89 I.R.A., *Annual Report,* 1887, p. 248; 1888, p. 43. One of the educational foibles current in the United States at the time was a mammoth indignation against the black heresy of teaching in non-English languages. ". . . if any Indian vernacular is allowed to be taught by missionaries in schools on Indian reservations it will prejudice the pupil as well as his parents against the English language." Commissioner Atkins in C.I.A., *Annual Report,* 1887, p. xxv.

90 Francis E. Leupp, *The Indian and His Problem* (New York: Charles Scribner's Sons, 1910), p. 29. Congressional prohibition, June 10, 1896, in 29 U. S. Stats., 345. For texts of Methodist-Episcopal, Baptist, and Methodist objections to later tribal-fund contract schools, see I.R.A., *Annual Report,* 1905, pp. 6–21, 48–53.

91 Women's National Indian Association, *Annual Report,* 1895, pp. 30–31; *ibid.,* 1903, p. 23; Report of Dr. Dorchester, superintendent of Government Indian Schools, May 23, 1893, C.I.B.A., New Mexico, 1911.

from a sectarian viewpoint both teaching occupation and particular Indian fields as vested interests.

No such carry-over of influence from previous missionary experience among the Navaho was possible for the Catholic Church, since no Catholic Navaho mission or school existed in the modern period.

Chapter II

La Cienega Ranch

Mother Katharine Drexel carried through successfully in midsummer of 1895 the modern attempt to establish a Catholic Navaho mission. Katharine Drexel, heiress of the fortune of Francis M. Drexel of Drexel & Morgan banking fame, had dedicated youth and wealth to aid the underprivileged.[1] Accompanying Joseph A. Stephan, Director of the Bureau of Catholic Indian Missions, on a tour of Western missions, she had learned a great love for the Indians in their wretched poverty and superstition.[2] Anything but maudlin, Miss Drexel decided to furnish her Church with an effective arm for specialized service among Indians and Negroes. After a twenty-month novitiate under the Mercy Sisters at Pittsburgh, Katharine founded her own community, February 12, 1891, under the protection of Archbishop Ryan of Philadelphia.[3]

Nine of her Sisters left the Cornwells Heights mother house near Philadelphia in 1894 to take over St. Catherine's Indian School in Santa Fe. Eight years earlier Miss Katharine had built this industrial school, which had been operated under government subsidy until the contract was terminated by Commissioner Morgan in 1893.[4]

At the close of the first school year Mother Katharine and Monsignor Stephan met at this New Mexican cradle of her projected mission enterprise to plan a new foundation for the Navaho. With Bureau finances overstrained to support numerous missions and schools, Monsignor Stephan knew he would have to rely on Mother Katharine's resources.

In early June, 1895, the Monsignor reported from Fort Defiance that Acting Agent Major Constant Williams, "an Episcopalian and a

[1] Interview with M. Philip Neri during visit with Mother Katharine Drexel, Cornwells Heights, November 8, 1950.

[2] Mother Katharine to community, April 21, 1897, C.H.A.

[3] Anselm Weber, in *St. Anthony Messenger,* 8:263, January, 1901.

[4] See C.I.A., *Annual Report,* 1892, pp. 158, 166.

most excellent gentleman," was willing and happy to assist. Investigation proved Wipo Spring near the Hopi villages too remote, and a doubtful mission site; several locations farther on in Arizona he wished to examine before returning to Santa Fe with a final recommendation.[5]

The following autumn, while en route to conclude the Navaho mission business, Monsignor Stephan stopped over at Santa Fe for the conferring of the *Pallium* and the consecration of the—at long last—debt-free cathedral of Archbishop Chapelle. Cardinal Gibbons and Apostolic Delegate Satolli headed the list of distinguished guests attending the special banquet given at St. Catherine's on October 16, 1895.[6]

Obviously the bluff old Monsignor, who had earlier studied military engineering in Germany, and who carried a Civil War ball in one heel[7] as a reminder of his chaplain service in the Union Army, was in rare crotchety mood. To his mind, poverty-stricken Indian missions, missionless Navaho, along with superstitious natives, did not jibe with outlandish Romanesque and with purple falderol. At the dinner in which the Sisters had outdone their resources by begging a venison roast and several bottles of burgundy and claret, the Cardinal was in poor digestion and utterly fatigued; he walked back to the Bishop's house immediately after dinner. The usual tedious after-dinner speeches, to Stephan's mind, lauded Archbishop Chapelle fulsomely while old Archbishop Salpointe "who did all the work . . . got no praise. . . . I had a fight with the Cardinal two weeks ago and I have been sick in bed ever since. I am going to have another this afternoon and then I am going to light out for the Navajoes!"[8] The doughty old mission campaigner was in smart military form to take on the pagan Navaho.

Arrived at Gallup, Monsignor Stephan hired S. M. Brown, livery-stable keeper, to drive him the twenty-eight miles to *La Cienega,* the location he and Mother Katharine had chosen.[9] West of the jumble of fantastic sandstone formations, across the gashed sage and greasewood flats of Bonito Valley, the rig labored to the crest of a rock-strewn outrunner of the Chuska Mountains, and halted. Below—

[5] J. A. Stephan to Mother Katharine, June 10, 1895, C.H.A.

[6] Jean Baptiste Salpointe, *Soldiers of the Cross* (Banning, Calif.: St. Boniface Indian Trade School, 1898), p. 280; report from St. Catherine's, Santa Fe, October 17, 1895, C.H.A.

[7] Sisters of the Blessed Sacrament, *Annals,* 6:205, 1899, C.H.A. Hereafter cited as *Annals,* C.H.A.

[8] Report from St. Catherine's, October 17, 1895, C.H.A.

[9] S. M. Brown to Stephan, August 24, 1898, C.I.B.A.

a quiet eddy beyond a tortuous maelstrom of butte, arroyos, and sand — lay the velvet-green alfalfa and the gold-flecked hoar green of autumn meadow. It was the spring-fed cove called by the Hispanos *Cienega Amarilla* (Yellow Marsh), and *Tsohotso* (Big Meadow) by the Navaho.[10]

Various Indians had claimed the rich bottoms. There they had raised good maize and melons, and there the mustangs grew sleek in the deep grama grass. But it was off-reservation land and soon the white outsiders, *Belagana,* were claiming the green strips and the springlands of even these scorched wastes where for decades the Navaho had grazed and made his corn.

Sam E. Day, who had assisted in surveying railroad and government lands north of the railroad in 1885, began the contest for the big meadow below the canyon mouth. He started to raise a log cabin and to string out a rail fence in the first days of 1887.[11] One previous squatter the Indians had already driven off; Sam Day, too, they threatened to kill and to fire his cabin, once he should try to fence off their horses and sheep.[12] Learning of the threat, Mr. Day enlisted the aid of the agent at Fort Defiance, and kept his Winchester handy. The Indian agent met with several Indians of the district and told them plainly that Cienega was just south of the reservation lands, and that men like Day had a right to homestead on the land which belonged partly to the United States and partly to the railroad.

White man's laws and agent's warnings notwithstanding, Short Hair and his outfit would not tolerate fencing off their best springs. Where *Naltsos naes,* "tall clerk," laid his rail fence, Short Hair made it clear, there they would lay the white man's bones. Sam Day tried to explain that the northern meadow would still be open, and plenty of water available; his best argument, and the one that won him his fence, was his sudden, direct offer to Short Hair of $1.50 per day for him and nine of his men to help split and raise his fence.[13] Dollar diplomacy again won the day!

In 1888 Joe K. Wilkin and J. M. Wyant teamed up for a time to

[10] Probably because of the heavy autumn bloom of golden *Gynnolonia Multiflora;* Weber, in B.C.I.M., *Indianer Wache,* 1908, p. 17. Lieutenant Simpson recorded the Spanish name in 1849 as *Sieneguilla de Maria.* J. H. Simpson, *Report of an expedition into the Navajo Country in 1849,* 31 Cong., 1 sess., Senate executive document, No. 64 (Washington, D. C.: Union Office, 1859), p. 111.

[11] Anna Burbridge Day, *Diary,* January 6, August 16, October 16, 1885; June n.d., 1886; January 13, 20, 21, 1887; S. E. Day, *Affidavit,* May 7, 1900, H.A.C.

[12] A. Weber, *Sendbote,* 26:379, May, 1899; Sam Day, Jr., interviewed for R. Wilken by Jewell Adams, November 7, 1951, P.A., CP.

[13] Sam Day, Jr., *ibid.*

settle and improve jointly two quarter sections, including most of the remaining unfenced meadowland at Cienega.[14] Subsequently Wyant took on another partnership arrangement with a rowdy called "Mug" Stevens; together they bought out a small trading post which had been opened by a man named Reeder. Competition between this store and the trading post run by Joe Wilkin led to a falling-out between Wilkin and the Wyant-Stevens combination. After a gun battle in which Joe Wilkin had his cheek creased, "Mug" left the area in a hurry when he learned that Joe was gunning for him. A Negro, George Overton, was hired by Wyant and Wilkin to help put up fences and improvements; he was given the use of a small log cabin on the north slope beyond Cienega, which Wilkin had purchased from a Mr. Carter.[15] Another disagreement between Wyant and Wilkin induced the latter to sell out his interests to Billy Meadows for $800. Joe next started a trading post east of the Chuska Range.[16]

It was this "Wilkin Ranch" of 240 acres more or less that Monsignor Stephan purchased in October of 1895. It lay six miles south of Fort Defiance, twenty-three miles north of Manuelito Station on the Atlantic and Pacific Railroad, a quarter mile below the south line of the reservation, in Apache County, Arizona.[17] As the area was officially unsurveyed, and hence not patentable homesteading land, the transaction entailed the purchase of improvements and personal property plus a quitclaim deed. Meadows thereby relinquished to the United States his pre-emptive rights as a squatter—once the land should be officially surveyed and opened to homestead filing. As agent for Mother Katharine the Monsignor paid the total sum of $3,600.[18]

As the survey eventually proved, eighty acres were railroad land, and parts of the remaining quarter section infringed Day's and Wyant's claims. What with later purchases of Day's and Wyant's

[14] J. M. Wyant, *Affidavit,* October 26, 1901, H.A.C.; see also Frederick Hartung, O.F.M., to J. A. Stephan, July 13, 1900, C.I.B.A.

[15] "Carter" or "Custer"; the cabin was on the northwest quarter of the southeast quarter of Section 14. J. K. Wilkin, *Affidavit,* July 19, 1901, C.I.B.A.; Sam Day, Jr., interviewed by Jewell Adams, November 7, 1951, P.A., CP. During the shooting feud, young Sam Day acted as runner for Joe Wilkin, and delivered the ultimatum written on the inside of an Arbuckle coffee bag which told "Mug" Stevens to clear out of the country before the sun went down.

[16] Frederick Hartung to J. A. Stephan, July 13, 1900, C.I.B.A.

[17] Quitclaim deed, October 26, 1895, H.A.C., and J. A. Stephan to D. Riordan, July 14, 1898, C.I.B.A.

[18] Deeds of sale and relinquishment, October 26, 1895, H.A.C. The deeds were drawn up and executed at the Albuquerque Office of Bernard S. Rodey, same date. *In re Sen. Bill 6528, 1908,* S.M.C., F-1 contains a résumé of land transactions concerning St. Michaels Mission.

interests for $4,000, purchase of two railroad forties for $200, besides locating and relocating Valentine, Forest Reserve, and Benson scrip, the total cost of acquiring clear title to Cienega Amarilla exceeded $10,000.[19]

En route back to Washington after the transaction Monsignor Stephan stopped off at Sedalia, Missouri, to enlist Father Andrew Gietl, C.PP.S., as missionary to the Navaho. This priest, who had earlier been stationed at Golden, Colorado, and previous to that at the Rennsalaer Indian Normal School, was anxious to take up the Arizona mission — if his superiors approved.[20] Apparently they did not, for the next two years were spent in a disappointing quest for missioners, or, an equally difficult task, their approval by the Tucson Ordinary. As usual the intrepid old army chaplain was frank: "St. Michels . . . is a lamentable case. I must frankly say that I have lost my cherished hopes for that mission. Bishop Bourgade wants only Saints fully canonized . . . before he accepts anyone for Indian missions."[21]

"St. Michel," named after the Torresdale, Pennsylvania, family estate of Mother Katharine's father, soon needed physical attention. With Billy Meadows, the former occupant, gone, fences were down in several places, the stone building stood unroofed, and there was rumor of claim jumpers eyeing the ranch.[22] Father George J. Juillard, Gallup pastor, inspected the place for Mother Katharine and hired J. B. Foley on a fifty-fifty proposition to protect and work the ranch.[23] While Father Juillard went abroad for a year, Father A. A. Martin transferred from Bernalillo, New Mexico, in mid-1897 to care for Gallup and its missions. Hard-pressed to make his numerous Indian and His-

[19] A. Weber, *Sendbote,* 27:637–642, August, 1900; *St. Michaels Mission Land,* folder, H.A.C. For exhaustive treatment, Emmanuel Trockur, O.F.M., in *The Provincial Chronicle of St. John Baptist Province,* 14:37–57, Fall, 1941; hereafter to be cited as *The Provincial Chronicle.* The eighty acres on railroad land was purchased in fee simple. Scrip was located on the one hundred sixty acres of government land to assure title, since the friars with their vow of poverty could not homestead, i.e., could not claim land in their own right. To avoid claim jumping, the government land of the Wilkin ranch was selected as lieu land for government land scrip. Only very valuable scrip, v.g., Valentine, issued by the United States as compensation to T. B. Valentine for valuable lands unjustly appropriated, could be placed on unsurveyed land. See 17 U. S. Stats., 649.

[20] J. A. Stephan to Mother Katharine, November 8, 1895, C.H.A.; for Gietl, see *Hoffmanns' Catholic Directory* (Milwaukee: Hoffmann Brothers), 9:287, 1894; 10:356, 1895. The Jesuits and the St. Louis Franciscans were also unsuccessfully approached according to Father Leopold Ostermann; see Emmanuel Trockur, in *The Provincial Chronicle,* 12:21, Fall, 1939.

[21] J. A. Stephan to Mother Katharine, June 2, 1896, C.H.A.

[22] George J. Juillard to Mother Katharine, May 14, 1896, C.H.A.

[23] *Ibid.;* J. B. Foley to "Dear Lady" (Mother Katharine), December 9, 1898, C.H.A.

pano missions — to the east and north as far as Cebolleta, and south to Atarque[24] — Father Martin found little time to visit " 'Seneca,' rich and lovely ranch."[25] Landgrabbers around Gallup and some near "Seneca," he wrote to Mother Katharine, were intending "to jump at your claim" and "Mr. Foley is not able to defend it."[26]

Although his contract held until April 26, Foley left to cook at an Arizona mining camp in March, 1898, after having roofed the stone house and put the fences and corral in order.[27] Colored George, "a great gambler," was in charge when Father Martin drove out in rain and snow on March 9 to spend the night. George claimed that he had been forced to brandish his Winchester only the previous Tuesday to scare off a claim jumper.

In order to lay the rumors and quiet the claim, Father Martin hired Tom Osborne at sixty-five dollars a month as ranchman.[28] After Osborne had taken over on April 19, the French priest felt the land was secure and in his quaint English assured Mother Katharine: "There is not anymore chance for intruders to jump at your place . . . and in his [Osborne's] respect for your grand *Oeuvre* . . . he will never have the idea to claim on it. . . . He is a good Irish Catholic."[29]

From the start everyone realized that these were mere stopgap remedies; a resident missionary would have to settle on the land both to establish claims, and, above all, to begin mission work. Monsignor Stephan confided his troubles over the Navaho mission to old "Padre Antonio" Jouvenceau of Park View, New Mexico.[30]

Playing on the embarrassed position of the Monsignor, who was confronted with a highly selective bishop in Tucson, together with the insecure mission ranch, Father Jouvenceau endeavored to have the Navaho mission relocated on the San Juan River within the Archdiocese of Santa Fe and within his own parish.[31] This was warranted, he believed, by the larger number of Navaho along the San Juan, especially in the vicinity of Chaco Cañon, Gallegos, Chico, and Blanco.

[24] George J. Juillard to Mother Katharine, April 7, 1897, C.H.A.; *Hoffmanns' Catholic Directory,* 11:203, 1896.

[25] A. A. Martin to Mother Katharine, August 2, 1897, and January 6, 1898, C.H.A.

[26] Same to same, February 25, 1898, C.H.A.; Mother Katharine to Charles S. Lusk, March 3, 1898, C.I.B.A.

[27] Martin to Mother Katharine, March 6 and 14, and April 4, 1898, C.H.A.

[28] *Ibid.*

[29] A. A. Martin to Mother Katharine, May 4, 1898, and May 21, 1898, C.H.A.

[30] J. A. Stephan to A. Jouvenceau, July, 1896, as referred to in Jouvenceau to Stephan, August 31, 1896, C.I.B.A.

[31] A. Jouvenceau, pastor of Park View, 1894–1906, St. Joseph Church, *Records.* A. Jouvenceau to J. A. Stephan, August 31, 1896, C.I.B.A.

Many Indians were farming on shares with the "Mexicans" and were settled permanently in agriculture. As these were favorably disposed to the Church, he had baptized many of their young ones. Everything considered, the San Juan seemed to him altogether more suitable than Cienega Amarilla.[32]

This attitude sat poorly with George J. Juillard, who was tending a scattered flock from Rio Puerco in New Mexico west across the Divide to the Rio Puerco in Arizona, a distance of 130 miles. From Gallup he wrote out a lengthy communication to the Santa Fe Archbishop based on facts as related to him by the half-breed Navaho, Frank Walker: "Rather few live on the Rio San Juan. There are more Indians coming to Gallup than to any other place of the territory."[33] Many live around Pino's, Dubois', and Newman's ranches; others have settled near Fort Defiance, Tuye, Ramah, La Posta, and Alamosa.[34]

Jouvenceau's letters in favor of Kutz or Gallegos Cañon "never met with any answer," he wrote, "so I have ceased to molest the Reverend Monsignor."[35] On his part the Monsignor had exhausted his list of prospective missioners for Cienega.

Toward the end of September, 1897, he dropped in for a visit with Father Godfrey Schilling, O.F.M., who was then engaged in building the imposing Franciscan Monastery at Washington, D. C.[36] Having explained his frustrating quest for Navaho missionaries, Stephan wondered if perhaps Father Godfrey could persuade his provincial in Cincinnati to undertake the neglected Navaho mission.

Father Godfrey's forthcoming letter of September 3, though generally short on fact and long on fancy, was a triumph in the proprieties of monastic political tactic.[37] Himself engaged in the centuries-long Franciscan crusade of guarding the Holy Places in Palestine, the holy friar could not but repeat the *Deus vult* of Peter the Hermit and recall the missionary glory of the Order and the Province. Thereafter, in sequence he listed the specific advantages of this waiting Navaho mission: a debt-free mission site with buildings, mounting pleas of the Navaho — so long unanswered by the secular clergy — no language problem since most all the Indians spoke some English, Mother

32 Jouvenceau to Stephan, *ibid.*

33 Frank Walker to Archbishop of Santa Fe (typed by Juillard on his parish letterhead), December 14, 1896, C.H.A. Letter forwarded to Mother Katharine by the Archbishop.

34 *Ibid.*

35 A. Jouvenceau to Juvenal Schnorbus, O.F.M., October 17, 1899, S.M.C., F-1.

36 Gottfried Schilling to Provincial Raphael Hesse, September 3, 1897, P.A., AF-1.

37 *Ibid.*

Katharine's promise to pay the friars' annual salary, and — confidentially — the good Mother hoped that the Cincinnati Province would not be outdone by the St. Louis Province,[38] or by the Benedictines who already had Indian mission fields.

Telling and grandiloquent as was this stirring crescendo, the rhetorician in Father Godfrey sensed the need for relief; the pounding staccato of his German softened and lengthened into sly innuendo:

> Monsignor Stephan further reveals that all of northern Arizona is to be erected into an Apostolic Vicariate over which one of the missionaries will be elevated, thereby placing the Province in a position to select parishes along the rail lines. . . . I beg you, Reverend Father Provincial, to embrace this opportunity to win God's blessing for the Order and for yourself by initiating your term of office with such a splendid work of social charity. Nor will the American Episcopate be able to deny our order and Province its rightful recognition when it again beholds our brown habit taking its place of honor among the poor abandoned natives of our land. . . . The monsignor will pay a personal call as soon as he receives favorable word from you.[39]

Few regular superiors — less so a newly elected provincial — could withstand the Scotistic cogency of the plea, much less the deft psychology of wise and lovable Godfrey Schilling. On October 12, 1897, the anxious Monsignor called on Father Raphael Hesse, O.F.M., in Cincinnati, and on the thirteenth a specially summoned definitorial conference voted unanimously to accept the Navaho mission.[40] Mother Katharine made a special trip five months later on March 12 to Mt. Airy, outside Cincinnati, where Father Raphael was confined to bed with rheumatism.[41] She explained the increasingly precarious status of the mission land in Arizona, pleading that he send "one of the volunteer missionaries at once." After she arrived there she planned to have the Father make the necessary affidavit of personal intent to homestead. It was most disappointing two months later to learn from the Provincial that he and the definitorium had decided that the

[38] Maricopa County, Arizona Territory, was officially taken over by St. Louis Province in 1896, and earlier still, the Franciscan Indian missions in Wisconsin and Michigan. See Maynard Geiger, O.F.M., *The Kingdom of St. Francis in Arizona* (*1539–1939*) (Santa Barbara, Calif., 1939), pp. 21–22.

[39] G. Schilling to R. Hesse, September 3, 1897, P.A., AF-1.

[40] A. Weber, *Sendbote,* 26:286, April, 1899; St. Michaels *House Chronicle,* S.M.C., p. 3. The early entries in this chronicle are in places inaccurate as to dates and past history of La Cienega. Hereafter this St. Michaels *House Chronicle* will be cited as *House Chronicle;* since entries are not always chronological, page numbers are cited.

[41] Mother Katharine to Charles Lusk, March 13, 1898, C.I.B.A., and Mother Katharine to Raphael Hesse, May 16, 1898, P.A., AF-1.

Franciscan vow of poverty precluded any such intent to take personal possession, a prerequisite for homesteading.[42]

To Mr. Lusk, who as secretary of the Bureau of Catholic Indian Missions handled legal and governmental affairs at the bureau office, this decision appeared critical. He advised the Sister Superior to induce a "secular priest to take the mission," one who could make the needed affidavit, comply with other legal requirements, and thus secure a patent.[43] He saw one alternative: if a survey showed the mission on a railroad section, it would be possible to purchase in fee simple from the railroad and settle this land business forthwith.[44]

Mr. Lusk met added discouragement when the general solicitor of the Atcheson, Topeka and Santa Fe Railroad, which had absorbed the old Atlantic and Pacific, informed Lusk that the railroad was definitely not willing to sign an option in favor of Mother Katharine's mission.[45] "From a business standpoint" first of all, the railroad did not want missions in the Cienega area because the company was trying to have the off-reservation Navaho put back on limits, thereby removing any encumbrances to sale or exchange of railroad lands; a school would contradict this policy since Navaho would tend to settle near their children. Second, there could be no option until a survey revealed the character of the land; adverse possession of springs or live water by the mission or by any homesteader or squatter would control thousands of acres of adjacent desert grazing lands.[46] Lusk immediately assured the solicitor that the proposed mission school would definitely not draw adult Indians and families; the missionaries would "minister to the spiritual needs at their homes on the reservations."[47]

Meanwhile Father Martin at Gallup and Bishop Bourgade at Tucson were endeavoring to have the mission land officially surveyed by the Land Office in Tucson, a service which would be undertaken only at the written request of three *bona fide* settlers of the township.[48]

Having been assured by Mr. Lusk that after the survey had been completed a congressional land grant would quiet the title for all time, Mother Katharine in May requested the Provincial to send the

[42] *Ibid.*

[43] Charles Lusk to Mother Katharine, March 15, 1898, C.I.B.A.

[44] Same to same, March 17, 1898, C.I.B.A.

[45] Same to same, April 16, 1898, C.I.B.A.

[46] Same to same, April 16, 1898, C.I.B.A.

[47] *Ibid.* This directly contradicted the missionary plans to-be of Father Provincial and Father Anselm Weber who later planned on a farming colony *à la* earlier California missions.

[48] A. A. Martin to Mother Katharine, May 4, 21, 1898, C.H.A.

Fathers to the mission in July.[49] Accordingly, at the July 25 chapter of the definitorium at Mt. Airy, three friars were assigned to the Navaho mission: Father Juvenal Schnorbus, pastor and superior; Father Anselm Weber, assistant; and Brother Placidus Buerger.[50]

On August 3, Father Juvenal left to put the place in order and to convert into a residence the empty stone building which Meadows had intended for his trading post.[51] From Gallup he contacted Charles Martinelli at Fort Defiance, employing him to plaster the bare stone walls and to raise two chimneys. José Kramer he hired by telegraph to come out from Albuquerque to partition off the one large rectangular room into six: a large end room to the west and another to the east to serve as chapel and kitchen, and four small bedrooms between.[52] In Gallup Father Juvenal stayed with the kindly and hospitable Father Martin, who aided in the renovation planning, and who, incidentally, would not allow the friar to pay even a single restaurant check.[53]

While making arrangements the erstwhile Latin instructor enjoyed the chance to botanize in the Fort Wingate area whither he had accompanied a hunting party. At Wingate he met Captain George B. Cooke, who insisted on immediate notification should the missioners ever need military help![54]

Father Juvenal returned to Cincinnati on August 26, and with the notice from Father Martin on September 15 that the mission would be ready within two weeks, the final preparations and farewells were concluded before departure for "Our Lady of Guadalupe."[55] Mother Katharine quickly reminded the Provincial that "some time ago it was christened St. Michael's."[56]

Monsignor Stephan, who had intended to accompany the first missionaries and stay for a few days,[57] was too exhausted from con-

[49] Mother Katharine to Raphael Hesse, May 16, 1898, P.A., AF-1. In July she further assured the Provincial that if the claim could not be perfected otherwise, Father Stephan would take a "Soldier's Claim" by reason of his Civil War service. Mother Katharine to Raphael Hesse, July 8, 1898, P.A., AF-1.

[50] *Tabula Definitionis,* July 25–27, 1898, P.A.

[51] Mother Katharine to Raphael Hesse, July 8, 1898, P.A., AF-1; *House Chronicle,* p. 3, S.M.C.

[52] *House Chronicle,* pp. 3–4, S.M.C.

[53] Raphael Hesse to Mother Katharine, August 26, 1898, C.H.A.

[54] A. Weber, *Sendbote,* 26:287–288, April 1899.

[55] R. Hesse to Mother Katharine, August 26, 1898, and September 20, 1898, C.H.A.

[56] Mother Katharine to R. Hesse, September 23, 1898, P.A., AF-1. Father Raphael agreed to the name "St. Michaels," in R. Hesse to Mother Katharine, September 30, 1898, C.H.A.

[57] Mother Katharine to R. Hesse, July 20, 1898, P.A., AF-1.

tinuous traveling among the western Indians and could not undertake the Arizona journey.[58]

This time Bishop Bourgade had not disapproved the Monsignor's choice of missionaries; from Las Cruces the Tucson diocesan Superior had telegraphed, "Reverend R. Hesse . . . would gladly accept your order for the Navajo mission."[59]

[58] Same to same, September 23, 1898, P.A., AF-1.

[59] No date, P.A., AF-1. *House Chronicle,* p. 3, S.M.C., dates the telegram as immediately following Mother Katharine's March visit to the Provincial.

Chapter III

First Friars at St. Michaels; Orientation and Adjustment, 1898

On Monday, October 3, 1898, the eve of their Founder's feast, the three Franciscans boarded the train for Kansas City, Kansas, where next morning they offered Mass in St. Anthony Church and enjoyed St. Francis' feast-day dinner with their confreres. Leaving the same afternoon by the Santa Fe Line they traveled on to Emporia, westernmost station of their Cincinnati Province. Wednesday at 3:30 p.m. they started on the final lap to Gallup, New Mexico, where they arrived thirty-six hours later to the minute.[1]

Through an oversight there was no ranchman waiting for them and their bulky luggage at the station. They made the best of it by hiring a barouche at Flahive's Livery Stable, and with only their suitcases and a few kitchen needs which Brother Placid had picked up at Ed Hart's Store, they drove off northwest across terrain which Father Juvenal described as "a most desolate country, if you except the picturesque rocks."[2] Father Anselm noted the "lone coyote that looked them over from the greasewood," and added with disappointment that they saw no Indians. They did pass a neighbor's wagon headed into town from Cienega, and "one lone hut and one trading post."[3] There was no commotion upon the arrival of the three tired Franciscans at Cienega. At 4 p.m. they reached the welcome sight of green meadows and had to inquire where the mission ranch might be.[4] Tom Osborne, the ranchman, surprised at their arrival, helped the Fathers make sleeping arrangements while Brother Placid busied himself over the cook stove. As they sat down hungry and tired around the kitchen table later that evening, the old stone trading post had become a Franciscan home.

[1] *House Chronicle,* p. 4, S.M.C.

[2] *Ibid.,* p. 5.

[3] A. Weber, *Sendbote,* 26:288, April, 1899.

[4] *House Chronicle,* p. 5, S.M.C.

At forty-six Brother Placid was the oldest in the new community. A strong, tall, jovial man, he had worn the brown habit and cord since he was sixteen, and was loved the province over as Brother "Aber Aber." He was thoroughly convinced of his ability to serve the Indians and win them to the Faith by medical administrations. His equipment in the medical field consisted of a large ten-pound sack of Epsom salts. A good, simple Brother was Placid.[5]

Both priests, ten years younger than the Brother, had been born in 1862, Juvenal Schnorbus in Cincinnati, and Anselm Weber at New Salem, Michigan. Juvenal had entered the Order when he was seventeen, and at twenty-three had been ordained. He had served in varying capacities since his ordination in 1885, his most recent as Latin instructor at the Franciscan Gymnasium in Cincinnati.[6] He was of slight build, with light hair, fair, almost anemic complexion, and a thin, somewhat boyish face. A serious, zealous, ofttimes moody man, he had a reputation for strict Franciscan observance and rather rigoristic theology.[7]

His assistant, and the future "Apostle of the Navaho," had been baptized Anton, but the name was changed to Anselm when he entered the Oldenburg, Indiana, Franciscan novitiate in 1882. Anton had studied Latin at home under his pastor, W. A. Tilik, until his transfer in October, 1877, to Detroit, where Anton then went to live while preparing for the diocesan seminary. Because of poverty he could not meet the fees. Several months later he returned to the farm home of his Prussian-born parents, Peter and Anna (Pfeiffer) Weber, until with Father Tilik's aid he was admitted to the Franciscan Gymnasium at Cincinnati. A fellow student recalled his "brilliant talents, retentive memory," and his quick grasp of problems.[8]

After ordination by Archbishop Elder of Cincinnati, December 28, 1889,[9] Father Anselm was assigned to teaching Latin at the Gymnasium and lecturing to the Franciscan clerics at St. Francis Monas-

[5] *Catalogus Fratrum Provinciae Cincinnatensis S. Joannis Baptistae, O.F.M.* (Cincinnati, 1933), p. 48; hereafter to be cited as *Catalogus Fratrum.* Placidus Buerger to A. Weber, December 23, 1901; Raphael Hesse to A. Weber, November 26, 1899. P.A., AH.; interview with John Forest McGee, O.F.M., September 5, 1951.

[6] *Catalogus Fratrum,* p. 41; *Tabula Definitionis Congregationis Capitularis,* 1897, P.A.; hereafter to be cited as *Tabula Definitionis,* P.A.

[7] Photos, P.A., AP.; letters from, to, about Juvenal Schnorbus, P.A., *Juvenal.*

[8] Leopold Ostermann, *F.M.S.,* 1922, pp. 1–2. Earlier details from letters, W. A. Tilik to A. Weber, February 28, 1899; Joe Weber (brother of Anselm) to J. Forest McGee, July 16, 1931, both in P.A., AY.; *Catalogus Fratrum,* p. 43.

[9] *'Celebret,'* Chancellor Henry Moeller, February 10, 1890, P.A., AP.

tery, Cincinnati. By disposition he was a thoroughgoing, deeply inquisitive student who spent long hours over his books, unashamedly enjoyed his teaching and giving the personalized attention to individuals which was only possible because of student loads of from six to ten clerics. One of the gymnasium students of the period characterized Father Anselm as "a born teacher, heart and soul in his work, with a genial character and genuine kindness that made him beloved by everybody."[10]

Excessively late hours at his desk and overwork to meet an impossibly broad schedule in college Greek, Latin, Philosophy, and Church History, plus week-end ministry, eventually broke his health. It was shortly after the doctor's verdict of approaching nervous breakdown, and recommendation of climate change, that the Navaho mission was accepted.[11] Father Anselm might regain his health in Arizona, it was hoped; so he was missioned to the Navaho. He was permitted to visit his parents and relatives in Michigan and Wisconsin before leaving.[12]

Anselm Weber was of medium height, had thinning brown curly hair, blue eyes set in a broad square face, and a wide mouth that tended to pull downward at the corners. He wore steel-framed spectacles and walked with head bent forward in the sloping-shouldered stoop so typical of the shortsighted student.[13]

In brief these were the three friar-missionaries who began community life in the converted trading post on the night of October 7, 1898. The mission resembled the squat, one-story stone buildings frequently in use at the time on government posts and Indian agencies in the Southwest. There were three doors on the north side, and four large and small windows pierced the field-stone walls. The roof was of cedar shingles. It stood on a slight rise off the northeast corner of the bottoms, diagonally across from the Wyant's homestead. The center door from the front of the building led into a passageway which separated the four bedrooms opening on this hallway. On the west end was the chapel room; on the east end was a combination kitchen-dining-living-reception room. Between cubicles and chapel ran low

[10] Edwin Auweiler, O.F.M., in *St. Anthony Messenger,* 29:452, March, 1922. For teaching assignments, *Tabula Definitionis,* 1889–1897, P.A.

[11] *Ibid.;* Leopold Ostermann, *F.M.S.,* 1922, p. 3; Maurice Ripperger, O.F.M., interview, January 14, 1951.

[12] Mrs. Mary Wellinghoff and Adeline Rauch, nieces of Anselm Weber, interview, February 16, 1951, P.A., AY.

[13] *Ibid.;* Sister Ignatius to community, May 29, 1902, C.H.A.; numerous photographs, P.A., AP.

flimsy, wooden partitions which, according to design, might easily be removed to provide schoolroom space.[14]

As the trunks and boxes containing fittings, chalice, and vestments were still in Gallup, the Fathers were unable to offer Mass for the first few days. Debris from plastering and carpentering had to be cleaned out and hauled away. Outside, the yard was a clutter of stone, wood litter, and tree stumps that needed disposal. Father Anselm knocked together a rough sledge on which they removed the rubble. Doorways had to be cut through the partitions, and cupboards, kneeling benches, and bookcases hammered into shape. A few curious Indians squatted in the shade at a distance and smiled as the perspiring "brown robes" dug fence-post holes in the rocky slope along the road. As Anselm Weber wrote, "we had built on rock, not sand."[15]

On October 9 the new chapel was blessed and officially dedicated to St. Michael the Archangel.[16] The first Masses were offered on Tuesday, October 11, with the table serving as altar, and salt and pepper cellars as wine and water cruets.[17] By November 3 they had the priestly happiness of celebrating Mass in fitting style on a standard altar presented by Mr. Firnstein of Pustets, and with the other proper appointments donated by Benziger Brothers, both religious-goods stores in Cincinnati.[18] Other liturgical needs of the chapel were furnished by gifts from Rosenthal, the Cincinnati printer, from the Oldenburg Franciscan Sisters, and from Joan Harter of Covington, Kentucky.[19]

Unable to preach to, or instruct, the curious Indians, as to what they were about, the friars on October 27 dramatized the main purpose of their mission by raising "a rude cross of pine, twenty three feet long," in front of the mission,[20] "openly declaring war on Satan and his followers," as Father Juvenal militantly recorded.[21]

Father Anselm meanwhile had been working in the ranch carpenter

[14] A. Weber, *Sendbote,* 26:380, May, 1899; photo taken by Mr. Hildebrand, carpenter at Fort Defiance, January 30, 1899, *House Chronicle,* p. 7, S.M.C. in P.A., PH.; see also Leopold Ostermann, in *St. Anthony Messenger,* 8:301, February, 1901.

[15] *Sendbote,* 26:382, May, 1899, which also describes work of first days.

[16] Zephyrin Engelhardt, *The Franciscans in Arizona* (Harbor Springs, Mich., 1899), p. 210.

[17] *House Chronicle,* p. 5, S.M.C. Father Martin of Gallup had likely offered the first Mass at Cienega on June 1, 1898, as planned. A. Martin to Mother Katharine, May 21, 1898, C.H.A.

[18] A. Weber, *Sendbote,* 26:380, May, 1899.

[19] *Ibid.; House Chronicle,* p. 6, S.M.C.

[20] Juvenal Schnorbus to Mother Katharine, November 5, 1898, C.H.A.

[21] *House Chronicle,* p. 5, S.M.C.

shop, turning out fourteen station crosses which Father Juvenal blessed and erected in the chapel on November 25. A new white cope, a used veil, and three used stoles arrived on the eve of Epiphany, a gift from the Oldenburg Sisters. With the beautiful Benediction service concluded, and with the incense-filled chapel ringing with the triumphant strains of *Grosser Gott,* the faraway mission seemed complete at last.[22]

In keeping with her wish to cover all costs incidental to opening the Navaho mission,[23] Mother Katharine met all expenses, including house renovation, travel, mission furnishings, host iron, Mass wine, Father Martin's horse and saddle ($25) — in all, $777 up to November 5.[24] As to maintaining day-to-day mission expenses of the friars, Mother Katharine requested an estimate from the Provincial,[25] but he felt that for him to fix a salary would run counter to the vow of poverty: "I would rather . . . leave it entirely to you to contribute towards supporting them. . . . We propose to observe holy poverty and hence will be satisfied with whatever you contribute."[26] She in turn suggested a thousand dollars as annual salary for the three missionaries, which agreement might be renewed annually if mutually satisfactory.[27]

Running the ranch introduced another problem in the material and mundane area where Father Juvenal felt ill at ease. Wishing to do full-time missionary work, and strong for strict poverty, he bridled at the idea of running the farming end of the mission. However, after the Provincial approved the simple supervision of Tom Osborne's activities, the mission superior reluctantly took over the ranch management and the books.[28] This became later a heavy, time-consuming chore, as all purchases and business had first to be cleared through the Sisters' office at Cornwells Heights, in strict Drexel banking tradition.[29]

[22] *Ibid.*, p. 6.

[23] Mother Katharine to Raphael Hesse, September 4, 1898, P.A., AH., and same to same, July 8, 1898, P.A., AF.

[24] Same to same, November (10–16), 1898, P.A., AH.; Juvenal Schnorbus to Mother Katharine, November 5, 1898, C.H.A.; Mother Katharine to J. Schnorbus, October 22, 1898, P.A., HA.

[25] Mother Katharine to Raphael Hesse, September 23, 1898, P.A., AF.

[26] Raphael Hesse to Mother Katharine, September 30, 1898, C.H.A.

[27] Mother Katharine to Raphael Hesse, November 28, 1898, P.A., AH.; same to same, November (10–16), 1898, P.A., AH.

[28] Mother Katharine to Juvenal Schnorbus, October 22, 1898, P.A., AH.; same to same, November 16, 1898, P.A., AH.; Mother Katharine to Raphael Hesse, November 28, 1898, P.A., AH.; A. Martin to Mother Katharine, October 12, 1898, C.H.A.

[29] See letters, several folders, P.A., AK.

Jealous as they were of their prime function as missionaries, and impatient to begin direct evangelical work, the friars nonetheless recognized the apparent stalemate facing them. They must learn the Navaho language to make headway with the Indians; as Navaho had not as yet been reduced to writing, they had to go to the Indians themselves to learn.

All the airy talk about the Navaho knowing either Spanish or English was pure fancy.[30] A few words like money, Washington, and Kishmus, along with a string of pungent cuss words, was the extent of their English, excepting the few at Fort Defiance and those who had been away to boarding schools.[31] It was the same in Spanish; in some areas of frequent contact with Spanish-speaking people, they could speak that language. At stores and trading posts run by Hispanos they could trade a blanket or sheep, or beg a handout; that was about all.[32] Government figures from Fort Defiance listed 500 Navaho out of a total of 20,500 as being able to carry on an English conversation in 1897, and 220 literates.[33] Five years later the same Navaho Agency report trimmed the earlier figures to 75 as able to converse and 45 literates.[34]

Before leaving Cincinnati Father Anselm had written to Dr. Washington Matthews, the noted anthropologist of the Navaho, for information regarding the Indians. The old Fort Wingate army surgeon had answered with a package of eighteen of his published treatises and with the far more practical advice:[35] "I would advise you to go to work at once and begin a vocabulary of your own. You will find the card system the best way to work it up. . . . As for my Grammar and Dictionary, I know not when it will be published, perhaps never." In a subsequent letter of November 22, Dr. Matthews restated his sound cultural approach for missionary endeavor:[36]

> My opinion is that if you want to reach the *hearts* of the people and gain a permanent influence over them, you cannot too soon begin to learn the Navaho language . . . one and all of you. You tell me you are not working for a day or for a year, but for a Century . . . for all time and Eternity, too. Then begin at once to learn the Navaho, and place no permanent reliance on any other means of communication (Ecclesiastes, XI, 1).

30 Washington Matthews to A. Weber, October 1, 1898, P.A., WM.
31 A. Weber, *Sendbote,* 26:551, July, 1899.
32 Washington Matthews to A. Weber, November 22, 1898, P.A., WM.
33 C.I.A., *Annual Report,* 1897, p. 482.
34 *Ibid.,* 1902, p. 630.
35 W. Matthews to A. Weber, October 1, 1898, P.A., WM.
36 To A. Weber, 1898, P.A., WM.

This advice became basic missionological dogma for Father Anselm and his confreres. Every meeting with an Indian in those early days was an opportunity to learn new words, to write down another Navaho expression.[37]

Brother Placid, smiling and friendly, ever willing to heat the coffee and set out food for visitors, proved himself the main attraction. Cooking to the Navaho was squaw work. Soon the neighboring Indians overcame their timidity and dropped by, half curious to see the "big, big squaw"[38] — and always hungry. While the "big squaw" demonstrated the traditions of a Franciscan kitchen, one of the friars with pencil poised sat on guard across the table, alert for new words and phrases.[39] Father Juvenal concluded the visits by giving the visitors, especially children, a bright scapular medal. These latter were quickly converted into earrings by the Navaho, while the words on the kitchen pad were copied and filed.[40]

From the start the Indians called the brown-robed Franciscans *e'nishodi,* literally, "those who drag their gowns," an expression carried over and translated from the Pueblo Indian term.[41] The Indians were amazed that the friars could make "paper words"; they laughed incredulously when Anselm would write down their sounds and at their request read them back to the mystified audience.[42]

"Black Mexican," as the Navaho named George Overton, the Negro who lived a quarter mile to the north of the mission, was also a frequent visitor. He added a few words, particularly gambling jargon, and induced some Indians to drop by to meet the friars.[43] When the number of objects to point to for new words was exhausted, and after pantomime also failed, the linguists would resort to the kitchen bible of every ranch home, the Montgomery-Ward "wishin' book."[44]

The weather favored indoor study for both missionaries and Indians. The hard winter of 1898–1899 was ushered in with a twenty-inch snow on December 8. Snow covered the ground for three months and on February 7 the temperature at St. Michaels fell to 32 degrees below zero.[45] While according to government figures no Indians

[37] A. Weber, in B.C.I.M., *Indianer Wache,* 1905–1906, p. 41.

[38] A. Weber, *Diary, 1899,* P.A., AF-2, notes at rear.

[39] A. Weber, *Sendbote,* 26:556, July, 1899.

[40] J. Schnorbus to Mother Katharine, November 26, 1898, C.H.A.; Leopold Ostermann, *F.M.S.,* 1922, p. 3.

[41] A. Weber, *F.M.S.,* 1913, p. 18.

[42] A. Weber, *Sendbote,* 26:552, July, 1899.

[43] A. Weber, *Diary, 1899,* P.A., AF-2, notes at rear; also same, *Sendbote,* 26:200, March, 1899.

[44] *Ibid.,* 26:556, July, 1899.

[45] J. Schnorbus to Mother Katharine, December 25, 1898, C.H.A.; A. Weber, *Sendbote,* 26:469, May, 1899.

actually died of freezing or starvation, 20 per cent of their sheep did,[46] and, rare for the independent Navaho of that day, a few Indians went to the agent for rations.[47]

The mission gave out as much hay and alfalfa as could be spared for Indian livestock, and fed the neighborhood callers,[48] especially the poor Ute Squaw and her boy, Percy Hayden. The Ute woman was a Navaho slave, and when her son noted the envy of the Navaho, and the rising ill will toward the *e'nishodi* who would feed Navaho slaves oftener than *Diné,* Percy discerningly cut down their visits.[49] From all the Indians the only payment expected by the friars for food and animal fodder was Navaho words, and more words.[50]

In the first of a series of monthly mission reports that ran almost uninterruptedly from March, 1899, until his death in 1921, Father Anselm described touchingly, and in detail, the Sunday of December 25, 1898.[51]

Outside it was black and cold as the friars creaked their way to the chapel where Brother Placid was filling the smoking maw of the hot blast. Piñon smoke sweetened the gloomy smell of kerosene from the wall lamp with its brightly polished reflector. At five o'clock, after the *Adoremus Te,* the *Veni Sancte,* and the reading of the meditation, Father Juvenal began his first of three Christmas Masses.

Hoping to soften the poignant memories of past years, of starry-eyed children singing around cribs glowing with scores of candles, Father Anselm sang wistfully and low the sweet German carols they all loved. It was lonesome — Christmas without crib and without rosy-cheeked *Kindlein* pouring out their folksongs of love to the *Christenkind.* The stove glowed and crackled while the house timbers complained of wind and cold.

At seven-thirty it was Anselm's turn to stand before the altar while Placid served and Juvenal sang. The mystery of ageless renewal restored his joy as he filled in spirit with the thrilling meaning of Incarnation: "By the mystery of the Word-made-flesh the light of Thy glory hath shown anew upon the eyes of our mind." In flowing cadence the Preface moved on, robbing the empty chapel of its loneliness as it joined him consciously with the world-wide communion

46 C.I.A., *Annual Report,* 1899, p. 156.

47 *Ibid.,* Part 2, 1899, p. 562.

48 A. Weber, *Sendbote,* 26:469–470, May, 1899.

49 *Ibid.,* 26:556, July, 1899.

50 *Ibid.*

51 The following account is a shortened paraphrase of the article "Eine Weihnachtsfeier . . . ," *Sendbote,* 26:199–203, March, 1899.

of Christ's Church — *"ut dum visibiliter Deum cognoscimus, per hunc in invisibilium amorem rapiamur. Et ideo cum Angelis et Archangelis . . . sine fine dicentes Sanctus. . . ."* Gray emptiness, the missioner's frustrated yearning for responsive souls, had lifted. Under the spell of the Mass he knew again, richly, the brotherhood of all men in Christ. He, Juvenal, Placid were part of the Church; they shared the endless stream of Christ's mission to man — German, American, Navaho.

After his thanksgiving he passed through the cold bedrooms to the warm, steaming kitchen where after cheering greetings the Brother served up Arbuckle coffee and last night's home-made fresh bread. The brotherhood of man was good.

Noiselessly the door widened, letting in a sweep of icy wind. Six half-frozen and hungry Navaho stalked in, their blankets pulled tight and close. "Kishmus, Kishmus!" The words had a strange, muffled sound, but their meaning was universally plain; and the Indians were smiling now as they moved toward the Brother, each with an outstretched palm. Made braver by the timeless fraternity of the skillet, an old squaw waddled up to Placid where he stood by the stove. Grinning widely and with begging gesture she giggled out — as only an old squaw can — her Christmas litany, "Kishmus! peso! money!" For all his six feet Placid was just a little confused. "No peso, no money . . . *aber, aber . . . froehliches Weihncht'n 'n gibts Kaffeekuchen 'n Fleisch,"* and he beamed wonderfully as he gestured them to the table.

Soon the men were sitting happily but stiffly around the unaccustomed table, while the women and children squatted Navaho style on the floor. All were laughing and chatting as they fell-to hungrily.

Anselm filled his corncob and pushed the tin of "Kanaster" tobacco to the center of the oilcloth-covered table. A black-eyed lad of seven munching a huge slab of the Brother's coffeecake walked hesitantly up to Father Anselm, shook his head slowly and appreciatively, and confided happily: "Bueno, bueno!" More Indians dropped in and the room became noisier. Father Juvenal gave them medals, which they clucked over approvingly. No one minded the wide-eyed infants peering from their cradleboards against the wall. When they whimpered, and the mothers nursed them, it was even more like Bethlehem and the shepherds.

Later Tom Osborne and George Overton led in a troop of sixteen more happy Navaho. Osborne had also been surprised by a troop of "kishmus" visitors, and fearing they meant trouble, had led his houseful over to the Negro's cabin, which also was crowded. So all in a group they had moved back to the mission when George ran out of food.

All day long they dropped by. One of the Indians who understood English from his days as a scout at Fort Wingate aided Anselm in trying to explain the meaning of Christmas. Using an illustrated Bible, along with a religious picture calendar on the wall, they attempted to describe Christ's birthday. It was grotesque, and possibly not too dogmatically sound, but it pleased the Indians as it mystified them. In the afternoon young Charley Day dropped in, and with his fluent Navaho explained to an Indian gathering in the chapel the meaning of statues, stations of the Cross, and the rosary. Charley did the talking after Father Juvenal made clear to him, a Protestant, the meaning of the various practices.

The Indians were rather disappointed that the *e'nishodi* did not put on a "sing" for the poor little God-baby. And several years later when the Sisters put up a crib at St. Michaels School, with only the Infant lying in a manger, the Navaho women "tsked" and scolded and clucked for hours because the "little boy's mother had walked away from the hogan and left her baby alone — without a blanket."[52]

Anselm and Juvenal were overjoyed: perhaps this was the opening drive. And Peshlakai Biye, the local silversmith, had asked the friars if they would instruct his son when he brought him to the mission! Anselm even wondered if possibly the silversmith's son might not be the first Navaho priest.[53]

Christmas was indeed an unusual experience for the missionaries that first year of 1898. It incidentally marked the housewarming of the mission, but, more significantly, the first genuine sense of belonging to the Navaho community.

[52] *Annals,* 7:100, C.H.A.

[53] End of the paraphrase from *Sendbote,* 26:199–203.

Chapter IV

Student of the Navaho, 1899

A WEEK before the first Christmas at St. Michaels the three Day boys had already joined in the general neighborhood effort to help the friars learn Navaho.[1] Charley was nineteen, Sammy sixteen, and Willie fourteen years old. Charley had been born in Iowa and the younger two in Colorado,[2] but having spent the past thirteen years, boyhood years, among the Navaho at Fort Defiance and at Cienega Amarilla, they spoke fluent Navaho.[3]

Both Sam E., Senior, and Anna Burbridge Day had received good schooling, and Anna had taught school before her marriage. She and Mr. Day now persuaded the friars to enter into an educational barter arrangement: they would be taught Navaho while instructing the three boys in English grammar, literature, geography, and mathematics. Arrangements were settled with Mr. and Mrs. Day on December 28, 1898, at the Day home, a quarter mile southeast of the mission.[4]

On January 23 classes began regularly.[5] Father Bernard Nurre, a close personal friend of Anselm Weber, and rector of the Cincinnati Gymnasium, furnished copies of *Webster's Speeches,* Hill's *Foundations of Rhetoric,* and was searching for McGuffy's *Sixth Readers.*[6] Father Anselm, who began the instructions, was just a little nettled when after two weeks he discovered that he was permanently saddled with the job.[7] After receiving instructions the greater part of the

[1] A. Weber, *Sendbote,* 26:637, August, 1899.

[2] Sam Day, Jr., interviewed by Silver Meyer, O.F.M., April 13, 1951; Emmanuel Trockur, O.F.M., in *The Provincial Chronicle,* 12:73–74, Winter, 1939–1940.

[3] A. Weber, *Sendbote,* 26:637, August 1899; Anna Burbridge Day *Diary,* October 4, 1885.

[4] *Ibid.* Father Anselm began brushing up on square roots as recorded in his personal day journal, January 17, 1899. This day journal for the year 1899 only will hereafter be cited as *Diary, 1899.* It is to be found in P.A., folder AF-2; Sam Day, Jr., interview, April 13, 1951.

[5] *Diary, 1899,* January 11 and 23; *House Chronicle,* p. 5, S.M.C.

[6] Bernard Nurre to A. Weber, February 26, 1899, P.A., BN.

[7] A. Weber, *Diary, 1899,* February 8.

morning the Day boys reversed the pupil-teacher status and taught the friars Navaho the remainder of the day. Informal tutoring of this kind took place Monday through Fridays, except for several days lost in February because of snow storms.[8]

By February 7 they hit on an arrangement for less haphazard Navaho instructions. Using a small *Webster's Dictionary,* Juvenal and Charley translated word for word, starting with "A." Sammy and Anselm worked backward from "Z." On April 26 the two teams met on the letter "L."[9] While Father Anselm and Sammy worked on further with adverbs, conjunctions, prepositions, and interjections, the other team revised the dictionary and added flora and place names of the locale. Common plant names were copied from Washington Matthews' list while unknown species were first identified by Markus Kreke, O.F.M., of Cincinnati.[10]

Constant application to the language sharpened the critical ear of the missionaries so that by the time they began on the dictionary they had abandoned the phonetic alphabet of the Bureau of Ethnology, the use of which Dr. Matthews had urged.[11] Instead, they tried out a new code which combined the phonetics of English, German, French, and Arabic. After practice they realized a new accuracy in recording sounds, tone inflections, and breathings. No longer did the Navaho visitors smile and chortle quite so exuberantly when the priests read back to them the new paper words.[12]

By the end of 1898 others besides Indians were beginning to visit the mission. Sunday Mass usually brought in worshipers from Fort Defiance. On New Year's Day, 1899, Mrs. Manning, Miss Molly Keough, and Miss Dennison drove over to increase the local congregation consisting of Tom Osborne and Charley Day. On that occasion Father Juvenal "kept the first sermon" at St. Michaels.[13] Mollie and Maggie Keough, Ethel and Eliza Jane Dennison, Mr. Maxie, Mr. Muse, and the Days, off and on, were the usual Sunday

[8] *Ibid.,* February 1–5.

[9] *Ibid.,* April 26; A. Weber, *Sendbote,* 26:638, August, 1899; Emmanuel Trockur, in *The Provincial Chronicle,* 12:74, Winter, 1939–1940.

[10] *House Chronicle,* p. 7, S.M.C.; Father Hugh Staud, O.F.M., copied in longhand the plant list of Washington Matthews published in the *American Naturalist,* 20:767–777, September, 1886; he did the copying at the Cincinnati Public Library. See also T. N. Glover to A. Weber, February 24, 1899, P.A., NL. Peshlakai gave the place names, as mentioned in *Diary, 1899,* March 5.

[11] W. Matthews to A. Weber, October 1, 1898, P.A., WM.

[12] A. Weber, *Sendbote,* 26:635, August, 1899.

[13] *Diary, 1899,* January 1.

visitors, weather permitting. Only the Keoughs and Tom Osborne were Catholic. An Indian or two also occasionally dropped in for the Mass "Sing."[14]

On January 4 George Thacker was introduced by Overton. Thacker clerked in a trading store at Corn Fields, and helped considerably with the Navaho vocabulary. Later, in attempting to translate the "Our Father," he confessed that he thought Navaho would not admit of expressions like "who," "heaven," "hallowed be Thy Name," or "trespass." Anselm Weber was beginning to understand the uncongeniality of Navaho culture with Christian concepts.[15]

Other traders dropping by to visit at this period were Mr. White, Mr. Meadows, former homesteader of Cienega and now trading northeast of the Chuskas, and J. Lorenzo Hubbell from Ganado.[16] Anson Chandler Damon, the old soldier and butcher from Bosque Redondo who had married a Navaho and settled at Fort Defiance, welcomed Anselm for long chats on Fort Sumner and the Navaho return to Fort Defiance. The missioner frequently dropped in on the old gentleman during his regular visit to the Fort on Saturdays.[17] Old Damon wanted to send two of his sons to classes at the mission school, suggesting at the same time his son, Ben, as farmer and interpreter.[18]

From traders and old-timers, and from government people and others, such as Reverend Herman Fryling, Dutch Reformed minister who had come to Fort Defiance in 1896, there was small encouragement offered the friars as to learning the Navaho language and teaching them Christianity.[19] But to Anselm Weber and Juvenal Schnorbus, who were practically finished with their "English-Navaho Dictionary" by May, these cautious people were overpessimistic.[20] Naïvely, Father Anselm wrote of a poor Indian missionary who spent fourteen years with his charges before attempting to translate the

[14] *Ibid.*, Sunday entries January through June.

[15] A. Weber, *Sendbote*, 26:557, July, 1899; *Diary, 1899,* January 4, February 8.

[16] *Diary, 1899,* Meadows on March 5, and Hubbell March 18; see also *ibid.*, notes at rear.

[17] A. Weber, *Sendbote,* 26:823, October, 1899. See Dane and Mary Roberts Coolidge, *The Navajo Indians* (Boston and New York: Houghton Mifflin Company, 1930), p. 28; *Diary, 1899,* January 28.

[18] *Diary, 1899,* January 28. His son, Frank Damon, had been farmer and interpreter since 1897 for the Methodist Mission at Jewett (Hogback), New Mexico. See Pauline Malehorn, *op. cit.*, p. 12.

[19] A. Weber, *Sendbote,* 26:639, August, 1899. Re Fryling see C. Kuipers, *Zuni Also Prays* (Grand Rapids: Christian Reformed Board of Missions, 1946), p. 104; *Diary, 1899,* January 28.

[20] Mother Katharine to J. Schnorbus, May 28, 1899, P.A., AK.

Catechism into the Skalzi Indian dialect. Thanks to the Days it would not be so with them at St. Michaels.[21]

"Yearning for an outlet to carry on direct mission work," as Father Anselm admitted,[22] the friars decided to take in a few Navaho boarding pupils at the mission. Some small start could thus be made toward the large mission boarding school contemplated by Mother Katharine. With Indian children at the mission they hoped also to improve their diction and learn everyday Navaho. Rumors had to be squelched, moreover: rumors that the Indian, Russell Sage, was spreading about St. Michaels Indian School of the future being only a day school; that the Indians would have to pay tuition and would have to walk through all weather to get a little schooling.[23] Possibly fearing that the devil was kicking up just a little too much trouble, Father Juvenal at this juncture wrote for, and received, faculties to use the rite of exorcism in private.[24]

Seemingly the neighborhood Indians were still unsure about the *e'nishodi.* Short Hair, Slinky, and others promised to send their boys and were highly interested in a school — when they came for food and hay; at their next call they gave scores of excuses for not bringing the pupils.[25] Father Anselm Weber's personal diary for 1899 carries in its telegraphic jottings something of the suspense of a Crusoe-and-Friday encounter as it tells how they won their first pupil: March 14, "Indian boy around the house"; March 15, "boy again on premises"; March 16, "little Indian visits us twice all by himself"; March 17, "Indian boy brings his sisters along"; March 18, "saw the mother of our 'lone' Indian boy — satisfied he should stay."

The eight-year-old tyke at first merely watched from outside the mission. On his third visit he allowed Father Juvenal to approach close enough to give him an apple. When finally he took the desperate plunge, entering the world of new kitchen smells and wonderful cooking turned out by Brother Placid, Challa Yazhe (Charley Shorty) was no longer the same. When finally he left, it was with a rosary around his neck and his blanket folds full of Placid's best. When Anselm and Charley Day visited the lad's widowed mother on Saturday, she agreed to let her boy stay with the *e'nishodi,* so long as they would not send her Challa away to school.[26]

[21] A. Weber, *Sendbote,* 26:640, August, 1899.

[22] *Ibid.,* 26:469, June, 1899.

[23] *Diary, 1899,* January 26, February 7. Russell Sage gave his source as Mrs. Wyant.

[24] Bishop Bourgade (Tucson) to Juvenal Schnorbus, February 11, 1899, S.M.C., F-1.

[25] *Diary, 1899,* February 4, March 6; A. Weber, *Sendbote,* 26:470, June, 1899.

[26] *Ibid.,* pp. 470–472.

Sunday, March 19, St. Joseph's feast, the chapel room was full. Besides the Fort Defiance whites and Mr. Day's family, Short Hair, Peshlakai and the poor widow had brought their families. Anselm with a full and thankful heart preached, and after services a special dinner was served in the kitchen for the widow and her large family. All of the undernourished family ate as probably never before or after.[27] In fact, it almost meant the widow's death, for at 9:30 that night, fearsome hour for Navaho, when *chindi* (ghosts) are abroad, Charley's older brother roused the mission to take his little brother to his dying mother.[28]

Father Anselm left the little fellow sleeping and, after dropping by to pick up George Overton, accompanied the older brother to the "dying" widow. No medicine men were there as the ghosts, the *chindi,* had frightened home the young Navaho dispatched to fetch help. With "Black Mexican's" good offices and Tom Osborne's stomach medicine, the woman was soon relieved, and the wailing children and relatives restored to happiness. An ancient grandmother smiled gratefully at the perspiring young missionary, calling him her "uncle." Status at last for the *e'nishodi!* If his stock continued to rise he would ascend *"vom Enkel angefangen, durch alle Stufen der Verwandschaft bis zum Grossvater."*[29] In less than two years Father Anselm, by that time known simply as *Chischilli* (Curly), had already graduated from the "grandfather" stage and was frequently addressed as *naa-tani,* or headman.[30]

On Sunday afternoon Anselm had ridden the countryside to find little Charley a companion. On Monday Slinky brought in his fourteen-year-old son, Chee (Red) Slinky.[31] In a rather pontifical style Father Juvenal solemnly recorded in the *House Journal* that "we concluded to permit him (Charley Yazhe) to retain his name 'Charley'—the second Indian boy—we gave the name 'Albert.' Both boys came of their own choice."[32]

The old Meadow's log cabin was soon to be vacated as Mother Katharine found the $65 monthly salary of Tom Osborne rather high and wanted a man around $40 or less.[33] Accordingly the two young-

27 *Diary, 1899,* March 19; A. Weber, *Sendbote,* 26:472, June, 1899.

28 A. Weber, *Sendbote,* 26:473, June, 1899.

29 *Ibid.,* 474.

30 In October, 1900. See Leopold Ostermann, in *St. Anthony Messenger,* 8:369, April, 1901.

31 A. Weber, *Sendbote, op. cit.,* p. 475.

32 *House Chronicle,* p. 6, S.M.C.

33 Mother Katharine to J. Schnorbus, March 16, April 13, and May 28, 1899, P.A., AK.

sters lived in one room of the log cabin, where Father Anselm instructed them in writing and reading Navaho and English.[34] Tom Osborne left after locating a "forty" about a mile to the northeast where he planned building a trading store. Charley Day used Reverend Fryling's camera to photograph this log cabin mission school with its first two pupils, both tousel-headed, and little Charley sphinxlike and owlish in his blanket.[35] The change from blanket to store clothes was made ten days after the boys' arrival when Father Juvenal returned from Gallup with shoes and complete boys' wardrobes.[36]

"Citizens'" clothes and short hair at this period took top billing in the civilizing program of the United States Indian Office. Major Hayzlett over at Fort Defiance had arrived to take over as Navaho agent one week after the friars opened St. Michaels Mission.[37] Like them he found the situation not a little perplexing, particularly the pet cultural program of Commissioner W. A. Jones who figured that, clothes making the man, a "wild" Indian shorn of his long hair and blanket would, Samsonlike, turn tame under the scissors.[38] Hayzlett's first task in this matter was to request shoes for his Indian police as they could not "present a dignified or commanding appearance when their toes and heels are exposed in mockinsons [sic]."[39] After more than three years he was able to report a modest success in his sartorial and tonsorial crusade: five hundred were wearing "citizens'" clothes in 1898, some ten thousand were doing so in 1902.[40] By offering a fawn-colored, western hat as a premium, he had induced about one hundred and fifty Navaho to cut their hair, and only one was sent to the guardhouse for refusal. "Scarcely one in a hundred paints his face."[41]

Over at the mission Father Anselm set a good example by getting

[34] *House Chronicle,* p. 7, S.M.C.; J. Schnorbus to Mother Katharine, March 26, 1899, C.H.A.

[35] *Diary, 1899,* March 13, 22, 26, 30 and January 16. This and other excellent photographs appear in the monthly *Sendbote* serial. Later, Anselm himself became adept at photography with equipment furnished by Max Schaefer, O.F.M., editor of the *Sendbote.* See A. Weber to Max Schaefer, March 10, 1901, P.A., *Sendbote.*

[36] *Diary, 1899,* March 29. Charley Yazhe kept kicking off the shoes, preferring bare feet even in snow. *Ibid.,* notes at rear.

[37] On October 15, 1898. W.R.C., Letter Books, p. 304.

[38] Haircutting order dated from 1896. See C.I.A., *Annual Report,* 1900, p. 291. From Washington, William H. Ketcham, director of the Bureau of Catholic Indian Missions, reported that Commissioner Jones had mellowed after the ridicule incurred by his haircutting campaign. In Ketcham to A. Weber, March 5, 1902, C.I.B.A.

[39] Hayzlett to Commissioner of Indian Affairs, November 11, 1898, W.R.C., Letter Books.

[40] C.I.A., *Annual Report,* 1899, Part 2, p. 562.

[41] Hayzlett to Commissioner, July 25 and August 16, 1902, W.R.C., Letter Books.

himself and his Indian charges properly trimmed shortly after the pupils arrived. Both for lack of space as well as because of age difference, two Indian boys, aged fifteen and seventeen, were refused admission to the mission boarding school at this time.[42]

While teaching the Navaho youngsters, classes for the Day boys and persistent work on the Navaho dictionary went steadily on. Under the indoor grind Father Anselm noticed an increase of his old nervous disorder. Alarmed over heightened tension and more frequent nervous twitching, he began checking up on possible factors. Smoking he had confined to a few daily corncobs of Kanaster, the only tobacco Father Juvenal provided.[43] Early in January he stopped completely, only to note a worsening. Again on the twenty-sixth he tried his first cigar since coming west, a present from Brother Meinrad in Cincinnati. On the last day of January he received a full box of cigars from Brother Ivo, but cut off smoking again three days later. On the following Sunday during Mass his arms jerked spasmodically again.[44]

He tried to relax and find relief at this time by outside work in the spring sunshine, planting trees and helping George Overton with the ranch.[45] Whether or not the outside work and the lowered nicotine intake were beneficial, the fact remains that these involuntary nervous seizures, which had developed already in 1891, continued to plague him periodically for the rest of his life.[46]

As to smoking, he often burned up ten to a dozen cigars a day, especially when under tension.[47] The self-appointed reformer of American morals, Carey Nation herself, tried to take a hand in Father Anselm's use of the cheroot. In Kansas City, Missouri, on one of Anselm's trips east, he lost a freshly lit cigar when Carey ruthlessly slapped it out of his mouth. Always calm, the rather stern-faced priest slowly turned to size up his crusading assailant. Unimpressed and noncommittal, he delighted the crowd at Grand and Ninth by casually pulling out another Selle's A-1, and relighting.[48]

In this same spring of 1899 Father Anselm discovered a new outdoor occupation which in the coming years was to consume more energy

[42] *Diary, 1899,* April 17, March 25.

[43] Berard Haile, interview with R. Wilken, September 2, 1949.

[44] *Diary, 1899,* January 9, 26, February 3, 5.

[45] *Ibid.,* March 2, 3.

[46] A. Weber to Dr. Braasch, October 1, 1919, Mayo Clinic, F. 202016.

[47] Berard Haile, interview, September 2, 1949. After 1900 the regular brand of cigars at the mission was Selle's "A-1," which sold at $26 per 1000; for special occasions the friars drew on Selle's "Bouquet," at $35 per 1000. See invoices from John N. Selle, 1900—, P.A., HA.

[48] John Forest McGee, interview with R. Wilken, September 5, 1951.

and time than perhaps any of his other manifold mission activities. When J. A. Lamport, Deputy Surveyor for Arizona Territory, reached Cienega after running his township line from near Manuelito,[49] Anselm spent March 24 through 26 with the surveyor, helping in the field work and learning the fundamentals of the craft.[50] Touched off accidentally by the unsettled mission land problem, practical surveying, and the instruments of the craft, came to symbolize along with cross, altar stone, and Navaho Catechism, his distinctive approach to winning The People.

The friars at the mission cleared another hurdle when on Good Friday, 1899, an old Fort Sumner Navaho, White Hair, took supper and spent the night at St. Michaels — even putting on a dance for Brother Placid.[51] Neighbors they had now become, and far more than mere curiosities; another old Navaho soon dropped by, all wrought up over the latest gossip: "Was it really so that the *e'nishodi* did not marry — not even once?"[52] Then from Slinky and the squaws, who enjoyed watching the teacher and the boys doing slate work, came news that Albert Slinky, the older boy, could never be an *e'nishodi:* he liked girls too much. Mr. Wyant had nicknamed Albert "E'nishodi Yazhe," "Shorty Long Gown."[53] Others were equally willing to explain why Peshlakai, up on the slope, was the wise one: the silversmith had three wives to weave and herd and give him a good living and many children; many rich ones did that. But Peshlakai had married three *sisters,* and had paid sheep to another Indian to keep his one and only mother-in-law far away; otherwise he might go blind in case he looked at the old woman. No fool, that one.[54]

With the youngsters always at hand or under foot, the missioners' ear for Navaho sharpened and new everyday phrases swelled the

[49] Lamport had been engaged for $100 by Monsignor Stephan already on November 25, 1898, to run his private survey. Lamport to Stephan, September 5, 1898; Stephan to Lamport, September 16, 1898, C.I.B.A. Lamport found a corner two miles north of Manuelito when surveying for the railroad, an earlier government survey marker for sections 7, 8, 17, and 18, T.14 N., Range 20 W., New Mexico Meridian. He came to St. Michaels on December 22, 1898, but deep snow prevented work at that time; on March 24, 1899, he reached Cienega. Juvenal to Mother Katharine, December 25, 1898, C.H.A., and *Diary, 1898,* March 24–26.

[50] *Diary, 1899,* March 24, 25; *House Chronicle,* p. 7, S.M.C. Mr. Sam E. Day later helped to point up Anselm's knowledge of practical surveying. Berard Haile, interview, September 2, 1949.

[51] *Diary, 1899,* March 31 and January 31.

[52] *Ibid.,* April 9.

[53] *Ibid.,* April 11, notes at rear.

[54] A. Weber, *Sendbote,* 26:556, July, 1899; *Diary, 1899,* May 21 and notes at rear.

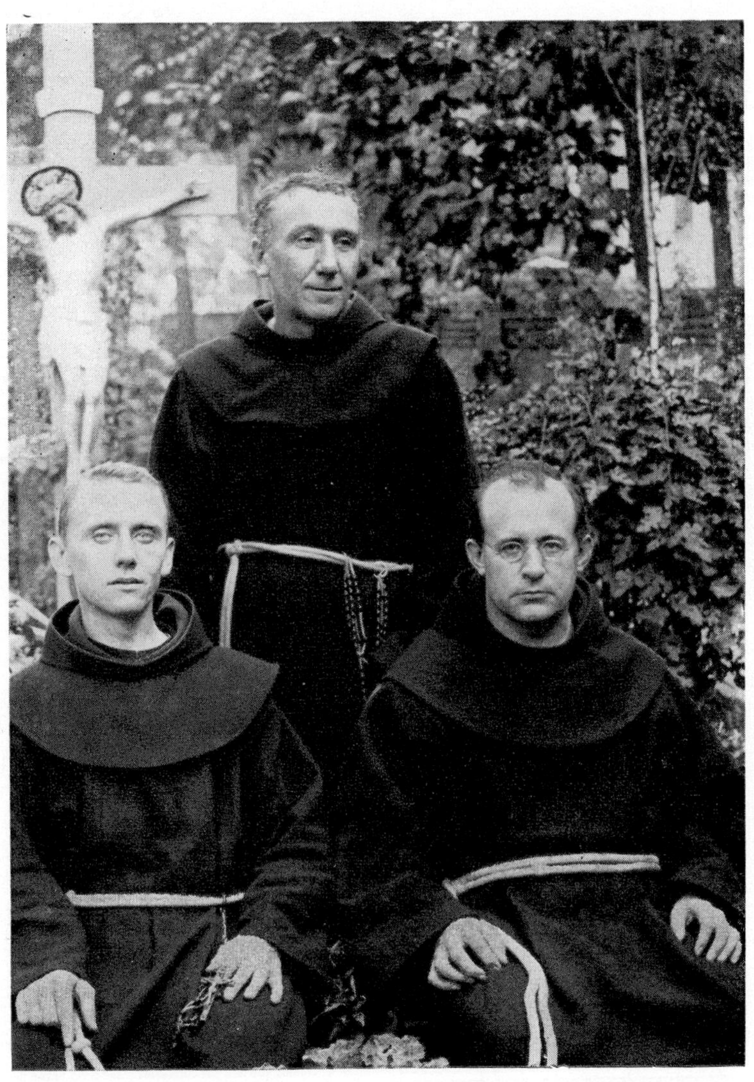

First missionaries to the Navaho: Fathers Juvenal and Anselm with Brother Placid (standing), at St. Francis Monastery, Cincinnati

Sammy, Charley, and Willie Day (rear) with first pupils at St. Michaels, Billie Yazzi and Albert Slinky flanking Blind Luke

growing word list.[55] Thirty-year-old Luke Everest, a poor Navaho who had gone blind when he was ten, joined the mission household in late May.[56] Having a smattering of English from his five years at Fort Lewis and Fort Defiance schools, he proved a great help in drawing out verb conjugations and in expanding the vocabulary.[57] Luke quickly won a warm place in the family circle by his sunny disposition, his easy, generous smile, snatches of Navaho song, and the happy chortle that was always spilling over.[58] A complete new outfitting for Luke in late June outbid the calico gift of a medicine man who needed Luke for "sings" and dances.[59] He did leave for vacation in summer but returned again in December.[60]

Anselm continued to correlate his practical study of Navaho culture with further research into the scant printed sources available. Peter Baptist Englert, O.F.M., of the Cincinnati Franciscans, while aboard ship for Rome to serve as Definitor General, had met Frank J. Polley of Stanford University and urged Anselm to contact the professor.[61] He in turn recommended Bancroft for bibliography, and introduced Anselm by letter to W. J. McGee of the Smithsonian Institution for a list of government publications on the Navaho.[62] Mr. Day and Agent Hayzlett at the Fort also obliged by freely opening their libraries. Around this period the Fathers opened a correspondence with M. Alphonse Pinart, early French traveler and ethnologist, who wished to publish the missioners' Navaho dictionary and catechism in his *Bibliothèque de linguistique et d'ethnographie Americaines.*[63]

A far cry it was, however, from the academic routine Anselm Weber had known in the Franciscan monasteries in Cincinnati. Something always upset routine. During a smothering sandstorm on May 19 a half-dozen Navaho had dropped in for shelter at St. Michaels and were trading words for black coffee and free tobacco when a troop

55 *Diary, 1899,* March 31, April 4; *House Chronicle,* p. 7, S.M.C.

56 *Diary, 1899,* May 24; Juvenal Schnorbus to Mother Katharine, December 20, 1899, C.H.A.

57 *House Chronicle,* p. 7, S.M.C.

58 A. Weber, *Sendbote,* 26:640, August, 1899.

59 *Diary, 1899,* June 12, 15, 19.

60 *Ibid.,* December 3, and A. Weber, *Sendbote,* 27:373, May, 1900.

61 Englert to A. Weber, June 11, 1899, P.A., NL.; *Diary, 1899,* April 18.

62 Polley to A. Weber, April 25, 1899, P.A., NL.

63 *Diary, 1899,* March 5, April 1. Regarding Pinart: Pinart had spent 1874–1876 in Arizona and New Mexico doing ethnological and linguistic work with the Navaho and other Indian groups. See A. L. Pinart to Reverend Father (Weber), April 19, 1899, P.A., LA. An account of these travels is published in Alphonse Pinart, *Voyage dans l'Arizona,* in *Bulletin de la Societe de geographie,* Paris, 6 Serie, Vol. 13, Mars, 1877, 16 pp.

of Negro cavalry clattered up. Inside, the Navaho froze in dismay at sight of the soldiers whose coming, they were sure, meant only trouble and arrest. Trying first to calm the Indians, the friars let in two officers, red-eyed and weather-burned, their clothes yellow with sand. Lieutenant McNamy was in charge of the troop of thirty from Fort Wingate who were heading for the Moqui (Hopi) villages on orders from the War Department.[64] At mention of Moquis, their ancient foes, the Navaho chattered happily again. In order to save the tired cavalry mounts, Father Anselm saddled up his buckskin, "Yellow," to bring information from Fort Defiance, which handled both Navaho and Hopi affairs. In Hayzlett's absence, Mr. Dennison rode back to confer at St. Michaels, bringing along his daughter, Eliza Jane, Mollie Keough, and Mr. Muse.[65]

Around the friars' kitchen table that night a curious military conference took place among the two army officers, Mr. Dennison, and the missioners, while Brother Placid trundled out coffee to the cavalrymen bivouacking in the barn.[66]

In January smallpox had broken out on First Mesa and fourteen Hopi had died, nine of whom refused vaccination. Dr. McKee, a woman physician, and S. E. Shoemaker, the government farmer in charge, had worked valiantly to stem the epidemic.[67] The Santa Fe Railroad doctor had been sent from Los Angeles and aided in the effort to inoculate and disinfect. Many Hopis refused white medicine, especially on Second Mesa, so that by February 26 twenty-eight had died on First Mesa and fifty-four on Second, where another one hundred and twenty-five cases raged. Oraibi on Third Mesa had no smallpox victims. In three months one hundred and eighty-seven had died, one hundred and sixty-three of these having refused treatment; the bodies of most of these the Indians simply pitched over the cliffs into the rock crevices. As the Hopis resisted carbolic-acid baths, clean clothing and fumigation of their homes, and insisted on breaking quarantine and visiting their children at Keams Canyon School, Agent Hayzlett had requested military assistance. Living apart in semi-isolation as they did, scarcely a dozen Navaho succumbed.[68]

[64] A. Weber, *Sendbote,* 26:999–1000, December, 1899; C.I.A., *Annual Report,* 1899, p. 383.

[65] *Diary, 1899,* May 19.

[66] A. Weber, *Sendbote,* 26:1000, December, 1899.

[67] Hayzlett to Commissioner of Indian Affairs, January 31, 1899, W.R.C., Letter Books.

[68] Same to same, February 1, 14, 26, April 25, June 6, May 8, 1899, W.R.C., Letter Books.

With this briefing Lieutenant McNamy led his men the hundred odd miles to Second Mesa where some sixty Hopi men holed up in a large adobe house in passive resistance. Leaving their horses and carbines, the soldiers attacked the adobe with pick and shovel until the Indians rushed out for a hand-to-hand engagement.[69] There was unnecessary violence according to some, even after the Indians submitted to vaccination.[70] Eight old die-hards were made prisoners and taken to the agent at Fort Defiance, who gave them four months at hard labor. More than all else the old Hopis feared the knife of the Navaho policeman assigned to guard them.[71] When released on September 28 their passive resistance was as strong as ever: they would under no circumstances support the government's educational program, they repeated, and they would resist sending children to Keams Canyon Government School.[72]

Ten weeks later Father Anselm traveled to Hopi, partly to write up the story of this independent, anarchistic tribe, and partly for health reasons.[73] As the Day boys were needed for farm work after July, and Charley Yazhe had run away from the mission on August 9, there were no classes to keep — and the Navaho conjugations could wait.[74]

Anselm rode horseback alongside the two-horse rig carrying Father Geo. J. Juillard and Mr. Weinert, an accomplished photographer. It was late afternoon, August 10, when the party left St. Michaels en route to Hubbell's for the night.[75] East of Bear Tank they joined another horseback party of three men and five women from Fort Defiance, who were also bound for the Hopi snake dance. At sundown Dennison and Manning of the Fort party took a ribbing for missing a close shot at a bear; their rifles had been unloaded.

While the Fort people drew up at sundown to make camp, the Juillard party rode on into the western twilight toward the steel-etched rim of Ganado Mesa. In the darkness they missed Hubbell's post and spent the night in a hogan with a surprised Navaho family. As there was no water there for the horses, they turned back next morning seven miles east to Don Lorenzo's store where they spent

69 Hayzlett to Commissioner, June 6, 1899, W.R.C., Letter Books.

70 Charles E. Burton, Keams School Superintendent, to Department of Interior, in C.I.A., *Annual Report,* 1899, p. 383.

71 *Diary, 1899,* May 28; A. Weber, *Sendbote,* 26:1001, December, 1899.

72 Hayzlett to Commissioner, September 28, 1899, W.R.C., Letter Books.

73 *House Chronicle,* pp. 7–8, S.M.C.

74 A. Weber, *Sendbote,* 27:373, May, 1900; *House Chronicle,* p. 7, S.M.C.; *Diary, 1899,* August 9, 4. He copied 800 conjugations before he left.

75 Account based on A. Weber, *Diary, 1899,* August 10–19 and *Sendbote,* 26:904–910, 27:106–111, November, 1899, and February, 1900.

the day. Anselm had his first opportunity to meet the Hubbell family whose "four children [Lorenzo, Romano, Barbara, and Adella] made an excellent impression."[76]

J. L. Hubbell was admired and loved widely by whites and Indians. Born in Pajarito, New Mexico, 1853, he had set up a trading post in partnership with Mr. Read at Fort Defiance when only eighteen.[77] At St. Johns, Arizona, he had later formed a vigilante group and furnished guns to clean out the lawless element. In the first week seventeen outlaws went to "boot hill" — along with seven vigilantes. After that, in 1885, he was made sheriff of Apache County. He had also figured prominently in the sheepmen-cattlemen-rustler wars of the 1870's and 1880's, and had personally known the Apaches, Victorio and Geronimo.[78]

As early as 1884 when Hubbell had his residence at St. Johns, Herbert Welsh had reported on the hospitality shown at the Clark and Hubbell tent store near Washington Pass, as well as at the Ganado Pillsbury and Hubbell post.[79] That hospitality was to become a byword in Navaho country. A man of rich experience and warm joviality, he spiced his hospitality with wit and an unending round of anecdotes.[80]

On this particular Friday of August, 1899, Don Lorenzo was at his best, and Mrs. Hubbell at her busiest. When Mr. and Mrs. Dennison, the Mannings, Mr. Muse, Dr. Parker and Pearl, Mollie Keough, and Ethel Dennison arrived, it simply meant two servings at the long table, and more voices around the melodeon that night. English, Spanish, French, and German — the collective repertory was at last exhausted. For Father Anselm, after long months of mission routine, the day and evening of conversation and song, the hominess of it all, stood out as the high light of the entire Hopi trip.[81]

Saturday the whole troop moved on together and in late afternoon made camp. Riding with Manning and Dennison, the missioner discovered that Mr. Dennison was deeply interested in religion, which they discussed all the way to Tuye Spring.[82]

[76] A. Weber, *Sendbote,* 26:907, November, 1899.

[77] J. Lorenzo Hubbell to Thomas Edwin Farish, n.d., in T. E. Farish, *History of Arizona* (Phoenix, 1918), Vol. 6, pp. 281–284. See Mrs. Le Charles G. Eckel, "History of Ganado, Arizona," *Museum Notes,* 6:49–50, April, 1934.

[78] *Ibid.* He became territorial senator and later Arizona state senator. See also Van Valkenburgh, *A Short History,* pp. 44–46.

[79] *Report of a Visit,* 1885, pp. 29, 32.

[80] Leopold Ostermann, in *St. Anthony Messenger,* 9:367, April, 1902.

[81] A. Weber, *Sendbote, op. cit.,* p. 907.

[82] *Diary, 1899,* August 13.

Early Sunday morning the two priests offered Mass on a huge oblong slab of rock in the canyon, and Father Anselm later rode cross-country with several others on a short cut that proved the long way around to Keams. At the canyon where Thomas Varker Keam, the Englishman and ex-Navaho agent, had settled in the 1880's, Anselm Weber became acquainted with Mr. Burton, the Shoemakers, the Keams, Raushes, and others.[83]

Tuesday, feast of Assumption, he and Father Juillard both said Holy Mass at Sitschomovi in the presence of some twenty-five whites and Hopi Indians, notwithstanding interference by an obtrusive Dr. Miller of Phoenix.[84] At Walpai on the sixteenth he watched, fascinated, the wizardry of the famous snake dance ceremony which the Hopi carry out yearly for rain.[85]

He left for St. Michaels on the following day and arrived home on Saturday afternoon. Later he would return often to Hopi country; never, however, under such pleasant circumstances.[86]

[83] *Ibid.*, August 13 and 14; for data on Keam see Van Valkenburgh, *A Short History*, pp. 39, 45.

[84] *Ibid.*, August 15.

[85] For detailed account, A. Weber, *Sendbote*, 27:106–111, February, 1900; in English, *F.M.S.*, 1918, pp. 15–22.

[86] *Diary, 1899*, August 17–19.

Chapter V

Experiments Toward a Mission Plan, 1900

Saintly Peter Bourgade who had invited the Franciscans to the Navaho mission, and so warmly encouraged them in their early language problems, announced his papal appointment to Santa Fe's vacant see early in 1899.[1] Father Juvenal Schnorbus left on Monday, October 2, to accompany Provincial Raphael and Father Charles Schoeppner from Lamy to Santa Fe for the solemn reception of the *pallium* by Archbishop Bourgade on October 4. Father Anselm could not attend as he was taking care of Gallup and its missions from September 20 through October 6.[2]

It was touching to watch the old Hispanos gather around the three brown-robed padres, kissing their hands in the Latin style and tearfully rejoicing that the friars were back again in Santa Fe.[3]

At a meeting with the Franciscans next day Archbishop Bourgade made the formal request that the Cincinnati Province accept missions in his new diocese. From his point of view the likeliest area would be on the San Juan River where he suggested the friars would be centrally located for parish, mission, and retreat work among both Navaho and Hispanos.[4] Padre Antonio Jouvenceau, who had preached the Spanish festive sermon, had already left Santa Fe for his Park View mission, so the Archbishop urged the friars to visit and plan with him a suitable parish on the San Juan in the Farmington-Largo area.[5]

[1] P. Bourgade to J. Schnorbus, February 11, March 2, 1899, S.M.C., CH. Appointment had been made January 7, 1899, *The Official Catholic Directory,* 1950 (New York: Kenedy, 1950), p. 213.

[2] *Diary, 1899,* September 20–October 6; *Franziskus Bote,* 8:178, November, 1899.

[3] *House Chronicle,* p. 9, S.M.C.; Bernard Nurre to A. Weber, October 16, 1899, P.A., BN.

[4] *House Chronicle, ibid.,* S.M.C.

[5] *Franziskus Bote,* 8:178, November, 1899; *House Chronicle,* p. 9, S.M.C.; George J. Juillard to A. Weber, March 1, 1900, P.A., GJ.

After visiting around picturesque Santa Fe, and spending several hours at St. Catherine's Industrial School, the three Franciscans came on to Gallup, where Anselm Weber met them.[6] At St. Michaels Father Raphael held official visitation at which Anselm had been advised to speak candidly regarding his anomalous status under Father Juvenal, and the denial of opportunity for initiative or even counsel in language and mission matters.[7] From Cienega, Provincial Raphael sent off letters to the Commissary Provincial, Louis Haverbeck, and to Bernard Nurre, a provincial definer, outlining the Bishop's San Juan project. Juvenal Schnorbus wrote to Padre Antonio at Park View regarding the same.[8] On October 9 Fathers Raphael and Juvenal left for San Diego where the rheumatic Provincial hoped to find relief at the Mercy Sisters' St. Joseph Sanatorium.[9]

The provincial political pot back in Cincinnati began to boil merrily over the new Spanish missions: Definer Bernard Nurre at the Gymnasium was all for adding a required course in Spanish to the curriculum. Decidedly, however, he disapproved the contemplated departure from "San Miguel" and the Tucson diocese in favor of the new San Juan mission. To keep both, he thought, would be wiser; it would mean a two-pronged campaign on the Navaho.[10] Father Juillard's earlier invitation to place a Franciscan at Gallup for training in Spanish and general acculturation appeared to be a splendid avenue to a future parish in Gallup.[11] The Definer also congratulated Anselm on being chosen by the Provincial to make the exploratory trip to the San Juan — it sounded as romantic as Karl Mai. He realized, of course, the ultimate reason for Anselm's trip was the need for locating suitable areas for *permanent Navaho settlements,* places, he suggested, not too far isolated in the hinterland for the good of the friars.[12]

In Louisville an old classmate and fellow Gymnasium instructor, Leopold Ostermann, was all aflutter over the prospect of going south-

[6] J. Schnorbus to Mother Katharine, November 1, 1899, C.H.A.

[7] *Diary, 1899,* October 6; B. Nurre to A. Weber, July 19 and September 23, 1899, P.A., BN.

[8] *Diary, 1899,* October 7; *St. Anthony Messenger,* 7:172, October, 1899, announces Father Haverbeck's selection as *pro-tem* provincial.

[9] J. Schnorbus to Mother Katharine, November 1, 1899, C.H.A.

[10] B. Nurre to A. Weber, October 16, 1899, P.A., BN.

[11] Same to same, September 23, 1899, P.A., BN.

[12] Same to same, October 31, 1899, P.A., BN. Karl Mai was the prolific German fiction writer who produced many western thrillers and a number of novels on travel and exploration in Asia and Africa. Father Anselm was one of many friars who were Karl Mai enthusiasts. RW.

west. He had located only one Spanish book in the Louisville convent, a series of meditations by St. Alphonsus. Leopold confided that none knew that Anselm had asked for him, but Father Pius Niehaus had likely guessed it. On reading the impersonal narrative part of Anselm's letter, Pius had gotten out a geography, studied northwestern New Mexico, and had proclaimed himself pastor of Farmington and Leopold his assistant at Aztec. "Then . . . he placed his right fist on the table, his hair standing on ends, looked about himself with the air of Richard III when he yelled for a horse. We . . . stood around in awe and admiration when he asked for . . . a Spanish book.[13]

The whole province was looking westward. Bernard Nurre, and even Father Chrysostom Theobald, preacher extraordinary, gave it out that they wanted to go to the new mission; Father Theodore Stephan was absorbing Spanish "with fanatical zeal."[14]

On All Souls' Day, just one week from the Thursday Father Juvenal had returned from San Diego, Anselm set out to explore the San Juan with Charley Day as guide.[15] After the past week's work with Navaho verbs, it was sheer relief to jog along north in the sunny autumn air, strong with the tang of piñon and juniper, and quiet as the desert blue above, save for the comforting rhythm of hooves and creaking saddle leather.[16]

By noon they reached Moore's Trading Post at Crystal, where they lunched and met Albert Thompson, who was likewise bound for the San Juan where he lived.[17] Northeast over the Chuskas by way of 9500 feet high, and ruggedly beautiful, Cottonwood (Washington) Pass brought them to Two Grey Hills where they met a kind reception at the Methodist mission.[18]

Mrs. Henrietta Cole who was in charge at the mission was engaged in medical and general field work, while Miss Sarah M. Munger taught a kindergarten for Navaho children.[19] Mrs. Cole had left

[13] L. Ostermann to A. Weber, October 19, 1899, P.A., LO.

[14] B. Nurre to A. Weber, September 23, October 31, 1899, P.A., BN.

[15] *Diary, 1899,* November 2.

[16] *Ibid.,* October 28–November 1. Anselm kept a day log of this seventeen-day journey and produced perhaps his finest descriptive material in his account published serially in *Sendbote,* 30:964–969 and 1076–1081, 31:34–39 and 125–129, November, 1903–February, 1904. The narrative given here is an account translated and briefed from *Sendbote* and edited with the aid of Anselm Weber's *Diary, 1899,* the *House Chronicle,* S.M.C., and other sources herein to be cited.

[17] *Sendbote,* 30:966, November, 1903; *Diary, 1899,* November 2 and October 30.

[18] *Sendbote, ibid.,* p. 968; *Diary, 1899, ibid.*

[19] The Women's National Indian Association, *Annual Report,* 1899 (Philadelphia, 1899), p. 22. Name changed to The National Indian Association in 1901. See also C.I.A., *Annual Report,* 1898, p. 123; 1899, p. 158.

Williams College at the behest of the Women's National Indian Association to take charge of the Two Grey Hills Mission which Mrs. Mary Eldridge had opened for the Association in March, 1898.[20] The government had contributed $100 toward furnishing the small mission cottage and in 1900 had appointed Mrs. Cole as Government Field Matron.[21]

Father Anselm retired almost immediately after supper as he felt poorly from the effect of the high crossing and the hard, fifty-five mile ride; Charley Day stayed up to visit since he was related to one of the ladies at this isolated mission outpost.[22]

Late next morning after visiting Noel's Store the party headed north across sand flats to Bennett Peak where they rested their horses and made a lunch on biscuit and canned peaches. Around four in the evening they reached an upthrust of vertical strata that pierced the desert like a dinosaur spine, and finding a break in the "Hogback," traveled its east flank across Chaco Cañon and the badlands. It was autumn dusk when the trio forded the swift, treacherous San Juan, and 6 o'clock when they reached the Jewett Mission, just east of the Hogback.[23]

Anselm Weber became deeply interested in the work carried on at this Hogback mission.[24] Mrs. Mary Eldridge and Miss Raymond (later, Mrs. Thomas Whyte) had opened the mission in 1891 under the auspices of the Womens Home Missionary Society of the Methodist Episcopal Church. Especially interested in social work and irrigation projects, both women had become Government Field Matrons with Mary Tripp taking over in 1894 to cover the direct Methodist missionary ministry.[25] Mrs. Eldridge concentrated on irrigation, industrial education of adults, and the establishment of the Jewett Hospital, all projects having the combined financial backing of the Indian Rights Association, the United States Indian Service, and the Women's National Indian Association.[26] Her industrial school for Navaho women which taught breadmaking and cooking, weaving and machine

[20] *Ibid.*, 1898, pp. 19, 26–28. See also W.R.C., Letter Book, 1898–1899, p. 477.

[21] W.N.I.A., *Annual Report,* 1898, p. 28; 1902, p. 27.

[22] *Sendbote,* 30:968, November, 1903.

[23] *Ibid., Diary, 1899,* November 3.

[24] *Sendbote,* 30:1076, December, 1903.

[25] Pauline G. Malehorn, *The Tender Plant,* mimeograph (Farmington, N. Mex., 1948), pp. 2–3; C.I.A., *Annual Report,* 1897, p. 107.

[26] Belle M. Brain, *The Redemption of the Red Man* (New York: The Board of Home Missions of the Presbyterian Church in the U.S.A., 1904), p. 76; Malehorn, *op. cit.*, pp. 8, 18; W.N.I.A., *Annual Report,* 1894, p. 17, lists $375 for Mrs. Eldridge's irrigation work on the San Juan; *ibid.*, 1898, pp. 26–28.

sewing was financed by the Indian Industries League.[27] Miss Tripp, working under the Methodist Episcopal Missionary Society, directed Sunday school work and education — first with a day school which proved unsatisfactory, and in 1898 by founding at her own expense a boarding school.[28]

During his visits to and from the San Juan country Anselm Weber formed a high estimate of the Hogback mission and of the socio-economic program of bouncing, stouthearted Mrs. Eldridge. To his mind her Navaho irrigation settlement on the north bank west of the Hogback proved that, given irrigation, the Navaho would live in farming communities.[29] While examining the industrial school for Navaho women under Miss Edith Dabb, and the fourteen Navaho youngsters under Fannie Rykert in the boarding school, he also noted the unconventional but practical bobbed hair of Miss Tripp and Mrs. Eldridge, and the short riding skirts of the latter.[30]

After a year in the sparse Fort Defiance country, and two days' travel across barren rock and desert, Father Anselm was entranced with the green alfalfa, the rich harvest and orchard lands, and the shimmering gold of cottonwood — as the party rode up the settled San Juan valley. By noon they reached the home of Albert Thompson's father, where they enjoyed fine western hospitality and sound advice from the old government farmer.[31] By evening Charley Day had brought the sharply observant, farm-bred missionary into Farmington. The countryside had been one continuous commentary on the possibility of desert farming, given irrigation facilities. At Farmington they stabled their horses at Frank Allen's livery, and since inquiry disclosed only three Catholic families, who were already cramped for space, they put up for the night at Tripletts Hotel.[32] To one searching for a likely mission location, a place where Indians might cluster in community around a mission, the San Juan seemed ideal; Father Anselm in a peaceful biblical mood recalled Lot's delight on beholding the well-watered valley of the Jordan.[33]

Trying to ford the river at the confluence of the Las Animas and the San Juan next morning, the Navaho whom they had picked up

[27] Board of Indian Commissioners, *Annual Report,* 1899, p. 335; W.N.I.A., *Annual Report,* 1899, pp. 15–16.

[28] Malehorn, *op. cit.,* pp. 13–15.

[29] *Sendbote,* 30:1076, December, 1903.

[30] Malehorn, *op. cit.,* p. 18; *Diary, 1899,* November 16; *Sendbote,* 30:1076, December, 1903.

[31] *Sendbote, ibid.,* p. 1077.

[32] *Diary, 1899,* November 4.

[33] *Sendbote,* 30:1077, December, 1903.

in Farmington as guide almost foundered in the quicksand. The two whites returned to town, where one of the McHenry boys directed them to King's Crossing, three miles west of Farmington. Navaho encountered on the left bank were already breaking summer camp for their winter migration southward. It came as a distinct disappointment to hear from the Indians that even in the growing season rather few Navaho lived along the river. The priest and his guide next turned eastward some three miles beyond the reservation line where they visited Eleuterio Vigil. He was willing to sell at $40 per acre — and with Navaho in the vicinity already, it was not an unattractive offer.[34]

Between Vigil's ranch and the river flamed a grove of golden cottonwoods which was pointed out as the former headquarters of Edward C. Vincent, the government official who had used up $60,000 running surveys and drawing blueprints for Indian irrigation works that never materialized.[35] Mr. McHenry of Farmington hoped to revive and complete the project; and on discussing it with the missionary McHenry received his enthusiastic support.[36]

Back in Farmington that same Sunday afternoon Anselm heard of the two abandoned valleys south of the river and eight miles upstream where Headman Mateo had farmed with his band until the irrigation dams and headgates had fallen to ruin. Mr. Allen drove him there next morning while Charley led the priest's horse. At Antonio Medina's ranch Charley fed the horses and prepared lunch while Mr. Allen drove around the old Navaho farming lands. Admittedly an excellent place for a large settlement, the missionary agreed, ". . . if we had the money, or the government would assist" in renewing the irrigation works![37]

On returning to Medina's they took kind leave of Mr. Allen and spent some time with Don Antonio who knew no English but conversed fluently in Navaho, and could manage a running Navaho translation of his Spanish Bible.[38]

Striking eastward they next rode to Kutz Canyon which they followed south to Dick Simpson's trading post where they were again disappointed at finding none of the expected Navaho communities. After a pleasant evening and a good sleep at the hospitable Simpson

[34] *Ibid.*, p. 1078; *Diary, 1899,* November 5.

[35] *Sendbote,* 30:1080, December, 1903; see Alban W. Hoopes, "The Indian Rights Association and the Navajo, 1890–1895," *N.M.H.R.*, 21:28–29, January, 1946.

[36] *Sendbote,* 31:126, February, 1904.

[37] *Ibid.,* 30:1080, December, 1903.

[38] *Ibid.*, p. 1081; *Diary, 1899,* November 6.

post, Charley and Father Anselm took a fix next morning for the northeast and started for Bloomfield and Aztec. At Aztec that evening they learned that Padre Antonio Jouvenceau was not expected until the following week. After inspecting the thriving orchards they retired to the Dalton Hotel for the night.[39]

With an extra week on hand Father Anselm decided to scout the country farther south. At Largo the next afternoon he was kindly received by the Hispanos, who regretfully informed him that it would be impossible to offer Mass since the kit was at Alcatraz. Contrary to Jouvenceau's letter, unexpectedly few Navaho families were working for Hispanos in the vicinity along Kutz Canyon. One of these he hired as guide for the south.[40]

With the orphan buttes, El Huerfano and El Huerfanito, as guides they bore southward past the Chico to Walling's store in the badlands. Here Charley and the friar parted with their Navaho guide, and on Friday morning rode on until they struck Chaco Cañon three miles above the mouth of Escavada Wash.[41]

Here the New York Hyde Expedition was at work excavating and photographing prehistoric Pueblo Bonito ruins. Anselm spent most of the day examining the archaeological treasures and in checking Navaho population in the adjoining canyons. He estimated between six and seven hundred Indians.[42] What with plentiful underground water and relatively dense Navaho population, Chaco seemed another apt spot for a mission — in fact, his first choice.[43] It lay fifty miles due west of Nacimiento and forty miles north from the Santa Fe rail line via Siete Lagunas; from Cabezon and La Posta it lay some sixty-five miles, and sixty from Farmington. Until it went bankrupt a few years previously, a mammoth cattle outfit had run thousands of head over this uplands plain that stretched nearly fifty miles in all directions.[44]

According to the friar's informants a newer institution in the area was in process of doing the Indians more lasting harm than the rowdy, stock-thieving cowpunchers.[45] The new device was allegedly a trading-

[39] *Diary, 1899,* November 7; *Sendbote,* 31:34, January, 1904. Anselm had written Padre Antonio October 23 but had received no answer by November 2 when he left Cienega. *Diary, 1899,* October 23, November 1.

[40] *Diary, 1899,* November 8; *Sendbote, ibid.,* p. 35.

[41] *Diary, 1899,* November 9, 10; *Sendbote, ibid.,* pp. 35, 36.

[42] *Sendbote, ibid.,* pp. 36–37; *Diary, 1899,* November 10.

[43] *Sendbote,* 31:126, February, 1904.

[44] *Diary, 1899,* November 10; *Sendbote,* 30:966, November, 1903.

[45] His opinion of the cowboys and cattle outfits he knew did not correspond to the pulp Westerner's version of a later date. See *Sendbote,* 28:725, 726, September, 1901.

post syndicate subsidized by the Hyde Expedition and managed by a Quaker named Wetherill. From numerous Navaho Anselm learned of the attempt to corner the Navaho blanket market, the overcrediting of Indians and subsequent foreclosures on horses, saddles, sheep, and jewelry. After buying out seven traders off the reservation, the company apparently tried to dodge the one-store-per-trader law operative on the reservation by setting up a holding company control over these traders who continued to manage and carry the reservation license.[46] The Indian agent recorded other objectionable practices not uncommon among traders of the period: the exclusive use of tin scrip, payment for work and freighting in trade only, selling pawned articles on short notice, the sale of "prehistoric" gems made in the back room, and random squawry.[47]

Leaving behind the Hyde Expedition store and Chaco, Father Anselm and young Day set out for Farmington on Saturday, November 11, making stops at Walling's, Simpson's, and Medina's. At Farmington on Sunday he noted the item in the *San Juan Times* respecting his visit and the industrial school and mission planned by "Miss Drexel" for "Navajos and Mexicans." On Monday Mr. Prewett, the editor, agreed to insert a correction in the next issue explaining that the school would be for Navaho only.[48]

On the same day he was done in on a horse trade with the mail rider at Farmington.[49] Back at Cienega the past July he had traded Reverend Martin's old buckskin, "Yellow," plus $2.50, for "Bird." Only later had he discovered that those Blue Mountain horse traders were rustlers. Bird had gone lame on the return from Chaco; now it was the mail pony's friskiness and bucking.[50] His "best trade ever" Anselm put through at Aztec on Wednesday when he swapped the half-broken bronc, plus $10, for "Swallow," the trim, fleet, little mare that carried him usually much too willingly until she turned wicked after foaling in 1902.[51]

At Aztec on Tuesday, before the final horse trade, Anselm failed to recognize a priest in the dust-covered old man who swung down from

[46] A. Weber to Charles Lusk, June 28, 1901, S.M.C., Traders.

[47] Navaho agents to Commissioner, September 5, 1902, December 9, 1909, November 17, 1910, W.R.C., Letter Books.

[48] *Diary, 1899,* November 11–13; *The San Juan Times,* November 10, 17, 1899.

[49] *Diary, 1899,* November 13; *Sendbote,* 31:38, January, 1904.

[50] *Diary, 1899,* July 9, 16, September 1, November 14; A. Weber to Mother Katharine, December 19, 1902, P.A., AK.

[51] *Ibid.,* November 15; A. Weber to Mother Katharine, December 19, 1902; P.A., AK. In 1902 Swallow was given to Charley Day for repairing the old Chin Lee trading-post chapel. A. Weber, *Sendbote,* 31:38, January, 1904.

the Durango stage. Nevertheless, good Padre Antonio Jouvenceau it was, pastor of San Juan and most of Rio Arriba counties. In a short while they were conversing animatedly on Indian missions as they shared their Mexican chili supper. On the fifteen-mile trip to Largo that evening their conveyance collapsed. Absolutely refusing Father Anselm's horse which Charley had been leading, the old priest insisted on continuing, in Anselm's words, *"auf Schusters Rappen."*[52]

That evening it was impressive to watch the excitement stirred up by the priest's visit; until late at night the Hispanos streamed in and out to visit and ask advice. Among them were several pupils from Fort Lewis School, sixty miles away in Colorado. Dr. Breen, the superintendent, whom Anselm Weber had met in Farmington on Monday, had brought them in so they might receive the Sacraments.[53] After a long inspiring conversation with the French missionary, Anselm was more than ever convinced that the Franciscans should begin work on the San Juan.[54] Padre Antonio's advice was based moreover on long experience in the Indian and Hispano mission fields. Arrived from France in 1870 after Salpointe's consecration in Clermont Ferrand, he had labored throughout Arizona until 1884 when he left Tucson to follow his dear friend, the Bishop, to Santa Fe.[55]

The return trip to St. Michaels from Farmington began on Thursday, November 16, with a short ride to Shoemaker's hut opposite Fruitland, a short visit there, and then back across the river to Jewett again, where the two spent the night in the new hospital.[56] Friday was a long day in the saddle, even riding such a gaited animal as Swallow, for the two friends rode first to the trading post of Joe Wilkin, some fifteen miles west of Bennett Peak, before dropping down along the Chuska foothills to Noel's Store at Two Grey Hills.[57] After sleeping here at Noel's place they rode over the mountain to Moore's for dinner, reaching St. Michaels Saturday, November 18, in mid-afternoon. They had traveled a distance of approximately 135 miles in two days, and on their trip had covered about 550 miles.[58]

Upon returning home Father Anselm spent two days drawing up a thirty-three page handwritten report to Provincial Raphael Hesse

[52] *Sendbote,* 31:39, January, 1904.
[53] *Diary, 1899,* November 13; *Sendbote,* 31:39, January, 1904.
[54] *Ibid.*
[55] Salpointe, *Soldiers of the Cross,* pp. 260–271.
[56] *Sendbote,* 31:127, February, 1904; *Diary, 1899,* November 16.
[57] *Diary, 1899,* November 17, 18.
[58] A. Weber to Mother Katharine, February 8, 1900, C.H.A.

in California.[59] Substantially the same report and recommendations he also forwarded to provincial definers, Bernard Nurre and Bernardin Wissler.[60] The missionaries at St. Michaels favored a large industrial school in the San Juan country because they feared that proximity to Fort Defiance compromised any possible success of a mission school at Cienega.[61] To attract pupils the government doled out premiums of wagons and tools through the headmen of a neighborhood furnishing a student quota. Indians untouched by government influence were considered more co-operative by the two missionaries.[62] Freedom from government influence they figured would be achieved by establishing a large school east of the reservation, preferably near Pueblo Bonito or Farmington, both well beyond the radius of pressure exerted by Fort Defiance or Little Water (Tohatchi) schools.[63] The river bottoms between Farmington and Fruitland would serve admirably, the report continued, if Mr. McHenry's irrigation project should win a government appropriation of some $40,000. Dr. Breen of Fort Lewis school would definitely send all Navaho at his school to such a San Juan establishment, as the health of the Indians fared poorly in the high altitude at Grand Junction.[64]

The Provincial agreed that a communal approach seemed the answer: Mother Katharine should secure a large strip of farming land where the Indians could be induced to settle permanently.[65] Anselm should exert every effort through Mother Katharine to convince Monsignor Stephan; then undoubtedly the McHenry irrigation project would go through.[66]

[59] *Diary, 1899,* November 20, 22; R. Hesse to A. Weber, November 26, 1899, P.A., San Juan. Twelve pages of shorthand and longhand assorted German and English notes, either the November 22 or January 18 report, are in S.M.C., F-3.

[60] *Diary, 1899,* November 22; list of the "Provincials, Custodes and Definitors, October, 1885 to January, 1948," *Provincial Chronicle,* January, 1948.

[61] *Franziskus Bote,* 8:247, January, 1900. Father Juvenal from time to time sent news releases to the *Franziskus Bote.* A. Weber to R. Hesse, November 22, 1899, S.M.C., F-3.

[62] *House Chronicle,* pp. 39–40, S.M.C.; A. Weber to Mother Katharine, February 8, 1900, C.H.A.; A. Weber, *Sendbote,* 31:125, February 1904.

[63] A. Weber to R. Hesse, January 18, 1900, S.M.C., F-3. Indians along the San Juan had always remained aloof from Fort Defiance agency. In 1878 they were investigated by Chee Dodge who was sent to learn why they did not appear for rations' issue. A Navaho-Ute conspiracy was also feared at the time. Frank D. Reeve, "A Navaho Struggle for Land," *N.M.H.R.,* 21:2, January, 1946.

[64] A. Weber to Mother Katharine, February 8, 1900, C.H.A.; *Sendbote,* 31:125, February, 1904; *House Chronicle,* p. 41, S.M.C.

[65] R. Hesse to A. Weber, November 26, 1899, P.A., San Juan.

[66] Same to same, January 23, 1900, H.A.C.; A. Weber to Mother Katharine, February 8, 1900, C.H.A.

Meanwhile, Father Raphael admitted, there was nothing definite he could do until Padre Jouvenceau's meeting with Archbishop Bourgade, December 12, on the matter of the friars taking over a mission territory among Hispanos and Navaho in New Mexico.[67] At that meeting he also hoped that Anselm's and Jouvenceau's insistence on complete separation between Navaho and Hispano foundations would be brought home forcibly to the Archbishop.

Mother Katharine, it was definitely known, would not support Mexican missions, nor would she have her Sisters study Spanish, since she had vowed to dedicate her means and herself exclusively to Indians and Negroes.[68]

As a result of the meeting in Santa Fe, Archbishop Bourgade sent a formal request to the Provincial, urging the dire need of his diocese for a religious community such as the Franciscans to undertake Indian and Hispano work. Such isolated places were definitely unsuited for young secular priests, and older men could not stand up under the physical hardships. Bourgade's letter, however, named no specific parish or mission area which he intended to turn over.[69]

Both the Provincial and the Definitorium, meeting under the Commissary Louis Haverbeck at the new monastery in Louisville in late December, agreed that the next step should be made by the Archbishop. On short notice the friars were ready to go to work anywhere — provided the parish or mission were well located and generally feasible. Three Fathers — Leopold not among them for all his Spanish meditations — were named to study Spanish and prepare to leave at the call of the Archbishop; meantime their identity remained a top secret. The Louisville meeting further stipulated that either Father Juvenal or Anselm would first investigate the proposed mission territory.[70]

For some time no definite offer was forthcoming relative to Father Raphael's official acceptance, sent to the Archbishop in early January; the Provincial reassured Anselm that the province would simply have to sit still *"und Thee trinken."*[71] With his wonted conservatism Father Louis took a dim view of expecting the New Mexico parish in anything like a near future.[72]

[67] R. Hesse to A. Weber, November 26, 1899, P.A., San Juan.

[68] W. Ketcham to Archbishop Bourgade, November 17, 1906, copy in C.I.B.A.; Mother Katharine to A. Weber, October 23, 1905, P.A., PB.

[69] B. Nurre to A. Weber, December 31, 1899, P.A., BN.

[70] *Ibid.*

[71] R. Hesse to A. Weber, January 23, 1900, H.A.C.

[72] L. Haverbeck to A. Weber, January 30, 1900, P.A., LH.

As to Anselm's effort to have one of the three secret selectees come west to assist Reverend Juillard and there at Gallup became acclimated — that was quite acceptable to the definers and to the Provincial in California.[73] To send a man as pastor to a Hispano parish who knew only "book Spanish" would be a serious loss of face.[74] However, Commissary Louis gloomily warned, to send a young friar for any long period to a secular rectory contradicted the statutes of the Order as completely as assigning neophytes to saloons![75]

Father Bernard Nurre wondered from the tone of the Provincial's letter to the December conference whether Raphael Hesse had decided to give up Cienega altogether. Such a suggestion he personally could not approve, and suggested that the province look for a better location — but within the Tucson diocese and in Arizona.[76] Anselm himself subsequently made a strong case against any such move, and promoted the idea that St. Michaels should continue as a center for the whole mission shed west and south of the Chuska range.[77]

As to a school at Cienega he was skeptical; he thought a school preferable at Ganado near Hubbells, or at Manuelito, since both places enjoyed a certain insulation from governmental influence.[78]

By late January the Provincial, too, had come around to the conclusion that St. Michaels be kept at least as long as McHenry's San Juan irrigation scheme had not found federal approval, and St. Michaels had not been proved utterly hopeless. He had already written Mother Katharine to do something in Washington which would settle once and for all time the uncertain status of land ownership at St. Michaels.[79]

While awaiting word from Archbishop Bourgade as to the new mission center, life continued much as before at St. Michaels. Classes with the Day boys resumed on December 4, but proceeded irregularly after Mr. Day accepted the position as chief clerk at Fort Defiance in late December.[80] Charley Yazhe who had skipped out during

[73] B. Nurre to A. Weber, December 31, 1899, P.A., BN.; R. Hesse to A. Weber, February 19, 1900, H.A.C.

[74] B. Nurre to A. Weber, December 31, 1899, P.A., BN.

[75] L. Haverbeck to A. Weber, January 30, 1900, P.A., LH.

[76] B. Nurre to A. Weber, December 31, 1899, P.A., BN.

[77] A. Weber to R. Hesse, January 18, 1900, in R. Hesse to A. Weber, January 23, 1900, H.A.C.

[78] A. Weber to R. Hesse, November 22, 1899, S.M.C., F-3; A. Weber to Mother Katharine, February 8, 1900, C.H.A.

[79] R. Hesse to A. Weber, January 23, 1900, H.A.C.; R. Hesse to A. Weber, February 19, 1900, H.A.C.

[80] *Diary, 1899,* December 4; *House Chronicle,* p. 43, S.M.C.; *Sendbote,* 27:373, May, 1900.

August returned to the mission shortly before Christmas; and Albert Slinky remained for a while after Christmas, then returned home. Luke and Father Anselm trained the boys well enough to have them sing a Navaho version of *"Ihr Kinderlein Kommet"* for Christmas services. A younger lad, Naat'ani Short Hair, aged six, came on January 15 to replace Albert who was considered a toughy and very obstinate.[81]

Progress on the dictionary was reported excellent as Blind Luke and Father Juvenal revised all previous entries. Exacting work began on a Navaho Catechism December 4 with the aid of Luke and Charley Day;[82] but not until Frank Walker was hired as interpreter in late January did they make much headway,[83] and then, largely, because Father Chrysostom Verwyst, O.F.M., an old Chippewa missionary, sent a sample prayer book and Catechism which he had worked out according to Indian religious concepts and thought patterns.[84] Chrysostom and Juvenal had met in California during October in a visit that proved of great value to St. Michaels. The experienced missionary had suggested teaching Navaho boys English as a means for the priests to learn Navaho; he optimistically estimated that the Fathers could learn to speak fluently in two years: "Try to spend all your spare time in the lodges of those people and in a few years you will master the language."[85] His advice stressed concrete, descriptive terms in paraphrazing Christian concepts into the Navaho idiom.[86]

With Frank Walker assisting Father Juvenal, Charley Day was released to help Anselm with the translation of Bible stories which were begun on February 8.[87] When Charley and Sammy Day in early March took over the Chin Lee Trading Post purchased for them by Mr. Day, Noe had just entered the ark. Now it would be a problem, Father Anselm wrote dryly, to get the patriarch back on dry ground.[88] By April Father Juvenal felt that the twenty-odd Navaho prayers from the *Roman Ritual,* and the Catechism as well, would be ready for publication after Chee Dodge helped them do a

[81] *Diary, 1899,* August 9 and December 17; *House Chronicle,* p. 43, S.M.C.

[82] J. Schnorbus, *Franziskus Bote,* 8:358, April, 1900; *House Chronicle,* p. 42, S.M.C.

[83] Father Anselm hired Frank Walker, Irish-Navaho government interpreter, on January 23, 1900. A. Weber to Mother Katharine, February 8, 1900, C.H.A.; F. Hartung to Mother Katharine, July 27, 1900, C.H.A.

[84] Letter and guides of Verwyst, December 13, 1899, in P.A., NL.; see also *House Chronicle,* pp. 40, 44, S.M.C.

[85] C. Verwyst to J. Schnorbus, December 13, 1899, P.A., NL.

[86] A. Weber, *Sendbote,* 27:376, May, 1900.

[87] A. Weber to Mother Katharine, February 8, 1900, C.H.A.

[88] *Sendbote,* 27:374, May, 1900.

revision.[89] When Chee did check over the work later on, he said the language was good but that the contents sounded as clipped and terse to a Navaho as a telegram would to white folks.[90]

In hiring Frank Walker as interpreter and ranchman, Anselm Weber had acted in his new capacity as Mother Katharine's agent and manager of the Cienega ranch, a position which had become irksome and too demanding for Father Juvenal.[91]

Twenty-five-year-old Frank Walker had already served as interpreter at Fort Defiance for seven years, had worked for C. N. Cotton at his abandoned boxcar trading post in Gallup, and had lately been employed as a *padrone* for the Santa Fe Railroad in recruiting and handling Indian labor.[92] His father, John Walker, was an old Oregonian who had later served as military courier between Santa Fe, Forts Wingate and Apache, and who had married Dominica, a Catholic Navaho slave girl of the Hispanos at Cubero.[93] He was the first to settle in the neighborhood of what later became St. Johns, Arizona.[94] Except for short intervals, occasioned at times by bouts with *tqodilgil* in the Gallup "Arcade" and elsewhere, and now and then with federal marshals, Frank remained uninterruptedly at St. Michaels, the constant friend, teacher of missionaries, and loyal fellow worker with the missionaries until his death in 1945.[95] Frank Walker hired in at $25 a month and lived with the Indian pupils in the renovated log cabin behind the stone mission building.[96]

Translation advanced rapidly with Walker interpreting, and largely because of his wide circle of Navaho friends, headmen such as Charley Mitchell (Challa Tso), Peshlakai, and Chee Dodge visited St. Michaels and offered their backing.[97]

About two months after Walker became interpreter, and a year and

[89] *Franziskus Bote,* 8:358, April, 1900.

[90] Letter of A. Weber, January 26, 1905, in B.C.I.M., *Indianer Wache,* 1905–1906, p. 41.

[91] A. Weber to Mother Katharine, February 8, 1900, C.H.A.; R. Hesse to A. Weber, February 19, 1900, H.A.C.; B. Nurre to A. Weber, July 17, 1899, P.A., BN.; Mother Katharine to J. Schnorbus, May 28 and July 15, 1899, P.A., AK.

[92] A. Weber to Mother Katharine, February 8, 1900, C.H.A.; I.R.A., *Annual Report,* 1890, p. 23; A. Weber, *Sendbote,* 30:400, May, 1903; Berard Haile, interview, June 20, 1950.

[93] A. Jouvenceau to A. Weber, September 18, 1905, P.A., Moqui; A. Weber, *Sendbote,* 27:206, March, 1900; F. Walker to Archbishop (Chapelle), December 14, 1896, C.H.A.

[94] Farish, *History of Arizona,* Vol. 6, pp. 275–276.

[95] St. Michaels Parish Records, March 20, 1945.

[96] A. Weber to Mother Katharine, February 8, 1900, C.H.A.; Mother Katharine to A. Weber, March 11, 1900, P.A., AK.

[97] *House Chronicle,* p. 43, S.M.C.

a half after the friars had settled at Cienega, the missionaries baptized for the first time. On April 4 Father Juvenal baptized an infant girl, whom he christened Mary; on April 10 Father Anselm baptized four young children of the Corn Merchant, whose son, Frank, had been staying at the mission for some time.[98] To fulfill a request of his old Latin teacher and pastor, Reverend Tilik, Anselm christened the first boy Wenceslaus, after Tilik's patron saint, and the first girl after Melania Dulzo, the faithful old housekeeper of Tilik, and Anselm's friend. All four babies died shortly after their baptism. Brother Placid became official undertaker for these and all such burials; the Indians dreaded the "ghosts" of the deceased, and burying their dead was taken over by the friars as another work of mercy.[99]

Four months after Anselm Weber's exploratory trip to the San Juan in quest of a New Mexico mission site, Archbishop Bourgade wrote to Provincial Hesse in California that he had chosen Peña Blanca as the Franciscan mission center for Navaho, "Mexican," and English work. The Provincial directed Anselm to visit the Archbishop for briefing, and then to scout the entire Peña Blanca country *"und fleissig notes machen"* so that besides his own good judgment the Provincial and the Definitorium could also judge intelligently on the desirability of the location.[100] In company with Father Juillard of Gallup, Anselm accordingly made a thorough investigation of Peña Blanca with its four Hispano missions, the Indian pueblos of Santo Domingo, San Felipe, and Cochití, and likewise the Anglo gold mining towns of Bland and Colle. On March 26, less than a week after leaving St. Michaels, Anselm sent in his first report, to be followed by a second on April 2.[101]

Encouraged by these reports Provincial Raphael Hesse accepted the new mission foundation, and urged Commissary Louis to send west one of the designated Fathers for a breaking-in period under Father Juillard. Somehow the secret appointments had leaked. The Archbishop knew about them; Father Raphael was not a little piqued. He also wondered if the friars could simultaneously do full justice to both the Navaho and the new Pueblo missions. It was no secret to the Provincial that the Definitorium's affirmative vote had un-

98 *Ibid.*, p. 45.

99 W. Tilik to A. Weber, February 28, 1899, P.A., AY.; F. Hartung, *Sendbote,* 27:552, July, 1900; A. Weber, *Sendbote,* 28:471, June, 1901.

100 R. Hesse to J. Schnorbus, March 15, 1900, P.A., PB.

101 See R. Hesse to A. Weber, April 6, 1900, P.A., PB.; *House Chronicle,* p. 44, S.M.C.

doubtedly been influenced by the Archbishop's underscoring of the health-resort possibilities of Peña Blanca for the ailing friars of the province.[102]

There is small doubt, if any, that Anselm Weber viewed the New Mexico parish of Peña Blanca as only one more move in his contemplated mission project to encircle the Navaho country with a series of missions.[103] That between themselves Archbishop Bourgade and Anselm Weber planned a perimeter of three strong missions bordering Navaho country is evident from Bourgade's successful report eighteen months later on "our contemplated project" of the St. Michaels, Nacimiento or La Posta [Cuba], and San Juan Navaho foundations.[104]

For the present, however, active work for Father Anselm on the Navaho mission was suspended by serious recurrence of his nervous troubles. In very poor health he left St. Michaels, April 25, 1900, to recuperate on the West Coast.[105] Anselm first lived with Father Victor Aertker, O.F.M., at St. Joseph's Church in Los Angeles until he transferred to the Santa Barbara Mission in order to bathe in the salt water. He also visited a short while in San Francisco, always enjoying the hospitality of the friars of the Santa Barbara Commissariat.[106]

Fortunately for Father Anselm his leaving at this time in no way embarrassed the mission work at St. Michaels since Frederick Hartung, newly ordained on August 19, 1899, had been stationed at the mission since September 9, 1899.[107] He had been suffering from a throat ailment and had been ordained beforehand and sent to Arizona on his physician's recommendation.[108] His good nature and cheerfulness had been a boon to St. Michaels, and his assured, businesslike way of handling farm and land matters compensated in great measure for Anselm's leaving.[109] Within a few short weeks after taking over as business manager he had provided Father Juvenal with a fast team

[102] *Ibid.*

[103] *House Chronicle,* p. 45, S.M.C.

[104] P. Bourgade to A. Weber, December 31, 1901, H.A.C.; *House Chronicle,* p. 45, S.M.C.

[105] R. Hesse to A. Weber, April 6, 1900, P.A., PB.; *House Chronicle,* p. 45, S.M.C.

[106] A. Weber, *Sendbote,* 27:990, December, 1900; F. Hartung, *Sendbote,* 27:550, July, 1900, and 27:642, August, 1900; F. Hartung to Mother Katharine, July 13, 1900, C.H.A.

[107] *House Chronicle,* p. 39, S.M.C.; *Catalogus Fratrum,* 1933, p. 15.

[108] B. Nurre to A. Weber, July 19 and October 31, 1899, P.A., BN.

[109] See George J. Juillard to A. Weber, May 30 and October 4, 1900, P.A., GJ.; B. Nurre to A. Weber, October 31, 1899, P.A., BN.; F. Hartung to Mother Katharine, July 13 and 27, 1900, C.H.A.

and buckboard, purchased from Don Lorenzo Hubbell at Mother Katharine's expense, and was supervising most capably the land transactions for Monsignor Stephan.[110]

Father Anselm Weber's plan to get a temporary assistant for George J. Juillard — by having the Peña Blanca missionary train at Gallup — went somehow awry; Father Francis de Sales Stuerenberg underwent conditioning for Hispano mission work at the Santa Fe Cathedral under the direct tutelage of the Archbishop. He took over as pastor of Peña Blanca on June 10.[111] In place of temporary assistance from the Franciscans, Juillard was soon to have a full-time young French helper, "bright, nice, lovely" Michael Dumarest.[112]

[110] For $240; F. Hartung to Mother Katharine, July 27, 1900, C.H.A.; Letters of Stephan to F. Hartung, July–October, 1900, H.A.C., and F. Hartung to A. Weber, September 2, 1900, P.A., AH.

[111] F. Hartung, *Sendbote,* 27:554, July, 1900; *House Chronicle,* p. 44, S.M.C.

[112] G. J. Juillard to A. Weber, October 4, 1900, P.A., GJ.

Chapter VI

Founding of St. Michaels Boarding School

The year 1900 marked a provincial election for St. John the Baptist Province of Cincinnati. On this account the usual annual visitation by the Provincial gave place to the special triennial investigation of the province by a direct representative of the minister-general of the entire Franciscan Order. Father Denis Schuler, O.F.M., of Germany, was sent to the United States and reached St. Michaels on his visitation tour, July 14, 1900.[1] He was accompanied by Father Leo Heinrichs of the New York Province who was assassinated in Denver, February 23, 1908, while distributing Holy Communion.[2] Denis Schuler was impressed with the Indian mission and personally visited the hogans near St. Michaels.[3]

Father Raphael Hesse had left the West Coast a month after Anselm Weber arrived in Los Angeles, and the Provincial had visited St. Michaels and Santa Fe en route to Cincinnati.[4] The chapter was held September 27–28 at Mt. Airy.[5]

Even prior to the chapter, provincial gossip indicated that Father Juvenal would not continue long "out West."[6] Temperamentally he seemed to be of the type that needed the reassuring rhythm of regularized monastic observance.[7] This cloistral area of religious equanimity he missed in the jumbled schedule imposed by mission

1 F. Hartung, *Sendbote,* 27:732–735, September, 1900; *House Chronicle,* p. 46, S.M.C.

2 Father Leo Heinrichs tried to climb the pine log to the nearby cliff dwellings but giddiness prevented him from more than viewing the ruins from the top of the improvised ladder. F. Hartung, *Sendbote,* 27:735, September, 1900. Regarding the assassination see C. J. McNeill, in *St. Anthony Messenger,* 46:4–6, November, 1938.

3 *House Chronicle,* July 14, p. 46, S.M.C.

4 F. Hartung, *Sendbote,* 27:554, July, 1900.

5 *Tabula Definitionis,* 1900, P.A.

6 B. Nurre to A. Weber, October 16, 1899, P.A., BN.

7 Bernardin Wissler, O.F.M., to A. Weber, December 19, 1900, P.A., BW.

trips, overcrowded quarters, and multiplied material interests. Moreover, he had been moody frequently and had requested to be relieved of the superiorship — even if it meant walking to get away.[8]

At his interview with the Visitor General in Los Angeles, Anselm Weber had explained the impasse and declared himself ready to return East if the chapter so wished.[9] Difference of outlook on mission philosophy, on treatment of Indians, and personal incompatibility[10] did not warrant their continuing together.[11]

Immediately before the chapter opening, Father Anselm in California had written a long clarifying letter to Father Bernard Nurre, who received it the very evening the new Provincial, Louis Haverbeck, had been elected.[12] With the electing of the new Provincial and the new definers, Father Bernard himself had gone out of office as a definer, so he gave the pertinent pages of the letter to Father Pax Winterheld, O.F.M., one of the new definers, with instructions to take it into the chapter room and to show it also to Father Louis.[13] Bernard Nurre knew by this time that the visitor himself did not favor Father Juvenal's continuance as superior.[14]

Realizing the incongruity of allowing Father Juvenal to continue on at St. Michaels under reversed status, the chapter transferred him to Fairmount, Cincinnati, and named Anselm Weber superior and pastor of the Navaho Mission, with Fathers Leopold Ostermann and Berard Haile as assistants.[15] In a personal, handwritten note Father Provincial notified Anselm of his appointment, urging him to return immediately from California to St. Michaels.[16] Subsequently, in giving Father Anselm permission to visit Santa Fe on his return from California, the new Provincial confided that directing provincial affairs was to him a genuine misery.[17]

[8] B. Nurre to A. Weber, July 19, 1899, P.A., BN.; A. Weber to J. Schnorbus, August 19, 1907, P.A., JS.; J. Schnorbus to A. Weber, January 21, 1901, P.A., JS.

[9] A. Weber to J. Schnorbus, August 19, 1907, P.A., JS.; A. Weber, *Sendbote,* 35:322, April, 1908, refers to his meeting with Visitor Denis Schuler at Los Angeles.

[10] A. Weber to Provincial Eugene Buttermann, May 29, 1912, P.A., JS.

[11] A. Weber to J. Schnorbus, August 19, 1907, P.A., JS.

[12] B. Nurre to A. Weber, November 18, 1900, P.A., BN. Vincent Trost, O.F.M., informed Anselm by telegram, card, and letters of chapter progress: of Louis Haverbeck's election with nine votes on the first ballot, and of Anselm's appointment, along with other provincial changes. V. Trost to A. Weber, September 28, 29, October 1, 2, 1900, P.A., VT.

[13] B. Nurre to A. Weber, *ibid.*

[14] Same to same, August 15, 1900, P.A., BN.

[15] *Tabula Definitionis,* 1900, P.A.; A. Weber to J. Schnorbus, August 19, 1907, P.A., JS.

[16] L. Haverbeck to A. Weber, October 1, 1900, P.A., LH.

[17] Same to same, October 10, 1900, P.A., LH.

There were now three friar priests in Arizona among the Navaho, and three from the same province at Peña Blanca, New Mexico. Father Theodore Stephan had already left in May,[18] and Father Arbogast Reissler traveled west with Fathers Berard and Leopold as far as Thornton, New Mexico.[19] The two new Navaho missionaries reached to St. Michaels with a serious problem:[27] A "bone shooter" medicine volunteered for the southwestern missions.[21] Two days after their arrival, Juvenal Schnorbus and Frederick Hartung, the latter much improved in health, returned eastward to their respective appointments in Cincinnati and Pekin, Illinois.[22]

With the sudden turnover in personnel there remained considerable unfinished business to handle, particularly the matter of procuring pupils for St. Catherine's Boarding School in Santa Fe. Sister Evangelist had begged Father Juvenal at the beginning of 1900 to enlist ten Navaho boys for St. Catherine's, and Mother Katharine had repeated the request.[23] In attempting to realize this Navaho schooling project Juvenal Schnorbus had fortunately enlisted the support of Charley Mitchell (Tso).[24]

Charley, an ex-army scout from Fort Wingate, had dropped by at St. Michaels on February 21 to size up the mission.[25] Apparently satisfied, and his curiosity whetted, he had returned shortly after with headmen Peshlakai and Chee Dodge to further analyze the *e'nishodi* situation at Cienega.[26] Their report evidently was good since a short while later members of Mitchell's outfit trooped in to St. Michaels with a serious problem:[27] A "bone shooter" medicine man, one of the Indian wizards who reputedly could shoot his darts irrespective of distance, had raped one of their women.[28] After she had subsequently fallen seriously ill, her menfolk had tracked down the dart shooter and forced him to treat the ailing woman. Under duress the old sorcerer had made an incision and sucked out the magic

[18] Same (as Commissary) to same, May 27, 1900, P.A., LH.

[19] Berard Haile, interview, September 2, 1949.

[20] *House Chronicle,* p. 47, S.M.C.; L. Ostermann, in *St. Anthony Messenger,* 8:301, February, 1901.

[21] B. Haile, in *The Provincial Chronicle,* 20:195, Summer, 1948; L. Ostermann to A. Weber, October 19, 1899, P.A., LO.

[22] *House Chronicle,* p. 47, S.M.C.; A. Weber to C. Lusk, October 8, 1900, C.I.B.A.

[23] Sister M. Evangelist to J. Schnorbus, January 7, 1900, P.A., AK.

[24] Mother Katharine to J. Schnorbus, August 30, 1900, P.A., AK.

[25] *House Chronicle,* p. 43, S.M.C.

[26] *Ibid.*

[27] F. Hartung, *Sendbote,* 27:639–640, August, 1900.

[28] See Kluckhohn and Leighton, *The Navaho,* p. 128; Coolidge and Coolidge, *The Navajo Indians,* p. 143.

pellets — several tiny arrowheads which he had previously concealed under his tongue. Nonetheless the woman died. The kinfold had kept the bone shooter captive ever since, and on their visit to the padres wanted to know what penalty to deal out.[29] Protesting that they held no judicial powers in civil matters, the missionaries convinced the Indians that they should deliver the faker to Agent Hayzlett.

Meanwhile Father Anselm had reported the matter to Hayzlett; he agreed to make an example of the dart shooter when the Indians should bring him to Fort Defiance. Probably too busy when the prisoner was brought before him, the agent on May 10 remanded the old codger into the care of the mission. There he remained as one of the household, explaining many religious ideas of the Navaho, and helping considerably with the language study.[30]

So the reputation of the friars had risen, but not to a point where the headmen would, out of hand, back the canvass for St. Catherine's desired pupils. Charley Mitchell, Peshlakai, and Chee Dodge had been among the Navaho who had visited the Chicago World Fair in 1893 with Lieutenant Edwin H. Plummer and who had all returned with liberal ideas on education.[31] Sending children away from the reservation was the hurdle.

In 1882 eleven boys and one girl had been sent off to Carlisle against furious opposition at a council in which young Manuelito had played a prominent role.[32] One of Chief Manuelito's sons had died at Carlisle, and another within a week of his return. Thereafter the Navaho dreaded all schools, especially off-reservation boarding schools. As a result Agent Dennis M. Riordan had hired a young Indian couple to reopen the Fort Defiance school in 1883. Robert Stewart, a Creek, and Antoinette Williams Stewart, a Navaho, were the second couple to be married at Carlisle.[33]

It was only after Charley Mitchell had visited Santa Fe and St. Catherine's, where he watched the Sisters at work with the children, that he wholeheartedly endorsed the proposal advanced so urgently by the Sisters and Father Juvenal.[34] He now, in fact, became the

[29] F. Hartung, *Sendbote,* 27:640, August, 1900.

[30] *Ibid.*

[31] Board of Indian Commissioner, *Annual Report,* 1894, pp. 30–31.

[32] D. M. Riordan to Chee Dodge (reminiscences), October 6, 1916, P.A., CD.; Board of Indian Commissioners, *Annual Report,* 1882, p. 2.

[33] Phelps Stokes Fund, *The Navajo Indian Problem,* p. 52; Board of Indian Commissioners, *Annual Report,* 1885, p. 214; Davida Woerner, *Education Among the Navajo . . . An Historical Study* (privately printed doctoral dissertation submitted at Columbia University, New York, 1941), p. 35.

[34] A. Weber, *Sendbote,* 28:109, February, 1901.

chief propagandist for St. Catherine's Navaho educational venture.[35]

Juvenal and Frank Walker had visited the three headmen on June 25, 1900, and again on July 27, on which date the missionary had instructed members of Charley's kinfolk and offered Mass.[36] His readiness to sit cross-legged around the fire, and his facility in fingering out his mutton from the common pot mightily impressed the Indians; the Long Dragging Gown from Cienega was a good one: he did not patronize the *Diné*.[37] Charley promised at their last meeting to have the children assembled at his Tseili camp in middle October.[38]

Anselm Weber arrived home at St. Michaels from California on the fifteenth of October, and on the seventeenth he and Father Leopold Ostermann struck out for Mitchell's place at Tseili, fifty-eight miles to the north. Leaving at 5:45 a.m. they skirted the western slopes of the Chuska as they passed Black Rock, Red Lake, Crystal, and finally crossed "Old Whiskey."[39] Frank Walker, who had left the day previously, had described Whiskey Creek as the third creek bed to be crossed. He had promised to post a guide there, but none was in evidence when the two friars passed by in the wagon. Toward evening they were overtaken by horsemen who had picked up their trail from Whiskey Creek. After greetings and the usual handclasps, these guides rode ahead toward Charley's. After nightfall Father Anselm had to lead the tired horses by the bridle along the narrow forest trail to guard against smashed hubs, and to keep the fatigued animals on the move. A blaze of fire through the trees finally led them to a hogan and hot supper. Squatting around the fire awaiting them were Charley Mitchell, Frank Walker, Naakai Dinae, Tsisch Chilli, and Mexican Navaho With the Black Moustache, the latter from over the mountains near the Shiprock.[40]

Charley offered his stone house for sleeping quarters, the same rectangular building he had previously suggested to Father Juvenal for mission purposes.[41]

At the council next day two new headmen put in their appearance, Braided Hair from the Lukachukai Mountains and Nataani Tsossi

35 *Ibid.;* L. Ostermann, in *St. Anthony Messenger,* 8:327, March, 1901.

36 *House Chronicle,* pp. 46, 47, S.M.C.

37 F. Hartung, *Sendbote,* 27:732–734, September, 1900.

38 L. Ostermann, in *St. Anthony Messenger,* 8:327, March, 1901.

39 *Ibid.,* pp. 327–328.

40 For detailed accounts, L. Ostermann, in *St. Anthony Messenger,* 8:328–329, March, 1901; A. Weber, *Sendbote,* 28:109, February, 1901.

41 L. Ostermann, in *St. Anthony Messenger,* 8:366, April, 1901.

(Slim Headman).[42] Braided Hair looked suspiciously at the strangers when he began his hour-long talk to the council. This Navaho Dewey wanted to know of what benefit or usefulness was education. Had it helped the Navaho to any better way of life, or to earn a living? In answer Father Anselm explained through Frank Walker that mission education would help the community, would develop honest, loyal men and women, devoted to family and to The People. He promised them that their children would love God more, and would thereby love their brothers more. Apparently the social note struck a responsive chord for Braided Hair dramatically shook hands, adding with conviction: "My father and headman, I like your words. I go now to bring my son." Outside the hogan he mounted and rode off.[43]

Thursday night, October 18, after the council concluded for the day, the campfire talk turned to tales and reminiscences in which all joined with great gusto and much laughter. To Leopold this conviviality from a supposedly taciturn people came as a delightful surprise.[44]

Next morning, Friday, when Nataani Tsossi asked the same questions and raised the same objections against education, Anselm Weber patiently answered each single doubt, never hurrying, never exasperated at the obvious repetitions.[45] Happy and satisfied, Slim Headman left two boys for St. Catherine's, and promised more from his outfit when the *e'nishodi's* school at Cienega should be ready.[46]

Old Billy, brother of Braided Hair, rode in to join the council that same Friday. He was twisted with rheumatism and old beyond his years, a man with a continual smile on his face, and the same Old Billy who had shot and killed a medicine man some time earlier.[47]

Chee Dodge had dropped by while en route to the Round Rock Store owned by him and S. E. Aldrich. On his return from Round Rock, Chee took Walker's place as interpreter Saturday evening after supper. Charley Mitchell had been explaining Navaho genesis through emerging worlds, Chee translating. To Charley's emergence theory Father Anselm put the question of the hen and the egg — which came first? A trifle balked, Charley replied that from the morning twilight came the first chicken; there was no special Creator, though plenty of gods,

[42] *Ibid.*, p. 368.

[43] A. Weber, *Sendbote,* 28:113, February, 1901; L. Ostermann, in *St. Anthony Messenger,* 8:369, April, 1901.

[44] L. Ostermann, *ibid.*, 8:401, May, 1901.

[45] *Ibid.*, 9:10, June, 1901.

[46] *Ibid.*

[47] *Ibid.*; Letter Book, 1898–1899, pp. 304–305, W.R.C.

in the genesis of the *Diné*. It was at this point that Chee from his reclining position on a sheepskin asked for the missionaries' belief.[48]

Frank Walker translated as Father Anselm unfolded the story of Creation and the Fall, of Incarnation and Redemption, of the Church of Christ, the Sacraments, and the Mass Sacrifice. He further explained the civilizing influence of Christianity in Europe, ending with the more modern impact of the Church in Paraguay and California. When the friar described the Resurrection and Ascension Chee "leaped to his feet, and, standing in midfloor, face aglow, and eyes sparkling . . . interpreted dramatically with word and gesture."[49] To Father Leopold it was obvious how Chee Dodge had gained such esteem and leadership status among illiterate primitives who ascribed wisdom and sagacity to oratorical prowess. All around from the circle of intent faces came nods and murmurs of approval as the handsome, black-haired interpreter dramatized the story of Easter and Ascension. Deeply impressed, the Indians rolled final cigarettes at the close of the friar's talk and soon turned over on their sheepskins for the night.[50]

After writing down the Indian names of the seven youngsters, Christian names were added as follows; Stephan Hashke, James Azhun, Paul Neinlinni, Joseph Choi, Willie Tgolli, Charley Dine Tsossi, John Foley Yazhe.[51] Finally after obtaining the signature (X mark) of the parents, as demanded by the 1895 federal statute regulating transporting Indian pupils beyond state lines, the whole troop of parents, friends, children, and the two missionaries set off south for Moore's trading post.[52]

Mrs. Moore graciously donated the flour, coffee, and sugar for the supper which the squaws in the party quickly made ready. She also furnished at cost complete wardrobes and shoes for the seven boys who quickly discovered that store clothes were too cramping, and shed them happily until within sight of the mission.[53]

From Moore's, Anselm and three Indians rode ahead to Fort

[48] L. Ostermann, in *St. Anthony Messenger,* 9:80, August, 1901; see *An Ethnologic Dictionary,* p. 346.

[49] *Ibid.,* p. 81.

[50] *Ibid.*

[51] *Ibid.,* p. 82; A. Weber, *Sendbote,* 28:202, March, 1901.

[52] A. Weber, *ibid.;* Law of March 2, 1895: "no Indian child shall be sent from any Indian reservation to a school beyond the State or Territory in which said reservation is situated without the voluntary consent of the father or mother. . . . Such consent shall be made before the agent of the reservation, and he shall send to the Commissioner of Indian Affairs his certificate that such consent has been voluntarily given. . . ." 28 U. S. Stats., 906.

[53] L. Ostermann, in *St. Anthony Messenger,* 9:120, September, 1901.

Defiance to report and register the departing pupils. On Thursday, October 23, after a touching farewell between parents and children, Charley Mitchell and Braided Hair accompanied Father Anselm and the seven pupils to Santa Fe. En route to Gallup they were overtaken by Chee Dodge, who also brought news that the agent's rig was in hot pursuit to recover two of the pupils. At Gallup Father Anselm had to surrender to a teacher from Fort Defiance Stephan and James who had attended the agency school during the previous year.[54] According to the curiously unconstitutional Browning Ruling of September 30, 1896, Indian parents could not change schools for their children: " . . . the Indian parents have no right to designate which school their children shall attend."[55]

With five instead of seven pupils, the headmen accompanied Father Anselm to Santa Fe, where they met Archbishop Bourgade, and spent two days observing classes, especially the industrial departments, at St. Catherine's School. It was here that the Franciscan met Mother Katharine for the first time. He was delighted with her gracious friendliness to the Navaho men, and her winning ways with the five youngsters whom she cajoled out of their shyness by personally challenging them to a rock-throwing contest with a tin can as target. Six-year-old John Foley further demonstrated his markmanship in the classroom the next day by scoring a direct hit with his slate pencil on a Sister who had reproved him for humming Navaho tunes during classwork.

The parting between Braided Hair and little Paul was tearful and pathetic, and only after a ringing public lecture by Chee on the train to Gallup did Braided Hair finally throw off his gloom. Train passengers were divided in their astonishment and admiration between the lecture and the imposing figure of handsome Charley Mitchell with his eyeglasses and the magnificent turquoise and shell necklace once worn by Chief Manuelito.[56]

Unfortunately the bad reputation of boarding schools off the reservation was reinforced when little Joseph Choi died of tuberculosis shortly

[54] *Ibid.*, pp. 120–121; *House Chronicle,* p. 48, S.M.C.; A. Weber to Chas. Lusk, October 26 and November 18, 1900, C.I.B.A.; A. Weber, *Sendbote,* 28:202–203, March, 1901.

[55] Abrogated by Commissioner W. A. Jones, January 17, 1902. Secretary of the Interior, E. A. Hitchcock, had promised its abrogation to Archbishop Ireland early in 1901 but delayed in acting. Already before his death President McKinley had ordered a canceling of the Ruling. Copy of abrogation from the Office of Indian Affairs, January 18, 1902, C.I.B.A.; Chas. Lusk to A. Weber, November 12, 1900, C.I.B.A.

[56] A. Weber, *Sendbote,* 28:293–296, April, 1901.

after returning from St. Catherine's in the following summer. Sister Evangelist had written of the doctor's verdict in May of 1901.[57] At the end of June Father Leopold had made the trip to Santa Fe to fetch home the five pupils. When they reached Cienega Joseph looked very poorly, so Leopold had baptized the little fellow before his parents came for him. Shortly afterward he died.[58]

Upon arriving back at St. Michaels from Santa Fe the October previous, Father Anselm had learned that the famous "Mountain Chant" would take place at Red Lake on October 31, 1900. Headmen from all over the reservation would take part. He telegraphed back to Mother Katharine in Santa Fe to come on to the mission at once with her cousin, Miss Josephine Whorton, and Sister Evangelist. The big "sing" would offer a splendid opportunity to enlist headmen in support of the projected boarding school at St. Michaels.[59]

The Sisters and Josephine Whorton arrived at Cienega on the evening of October 30 and lodged with the Days.[60] Miss Josephine left almost at once by carriage with Mrs. Wyant, Father Leopold, and Frank Walker to attend the "Mountain Chant." Father Berard and Little Bone Shooter, the shaman, accompanied on horseback.[61] Anselm Weber left on the mare, Swallow, at 6:30 p.m., and made the twenty-five miles to Red Lake in two and one-half hours. From miles off the roaring ceremonial fire was a beacon.[62]

Near midnight, toward the height of the dance, a fight broke out back among the wagons between two Navaho who had been imbibing freely of the "dark water" which was being sold to the Indians at 75 cents a nip. Charley Mitchell grabbed one of the brawlers in the act of drawing his revolver; Anselm, who had accompanied Mitchell from the thronged spectators, stepped between and relieved both of their six-shooters.[63] The missionaries and their party left the dance as the first streaks of dawn were silhouetting the craggy, pine-burred Chuska rim, early on All Saints' Day.[64]

57 To A. Weber, May 7, 1901, P.A., SE.

58 L. Ostermann, in *St. Anthony Messenger,* 9:264, January, 1902; *House Chronicle,* p. 51, S.M.C.

59 A. Weber, *Sendbote,* 28:293, 297, April, 1901.

60 *Ibid.,* 28:637, August, 1901.

61 *Ibid.,* 28:297, April, 1901.

62 A. Weber, *Sendbote,* 28:377, May, 1901. The ceremonial is detailed in this issue, pages 376–380. See Washington Matthews, "The Mountain Chant: A Navajo Ceremony," *Fifth Annual Report of the Bureau of Ethnology to the Secretary of the Smithsonian Institution,* 1883–1884 (Washington, D. C.: United States Printing Office, 1887), pp. 379–467.

63 A. Weber, *Sendbote,* 28:380, May, 1901.

64 *Ibid.,* 28:554, July, 1901.

Charley Mitchell and Frank Walker had induced all the headmen attending the dance to meet in council at St. Michaels during the day. Around ten o'clock in the morning they began to drift in, blear-eyed from loss of sleep. Behind the mission they threw down saddles and blankets in a long line near the log house where they slept while their horses munched good alfalfa hay. Toward sundown the fragrance of roasting mutton and fresh pan bread drew them to the feast which had been prepared by neighborhood squaws at Mother Katharine's expense.[65]

At the All Souls' Day council the next day the missionaries, the Sisters, and Miss Whorton took places on the porch of the log cabin while the headmen squatted on the ground in a semicircle. Peshlakai opened the talks in his usual blunt, factual style: Graduates from the various schools had thus far distinguished themselves, he said — and Walker interpreted — only by their dissatisfaction, their craftiness and poverty. While at school learning reading, writing, and numbers, their companions at home were raising sheep and children. As Peshlakai, the Silversmith, concluded by insisting that education had only harmed the Navaho, the Sisters were feeling quite uncomfortable; the missionaries already knew the attitude of the Indians.[66]

Charley Mitchell spoke next and in a tone indicating that his visit to St. Catherine's School had raised his hopes for a new kind of education, one that would stress practical skills and crafts. Seven more headmen addressed the council, some from the north and northeast who were strangers to the Fort Defiance area; all were somewhat skeptical of education but hoped that the Sisters' school would raise the living conditions of the *Diné*.[67]

Mother Katharine replied that she had always admired the Navaho for their spirit of independence and for the intelligence and weaving skill of their womenfolk. She did not believe the headmen were entirely convinced of all they said against education; they had men like Chee Dodge to prove the benefits of schooling to their own. She knew many other great Indian peoples, she continued, whom moral and religious education had bettered in many ways.[68] To Sandoval's complaint that

[65] *Ibid.* Preparations for the council and feast had been planned two weeks previously. Sister Evangelist to J. Schnorbus, October 15, 1900, P.A., SE.

[66] A. Weber, *Sendbote,* 28:555, July, 1901.

[67] *Ibid.*

[68] *Ibid.* On this occasion, and not infrequently, Mother Katharine was traveling incognito as "Sister Mary," and Miss Whorton as Miss Warden, to avoid the publicity with which the newspapers tried to surround the names of Drexel and Whorton. See A. Weber, *Sendbote,* 28:293, April, 1901.

Don Lorenzo Hubbell's Trading Post at Ganado

Solid stone altar in Keams Canyon for Father Anselm's Mass. Serving, Father Juillard

Brother Placid, Father Juvenal, and Father Anselm, 1899, before first St. Michaels Mission

school people made all sorts of overtures to Indian parents in order to get their children — and then later refused them horse feed and supplies for the parents when they visited their children — Mother Katharine promised emphatically that both the Indians and their horses would be given cordial hospitality at her proposed new school.[69]

Almost every Indian speaker had stressed the treatment given the Indian children when sick at school. Would the St. Michaels School allow the Indians to take their sick children home for treatment, or would the Sisters, too, insist on keeping the children to die at school without good Indian medicine? Aware that this was at the heart of their objections, and most touchy, Father Anselm signaled Mother Katharine that this was his province. He assured them that by all means the parents would be notified of their child's sickness. He argued, however, against sending seriously sick children home to drafty hogans and earthen floors. Nor did he believe the headmen realized that the *e'nishodi* were also powerful medicine men with good prayers and strong medicine.[70]

With a display of oratory he next painted a vivid picture of dedicated Sisters and priests who for God's sake had foregone marriage and family in order to dedicate themselves to the education and care of all children. St. Michaels Mission was founded simply and exclusively to serve the Navaho, without compensation, for love of them and their children. St. Michaels would educate the children not only in reading and writing, but in farming, stock raising, building trades, and other useful crafts.[71]

With a flourish Father Anselm finished, and stepping down from the porch of Walker's home, motioned the Sisters and priests to do likewise. The council was over. All around there was handclasping and promising by the headmen to back the future mission school. Mother Katharine promised to begin building next year (1901), and to open a large boarding school the following year. By that time she hoped to have Sisters enough in her community to open the Navaho foundation.[72]

Both Father Anselm and Mother Katharine were direct actionists. With prospects for a new school in the foreground, she traveled on to Keams Canyon to inspect the government school then under construction by the Owen Company of Minneapolis;[73] Anselm Weber

[69] *Ibid.,* 28:556, July, 1901.
[70] *Ibid.,* p. 558.
[71] *Ibid.,* p. 559.
[72] *House Chronicle,* pp. 48–49, S.M.C.
[73] Mother Katharine to Cornwells Heights, October, 1900, *Annals,* 6:110, C.H.A.

undertook to write a stirring appeal for vocations to the Sisters of the Blessed Sacrament for Indians and Colored People.[74]

Difficulties over title to the mission lands engaged the close attention of Anselm Weber for most of the following year of 1901. Mr. Sam E. Day, who had chained for Lamport's earlier (March, 1899) private survey, maintained that Lamport had "allowed too much" for rough ground — one chain for every five miles.[75] Lamport's official government survey of early September, 1900, proved Day's contention correct: the east-west lines were seventy feet off, bringing Wyant's buildings on the same forty as the mission buildings.[76]

The survey was again checked by government inspector at George Overton's request; he claimed fraud in the previous surveys and insisted that "Reverend Berard after divine services puts in the rest of the day destroying [my] improvements."[77] Bert McJunkins, who had trespassed on an Indian's land to build his store, complained that the priests "represent themselves as teaching the Christian religion to the Indians, but more of their time is spent in creating discord."[78]

Colored George's claims were finally disposed of through affidavits by Billy Meadows and Joe Wilkin, both testifying that George had merely worked for them, and had made no improvements entitling him to squatters' rights for himself.[79]

With Day and Wyant it was necessary to buy off their improvements for $1,500 and $2,500 respectively, thereby obtaining formal quitclaims.[80]

It was further necessary to force the eviction of traders Halloday, McJunkins, the two Weidemeyer brothers, and Sampson — all having successively owned and operated a trading post on Indian land, about three hundred yards from the old Wyant store. Balked in a move

[74] Mother James to A. Weber, November 15, 1900, P.A., AK. The English article appeared in *St. Anthony Messenger,* 8:262–268, January, 1901.

[75] A. Weber to Monsignor Stephan, July 30, 1900, C.I.B.A.

[76] J. Schnorbus to Mother Katharine, September 6, 1900, C.I.B.A.; F. Hartung to Monsignor Stephan, September 17, 1900, C.I.B.A.

[77] Quoted in A. Weber to Chas. Lusk, August 12, 1901, C.I.B.A.

[78] Bert McJunkins to Commissioner of Indian Affairs, August 16, 1901, B.I.A.L.R., 45948, 1901; Major Hayzlett to Commissioner of Indian Affairs, May 20, 1901, B.I.A.L.R., 28268, 1901; Inspector F. M. Consor, Report from Navaho Agency on trespass of Indian land at Cienega, August 4, 1902, B.I.A.L.R., 47379, 1902; A. Weber, *Affidavit,* attesting to collusion between Halloway, McJunkins, and Weidemeyer, August 17, 1901, B.I.A.L.R., 46098, 1901.

[79] *Affidavits,* W. Meadows, August 3, 1901, P.A., MS.; J. K. Wilkin, July 16, 1901, P.A., MS.; A. Weber, *Sendbote,* 28:820, October, 1901.

[80] *House Chronicle,* p. 50, S.M.C.; A. Weber, *Sendbote,* 29:642–643, August, 1902; Mother Katharine to A. Weber, December 12, 1900, February 12, 1901, February 22, 1901, May 16, 1901, S.M.C., F-1; see above, pp. 25–26.

to take over Wyant's store when he left, these men had tried at all costs to undersell and close down G. Manning, Tom Osborne, and, subsequently, John Walker, when they leased the original Wyant trading post through Father Anselm.[81]

This entailed survey work on the part of the missionary to furnish a description of the disputed land on which Peshlakai Biye and Woody wished to file. Neither Agent Hayzlett nor the county judge at St. Johns, Arizona, realized that Indians could file on public lands off the reservation, so Father Anselm took the two Indians to St. Johns personally and handled their homestead claims.[82] For twenty-five years already the law enabling both reservation and allotted Indians to homestead had lain dormant, largely because the measure had passed as an unnoticed and undebated rider attached to an Indian appropriation bill.[83]

It was not until June, 1902, that the final clearing of title to mission land was settled. This had involved the purchase of land script to cover three hundred and sixty acres, and the purchase in fee simple of eighty acres of railroad land.[84] It was believed that that much land was needed for training the Indians in farming and irrigation, as well as for the support of the future boarding school.

Mother Katharine by the autumn of 1901 felt secure enough in her title to begin actual planning for the school.[85] Bids were opened on November 1, 1901, at St. Michaels, with the bid of $51,000 by J. H. Owen of Minneapolis winning out over Mr. Henry of Las Vegas, New Mexico, and Mr. Reiland of Gallup.[86] The contract was finally put into effect, and building operations started, only after Mother Katharine had instructed Anselm Weber to place guaranteed Valentine scrip

[81] Hayzlett, Order to vacate, directed at C. F. Weidemeyer and Bert McJunkins, May 14, 1901, B.I.A.L.R., 28268, 1901; Inspector F. M. Consor, Order to vacate, directed at G. V. Sampson, August 4, 1902, B.I.A.L.R., 47379, 1902; J. Walker to Commissioner, June 6, 1902, B.I.A.L.R., 34269, 1902.

[82] S. E. Day to A. Weber, May 15, 1901, P.A., FO.; A. Weber to C. Lusk, June 19, 1901, C.I.B.A.; A. Weber, *Sendbote,* 28:642, August, 1901, and 28:722–727, September, 1901. At St. Johns Father Anselm learned for the first time that the Puerto Rican pastor, Pedro Badillo, a giant of a man, had died and had been buried the previous month. Wearing his tentlike cassock, Anselm sang Mass for the grateful congregation. A. Weber, *Sendbote,* 28:727, September, 1901.

[83] Loring Benson Priest, *Uncle Sam's Stepchildren: The Reformation of United States Indian Policy, 1865–1887* (New Brunswick: Rutgers University Press, 1942), p. 181.

[84] A. Weber, *Sendbote,* 29:643–644, August, 1902; Mother Katharine to A. Weber, January 9, 1902, P.A., MS.

[85] A. Weber to C. Lusk, October 17, 1901, C.I.B.A.; R. E. Morrison (U. S. Attorney) to A. Weber, December 9, 1901, P.A., MS.

[86] *House Chronicle,* pp. 51, 52, S.M.C. Alterations raised figures to $56,000.

on the school forty as a final precaution. Valentine scrip which sold at $20 per acre could be located on any open public-domain lands.[87]

Construction work on the school began March, 1902, near the Day homestead, about three quarters of a mile from the mission. The first lumber was freighted in on March 19, feast of St. Joseph, and the limestone quarrying began April 16.[88] To Father Anselm fell the work of inspecting the job, checking materials and freighters; all decisions and arbitration regarding the work were sent for settlement to Mother Evangelist at Santa Fe, as she had been named superintendent.[89] To facilitate legal work relative to land, taxes, and contractual matters in general, Anselm Weber was shortly after chosen as agent for the newly chartered Sisters of the Blessed Sacrament Corporation in Arizona.[90]

Indian labor supplemented the Owen Company construction workers who pushed the job rapidly ahead. By June 24, 1902, the rough-dressed stone walls were nearing first-story proportions, outlining the spacious school which was to consist of a main, three-story building, one hundred and thirty-six by sixty-nine feet; a south wing of two stories, seventy-seven by twenty-two feet; and a chapel measuring seventy-four by thirty-four feet.[91]

During the busy months devoted to settling land claims and assisting later in the building program, the Franciscan Fathers were expanding on their mission work, especially the constant study of the Navaho language and orthography.[92] There were also occasional sick calls by this time, such as the ninety-mile trip Father Leopold made to ailing Charley Mitchell, and Father Berard's even longer trip to administer the Sacraments to Mrs. Barnes at Keams Canyon.[93] Father Leopold was called back temporarily to help out at Lafayette, Indiana, during Eastertide, 1901, when Father Samuel Gelting lost his voice. Father Samuel after spending several weeks at Colorado Springs completed his recuperation at St. Michaels.[94]

[87] A. Weber, *Sendbote,* 29:642, August, 1902; Mother Katharine to A. Weber, February 26, 1902, P.A., MS.; C. C. Manning to A. Weber, February 26, 1902, P.A., MS.

[88] *House Chronicle,* p. 52, S.M.C. Freighting from Gallup averaged 35 cents per hundred.

[89] Mother Katharine to A. Weber, April 9, 1902, P.A., MS. See folders "MS" in Provincial Archives for extensive correspondence covering progress of building.

[90] Mother Katharine to A. Weber, September 30, 1902, P.A., MS.; R. E. Morrison to A. Weber, November 30, 1901, P.A., MS.

[91] A. Weber, *Sendbote,* 29:644, August, 1902; *House Chronicle,* p. 53, S.M.C.

[92] *House Chronicle,* p. 49, S.M.C.

[93] *Ibid.,* pp. 50, 52.

[94] Provincial L. Haverbeck to A. Weber, April 9, 1901, P.A., LH.; S. Gelting to A. Weber, June 20, 1901, P.A., AH.; A. Weber, *Sendbote,* 28:996, December, 1901.

At the summer chapter, 1901, Brother Placid transferred to Batesville, Indiana, being replaced at St. Michaels by Brother Simeon Schwemberger.[95] The same chapter brought Father Leander Schell as the second superior to Peña Blanca along with two Brothers, Arnold Holtmann and Vital Huelshorst.[96] After the fiesta at Peña Blanca, December 12, 1901, attended by Father Juillard and Anselm, the latter stayed on to lead in retreat exercises for Friars Leander, Theodore, Francis, and Arbogast.[97] Between the two friaries of the Southwest existed a close fraternal bond. During the repairing of the rectory at Peña Blanca during Lent of 1901, Father Francis de Sales had lived with the Franciscans at the Navaho Mission.[98] Similarly when Leopold or Berard traveled to or from Santa Fe to chaperon Navaho pupils, there was always a stopover at Peña Blanca.[99]

Excavation work was just getting under way at the new school when Father Anselm achieved the long-awaited permission to give instructions at the government school at Fort Defiance. To his request of January 31, 1902, Major Hayzlett had replied that Superintendent Lamar's school schedule would permit of no interruption for evening religious instructions.[100] Through Father William Ketcham, new Director of the Bureau of Catholic Indian Missions, the friar approached Indian Commissioner W. A. Jones for the same permission.[101] On April 2 approval came from Major Hayzlett, and the very next evening, a Thursday, Father Leopold began the nonsectarian religious class at the Fort school.[102] Thereafter, instructions were given Wednesday evenings from seven to eight o'clock. Reverend Fryling of the

[95] *Tabula Definitionis,* 1901, P.A.

[96] *Ibid.* Brother Vital, skilled builder, farmer, and cook, is stationed at the present (1953) at Jémez Pueblo. RW.

[97] Leander Schell to A. Weber, November 3 and 26, 1901, P.A., LS. In assuring Anselm that there were English meditation books at Peña Blanca, "and dry enough for any retreat," Leander suggested that "wenn Sie uns anshauen wird's Stoff genug zu ein Parr traurige Betrachtungen geben."

[98] L. Ostermann, in *St. Anthony Messenger,* 9:366, April, 1902.

[99] *House Chronicle,* pp. 50, 51, S.M.C.; L. Ostermann, in *St. Anthony Messenger,* 9:154–157, October, 1901.

[100] Hayzlett to A. Weber, January 31, 1902, B.I.A.L.R., 13761, 1902; A. Weber, *Sendbote,* 29:831, October, 1902.

[101] A. Weber to W. Ketcham, February 2, 1902, and W. Ketcham to Commissioner, March 5, 1902, both in B.I.A.L.R., 13761, 1902. Father Ketcham had replaced Monsignor Stephan as Director of the Bureau of Catholic Indian Missions after the latter's death, September 14, 1901. The old Civil War chaplain died on the same day as the assassinated President McKinley, his close friend. McKinley had told Stephan to pass up any line of visitors in coming to the president's office, and merely to say that "that bullet in your heel hurts too much to wait." *Annals,* 6:205, C.H.A. The Monsignor was buried at Cornwells Heights as he desired.

[102] *House Chronicle,* p. 52, S.M.C.

Dutch Reformed Mission came to St. Michaels several days later to protest against the encroachment into his field, especially since it was mere duplication, he said, to have both himself and Father Leopold giving the same moral and nondenominational instructions.[103] Only the previous month in Santa Fe, the Sisters of the Blessed Sacrament had resumed instructions at the government school there.[104]

By June of 1902, besides St. Michaels, the Dutch Reformed Mission, and the Episcopal Hospital in the Fort Defiance area, the following missions were serving the Navaho either within or on the fringe of the reservation: the Baptists at Two Grey Hills, the Presbyterians at Jewett, the Methodists at Farmington, the Dutch Reformed under Reverend Brink at Tohatchi, Charles H. Bierkemper (The Man With the Whiskey Name) at the Ganado Presbyterian Mission, and W. R. Johnson at Cañon Diablo on the Little Colorado, an independent.[105]

St. Michaels as an expanding mission center gained official recognition as a settlement on September 1, 1902, when a United States post office was established with Hampton-schooled John Walker, Frank's brother, as the first postmaster.[106] Charles Lusk of the Bureau of Catholic Indian Missions had pushed Anselm Weber's petition, as did J. L. Hubbell who worked for, and eventually in 1903 obtained, daily service from Gallup to Chin Lee via Ganado.[107] Provincial Louis Haverbeck had refused permission for any of the priests or Brothers to serve as postmaster on the score that this would run counter to the Franciscan Rule.[108] If the postal authorities should have objected to the name St. Michaels, Father Weber had suggested "Cienega," "Meadows," or, preferably, "Drexel."[109]

One of the first pieces of mail to pass through the new post office was the good news from the Provincial that Bishop Granjon had approved and signed the *beneplacitum.*[110] Father Anselm's request to

[103] A. Weber, *Sendbote,* 29:831, October, 1902; A. Weber to W. Ketcham, March 27, 1907, C.I.B.A.

[104] Sister Evangelist to A. Weber, April 10, 1902, P.A., CI.

[105] Report for 1902, Letter Book, 1902, p. 146, W.R.C.; C.I.A., *Annual Report,* 1903, p. 130; see Cora B. Salsbury, *Forty Years in the Desert, A History of Ganado Mission 1901–1941* (Ganado, n.d.), p. 16. For an account of W. R. Johnson who began at Tuba in 1890, see I.R.A., *Annual Report,* 1903, p. 56, and 1904, pp. 66–68.

[106] *House Chronicle,* p. 53, S.M.C.

[107] A. Weber to C. Lusk, May 29, 1901, C.I.B.A.; C. Lusk to A. Weber, August 2, 1902, C.I.B.A.; J. L. Hubbell to A. Weber, March 15, 1901, and August 15, 1902, P.A., JLH. Daily service was inaugurated May 25, 1903, in A. Weber to Mother Katharine, May 18, 1903, P.A., BU.

[108] L. Haverbeck to A. Weber, February 22, 1901, P.A., LH.

[109] A. Weber to C. Lusk, May 29, 1901, C.I.B.A.

[110] *House Chronicle,* p. 53, S.M.C.

the summer chapter for permission to build a new mission house for the friars had been granted on condition that the friars first obtain the canonical approval and guarantee from the Bishop respecting the parochial status and limits of the Navaho Mission. Unless the friars secured such an official approbation, it seemed unwise to the definers and the Provincial to invest provincial funds in a friary and mission chapel.[111] Anselm Weber, accordingly, drew up the canonical document in precise Latin which specified the rights and limits of the mission to the Navaho.[112]

After this document was approved at provincial headquarters it was taken to Tucson for Bishop Granjon's decision by Father Anselm. Arrived at Tucson, via railway from Albuquerque and Deming, the friar learned that the Bishop was in Mexico City at the time.[113] Having forwarded the document to Mexico City, he spent his furlough visiting San Xavier del Bac Mission, and examining the agricultural exhibits at the university. On August 25 came the response from the Bishop, a wire from Mexico City, *"Beneplacitum* granted as per request."[114] Pope Leo XIII at Rome gave his formal apostolic approval to this ecclesiastical "quasi franchise" whereby the friars were given, *"in perpetuum,"*[115] charge of a parish including all Navaho in the diocese, the chaplaincy and spiritual direction of St. Michaels School, charge of all present and future missions and schools within the reservation, and also for fifteen miles south of the reservation in Apache County. All whites within the reservation and the fifteen miles southern extension in Apache County were also included under St. Michaels parochial jurisdiction: *"pro Navajoensibus . . . et pro aliis infra limites supra descriptas degentibus."*[116]

Returning successful from his Tucson visit, Anselm Weber stopped over at the Flagstaff home and lumber mill of T. A. and M. J. Riordan who were giving a 25 per cent discount on all lumber destined for the mission building program.[117] At Prescott he likewise made the

111 L. Haverbeck to A. Weber, July 24, 1902, S.M.C., CH.

112 A. Weber to L. Haverbeck, August 1, 1902, P.A., AH., and S.M.C., CH.

113 A. Weber, *Sendbote,* 29:909, November, 1902.

114 Addressed to A. Weber at Catholic Cathedral, Tucson, S.M.C., CH.

115 Papal *beneplacitum,* P.A. This document was approved at an audience with Leo XIII, November 17, 1902.

116 Text of episcopal *beneplacitum* was signed and dated August 25, 1902, and was returned directly to Cincinnati from Mexico. See P.A., *Beneplacita;* also L. Haverbeck to A. Weber, December 15, 1902, S.M.C., CH.

117 A. Weber, *Sendbote,* 29:909, November, 1902; *House Chronicle,* p. 53, S.M.C.; Mother Katharine to A. Weber, November 19, 1901, P.A., MS.; T. A. Riordan to A. Weber, March 24 and August 7, 1903, P.A., BU.

acquaintance of the head of the territorial United States Land Office.[118]

Not without many delays after the securing of the *beneplacitum,* the building of a modest new Franciscan mission house eventually got under way.[119] The Provincial and the definers, agreeing that overcrowding made the stone house unsatisfactory, vetoed out of hand the suggestion of a "mud" or "adobe" house: "it must be of stone or brick!"[120] Custos Raphael Hesse opposed flatly Bernard Nurre's proposition that the province provide the new mission residence; as provincial he had received Mother Katharine's assurance that she would cover all expenses of the mission. Not by any means, he further insisted, should the province contribute so long as the province itself held no title to the building site.[121]

After Father Anselm proved that local clays were unsuited for brick, permission for adobe was granted.[122] Mother Katharine's architect, Mr. Burns, had rejected local kilned brick, even for inside work on the school.[123] Stone was rejected because of costs; for the same reason the one-floor, ranch-style *convento,* with enclosed patio, was abandoned.[124] Approved finally was a conventional, two-story, Midwestern-style house, with a chapel wing letting out to the east.[125] Special visiting, dining, and sleeping quarters for Navaho were included. It was one year later, April 15, 1903, when actual construction began on the knoll some fifty yards northwest of the stone mission.[126] Final cost of building and water system ran to $14,000, toward which Mother Katharine generously donated $4,500, and the province the balance.[127] Anselm Weber dedicated the building on October 25, 1903, but the friars did not occupy it until February, 1904.[128]

[118] A. Weber, *Sendbote, ibid.*

[119] March 21, 1903, L. Haverbeck to A. Weber, July, 1902, through March, 1903, P.A., LH.

[120] L. Haverbeck to A. Weber, June 10, 1902, P.A., LH.; Mother Katharine to A. Weber, September 26, 1902, P.A., BU.; L. Haverbeck to A. Weber, July 24, 1902, S.M.C., CH.

[121] B. Nurre to A. Weber, July 7 and 12, 1902, P.A., BN. The Custos' stand lost; the second mission building, as well as the third, in 1937, were constructed on land belonging to St. Michaels School. RW.

[122] Telegram, P. Louis to A. Weber, September 8, 1902, P.A., BU.

[123] C. M. Burns to A. Weber, August 12, 1902, P.A., MS.; A. Weber to L. Haverbeck, August 1, 1902, S.M.C., CH.

[124] A. Weber to Mother Katharine, May 18, 1903, P.A., BU.; A. Weber to L. Haverbeck, August 1, 1902, S.M.C., CH.

[125] A. Weber to Mother Katharine, June 18, 1903, P.A., BU.; plans of architect A. Kunz of Cincinnati and Definer Pius Niehaus, enclosure with letter of L. Haverbeck to A. Weber, September 4, 29, 1902, P.A., LH. See "Photos" in P.A.

[126] *House Chronicle,* p. 54, S.M.C.

[127] Memo of payments to J. H. Owen by A. Weber, 1903, P.A., BU.; Mother Katharine to A. Weber, June 5 and July 10, 1903, P.A., BU.

[128] *The Provincial Chronicle,* 15:18, Fall, 1942.

Chapter VII

Teachers and Pupils Arrive at St. Michaels School

In late May of 1902 Mother Katharine and Sister Ignatius, accompanied by Mr. Didier, the carpenter at St. Catherine's School, inspected the construction work at St. Michaels.[1] Sister Ignatius was keenly observant of all details concerning her trip, the missions, and the friars. Her letters to her Sisters at Cornwells Heights give such a photographic description of Father Anselm, and so intimate and homey a glimpse of St. Michaels in the summer of 1902, that they defy briefing or paraphrase. After detailing the trip from Cornwells Heights to Lamy, New Mexico, she writes of their 5:35 a.m. arrival in Gallup:[2]

> . . . we stepped off the westbound train, with our black valise, grey telescope and big chip basket. The carpenter, getting off another car, stepped briskly up and relieved us somewhat of the luggage; and in the distance I discerned coming down the platform hastily, a priestly figure (this recognition was made by seeing his collar) with grey trousers, an old-time (fifty years ago style) swallow tail coat, somewhat green, and a black slouch hat, bearing full evidence of the frequent incursions of Arizona sand and dust. This was the holy Franciscan, Father Anselm Weber, who had driven thirty miles the night before and had said his first Mass of that morning at 4:00 A.M. In his holy humility he wished to carry the telescope but I held on to it firmly. He led the way up the platform, Reverend Mother and I followed, while the carpenter completed the procession back of us. With head bent forward and body also, slouch hat pressed down pretty closely to his ears, he wended his way up a little hill, his followers doing likewise, until after a fifteen minutes' walk, we found ourselves ushered into a library belonging to the priest of Gallup, New Mexico, a rather

[1] *House Chronicle,* p. 52, S.M.C.

[2] Sister Ignatius to community, May 29, June 1, 1902, *Annals,* 6:267–276, C.H.A. Introductions and conclusions omitted; footnotes added for clarification; parentheses as in original.

nice one, I must own, for such a neighborhood. Here our luggage was deposited, and Father brought us to the church. Such a church! such a home for the King of kings! There are no side altars to this church. Over the main altar they have a Sacred Heart statue, enclosed in a niche, the background of which is draped in red, and the canopy and side portions covered over with some light material cut in scallops. On the floor of the altar is a large rug which, being too large, is spread down over the steps without tacks or anything else. This floor is very shaky, and the priest's movements always seem to sink the floor. Leading up the aisle of the church is an old piece of grey matting, edge unbound, and placed loosely on steps leading up to altar railing. In the corner of the sanctuary a bishop's canopy has been created of some kind of cherry wood, and the cushion of this is a grey Smyrna rug. I do not think the dust brush is ever used in this country.

Well, thanks be to God, we heard Mass and received Holy Communion here, and after our thanksgiving, an old lady came in, bareheaded, and in broken English told us to come to breakfast. Father Weber sat at one end, the carpenter at the other, and Reverend Mother and I sat at opposite sides. Breakfast over, Father Weber, the carpenter, Mother and myself went back to the freight station. We went into the trunk room and took out clean clothing to carry with us to St. Michaels. Meanwhile, Father and the carpenter had gone back and by the time we had made sufficient inroads into the trunk they had the team down at the station for us.

We started off at 7:45 A.M., for over four hours' drive. Nothing transpired on the way to disturb the harmony which Nature had bestowed, and our ride over gullies, elevations and level sandy roads was an uneventful one.

Now before I begin to say one word about the holy Franciscans' abode on the hill, I protest strongly and emphatically against what may seem irreverent in my remarks. On the contrary, I have the highest reverence for the beautiful spirit which characterizes the four sons of St. Francis here, the spirit which St. Francis wished to bequeath to his followers, the spirit of poverty and humility. Now, all you future missionaries, listen to my tale. Getting nearer to our destination, I descried on the top of the hill, a little rectangular shaped building, one story high, the stones of which, although originally light, had turned brown. Of course, you understand the architecture could not compare with the brown stone mansions of Fifth Avenue, New York.

As our carriage rolled up, a brown-robed Franciscan, quite portly in dimensions, appeared on the scene to greet us.[3] Shortly after this, the good-hearted Brother[4] who is chief cook, singer in choir, head housekeeper and farmer, poultry raiser, laundry man, baker, altar-server, etc., and generally useful everywhere, it seems to me, appeared

[3] Leopold Ostermann, O.F.M. [4] Simeon Schwemberger, O.F.M.

also, and with sleeves rolled up disclosing a brawny arm, strong and well developed from frequent use in the Master's service, shook hands graciously.

From this first close observation of the Brown Franciscans, I discovered that they have no little book which reads: 'Did I brush the habit daily, and cleanse it thoroughly every week?'

Shall I continue to describe? Well, they wear sandals in the house. One of them I notice wears black stockings; another, stockings which I think were once white; another wears shoes which are almost as red as auburn, have pretty big holes in them and make a great deal of noise.

The cords are ash color, to me. Perhaps they once were white. You know, they have the cowl attached, and I must own that they are rather picturesque, real representations of the habit you see on holy St. Francis of Assisium [sic].

All this is from outside. We were ushered into the kitchen, there deposited our bag and baggage on the kitchen floor, and asked to go to the Chapel. To reach the Chapel you are obliged to pass through three rooms, all about the same size, — I think about nineteen feet across, which are occupied by the holy men. Each room contained a bed, a table, paper, two or three pairs of trousers hanging on the door, an overcoat, a hat or two, a pair of shoes or sandals near the bed, a chair, a number of cigar boxes cut in halves to hold letters, a few cigar stubs and (the rooms) are lighted by a small window about 3 feet x 4. One of the beds I noticed was made up on boxes. I do not know who occupies this room. On the door of the first room you enter is hanging a crucifix.

For the Stations of the Cross they have fourteen little wooden crosses about 4 inches long and 2 inches wide, nailed along the walls. There are four kneelers in the Chapel, two of which are long ones, and the other two smaller, all plain wood, no finish of any kind.

A little wood stove about three feet long is on the left side of chapel. It is not a heater, looks more like a kitchen stove. On the wall next to this, the battered down dust pan hangs. It looks like one which the Holy Providence boys might have used.[5] It is hanging with scoop facing you, and beside it, its companion, a well worn dust brush, hangs in same position.

Supper was next announced. We went through the three rooms mentioned, and out to the kitchen. The table was set for the four Franciscans, our carpenter, Mother and myself, and an Indian interpreter, also a farmer who, I believe is of Irish descent,[6] — a number of

[5] Holy Providence is a boarding school for Negro children at Cornwells Heights.

[6] The interpreter was Frank Walker; the farmer probably Tom Osborne who was renting the old Wyant store at this time and acting as paymaster and trader-cashier for the Indians working for the Owen Company, as agreed on in a letter of Mother Katharine to A. Weber, November 19, 1901, P.A., MS.

nationalities for the little supper board. The tablecloth which I believe is never taken off, is of yellow oilcloth, with black figures running through it. In the center of this are placed in stately array, and they seem to remain so, a large catsup bottle, a large vinegar bottle, a little cup containing toothpicks, a sugar bowl with broken handle, and a couple of other bottles, contents of which I failed to recognize. Each person's coffee was poured out by the venerable Brother, and to make things more convenient, he always puts the spoon in the cup when he sets the table.

We who sat at the upper portion of the table, got cups, but I noticed that those at the lower ends, had bowls. Water is not served here. Large platters, about two sizes larger than those we use in our refectory, were piled up with food, and each one was to help himself, and then shove down the dish. . . . May 29, 1902.

Sunday, June first, 1902.

Opposite the table where we were seated the stove is placed, and the floor underneath, which has neither zinc nor oilcloth, bears strong evidence to the Brother's frying ability, for it is deeply tinted with grease. Poor Brother! He is the best-hearted person you ever saw— truly serving the Lord in gladness, for his hearty laugh is heard very frequently through the one-story mansion. I must confess that he is not very quiet. He tells us that he only keeps still when the Father Provincial and the Sisters are around. The Father Provincial visits them once a year. He also tells us that the Superior told him about a year ago that he was only half-civilized, so he believes it. Providential that he is out among barbarians where he can, as he expresses it, holler and yell to his heart's content.

An amusing thing occurred the other night. He does not sleep up at the house, but occupies a room in an empty house which belongs to Mother's property, about three quarters of a mile away, in order to keep out invaders. Well, hearty and happy as a lark, he walked down and had a blanket and an old bag, sackcloth, wrapped around him. The contractor who has the work for Mother, is called Mr. Owen, and he has a number of small wooden houses built around for his men. Mr. Owen has rules and regulations up for orderly conduct on the part of the men, and he issued verbal orders for extreme care in this respect during the Sisters' stay, as they slept right near this little house, in what is called 'The Day Mansion.'

Brother came along about dusk and for fun called out at the top of his voice, 'Rags! Rags! Rags for sale!' Mr. Owen popped out in great consternation, thinking it was one of his men. 'Say, what does this noise mean, and the Sisters sleeping so near,' etc., etc., a good scolding. As soon as he saw it was Brother, he said, 'Oh, excuse me, I thought it was one of the men.' Brother said, 'Well, what would you have done?' 'I would have called him down, somewhat,' replied Mr.

Owen. 'What are you going to do now?' asked Brother. 'Oh, I can't do anything with you,' was the reply.

Brother calls the place 'Owendale,' and the men, 'Owendale rascals.' You may know how good-natured he is when I tell you that he cooked for all the men before they had what they call their 'mess house' erected. . . .

I did not tell you that we walk up three-quarters of a mile for Mass, at 6:30 A.M., return again to building, up for dinner again, return and up again for supper. After supper we make up our prayers, and then down we come to our mansion.

The names of the Franciscans are Father Weber and Leopold (who occupies a little log house by himself and usually has about ten or fifteen Indian night visitors), Father Berard and Brother Simeon.

We have had Benediction every morning since Corpus Christi. Father Leopold plays the organ which is in a room next to the Chapel, and Father Weber and Brother Simeon join in the singing. Their life is surely one of apostolic simplicity, and poverty. Father Weber is a most disinterested man. . . . Nothing is a trouble. He tries to get as much information as possible for Mother. All of you who are to be future penitents of these holy Franciscans should begin to pray for your ghostly Father.

When we went to Confession the other day Father took down a little screen about four feet square, placed it on top of the priedieus in the Chapel, — while Mother vacated the Chapel to give me a chance to confess my iniquities. I had to do the same with her.

Now I shall close. It may be a long time before this letter reaches you, as reports say that there was quite a wash-out on the railroad at Trinidad, Colorado. No mail has come here for four days. We are awaiting our tickets. Goodbye. God bless and keep you all!

Additional descriptive material on the same period is provided in a lengthy report of Mother Katharine covering a subsequent inspection tour in September.[7] On that occasion the foundress and (now) "Mother" Ignatius put up at the European Hotel in Gallup at 2:20 a.m., where they rested until 7:00 o'clock Mass, which was offered by Father Anselm at Sacred Heart Church. After assisting also at Masses of Father Juillard and Michael Dumarest, they breakfasted with the Fathers, with Mr. Didier who had accompanied them, and with Albert Slinky, who had attended St. Catherine's the past year.

Leaving Gallup at 2:00 p.m. they drove the last few miles to St.

[7] Letter undated, *Annals,* 7:7–15, C.H.A.; a letter of Mother Katharine to A. Weber, September 5, 1902, P.A., AK., notifies of a visit planned for "next Friday," i.e., September 13, 1902.

Michaels into the awesome, humbling glory of a purple sunset while they recited the rosary. With a light touch Mother Katharine depicted the supper at St. Michaels, and the moonlit road to Day's log house, where Anselm Weber fumbled around in the blackness to locate the oilcan and the matches for the empty lamps. The floor of the "Day Mansion" was of tamped earth, and near the window waited the comfortable handmade cradle chair, Mr. Day's favorite, which had been left behind for the Sisters.[8]

On this visit Mother Katharine fixed October 19 as the date for the Sisters' arrival at their convent quarters in the new school; classes, it was planned, would take up on December 3, feast of St. Francis Xavier.[9]

According to schedule on Sunday morning, October 19, Mother Katharine, Mother Evangelist, Sister Agatha, and Sister Angela reached Gallup at eight o'clock, with ample time to assist at Father Berard's ten o'clock Mass at Sacred Heart Church.[10] After breakfast at the European Hotel Father Berard drove them out to Cienega in an open, two-seated buckboard. On their arrival at 6:30 p.m. they were met at the new school by Mr. Owen and Tom Osborne. Father Anselm hurried down from the mission, three quarters of a mile northwest; "he could not have been kinder" in offering his services. The Sisters bustled about, tacking up blankets and papers over bare windows and generally readying their half-finished quarters for the night. The prospect of uninhibited Indians peering in did not appeal.[11]

The next morning after Mass and Office "in the dear little holy poverty chapel" at the friars' stone mission, they took breakfast with Father Anselm, Frank Walker, Charley Curley, and two other whites. As the new stove in the Sisters' apartment at the school came with no top, Sister Angela fussed about trying to adapt it, but finally had to settle for a heating stove on which to do her cooking. Her hot-water system was ingeniously rigged out by strapping a hogshead to the rear of the kitchen stove.[12]

Miss Josephine Whorton Drexel arrived on Wednesday with Sister Mary of the Annunciation and Sister Ambrose. By Friday, when

[8] Preceding notes are all from the September, 1902, letter of Mother Katharine to her community, *Annals,* 7:7–15, C.H.A.

[9] Mother Katharine to A. Weber, August 9, 1902, P.A., MS.; same to same, September 26, 1902, P.A., BU.

[10] Sister Agatha to community, October, 1902, *Annals,* 7:63–71, C.H.A.

[11] *Ibid.;* Mother Katharine to A. Weber, June 5, 1903, P.A., BU.

[12] Sister Agatha to community, October, 1902, *Annals,* 7:63–71, C.H.A. Sisters Angela, Crescentia, and Mary of the Annunciation, interview at Cornwells Heights, November 7, 1950.

Sisters Inez, Gertrude, Theresa, and Josephine struggled in with the last of the bags and boxes, the Sisters' quarters already reflected the convent touch.[13] Much work remained, however, before the buildings would be readied for the opening of school.

On Saturday after the Sisters' arrival Father Anselm and Frank Walker drove Miss Josephine and Sister Agatha to Chin Lee for an excursion into beautiful Cañon de Chelly. At Hubbell's they enjoyed the trader's usual warm hospitality. While there it was a novelty to watch Don Lorenzo pay out his own money "chips" for blankets, and then observe how the Indians purchased their own supplies with this scrip.[14] It was so much more real for the Indians to barter with hard money than merely to have book credit.

Sunday morning after Mass on the dining table at the far end of the huge Hubbell hall, it was found necessary to send Frank back to St. Michaels for new horses. During the day Miss Josephine and the young Sister visited the neighboring hogans, where they provoked much laughter by their attempts at weaving. One handsome Navaho buck, wearing a peacock-feathered hat, curiously examined Miss Josephine's Isleta Indian belt, her rings, and dress, and was more than mystified by Sister Agatha's watch, rosary, and crucifix.[15]

Frank Walker returned late Sunday night with a fresh team so that the party made an early start on Monday, arriving at Day's trading post near Chin Lee at 4:30 p.m. On Tuesday, with Father Anselm and Charley Day on horseback, Mrs. Sam Day drove Josephine and the Sister through the ever changing beauties of the sheer-walled gorges of Cañon de Chelly where ancient cliff dwellings clung like wasp nests, and where for decades the Navaho had been able to hold off the forces of Spain, Mexico, and the United States. After a wonderful picnic dinner packed by Mrs. Day the sight-seeing party was forced to speed home to the trading post by a frightening thunder and lightning storm.[16]

Having returned Wednesday evening to Hubbell's, they borrowed one fresh horse named "Billy" before leaving Thursday morning for St. Michaels. Halfway home, at the top of the mountain, the other horse went lame. This time Father Anselm walked the fourteen miles

[13] *Ibid.* On December 16, two additional Sisters joined the St. Michaels community, making eleven in all. *House Chronicle,* December 16, 1902, p. 53, S.M.C.; see A. Weber, in B.C.I.M., *Indianer Wache,* 1908, p. 21.

[14] Sister Agatha to community, November 2, 1902, *Annals,* 7:71–77, C.H.A.; A. Weber, *Sendbote,* 30:35–38, January, 1903.

[15] *Ibid.,* p. 74.

[16] A. Weber, *Sendbote,* 30:37, January, 1903.

to Cienega for another fresh team, while Sister Agatha caught up on notes for her letters, and Miss Josephine took down Navaho words dictated by Frank Walker. Besides the blazing fire "for protection against stray bears, Miss Drexel has her Apache dagger . . . and we have Father's revolver in the carriage."[17]

Without further mishap the delightful excursion for Sister Agatha and Miss Josephine ended; for Father Anselm, however, the trip had opened prospects for a new mission in the heart of the Navaho community, at Cañon de Chelly.[18] On her part Miss Josephine gave such a glowing account of her visiting around the Ganado hogans that her mother, Mrs. Joseph Drexel, offered $600 annually to support a day school at Hubbell's.[19]

The immediate task ahead in the fall of 1902, however, concerned the opening of St. Michaels Boarding School. The problem, scarcely less imposing than solving the land difficulties, and rearing the buildings, focused on the enrollment of Navaho pupils.

In organizing the 1899 mission school, and in collecting children for St. Catherine's School in Santa Fe,[20] the friars, it is true, had broken down much of the traditional antipathy of the Navaho against sending children away to school. To refresh the memory of promises made on earlier trips into the reservation, Father Anselm rode off with Frank Walker, Charley Mitchell, and another Navaho on October 7, 1902, to recheck and reconnoiter.[21]

Thirty-five miles north from St. Michaels, at Silversmith's, they stopped over for the first canvass. To the question as to whether Peshlakai himself would send any children, he answered almost indignantly that he had always classed himself as one of the *e'nishodi's* first friends: *E'nishodi Chischilli* (Long Gown Curly) could pick at will from his nineteen children! Other family heads of Peshlakai's outfit were of the same mind.[22]

From Mitchell's place at Tseili, where prospects for pupils were also excellent, Charley on muleback guided Father Anselm and Frank over the mountains via Tseili Pass which divides the Tunicha and Lukachukai ranges. The northeastern drop-off which they reached in late afternoon looked out on a breath-taking panorama below: the beckoning arms of the two Lukachukai outrunners, with the shimmer-

[17] Sister Agatha to community, November 2, 1902, *Annals,* 7:71, C.H.A.
[18] A. Weber, *Sendbote,* 30:126, February, 1903.
[19] As proffered in Mother Katharine to A. Weber, July 2, 1903, P.A., AK.
[20] See pp. 75–81.
[21] A. Weber, *Sendbote,* 29:997–1002, December, 1902.
[22] *Ibid.,* p. 998.

ing Red Rock desert intervening, and far off, suspended above tawny, swirling sandstorms, the phantom Carrizos.[23]

That night at Red Rock they put up with Naakai Dinae, father of two St. Catherine students.[24] He served corn bread and black coffee to the weary horsemen upon their arrival. At the meeting next morning, October 11, Anselm's request for pupils met a favorable response from the headman's people. The children would be ready when Chischilli returned before the first snows.[25]

That same Saturday afternoon Charley Mitchell led northeast on dead reckoning across the desert, past Shiprock which was veiled behind sheets of blinding sand, until they reached the San Juan. After visiting various outfits and camps along the river, they recrossed the mountains farther south on October 15, and spent the night with a kindly old Tseili Navaho named "Grandfather."[26] Besides Grandfather, his wife, and daughter, eleven sheepherders occupied the same hogan that night with Anselm and Frank Walker — Charley Mitchell having ridden on home.

While reclining on their sheepskins around the fire, chatting before falling off to sleep, old Grandfather grew suddenly excited and fearful as he pointed up through the smoke hole in the roof to an eclipse of the moon. In a moment all were chattering in great fright. The moon was dying! Calling them back to the fire the priest patiently demonstrated an eclipse by interposing an onion between the fire (sun) and a potato, symbolizing the moon. The onion nearest the fire shut off light from the more distant sphere, Father Anselm explained. So, too the earth tonight was shadowing the moon. Grandfather showed his relief and admiration in the pleased smile of comprehension.[27]

Five weeks after this reconnaissance, on Monday, November 24, the missionary and Frank Walker again turned north from St. Michaels toward Red Rock.[28] This time they rode in a big farm wagon loaded with hay, blankets, and provisions for themselves and the pupils they hoped to fetch for St. Michaels School.[29] Late on the first evening they reached Moore's trading post, and the next

[23] *Ibid.*, p. 999; see Dr. Washington Matthews, in *The Land of Sunshine,* 10:113–125, February, 1898.

[24] A. Weber to Mother Katharine, December 19, 1902, C.H.A.

[25] A. Weber, *Sendbote,* 29:1001, December, 1902.

[26] *Ibid.*, p. 1002.

[27] *Ibid.;* A. Weber, *F.M.S.*, 1916, pp. 43–44.

[28] Detailed and practically identical accounts are to be found on this trip in A. Weber, *Sendbote,* 30:214–220, March, 1903, and A. Weber, "Opening of St. Michaels School," *F.M.S.*, 1917, pp. 10–19.

[29] *F.M.S.*, 1917, p. 10.

morning crossed the mountains over Washington Pass, a precarious business with the bulky wagon on some of the sharper descents. Frequently Anselm led the way on foot, seeking the safest trail.[30] In the afternoon, numbed from the mountain cold, they rested and warmed themselves at Lynn Wetherill's store before pushing on from Two Grey Hills to the hogan of one of Grandfather's sons-in-law to spend the night.[31]

In loose shifting sand they creaked along the next day at a walk past Bennett Peak until reaching the store of Joe Wilkin, earlier a settler at Cienega.[32] Naakai Dinae had waited there most of the day for the *e'nishodi* before leaving; Naätani Tsossi had waited.[33] Twenty miles farther north they reached Red Rock, their destination, one day behind schedule. At the hogan of Naakai Dinae, where various Navaho were gathered for a "talk," the two tired men slept with the Indians around the hogan fire.[34]

On Friday morning, November 28, council day and a decisive one for the new school, Father Anselm offered Mass for God's blessing on his quest, and for clear weather on the return trip.[35] By noontime about fifty Navaho were gathered; two sheep purchased at the camp, along with flour, sugar, and coffee from the wagon, furnished a festive dinner for all.[36] After smoking was started Anselm began his talk in which he explained the purpose of the new school: moral, religious, and industrial training which would develop worthy and brave men for the *Diné*. Most explicitly and repeatedly he stated: "No one will be forced. . . . You may visit the children at any time and stay with us. When you come to us you will always have free food and hay."[37]

To these fiercely independent men of Red Rock Valley the allusion to force in procuring school pupils rang back proud memories of their successful stand against white man's force ten years earlier. In 1892, Agent Dana Shipley had tried to compel these very people to grant his Fort Defiance School twenty-five children.[38] Seventeen-

[30] *Sendbote,* 30:214, March, 1903.

[31] *Ibid.* They had planned to stay overnight at the camp of a friendly outfit, but finding the camp and neighborhood deserted, had moved on to the next inhabited hogan which happened to be that of the Grandfather's relative. *F.M.S.,* 1917, p. 12.

[32] *Sendbote,* 30:215, March, 1903.

[33] *F.M.S.,* 1917, p. 13.

[34] *Sendbote,* 30:216, March, 1903; *F.M.S.,* 1917, p. 13.

[35] *Ibid.,* A. Weber to Mother Katharine, December 19, 1902, C.H.A.

[36] *F.M.S.,* 1917, p. 13.

[37] *Sendbote,* 30:217, March, 1903.

[38] C.I.A., *Annual Report,* 1892, pp. 156–157.

year-old Frank Walker had interpreted for Shipley on that occasion as he now did for Father Anselm.[39]

When Agent Shipley had reached Tseili with his contingent of Navaho police, and had held a council to explain his designs, his intention of using force, if necessary, to gather children was disclosed. Among those present at the council had been Mr. Black, or Blacky (Hastqin Zhin), sent by the Carrizo community to spy.[40]

By the time the agent reached Round Rock Store, which Charley Hubbell ran for Chee Dodge and S. E. Aldrich, Headman Black Horse was on the scene with fifty of his Carrizo band, all apparently very friendly.[41] Having previously planned every move in council, Black Horse's men had cached their arms a few hundred yards from the store to dispel any suspicions, and now in good Navaho tradition passed — not the peace pipe which Navaho rarely use, and then only in ceremonial sings[42] — the playing cards for a bout of gambling.[43] Revolver cartridges were the stakes since almost every Navaho brave packed a belt of this modern wampum. One could not have found a more convivial gathering of policed and police than these agency worthies as they blissfully handed over their six-shooter ammunition.[44]

In council next day with Shipley, Black Horse ran the gamut of arguments against sending off their Navaho children: arguments drawn from the depleted ranks of their children occasioned by a recent diphtheria epidemic, down to emotional appeals based on Navaho family solidarity. He concluded with a flat disavowal of the Navaho intention to accept white civilization: "We do not want your education. We do not want anything to do with the white men. We want none of the white man's ways. We ask nothing of the Government but to be let alone, and you shall not take those children."[45]

[39] Frank Walker furnished full details, supplemented by the accounts of Black Horse, Mr. Black, and Navaho Killer. See A. Weber, *Sendbote,* 30:400–405, May, 1903, and *F.M.S.,* 1917, pp. 13–18. Lieutenant Suplee fixes the date in his log as the last week in October, 1892; he received reports of the riot on November 2, 1892. See *Message from the President of the United States Transmitting Reports Upon the Condition of the Navaho Indian Country* (Washington, D. C.: Government Printing Office, 1893), p. 20.

[40] *Sendbote,* 30:400, May, 1903.

[41] *Ibid.,* pp. 400–402. Van Valkenburgh, *op. cit.,* p. 51.

[42] *An Ethnologic Dictionary,* pp. 287, 395, 506.

[43] Cards and gambling were favorite pastimes among Navaho. "The Navajo is a born gambler, wasting his time and energy and property over the gaming tables." Charles E. Burton in C.I.A., *Annual Report,* 1900, p. 476. Major Hayzlett noted the same in Hayzlett to Commissioner, 1899 Report, W.R.C., Letter Book, 1898–1899, pp. 476–477.

[44] A. Weber, *Sendbote,* 30:402, May, 1903.

[45] Board of Indian Commissioners, *Annual Report,* 1892, p. 134; A. Weber, *ibid.*

But Shipley held adamant: he would take pupils back to Fort Defiance, by force if necessary. At a prearranged cue from Black Horse, "I will bet my head against yours," the Navaho surrounded the agent and began pummeling him. Hastqin Black and Navaho Killer tried in vain to break through the ranks to reach the agent with knife and short ax. With high courage the Indian police, aided by a few other cooler-headed Navaho, managed to convoy the mauled agent inside the nearby store. By the narrowest of margins one policeman escaped on horse to the San Juan for ammunition, while another rode his horse to death in a wild twenty-five mile race to notify Cavalry Lieutenant Brown, encamped at Tseili.[46]

Brown rode into Round Rock early the next morning with twenty troopers and released Shipley who, along with Hubbell, Chee Dodge, Walker, Mitchell, and Alfred Hardy, had spent an uncertain night under siege.[47] Before the cavalry rode up Shipley had been forced by Black Horse to give his solemn promise neither to solicit pupils by force, nor to take action against the Indians for the riot.[48] As it turned out, Lieutenant Brown, who had discussed the whole affair with Black Horse, had to send a telegram to the Secretary of War in order to counter Shipley's message demanding a punitive expedition against Black Horse and his band.[49]

At the council ten years later, November 28, 1902, Black Horse,

[46] First Lieutenant H. C. Brown, First Cavalry, was at the time in charge of the Navaho reservation irrigation survey which was being carried out during September and October, 1892, under Lieutenants Brown, Suplee, and Gurovits. See *Reports Upon the Condition of the Navajo Indian Country, op. cit.* Black Horse and twenty-five Indians of his band challenged Gurovits' right to penetrate the Carrizo Mountains, and demanded that he pay for the wood he used. *Ibid.*, p. 18. Suplee admitted that the Navaho gave no co-operation in mapping springs and water holes because the Indians insisted that this was only a ruse to discover Navaho children and to force them to school. Suplee noted: "This compulsory attendance of his children [at school] will send him [the Navaho] on the warpath quicker than anything else." *Ibid.*, p. 26. Note how Commissioner T. J. Morgan suppresses these damaging remarks on compulsory school attendance. *Ibid.*, p. 44.

[47] A. Weber, *Sendbote,* 30:402–403, May, 1903. Alfred Hardy was the industrial teacher at Fort Defiance who in 1895 was hired by the Indian Rights Association to investigate the ineptitude and possible graft of E. C. Vincent, the engineer commissioned to carry through the government's irrigation project of 1894. This irrigation project had been urged by General McCook and Commissioner Morgan to relieve the economic distress of the Navaho. An appropriation of $64,500 was passed to implement the recommended irrigation projects of Lieutenants Brown, Suplee, and Gurovits. See Alban W. Hoopes, "The Indian Rights Association and the Navajo, 1890–1895," *N.M.H.R.*, 21:28–46, January, 1946.

[48] A. Weber, *ibid.*

[49] *Ibid.*, pp. 404–405. General A. McCook backed his lieutenant's request that no troops be sent. C.I.A., *Annual Report,* 1892, p. 171.

Navaho Killer, and Hastqin Black were on Anselm Weber's side as he earnestly detailed the objectives of St. Michaels School and asked for their co-operation. After his talk one squaw approached the priest to clasp his hand. "Three I go to bring," she said with a smile, and strode off amid the applause of the large assembly. She was the wife of Mr. Black.[50]

The next morning twenty-one youngsters, warmly wrapped in blankets, rode off in the farm wagon while a mixed group of twenty adults accompanied Anselm on horseback. Up the steep, icebound trail over Washington Pass the horses slipped constantly as they dragged the cumbersome, sliding wagon, while the missionary prayed and Frank Walker muttered his choicest mule-skinner invectives. In several places Anselm roughed the ice with a pick while the Indians carried earth in their blankets to lend traction. Up the steepest grades the older children walked and the youngest rode double behind their elders.[51]

Lowering skies held off until the party cleared the pass, when a heavy snowstorm broke. Kindly traders gave shelter each night to the entire party: Wilkin on Saturday, Lynn Wetherill on Sunday, and Moore the night before reaching St. Michaels in the heavy Tuesday snowstorm. Each evening Father Anselm and a vanguard had cantered ahead to purchase and prepare hot food for the band of over forty.[52]

The next day, December 3, 1902, feast of St. Francis Xavier, St. Michaels School solemnly opened with a High Mass sung by Father Berard Haile, the chaplain. After a visit of several days, during which the snow melted, the Red Rock Indians returned home, satisfied with the new school at Cienega.[53]

With a rest of only two days Anselm Weber set out again for pupils, this time with Walker and Brother Simeon as companions, and with the Sisters' team of heavy mules drawing the freight wagon.[54]

Silversmith was at a second of his hogans when the three reached his place the first night. As his was a unique modern hogan, boasting door and lock, Brother Simeon had to climb through the smoke hole

[50] *Sendbote,* 30:217, March, 1903.

[51] *F.M.S.,* 1917, p. 19; A. Weber to Mother Katharine, December 19, 1902, C.H.A.

[52] *F.M.S., ibid.,* and *Sendbote,* 30:219, March, 1903.

[53] *Sendbote, ibid.* Father Berard took an excellent photo of the troop of Navaho men and women about to take their leave. See A. Weber in B.C.I.M., *Indianer Wache,* 1908, p. 21.

[54] A. Weber, *Sendbote,* 30:301, April, 1903. The team of freighting mules which J. L. Hubbell "coveted," according to Anselm, as well as the heavy freight wagon, were purchased from Mr. Wyant when he left Cienega. A. Weber to Mother Katharine, December 19, 1902, C.H.A.

in the roof to unscrew the lock from the inside.[55] At Charley Mitchell's next day they found his wife sick with a high fever. Simeon's quinine lowered the fever; Charley and Silversmith, the sick woman's brother, held nonetheless with the verdict of Mitchell's brother, a stargazer, that the poor woman had been bewitched by magic shots in the breast and neck by splinters of fang and antler. Local medicine men were hopelessly outclassed; there was nothing to do but wait for the specialist who dealt in anti-bone-shooter remedies. To show his affection and concern for his sister, Silversmith himself had to ride ninety miles over the mountain to fetch the wizard.[56] No concern was paid Father Anselm's plea that the woman be given rest and quiet. On went the "sing" of the local medicine man, with chanting, rattling, washing, and magic wand-waving over Charley's wife, who sat impassively in the middle of the beautiful sand painting, hands in lap, fatalistically awaiting the inscrutable pleasure of the "supernaturals."[57]

Later Anselm learned that the anti-bone-shooter from over the mountain had succeeded in sucking out the two sorcerer's darts (hidden actually under his tongue), and the woman had recovered.[58]

Meanwhile Father Anselm had offered Mass on December 8, feast of the Immaculate Conception, in Charley Mitchell's stone house, before bundling the nine children into the wagon for the return trip. Before departure, an old Navaho delivered a touching commencement talk to the youngsters on uprightness in mind and heart. As it was a hard, poor year for the Indians, the friars distributed warm clothing to the many poor and flockless ones of the valley.[59] It was the beginning of the lean era during which Major Hayzlett gave orders that any needy Navaho might kill for food any unbroken range horse; this he hoped would stave off actual starvation, and simultaneously reduce the serious overgrazing brought on by unnecessarily large herds of horses. Though economically ruinous, these large herds were treasured as conspicuous status tabs by the wealthy Navaho families.[60]

Additional children were brought in from Tseili, Tohatchi, and

[55] *Sendbote, ibid.*

[56] *Ibid.*, p. 303; see Washington Matthews, *Navaho Legends*, p. 56; Clyde Kluckhohn, *Navaho Witchcraft* (Vol. XXII, No. 2, Papers of the Peabody Museum, Harvard University, Cambridge, Mass., 1944), pp. 20, 93.

[57] A. Weber, *Sendbote, ibid.*, p. 302.

[58] *Ibid.*

[59] A. Weber to Mother Katharine, December 19, 1902, C.H.A.; A. Weber, *Sendbote, ibid.*, p. 305. Hayzlett reported after one year as agent that "Many have no flocks — they are the poor." C.I.A., *Annual Report*, 1899, p. 157.

[60] C.I.A., *Annual Report*, 1903, p. 126. He listed 47,260 horses, mules, and burros for 14,000 Navaho on and off the reservation. See Tables, *ibid.*, pp. 630, 650–651.

other points during the next few days, so that by late December there were fifty children at St. Michaels.[61] Considering that the water system was not yet in operation, this was more than a capacity crowd.[62] By the close of school on August 26, 1903, fifty-six pupils in all had enrolled, thirty-six boys and twenty girls.[63]

Advisedly Anselm Weber had scheduled vacation from late August until October 15, to cover the Indian harvest period for fresh corn, melons, vegetables, and peaches. With supplies running low in mid-October, parents were more inclined to send their children back to school.[64]

From the very start Navaho was used exclusively in teaching religion, and when Father Anselm visited the children during playtime, as he frequently did, they came running to chat and joke in their own language.[65] Gentleness he demanded above all in dealing with the children and, if serious infractions of discipline required his attention, he was accustomed to call the offender to his office up at the mission for a thorough "talk."[66] He strenuously opposed corporal punishment, especially since Navaho parents themselves rarely used it. One of the Sisters, whose brother, Jack O'Brien, had a national reputation in boxing, inclined toward demonstrating the family prowess with some of the obstreperous older Navaho — until blocked by Father Anselm. His letters to priests and others connected with Navaho education indicate unyielding consistency in this respect.[67]

Language handicaps proved the most difficult obstacle in schoolwork. Where Navaho was used, as in religious instructions, it was obvious that the pupils were the equal of white children in quickness of grasp and in memory.[68]

Francis M. Neel, superintendent at the Fort Defiance School, had forbidden the children to speak Navaho during work and school hours,[69]

61 A. Weber, *Sendbote,* 30:305, April, 1903; Marcellus Troester, O.F.M., *F.M.S.,* 1917, p. 39. 62 A. Weber to Mother Katharine, December 19, 1902, C.H.A.

63 Sister M. Evangelist to Major Hayzlett, August 8, 1903, W.R.C., Letter Books.

64 A. Weber, *Sendbote,* 30:877, October, 1903. 65 *Ibid.,* 30:305, April, 1903.

66 Sisters Angela, Crescentia, and Mary of the Annunciation, interview November 7, 1950.

67 *Ibid.;* A. Weber to J. Schnorbus, August 19, 1907, P.A., JS.; Sue McCullen to A. Weber, November 5, 1911, P.A., CI.; A. Weber to Chas. Lusk, March 4, 1916, P.A., CI., "an Indian School is not a Prussian soldiers' camp"; and A. Weber to Chas. Lusk, February 24, 1919, P.A., AP., are good samples of his opposition to physical punishment of pupils.

68 *F.M.S.,* 1917, p. 20. Charity Gaston in appraising her Fort Defiance children in 1869 and 1870 used almost identical words, "they are quick to learn and have retentive memories." C. Gaston to Major W. Clinton, August 23, 1870, in C.I.A., *Annual Report,* 1870, p. 618. 69 A. Weber, *Sendbote,* 35:36, 38, January, 1908.

and required a single English sentence from each pupil after daily industrial chores as a device to encourage English speaking.[70] When Major Hayzlett visited St. Michaels School shortly before Superintendent Leavengood took over at Fort Defiance, he pleased the Sisters no end by telling them that the mission school was "way ahead of ours" at the Fort.[71]

As with the government school at Fort Defiance, St. Michaels operated on what was euphemistically called an industrial-school discipline, with half the day spent at classwork and the remainder divided between house and ground chores. Some training, it is true, was given in hygiene, housekeeping, nursing, cooking, sewing, needlework, and — table setting and serving. The weaving course at St. Michaels, taught by an expert Navaho squaw from the neighborhood, was excellent. Reverend J. Dolfin of the Dutch Reformed Church, when inspecting Christian Indian missions, paid high tribute to the tradition of artistic weavers trained at St. Michaels, and urged similar craft training at Rehoboth.[72]

For the boys there was some training in gardening and irrigation derived from their chores on the mission farm; and when building was under way, they worked as helpers in stone and brick masonry, and in carpentry.[73] In large measure vocational training in Indian boarding schools of the period generally meant productive work, such as gardening, cleaning, laundry and kitchen chores.[74]

School had but recently opened at St. Michaels when on December

[70] C.I.A., *Annual Report,* 1899, p. 160, in which Mr. Neel reports that the forty girls were in better health than the ninety-four boys, four of whom were sent home with tuberculosis. This obviously was not the case at St. Michaels where six girls and no boys died in 1903. It was simply that the less healthy among the boys were sent to school, according to Dr. Wigglesworth, Fort Defiance physician at the turn of the century. Interview, October 30, 1950, Washington, D. C.

[71] A. Weber to Mother Katharine, May 18, 1903, C.H.A.

[72] *Bringing the Gospel in Hogan and Pueblo,* 1896–1921 (Grand Rapids, Mich., 1921), p. 238. Rehoboth, which means "the Lord hath made room," was founded in 1903, six miles east of Gallup after the Dutch Reformed minister at Fort Defiance sensed the "encroachment upon our privileges and liberties" at the Fort. *Ibid.,* p. 312. See similar account in Elma R. Smith, *Private Schools for the Navajo Indians* (published Master of Arts thesis, University of Arizona, 1947), pp. 25–26. According to A. Weber to Charles Lusk, August 24, 1903, C.I.B.A., trouble began when Mr. Leavengood brought about the discharge of the Misses Keough and Miss Snow. Leavengood's charges against the employees and against Major Hayzlett were strongly backed by the Reformed minister. After the investigation, Leavengood was transferred. Mr. Reuben Perry took over, and shortly afterward the Dutch Reformed Mission was abandoned. See also W.R.C., Letter Books, June–September, 1903; Sallie Snow to A. Weber, September 29, 1902 and March 15, 1903, P.A., SN.

[73] A. Weber, *Sendbote,* 35:37–38, January, 1908.

[74] Schmeckebier, *The Office of Indian Affairs,* pp. 217, 218.

12, 1902, Sampson's store and saloon burned to the ground. The next morning the charred and mutilated remains of the clerk, C. M. Kiel, were found in the ruins.[75] After Weidemeyer vacated the much-debated "spite" store, Sampson had continued to operate it as a combination store and saloon, notwithstanding Inspector Conser's order to vacate.[76] Drunken Indians were suspected at the inquest, but no indictments were returned.[77]

To prevent future sale of liquor in the St. Michaels area, Father Anselm, aided by teetotalers S. E. Day and J. L. Hubbell, initiated a petition for a local-option election.[78] At this election on May 5, 1903,[79] the vote went overwhelmingly dry, twelve votes to one, the one negative vote being cast "no doubt," as Father Anselm twitted Mother Katharine, "by your esteemed friend, the Negro [George Overton]."[80] Regardless of land troubles partially occasioned by George, Mother Katharine had wished him under the employ and influence of the mission.[81]

Nothwithstanding the regular visits of the agency physician to St. Michaels School, two children died during the 1902–1903 term.[82] Little Agatha who died on March 10, 1903, was buried the next day at a Solemn Requiem High Mass, likely the first Navaho-attended Catholic burial service.[83] Fearing to offend Navaho taboos controlling corpses and ghosts Father Anselm explained death and eternity to the children beforehand, stressing the freedom of the pupils to absent themselves if they so wished. Impressively, every one of the pupils paid Christian

[75] Office Diary, December 13, 1902, W.R.C.; *House Chronicle,* S.M.C., gives December 6, 1902, as the date. [76] See p. 84.

[77] C. C. Manning to A. Weber, January 13, 1903, and J. L. Hubbell to A. Weber, January 13, 14, 1903, P.A., Traders. See A. Weber, *Sendbote,* 30:490, June, 1903.

[78] J. R. Armijo, clerk of the Board of Supervisors, Apache County, to A. Weber, January 13, 1903, P.A., PL.; two months before the arson and murder, Father Anselm had already requested an election on local option, as the only conclusive way of closing Sampson's gambling and drinking place near the school. Alfred Ruiz to A. Weber, October 24, 1902, and November 12, 1902, P.A., PL. Re Day and Hubbell, Dr. Wigglesworth, interview, October 30, 1950.

[79] Order of Election, County Board, April 8, 1903, P.A., PL.

[80] A. Weber to Mother Katharine, May 18, 1903, C.H.A. George Overton himself was murdered ten years later, October 24, 1912, at his cabin near the mission. See *The McKinley County Republican* (Gallup, N. Mex.), October 25, 1912. The inquest hearing which was held under Sam E. Day placed the guilt on a half-breed Laguna teamster who worked for J. L. Hubbell. Emmanuel Trockur, in *The Provincial Chronicle,* 14:41–42, Fall, 1941.

[81] Mother Katharine to A. Weber, September 26, 1902, P.A., BU.

[82] A. Weber, *Sendbote,* 30:877, October, 1903. Similar gratis physician care by the agency doctor was rendered to the Episcopal Hospital at the Fort. See A. M. Wigglesworth, printed appeal for funds, n.d., C.I.B.A. letters, 1905.

[83] A. Weber, *ibid.*

respects to their playmate at the Mass. Thomas Morgan stood unafraid at the coffin, interpreting for Father Anselm at the sermon after Mass.[84]

Out of eighty-seven pupils in the 1903–1904 term, six girls died in close succession.[85] Though many of the parents attended the funerals and listened to Anselm Weber's talks on the resurrection and eternal life, they were far from reconciled, and against the agent's and doctor's advice, one of the parents insisted that his sick child should be sent home for treatment by the medicine men. All sermons of the missionary to the contrary, it was plainly suicidal to almost all Navaho to force sick children to live in the same haunted infirmary where others had died.

Some Navaho were soon spreading the rumor that the *e'nishodi,* for all their prayers, were out-and-out wizards;[86] as a result, enrollment at St. Michaels in October, 1904, was only fifty,[87] and rose to no more than eighty-two by August 15, the closing date.[88]

Except those in serious danger of death, and two tiny orphans, no children were baptized at St. Michaels until June 12, 1904, when eight girls and fifteen boys requested this Sacrament.[89] These and a few additional children who were baptized June 2, 1906, made up the earliest First Communion class at the mission, receiving in a solemn Pentecost ceremony, June 3, 1906.[90]

Malcontents complained that the priests cared only to baptize the children, and did not mind if they died, so long as the water was poured.[91] The enrollment which had remained almost static in 1905 regained its expected increase in 1906, when thirty new pupils were added from the Sanders-Houck district, off the reservation. In this region Anselm Weber had recently surveyed Indian lands, and aided in the paper work required for filing on, and securing, allotment patents. The total count in November, 1906, was one hundred sixteen children at St. Michaels School;[92] by 1909 and thereafter until 1915 an average of one hundred and fifty pupils was maintained at St. Michaels School.[93]

[84] Sister Evangelist to community, March, 1903, *Annals,* 7:136, C.H.A. See *An Ethnologic Dictionary,* pp. 455–456.

[85] A. Weber, *Sendbote,* 31:681, August, 1904.

[86] *Ibid.,* pp. 682–683; L. Ostermann to A. Weber, November 9, 1905, P.A., CL.

[87] *House Chronicle,* October 18, 1904, p. 55, S.M.C.

[88] *Ibid.,* August 15, 1905, p. 57.

[89] A. Weber, *Sendbote,* 31:684, August, 1904.

[90] *Ibid.,* 33:902–903, October, 1906.

[91] A. Weber to W. Ketcham, October 20, 1905, C.I.B.A.

[92] A. Weber, *Sendbote,* 34:514–515, June, 1907.

[93] Mother Katharine to A. Weber, April, n.d., 1909; P.A., MS. A. Weber, Report to E. Buttermann for 1909–1915, P.A., MI.

Chapter VIII

Chin Lee and Lukachukai Missions

WITH the opening of St. Michaels Boarding School the first phase of mission endeavor was concluded for the friars at St. Michaels. The second stage focused on the need to extend the direct effectiveness of the mother mission at Cienega by establishing mission posts throughout the hinterland and along the perimeter of the Navaho country. It was hoped first of all that through such a network of branch missions adults would be Christianized, and second, that boarding-school graduates might be encouraged to colonize around the new mission centers. For this reason irrigation and agricultural opportunities featured in the selection of suitable sites for these outposts of St. Michaels central mission. With such Navaho communities in mind the friars envisioned simple mission projects including small residences and day schools.

Shortly after the new school opened in December, 1902, Anselm Weber revealed that the Franciscans' first experiment in a branch mission and day school would be tried at Chin Lee, at the mouth of Cañon de Chelly.[1] Doubtlessly the contacts made in and around the Cañon while chaperoning Sister Agatha and Josephine Whorton Drexel had emphasized the likelihood of that region for a mission colony.[2] What induced the friars, however, to give priority to Chin Lee over the more attractive features of the San Juan site hinged on the matter of a note from Mr. Sam E. Day. The Chin Lee trader wrote that the corn husks for the school mattresses were sacked and ready, mentioning obliquely that Reverend Bierkemper of Ganado had been sizing up Chin Lee as a prospective Presbyterian mission.[3]

Berard Haile wrote forthwith to the Bureau of Catholic Indian

[1] *Sendbote,* 30:127, February, 1903.

[2] See pp. 96–97.

[3] To A. Weber, December 8, 1902, P.A., CL.

Missions in Washington, asking if the missioners could apply to the government for both the San Juan and the Chin Lee mission sites: "We intend to commence on San Juan next spring . . . we must extend over the whole reservation [in order to promote] effective missionary work."[4]

An earlier offer of Don Lorenzo Hubbell to begin at Ganado in 1899 had been delayed for lack of a decisive mission policy.[5] As a result Reverend Bierkemper had found a clear field to move into the original picket-adobe trading post at Hubbell's in 1901, closing out the friars from their projected day school there.[6]

Mr. Day and his two older boys, Charley and Sammie, prepared the Indians to give a favorable vote to the friars' request for a Chin Lee mission site.[7] On April 16 Father Anselm and Father Berard left for Chin Lee, where after a feast and council on April 20, 1903, they received the signatures (X marks) of sixteen principal men for a mission site. Father Berard acted as witness and Charley Day interpreted.[8]

The site, which was surveyed by Father Anselm and Mr. Day, lay not quite three miles due west of Charley's store, and three quarters of a mile south of a beautiful cottonwood grove near which the Indians cultivated and irrigated their farm lands.[9] "With supervision and encouragement," wrote Anselm to Father Ketcham,[10]

> the Indian farms could easily be doubled. This is one reason we selected it, since we can colonize a number of Indians there and establish a day school; besides it is a central point from which the Indians on three different mountain ranges can be reached in a day.

Two days later, having drawn up the official petition to the Commissioner of Indian Affairs, and on the point of leaving, the friars were surprised to see Reverend Bierkemper and the Presbyterian

[4] B. Haile to W. Ketcham, December 15, 1902, C.I.B.A.

[5] See A. Weber to R. Hesse, November 22, 1899, S.M.C.; Mrs. Barbara Hubbell Goodman, interview, July 16, 1950.

[6] Since Mrs. Bierkemper began a Presbyterian day school at Ganado in 1902, and a quarter section of land was granted by the government for a Presbyterian mission site in the summer of 1902, no further thought was given to setting up a Catholic mission by the friars. See Cora B. Salsbury, *Forty Years in the Desert,* pp. 14–16; Elma R. Smith, *Private Schools for the Navajo Indians,* pp. 32–33. G. W. Hayzlett to Commissioner of Indian Affairs, July 26, 1902, W.R.C., Letter Books.

[7] S. E. Day to A. Weber, January 7, 1903, P.A., CL.

[8] *House Chronicle,* p. 54, S.M.C.; Indians' petition, April 20, 1903, 26941, 1903, B.I.A., SC 143.

[9] G. W. Hayzlett to Commissioner of Indian Affairs, June 24, 1903, 36141, 1903, B.I.A., SC 143; A. Weber to W. Ketcham, April 25, 1903, C.I.B.A.

[10] A. Weber to W. Ketcham, April 25, 1903, C.I.B.A.

superintendent of New Mexico and Arizona drive up from Ganado in a buggy. They had come for the identical purpose of selecting a site; after sizing up the situation, however, they left.[11] Without delay Anselm and Berard rode horseback to Fort Defiance over the old Indian trail in order to submit their application to Agent Hayzlett before the ministers should enter any complaint.

Mrs. Henrietta Cole, government field worker and Methodist missioner, wrote to Commissioner Jones the next month to protest the granting of the Chin Lee mission site to the Catholics:[12]

> I thought I would write you this line for fear that you folks at Washington would not notice it was the same place I was to go — and perhaps grant their request. Of course a Catholic mission and Protestant at the same place would not be advisable.

After investigation, Major Hayzlett on June 5, 1903, approved the selection near the canyon mouth. He estimated that the Franciscans with much labor might extend the Indians' irrigation ditch, and thus colonize many families on their quarter section and nearby. "So long as the government does not intend to locate a school at Chin Lee," he recommended approval of their selection.[13] Official Washington approval followed on June 20, a few days later.[14]

Father Leopold Ostermann took over the mission work among the Cañon de Chelly Navaho not long after the site was approved. He lived with the Day family off and on for two- and three-week periods while visiting with the Indians in and near the Cañon. It was during this early period that Leopold satisfied his curiosity regarding the oddly named canyon: Chin Lee, which had rather a Chinese ring, was the Anglicized form of the Navaho word, *Ch'inli,* meaning "flowing out place"; Cañon de Chelly was simply the Hispanic spelling for the Navaho, *Tseyi,* which meant "in the rocks" and referred to the magnificent labyrinth of gorges and crevasses slashing back through the brilliant sandstone of the canyon.[15]

Beginning August 15, 1904, Father Leopold took up residence about one mile east of the future mission, in an abandoned stone and log building originally intended as a trading post. This he rented from a Navaho and fitted out roughly as a combination chapel and part-

[11] *Ibid.;* A. Weber, *Sendbote,* 30:487–488, June, 1903.

[12] [May, 1903], 31906, 1903, B.I.A., SC 143.

[13] G. W. Hayzlett to Commissioner of Indian Affairs, June 5, 1903, 36141, 1903, B.I.A., SC 143.

[14] Commissioner of Indian Affairs to G. W. Hayzlett, June 24, 1903, 54187, 1903, B.I.A., SC 143, with enclosure, Land Authority 82189.

[15] L. Ostermann, *F.M.S.,* 1914, pp. 25–26.

time residence for himself and Brother Gervase.[16] Both roof and floor were of adobe mud, and frequently during their periodic mission trips there, the rains forced the friar to offer Mass while standing on a plank, his alb tucked up above his boot tops. When Father Anselm took a turn at the mission in July of 1905, he heard the dry, ominous vibration of a rattler as he approached the altar. Charley Day drew his Colt swiftly and dispatched the coiled snake before it could strike.[17]

Leopold Ostermann held his first public service in Chin Lee on September 23, 1903.[18] During the more frequent visits which became possible after the renting of the stone store, he had many "talks" with the Navaho, with one or the other of the Day boys interpreting. During one such sermon on the origin of the universe, an old chanter, or medicine man, who was sitting uncomfortably and unaccustomedly upright in a front pew, observed dryly to his companions: "He is pretty near accurate." Regarding the story of Adam and Eve the same leathery old singer nudged his partner, and pointing Navahowise with his puckered mouth to somewhat disconcerted Leopold, cautioned: "He is a little way off now, but the 'Big Fellow' (Tso) will get it straight again soon."[19]

Father Leopold soon realized that primarily the Navaho expected the *e'nishodi* to supply their material wants. Life for the Indian was one constant grubby search for food, clothing, and shelter. On one occasion when Leopold had given his best to dramatize the continuity of the Mass and Calvary, and had asked for questions to clarify obscure points, he was pitiably undeceived as to the deep spiritual impression he had created when the one and only questioner spoke up — wondering whether the *e'nishodi* would now give them food and clothes.[20] The Navaho, he was eventually to understand, were through and through a pragmatic people, little given, by culture and thought categories, to theological abstractions.[21]

[16] Gervase Thuemmel, O.F.M., along with Father Herculan Zeug, O.F.M., were appointed to St. Michaels in the summer chapter, 1904. *Tabula Definitionis,* 1904, P.A. The old store-building mission stood where the Garcia trading post is now (1952) located.

[17] L. Ostermann, *F.M.S.,* 1914, p. 27; A. Weber to Provincial C. Theobald, July 13, 1905, P.A., CL. [18] *House Chronicle,* p. 54, S.M.C.

[19] L. Ostermann, *F.M.S.,* 1914, p. 29. [20] *Ibid.,* p. 30.

[21] See Dorothea Leighton and Clyde Kluckhohn, *Children of the People* (Cambridge: Harvard University Press, 1947), pp. 112–113, and Gladys A. Reichard, *Navaho Religion, A Study of Symbolism* (Bollingen Series XVIII, New York: Pantheon Books Inc., 1950), p. 3. Hereafter the Reichard work will be cited *Navaho Religion.*

As he divested after Mass on another occasion an old Navaho singer patted his shoulder and smilingly and kindly explained the manward and utilitarian Navaho outlook on prayer: "The *e'nishodi's* prayer was t' a yisi qozho', very happy." And opening his pollen pouch he sprinkled sacred pollen around the sacristy. Another Navaho explained to Leopold that prayer was very good for all, for Americans and for the *Diné:* "If we pray much we shall see much rain; if we see much rain the corn and everything will grow fine; if everything grows fine we will have plenty to eat." Leopold did his utmost to throw off his sense of frustration and tried to explain simply to the Indians that the friars would help with food and clothes as best they could, but that first and foremost they were among the Indians to help them come closer to God.[22]

Financial barriers prevented any attempt to build even a small mission or day school at Chin Lee until 1905. After the San Juan experiment Anselm Weber requested Mother Katharine to divert the $500 she had pledged for that mission to Chin Lee.[23] Previously Anselm had received $100 of the $600 originally promised by Mrs. Joseph Drexel for a day school at Hubbell's.[24] This sum added to the $900 he had collected on a lecture and begging tour back East in 1905 provided the building fund.[25] Fathers William Ketcham, Anselm, and Leopold selected a slightly elevated ridge on the quarter section at Chin Lee August 15, 1905, as the location for the mission. Work began the next day.[26]

Brother Placid, who had left St. Michaels in 1901, happily returned in August to his "Nanahoffs" after serving for some time at Jémez, New Mexico. Father Anselm had requested Placid's return in his usual prechapter letter to the Provincial.[27] Leopold and Placid lived in the old stone store-mission from August until the first week of January,

22 L. Ostermann, *F.M.S.*, 1914, p. 31.

23 A. Weber to Mother Katharine, July 25, 1905, C.H.A.; Mother Katharine to A. Weber, August 7, 1905, P.A., CL.

24 Stewart Culin, the ethnologist, and a non-Catholic, had been triumphant over his successful psychological campaign in which he casually brought Mrs. Drexel to remember her promise of financial assistance. S. Culin to A. Weber, January 22, 1904, P.A., SC.

25 Mrs. Henry Nurre of St. Bernard, Ohio, had given $300 with the stipulation that Indian labor only be employed. A. Weber, in B.C.I.M., *Indianer Wache,* 1908, p. 25. Anselm had given stereopticon lectures and sermons at St. Bonaventure College, New York; at Chatham, Ontario; Cincinnati; Louisville, Kentucky; Hamilton, Ohio; and Kansas City, Missouri. A. Weber, *Sendbote,* 32:990–991, October, 1905.

26 L. Ostermann, *F.M.S.*, 1914, p. 29; A. Weber to C. Theobald, July 13, 1905, P.A., CL.; *House Chronicle,* p. 56, S.M.C.

27 A. Weber to Provincial, July 13, 1905, P.A., CL.

1906, while they supervised the making of adobes, carpentering, and general construction of the rectangular mission building.[28] It contained six twelve by twelve rooms and a larger twelve by twenty-four chapel room, the whole having been designed to specification by Anselm Weber. Advisedly the building was located so as to leave space for the contemplated mission day school on a nearby rise.[29]

After attending the annual retreat given at St. Michaels in November, 1905, by Provincial Chrysostom, good Brother "Aber Aber" Placid never did return to see the completed Chin Lee mission.[30] Stricken with severe stomach pains while at St. Michaels — thought to be liver trouble by the friars — Placid was sent on to St. Joseph Hospital in Albuquerque where after an operation on February 19, 1906, he died at the age of fifty-four. Carcinoma of the stomach was listed as the cause of his death.[31] Fathers Albert Daeger and Arbogast Reissler had visited him and administered the Last Sacraments during Placid's illness, and Anselm had sent him money and a box of St. Michaels favorite cigars, Selle's A-1's.[32] He died before Anselm was able to reach his bedside, so there was left for the friar superior only the last kindness of accompanying the body of the faithful Brother to Peña Blanca. There among his confreres Placid was laid to rest in the windswept parish cemetery on February 22, 1906.[33]

After Brother Gervase Thuemmel finished his year of novitiate and made his simple profession on August 15, 1905, he returned to the Navaho mission and went immediately with Father Leopold to Chin Lee where they took up full-time residence at the mission.[34] On their third try they struck water at fifteen feet on September 14, thus relieving them of the burden of using water from Chin Lee Wash or from the water hole a half mile over the ridge, which they had been sharing with the Indian dogs and sheep.[35] Though the Indians pronounced the well water "very good" some friars for years

[28] L. Ostermann to A. Weber, eight letters, September 3 through December 31, 1905, P.A., CL.

[29] A. Weber to Provincial, July 13, 1905, P.A., CL.; A. Weber to W. Ketcham, December 8, 1915, C.I.B.A.

[30] A. Weber, *Sendbote,* 32:317–319, April, 1906; A. Weber to W. Ketcham, January 22, 1906, C.I.B.A.

[31] P. G. Cornish, Coroner's Certificate, February 19, 1906, P.A., PB.

[32] Brother Placid to A. Weber, January 31, 1906, P.A., PB.

[33] O. W. Strong's Sons, bill for $37.50, for embalming and ambulance service to Peña Blanca, February 20, 1906, P.A., PB.; Provincial Death Notice, printed by *Albuquerque Morning Journal,* February 20, 1906, P.A., PB.

[34] *Catalogus Fratrum,* 1933, p. 32; L. Ostermann, *F.M.S.,* 1914, p. 29.

[35] L. Ostermann to A. Weber, September 15, 1906, P.A., CL.

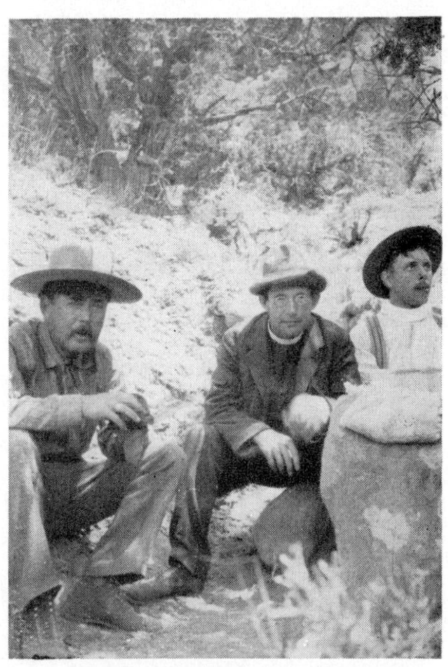

Interpreter Frank Walker with rumpled Father Anselm and cherubic Father Mike Dumarest

Charley Mitchell, Indian scout, wearing necklace handed down from Manuelito

Mother Katharine Drexel

Father Leopold Ostermann

complained of the alkali effects, even ascribing Brother Placid's death from cancer to the high alkali content.[36]

At the summer chapter of 1907 Father Marcellus Troester was assigned as assistant to Leopold, with Lukachukai, Tseili, Red Rock, and Naazlini as his mission circuit.[37]

Ever since 1905, when Anselm Weber had heard from Commissioner Leupp's own lips in Washington that the government would back no new boarding schools — he called them educational almshouses[38] — but would introduce Indian day schools to keep children and parents together, Anselm had dreamed of financing a mission day school at Chin Lee.[39] The financing always remained in the realm of wishful thinking, while Father Leopold grew ever more deeply convinced that despite all efforts "no progress could be made christianizing the adults who are thorough and intense heathen."[40] Quite frankly he informed his superior at St. Michaels that so far as he could figure after five years of experience the Chin Lee Mission was utterly disheartening without prospect of a government school, which would at least allow some groundwork for the future harvest.[41] In four years of mission work he could meagerly report one baptism, and that of an infant in danger of death. "We have no other encouragement but a faint hope for the rising and coming generation."[42] It was a numbing commentary for a missioner with the zeal of Father Leopold.

With mission finances ever a minus quantity, Father Anselm had

[36] M. Troester to Provincial, n.d., P.A., CI.; Fintan Zumbahlen, O.F.M., to C. Theobald, August 27, 1910, and A. Weber to C. Theobald, August 27, 1910, P.A., CL. Father Anselm seconded Fintan's plea to be released from his 1910 chapter assignment to Chin Lee. The water, Anselm related, had caused him personally much illness, and Father Fintan had never been in good health. See *Tabula Definitionis,* 1910, P.A.

[37] *Tabula Definitionis,* 1907, P.A.; A. Weber, *F.M.S.,* 1915, p. 41, and "Catholic Missions and Mission Stations Among the Navajo," *The Indian Sentinel,* 1:19, April, 1918. Father Marcellus, after official transfer to St. Michael's, was delayed several months at Carlsbad to fill in. To Anselm's urgent plea that Marcellus request immediate release, he epitomized his life of beautiful humility and selflessness by replying: "Allerdings bleibe ich aus Prinzip ganz and gar passiv. Es gefaellt mir ganz gut in New Mexico, und sollte ich nach Arizona gehen, so wird es mir wohl da auch gefallen." M. Troester to A. Weber, November 25, 1906, P.A., MT.

[38] Francis E. Leupp, *The Indian and His Problem* (New York: Charles Scribner's Sons, 1910), p. 137.

[39] A. Weber to W. Ketcham, September 18, 1907, C.I.B.A. Details of the interview are given in A. Weber, *Sendbote,* 32:498–500, June, 1905. On this occasion Anselm also received permission from the new Commissioner to give religious instructions at Fort Defiance in Navaho contrary to existing rules. *Ibid.*

[40] Report of L. Ostermann to Bureau of Catholic Indian Missions, 1910, C.I.B.A.

[41] L. Ostermann to A. Weber, May 14, 1908, P.A., NL.

[42] Report of L. Ostermann to Bureau of Catholic Indian Missions, 1907, C.I.B.A.

taken pains to promote a government school at Chin Lee in default of a mission school. He had even driven Agent Perry and Inspector Pringle to Chin Lee in 1906 to help select a site "only one quarter mile from our mission."[43] He had cultivated Commissioner Leupp on his visit in June of the same year, and heard again from him a promise of a school for Chin Lee; at this stage the Commissioner had conceded that a small local boarding school would accommodate nicely to Navaho institutions. Yet after the plans were drawn he could not bring himself to add his signature: boarding schools simply went against his grain.[44] Nonplused, and with mission finances exhausted, Anselm Weber actually turned to prospecting for gold on a tip given by the Indians. He thought he had struck a rich lode which would guarantee a mission boarding school. Subsequent assay, sadly, burst his dream.[45] Finally in the fall of 1909, after Commissioner Valentine came into office, the building of a boarding school with a capacity of eighty pupils went into construction a mile from the Chin Lee Mission.[46]

Simultaneously, on the part of the friars, building operations began on a chapel to provide Sunday Mass and instructions for the school children. Lumber Father Anselm purchased through the government from the Indians' saw mill at $10 per 1000 feet, and rock was quarried nearby. In a remarkably short time Brother Gervase was displaying skill at quarrying, masonry, and carpentry under the guidance of W. E. Hildebrand, the contractor. Plans for the mission chapel were drawn by Roy Bradley, the building inspector for the Chin Lee government school, then nearing completion.[47]

After a personal visit from Father Anselm upon his return from Europe in the autumn of 1911, the New York Marquette League donated $1,000 on condition that the chapel be named "The Annunciation."[48] At that time long finished, but as yet unnamed, the chapel was accordingly dedicated solemnly by Anselm Weber on the feast of the Annunciation of the Virgin Mary, March 25, 1912. Father Egbert

[43] A. Weber to Mother Katharine, June 10, 1906, C.H.A.

[44] A. Weber to Chas. Lusk, June 12, 1906, C.I.B.A.; A. Weber, *Sendbote,* 36:412, May, 1909; Davida Woerner, *Education Among the Navajo,* pp. 50–52.

[45] A. Weber to L. Ostermann, May 4, 1908, and L. Ostermann to A. Weber, May 14, 1908, P.A., NL.

[46] *F.M.S.,* 1913, p. 21; A. Weber, *Sendbote,* 37:396–397, May, 1910.

[47] Agent Peter Paquette to Commissioner, October 7, 1909, W.R.C., Letter Books; A. Weber to Chas. Lusk, July 11, 1910, C.I.B.A.

[48] E. R. Byrne, Marquette League, to W. Ketcham, November 22, 1911, C.I.B.A. This donation was originally intended in 1905 for the Hopi mission. *House Chronicle,* p. 57, S.M.C.

Fischer preached, Marcellus was deacon, and Leopold presided at the melodion, covering for the choir which was composed of printer George Connolly and several Indian Service employees.[49]

The written consent of the parents of practically every one of the eighty pupils having been secured, the children were chaperoned the half mile to and from Mass and given instructions every Sunday.[50] By 1918, with an enrollment of one hundred and sixty-five children, all but five received Catholic instructions twice each week at school from the missionary, and attended Sunday services at the mission chapel.[51]

It was not until May, 1914, after eleven years of work in and about Chin Lee, that Father Leopold felt ready to accept any Navaho converts. On this joyous occasion eighteen young men and twenty-four girls were baptized and received their First Communion. On June 12 nine more boys and three girls were added to the tiny Christian community, called the Chin Lee Annunciation Mission.[52]

During the long hard years Leopold Ostermann spent countless hours in the field and at his desk working at Navaho etymology and orthography. To the Indians the heavy quiet man was simply *E'nishodi Tso,* "Big Long Gown," who wore his brown habit whether astride his "Frank Horse," whether behind the counter as the friendly postmaster of Chin Lee, or engaged in manual work.[53]

His lengthy letters to Father Anselm, especially during 1908, when the *Ethnologic Dictionary* was being promoted by Anselm under the editorship of Berard Haile, show Father Leopold for the thoroughgoing and scientific student he was. He stressed derivation and etymology rather than reliance on acoustics; he argued against complete reliance on the diction and phonetics of good interpreters, but untrained linguists, such as Frank Walker and Chee Dodge — unless, as he warned, "you wish to publish a handbook of Navaho patois." Blessed with great patience and sly wit he was able to stomach the sarcasm occasionally directed at his "pedantic insistence," and continued to send in his lists of phrases and words. "St. Michaels seems to be Attica. . . . [However] we are not bound by vow to conform, in

49 L. Ostermann, *F.M.S.,* 1914, p. 34.

50 A. Weber, *F.M.S.,* 1913, p. 19. Peshlakai and Charley Mitchell were invaluable in obtaining signatures for Catholic instructions. A. Weber, *Sendbote,* 37:900, 1072, October and December, 1910.

51 A. Weber, in B.C.I.M., *The Indian Sentinel,* 1:19, April, 1918.

52 A. Weber, *F.M.S.,* 1915, pp. 39–44.

53 Mrs. Barbara Goodman and Roman Hubbell, interview, July 16, 1950; *F.M.S.,* 1913, pp. 41–44.

private use, to localisms," he retorted with a chuckle to ribbing from Father Berard.[54]

Father Berard Haile during his ten years at St. Michaels headquarters, where he served as chaplain at the boarding school, had worked steadily ahead in his investigation of Navaho language and culture. During his first two years after arrival in 1900 he had reneged at the attempt of Juvenal and Anselm to compress Navaho grammar and syntax into the rigid forms and structures of classical languages as taught in the Franciscan Gymnasium. Instead, as he disparagingly put it, he devoted his time to more useful chores, such as farming, chicken raising, and the extermination of lice and bedbugs.[55]

Largely through Stewart Culin, Father Berard in 1902 developed an engrossing interest in Navaho ethnology and linguistics.[56] With the constant service of Frank Walker, the aid of Chee Dodge, and various medicine men, along with the collaboration of Anselm, Leopold, and Marcellus, Berard planned and edited during 1907–1909 *An Ethnologic Dictionary of the Navaho Language*. This they printed on a press purchased through the good offices of Mr. Culin.[57] Father Anselm had to argue strenuously with Provincial Eugene Buttermann to prove the missionary value of linguistic studies before he gained permission to loan $500 to finish printing the *Ethnologic Dictionary*.[58]

George Connolly, a Cincinnati printer who was out West for his health, took over the formidable task of setting and printing in the log cabin printery.[59]

Mother Katharine subsidized the printing, also in 1910, of the Navaho-English Catechism, which was the cumulative product of Anselm Weber's twelve years of preparation and experience.[60] The two-volume work, *English-Navaho* and *Navaho-English Dictionary*

[54] L. Ostermann to *Carissime* (A. Weber), January 10, April 19, May 14, 1908, P.A., LO.; A. Weber to L. Ostermann, May 8, 1908, P.A., CL.; L. Ostermann to B. Haile, December 24, 1905, P.A., LO.

[55] B. Haile, in *The Provincial Chronicle*, 20:195, Summer, 1948. Marcus Kreke, O.F.M., science instructor at the Franciscan Gymnasium, was enlisted in the bedbug campaign: "Also auch endlich als Wanzendoktor muss der alte greise aus dem Kopfe barfuessige Professor auftreten." He suggested in reverse importance: Brother Martin, Persian Insect Powder, and carbon bisulphide. M. Kreke to Anselm Weber, August 12, 1903, P.A., MK.

[56] B. Haile, *ibid.*, p. 196; A. Weber, *F.M.S.*, 1913, p. 18.

[57] *Ibid.*

[58] A. Weber from Duesseldorf, Germany, to B. Haile, August 27, 1911, P.A., PP.

[59] B. Haile, in *The Provincial Chronicle*, 20:196; letter drafts of B. Haile to Provincial Buttermann and to A. Weber, July, 1911, S.M.C., Letter Book-1.

[60] A. Weber to Mother Katharine, February 2, 1910, P.A., PP.; A. Weber, *F.M.S.*, 1913, p. 20.

was ready for the press at the close of 1910, though not published until 1912.[61] Though the province viewed with some skepticism Berard Haile's interest in ethnology and anthropology, Father Anselm realized the essential missionological contribution involved, and consistently backed Berard's research and publishing in these fields.[62] Provincial Buttermann and the definers of the province limited him in 1911 to the publishing of a Navaho dictionary and grammar; other works to concern religious topics only, such as catechisms and Holy Scripture. Printing was to be done by outside printers. Eighty dollars a month for Connolly was out of the question![63]

Much of the earlier linguistic work of Anselm had to be discarded: extended study revealed numerous wrong approaches, many of them due to difficulties with phonetics, and with the extremely elusive problem of dealing in Navaho thought categories which in their pictorial concreteness admitted of no direct conversion with European conceptional patterns.[64] During his twenty-three years among the Navaho, Father Anselm never lost his deep conviction concerning knowledge of the Navaho language for effective mission work. A year before his death, while undergoing extremely painful treatment for cancer at Rochester, Minnesota, he wrote for copies of Hossfeld's *Spanish Grammar:* "I intend to publish the savage Navaho tongue according to that method, if it suits me. That is one 'job' I wish to finish before I cross the Styx."[65] It was a "job" unfinished by Father Anselm; five years after his death a *Navaho Grammar* appeared, the work of his confrere, Berard Haile, who incorporated the joint labors of Anselm and Leopold.

Lukachukai

Some thirty-five miles northeast of Chin Lee rise the majestic Lukachukai Mountains, the northwestern bastion of the Chuska range

[61] A. Weber, printed letter to subscribers of the Franciscan Press, December 28, 1910, P.A., PP.; B. Haile, in *The Provincial Chronicle,* 20:196.

[62] B. Haile, answer to questionnaire, January 27, 1951, P.A., CP. Except for the printing of the annual mission magazine, *Franciscan Missions of the Southwest,* 1913–1922, the Franciscan Fathers' Press at St. Michaels was idle for more than ten years after 1914. The discovery of new tones in the Navaho language in 1926 required a new orthography and the re-editing of the previous works. See listing of B. Haile's works in the bibliography, pp. 242–243.

[63] Provincial Buttermann to B. Haile, August 7, 1911, P.A., BH.

[64] A. Weber, *F.M.S.,* 1913, pp. 18–19; see Kluckhohn and Leighton, *The Navaho,* pp. 122, 199, 208–215.

[65] A. Weber to Urban Freundt, O.F.M., February 14, 1920, P.A., NL. On Berard Haile's later labors at St. Michaels Franciscan Fathers' Press, see Ammian E. Lutomski, O.F.M., "A Padre of the Trail," *Arizona Highways,* 23:11–15, July, 1947, a popular treatment.

which lies along the boundary line between New Mexico and Arizona.[66] On his various trips to Round Rock, and in recrossing Lukachukai Pass to and from Red Rock Valley, Father Anselm had become acquainted with the thriving farm community spread out along Lukachukai Creek. Here where higher annual rainfall plus live water had conspired naturally to create attractive agricultural conditions, and had drawn a relatively dense Navaho population, the missionary visualized a future Christian center: "We ought to have a mission and day school at the Lukachukai, and chapels at Tseili and Tselchidahaskanni [Red Rock]," he wrote in 1908.[67] Even after he became skeptical of day schools for the San Juan and for Chin Lee, he still held out for such a community school at Lukachukai, obviously because in this beautiful, watered valley thrived a true community.[68] Even with irrigation these Navaho farmers made up a community not in the sense of a clustering of families living in a village pattern the year around, but a true community of families grouped closely on irrigated farm land and bound by common ties of neighborhood, occupation, and culture.

Prior to 1909 Father Anselm occasionally visited the Lukachukai Valley in order to offer Mass and to keep alive the faith of those who had finished their schooling at St. Michaels. Frequently services were held at Tsishbizhi's, the home of one of these returned students.[69] At a Yeibichai dance held at the foot of the mountains on October 9, 1909, Charley Mitchell requested land for a chapel and, under proper circumstances, for a day school as well. Warmed by the obviously favorable response in the faces of the assembled Navaho, Anselm further explained his earlier promise to keep in contact with St. Michaels graduates. This mission, he explained, would make it possible to expand and put to work the schooling given at St. Michaels if the site were centrally located.[70] After unanimous approval, the Indians conferred as to the best location, and then in a group rode over to their sacred, and unused, legendary spring, *"Qabó ol aesi."*[71] The ceremonial spring was truly a beautiful spot, with its tiny meadow

[66] Lukachukai, according to Father Berard, means "white reed patches"; better, "at the reeds where (the mountainside is) white (with) spruce." B. Haile, *F.M.S.,* 1916, p. 21; *An Ethnologic Dictionary,* p. 31.

[67] A. Weber to Bishop Granjon, November 23, 1908, P.A., MM.

[68] See A. Weber, *Sendbote,* 36:412, May, 1909; A. Weber to Chas. Lusk, October 13, 1909, C.I.B.A.

[69] M. Troester, *F.M.S.,* 1915, p. 31.

[70] A. Weber, *Sendbote,* 36:1082–1084, December, 1909.

[71] M. Troester, *F.M.S.,* 1915, p. 32.

glistening green and bright in the sea of gray-green sage. In the background lifted the masses of tawny, orange-red sandstone which buttress the soaring pine-clad heights of the Lukachukai.

Anselm was deeply impressed by this display of generosity, and told them how grateful the *e'nishodi* were. With tape and pocket compass he next measured off forty acres surrounding the ceremonial spring and set up his monuments. Thirty-three family heads, including one woman, signed the petition for the mission site.[72] On December 18, 1909, the Office of Indian Affairs approved the selection.[73]

As soon as the walls of the Chin Lee Mission were raised, Anselm was on hand at Lukachukai to break ground for the building of the mission chapel there. Work began July 18, 1910.[74] Roy Bradley's plans for Chin Lee were likewise used for Lukachukai, and the work was carried out under W. E. Hildebrand, the contractor for Chin Lee. Two small, eight by eight-foot rooms were added in the rear for the use of the visiting missionary.[75] Five hundred dollars from Mrs. Theresa Huss of Buffalo began the work, and another $500 from James J. Condon, in memory of his wife, Isabella, helped to cover the final cost of $2,240.[76] Through experience gained while at St. Michaels, and by their work at quarrying, dressing, and laying stone for St. Isabel's Chapel, many Indians of the Lukachukai area became fairly adept at stonework as evidenced by the stone houses they have since raised in that community.

Lukachukai chapel was also undertaken on the prospect of a large government boarding school which was to be built in the neighborhood of the mission.[77] Though the chapel building had been roughed out by the autumn of 1910, finishing work dragged on through the next eighteen months.[78] Solemn High Mass followed the June 22, 1910, dedication by Father Anselm who was assisted by his confreres, Leopold and Marcellus. The choir was composed of Fathers Egbert

[72] A. Weber, *Sendbote,* 36:1085, December, 1909; Indians' petition to Commissioner R. G. Valentine, October 10, 1909, copy in P.A., LM.

[73] Land Uses, 93008, 1909, RTB, copy in P.A., LM.; Peter Paquette to Commissioner, November 15, 1909, W.R.C., Letter Books.

[74] A. Weber to Dennis Engelhard, O.F.M., July 21, 1910, P.A., LM.; A. Weber to Chas. Lusk, July 11, 1910, C.I.B.A.

[75] M. Troester, *F.M.S.,* 1915, p. 33; B. Haile, *F.M.S.,* 1916, p. 24.

[76] A. Weber to D. Engelhard, January 30, 1910, P.A., LM. The Condon family later supplied mission bell and various appointments for the altar. See Condon letters, 1911–1916, P.A., LM.

[77] *F.M.S.,* 1913, p. 21.

[78] Supplementary Report, October 27, 1910, W.R.C., Miscellaneous Letter Books.

Fischer, Fintan Zumbahlen, and Florentin Meyers who had driven out with Anselm on the previous day.[79]

Marcellus Troester continued to attend St. Isabel's with monthly visits until Berard Haile was appointed resident pastor at the August, 1915, chapter, with Brother Gervase transferring from Chin Lee as companion and building assistant to Father Berard. Marcellus Troester returned to St. Michaels where he took over Father Berard's previous mission work at Tohatchi.[80]

Building of a residence began almost immediately at Lukachukai. Logs were ordered but turned out to be such slender poles that Berard Haile shifted to stone instead, using the poles for corral and stables. Indian freighters furnishing wagons and teams hired in at $2.50 per day, and stone workers at $2. With this Indian help Gervase was able to lay a perch of stone daily, once he had taught the Navaho the trick of quarrying and cutting stone. Father Berard put in full days alongside the lay Brother at both masonry and carpentry work. By Christmas time the walls were finished and rafters in place.[81]

During the rush to finish up the masonry work before the bitter Lukachukai winter set in, Father Berard heard reports that Peshlakai was ill. Headman and dramatic spokesman for the Navaho, and earliest influential friend of the *e'nishodi,* Old Silversmith had advanced the mission cause on many fronts. Before *E'nishodi Yazhe* could make the trip south to visit and attend him, the bespectacled old leader unexpectedly died. All over the reservation and beyond, there was deep grief. The Silversmith, to Berard's mind, outranked in prestige both Charley Mitchell and Chee Dodge in the eastern, southern, and northern sections. Charley Mitchell, now policeman and Navaho judge, carried the greater influence in the west. Father Anselm at St. Michaels could not at the time make the trip to Peshlakai's deathbed as he was incapacitated by a serious spell of nervous exhaustion.[82]

The government day school was built on the rise above the mission in 1915, and opened for classes the next spring, after the Navaho

[79] Fort Defiance Office Diary, June 21, 1912, W.R.C.; M. Troester, *F.M.S.,* 1915, p. 37.

[80] B. Haile, *F.M.S.,* 1916, p. 24; A. Weber, in B.C.I.M., *The Indian Sentinel,* 1:19, April, 1918. Berard Haile had begun instructing at Tohatchi Boarding School in 1914, making weekly mission trips which included Saturday evening and Sunday morning instructions, and Sunday Mass. Marcellus Troester erected a chapel at Tohatchi in 1917. M. Troester, *F.M.S.,* 1917, pp. 39–41.

[81] B. Haile to A. Weber, August 24, September 5, 6, 11, December 23, 1915, P.A., LM.

[82] B. Haile to A. Weber, December 12 and 19, 1915, with undated enclosure, P.A., B.H.

returned from their annual winter exodus.[83] To the Navaho mind this day school was queer business: the parents had no work from their child and yet had "to keep half of their child at home." By September the original twenty-one day pupils had dwindled to three and sometimes four. Father Berard still hoped, however, that the appeal of the nearby Red Rock district for a small Sisters' community school would materialize.[84]

Lukachukai gave the friars a rather objective mission case study on the effectiveness of mission boarding-school environment on young Christian Navaho after their re-entry into native community life. Father Anselm had planned the Chin Lee and Lukachukai Missions advisedly to serve as extensions of St. Michaels into the hinterland, field missions which would aid in the process of cultural infiltration, cross fertilization, and even eventual assimilation of primitive paganism by Christianity.[85] If with the mission center's aid, returned Christian boys and girls could personally maintain essential Christian Faith with its practices, the process of cultural change would be under way. Especially would this process be hastened if the returned students intermarried and founded Christian families. That in time would mean the transition from paganism to Christianity.

In this respect it is significant that the Navaho offered little or no resistance to technical advance, and readily accepted new tools and mechanical methods of white civilization. The missionaries hoped that in accepting civilizational change the Navaho, like most other Indian groups, would easily and painlessly adopt Western, or European thought ways and culture.[86]

By 1917, however, there was small evidence of any deep-seated carry-over of Christian boarding-school influence into Navaho home communities. True, returned students could read, write, use a mowing machine or binder, and enjoy a ball game; but evidently the freedom from detailed boarding-school regimentation and supervision attaching to life at St. Michaels meant a release also from the religious aspects of their controlled school life. Ceremonial rites and camp life, like open skies and all-night sings, were apparently a part with freedom and the joy of easygoing, wholesome home and community life.

[83] M. Troester, *F.M.S.,* 1915, p. 37.

[84] B. Haile, *F.M.S.,* 1917, pp. 51–52; B. Haile to A. Weber, November 12, 1916, P.A., LU.

[85] A. Weber to W. Ketcham, April 25, 1903, C.I.B.A.; see A. Weber, *Sendbote,* 30:122–127, February, 1903, and 36:1084, December, 1909.

[86] See A. Weber, *Sendbote,* 37:787–788, September, 1910; Kluckhohn and Leighton, *The Navaho,* p. 28.

At least the facts as of 1917 would seem to indicate this: rarely would the returned graduates assist at Sunday Mass, and the pupils home on vacation hid themselves when the missioner sought them out to encourage their attendance. Several St. Michaels graduates were leaders at the Yeibichai dances; another was already training as a medicine man, or singer, and some of the married graduates were skittish about having their babies baptized.[87]

Good Archbishop Bourgade in 1906 had noted similarly disappointing results among the Pueblo Indian children. At the boarding school, the good Bishop maintained, a forced, hothouse variety of piety, not true religious conviction, was fostered. "Stuffing these little Indians with an endless number of pious practices is simply calculated to give them a lasting aversion for practicing their religion later on."[88] He argued against the "novitiate method" of teaching Catholicism, with no planned nor intelligent effort to adapt the training to Indian problems and culture. "I and the priests who have spent their lives among the Indians are not consulted as a rule."[89]

The Lukachukai Mission on its part served in a limited capacity as a minor Indian agency where family controversies were settled, native pagan marriages were registered,[90] and from where the missioner hoped eventually to organize communal management of water rights to replace the existing individual control system.[91]

From a sociological viewpoint community houses which might be used for religious services, as well as social events, neighborhood politics, and as Navaho gossip centers, apparently would have answered better and more functionally the needs of widely scattered families than did the formal chapel of parochial tradition. Economically, the construction of rarely used, but costly, stone chapels for the Navaho seemed ill-advised.[92]

It was, however, the old story of church and mission support: benefactors could be induced to give for the erection of buildings, especially as memorials in stone, while they remained indifferent to appeals for the support of the missionary himself or for unconventional forms of mission service, such as language and cultural studies, or for socio-economic projects calculated to offer economic security.

[87] B. Haile to A. Weber, November 4, 1917, P.A., BH.; see also same to same, November 12, 1915, P.A., BH.

[88] Archbishop Bourgade to W. Ketcham, April 23, 1906, C.I.B.A. See Archbishop Bourgade to Mother Katharine, *Annals,* 7:268, C.H.A.

[89] *Ibid.;* Archbishop Bourgade to W. Ketcham, November 8, 1906, C.I.B.A.

[90] B. Haile to A. Weber, Christmastide, 1915, P.A., LM.

[91] Same to same, November 12, 1915, P.A., BH.

[92] Same to same, November 4, 1917, P.A., BH.

Chapter IX

San Juan and Jémez Missions

THREE years before the Chin Lee Mission was established in the spring of 1903, plans had been under way for a like foundation on the San Juan River. What Anselm Weber in 1899 and 1900 had hoped would grow into a combined Navaho-Hispano mission on the San Juan evolved into the Peña Blanca mission base for Hispanos, Pueblo Indians, and Anglos.[1] From St. Michaels, however, the missionary continued to keep the San Juan in close focus. Through General Morrell, congressman from Pennsylvania, and brother-in-law of Mother Katharine, he argued insistently for irrigation appropriations. When General Armstrong visited the reservation in 1901 Anselm prevailed on him to visit the San Juan area, a trip which so convinced Armstrong as to possibilities there that the general strongly urged Mother Katharine to open a second Navaho mission along the river.[2]

Samuel Shoemaker, the government farmer and irrigation expert on the San Juan, scouted the river for prospective mission land. He had in mind an eighty-acre tract near Fruitland which in 1901 could have been purchased for seven or eight hundred dollars.[3] Mother Katharine agreed to buy the land for a day school, provided Father Anselm would himself check to avoid the encumbrances burdening the St. Michaels land site.[4]

From Santa Fe, Archbishop Bourgade congratulated Father Anselm, and himself, over the approaching fulfillment of "our contemplated project including Jémez and ranging from St. Michaels to the San Juan."[5] Two weeks later, after the Archbishop had talked over matters

[1] See pp. 70–71.

[2] A. Weber, *Sendbote,* 31:125–129, February, 1904.

[3] S. Shoemaker to A. Weber, December 17, 1901, P.A., SJ.

[4] Mother Katharine to A. Weber, January (n.d.), 1902, and February 26, 1902, P.A., SJ.

[5] Archbishop Bourgade to A. Weber, December 31, 1901, H.A.C.

with Provincial Louis Haverbeck, prospects for the friars' taking over Jémez had dwindled.[6]

Nor was it small wonder that the Provincial was at an impasse: one, possibly two, of the Peña Blanca friars would have to be recalled as unsuited for the New Mexico work,[7] and simultaneously Bishop Matz was begging the province to take over Durango, Colorado.[8] However, Father Louis did manage to find two apostolic young priests to mission at Jémez after the definers voted on February 4 to accept the pueblo and its missions.[9] Within two weeks Barnabas Meyer and Florentin Meyers had arrived at headquarters in Peña Blanca where they lived until orientated and physiologically calloused for mission wear and tear.[10] On March 24, 1902, Father Barnabas moved into the bunk-house-style convento at Jémez which had been built by Father Cellier, the last secular priest in charge. The convento had been constructed out of materials stripped from the defunct day school founded by Mother Katharine.[11]

With Jémez in Franciscan hands it remained to found the San Juan Mission — if the "contemplated project" to surround the Navaho with missions were to be realized. For the remainder of 1901 and 1902, however, Father Anselm found little leisure for any business outside the contentious mission-land matters, supervising construction of St. Michaels School, and rounding up pupils.

Quite by coincidence in the winter of 1902–1903 the government had been finally compelled to grant funds for Shoemaker's irrigation works along the San Juan. Successive drought years had forced many Navaho to subsist on horses and what few piñons they could store. Stories of privation sent in by traders to the newspapers had ballooned into famine stories, so that the Office of Indian Affairs was pressured into granting $10,000 as a work loan, to be repaid by road and

[6] Same to same, January 15, 1902, P.A., PB.

[7] G. Juillard to A. Weber, October 4, 1900, P.A., GJ.; B. Nurre to A. Weber, December 31, 1900, P.A., BN.

[8] B. Nurre to A. Weber, *ibid.* Durango was offered to the Cincinnati Province again in 1903 by the same Bishop Matz who the following year in 1904 asked the Provincial to have Anselm Weber take over the Ute Indians in southwestern Colorado, as well as the Hispanos' missions west of the Cumbres, along the New Mexico-Colorado line. B. Nurre to A. Weber, September 21, 1903, July 1, 1904, P.A., BN.

[9] Pius Niehaus, O.F.M., to A. Weber, February 8, 1902, P.A., PN.; Archbishop Bourgade to A. Weber, February 10, 1902, P.A., PB.

[10] "Die zwei R.P. missionarii ad Indios Mexicanosque sind schon 10 Tage hier und haben schon plenty petroleum jelly gebraucht um eine gewisse Stelle des Koerpers zu beruhigen die durch das Reiten am meisten aufgeregt war." Leander Schell, O.F.M., superior at Peña Blanca, to A. Weber, March 4, 1902, P.A., LS.

[11] B. Meyer to A. Weber, March 17 and June 9, 1902, P.A., BM.

irrigation work.[12] Mr. Shoemaker could in January of 1903 move from opposite Fruitland where during three years he had opened up shallow ditches and improvised head gates to furnish water for some sixty Indian families. He now set up headquarters at Sandoval's Place below the Hogback where he put fifty Indians to digging a twelve-foot deep main ditch that ran four and a half miles in length, and was planned to irrigate some 3000 acres of land.[13]

To Anselm Weber's query of December 30, 1902, as to prospects for land on the south side of the San Juan, Shoemaker replied that Sister Tripp had bought the forty-acre tract opposite King Ranch for a Methodist industrial school.[14] Shoemaker suggested an excellent location three miles down the river which he would aid Anselm in obtaining.[15] This was in line with the missionary's intention to found the new mission close to Farmington in order to serve the Navaho camps that spread fanwise east, west, and south of Farmington.[16]

Anselm Weber waited until late May of 1903 to check personally on possible mission and day-school sites along the San Juan. Fathers Berard Haile and Michael Dumarest left by wagon on May 19 for Round Rock, accompanied by Frank Walker, who rode horseback.[17] Father Anselm and Stewart Culin rode via Ganado, and from there by Indian trail through a petrified forest, to Chin Lee.[18]

Mr. Culin had come out from New York on a six-month leave of absence for field work in behalf of the Brooklyn Institute Museum. One of his intentions, among others, was to purchase the Sam E. Day ethnological collection for the Brooklyn Museum where he was curator of ethnology.[19] The year previous, as ethnologist for the University of Pennsylvania Museum, Culin had visited at St. Michaels where he

[12] S. Shoemaker to A. Weber, January 6, 1903, H.A.C.; A. Weber, *Sendbote,* 31:129, February, 1904.

[13] A. Weber, *ibid.;* C.I.A., *Annual Report,* 1903, p. 127. See Hayzlett's praise of Shoemaker's work in August, 1902, in W.R.C., Letter Book, 1902, pp. 159–160.

[14] S. Shoemaker to A. Weber, January 6, 1903, H.A.C.; *The Farmington Hustler,* October 2, 1902, as cited by P. G. Malehorn, *The Tender Plant,* p. 23, describes the purchase by Miss Tripp.

[15] S. Shoemaker to A. Weber, January 6, 1903, H.A.C.

[16] A. Weber to W. Ketcham, August 21, 1903, P.A., SJ.

[17] A. Weber to Mother Katharine, May 18, 1903, C.H.A.; A. Weber, *Sendbote,* 31:224, March, 1904.

[18] A. Weber, *Sendbote, ibid.,* p. 225.

[19] S. Culin to A. Weber, March 9, 1903, P.A., SC. Berard Haile sent many valuable data on Navaho ball games; see S. Culin to A. Weber, June 11, 1902, and December 10, 1903, P.A., SC. A. Weber sent twelve prehistoric bone dice from Tanner Springs to the Brooklyn Museum. Professor Franklin W. Hooper to A. Weber, March 21, 1903, P.A., AR.

had enlisted the assistance of the missionaries for his study of Indian games.[20]

Arriving with Anselm at Day's trading post, after losing the trail in a sandstorm, Culin haggled and fumed with Mr. Day until they met at a figure of $4,000 for the excellent Day collection.[21] This included a wide variety of mummies, clothes, basketry, pottery, bows, arrows, and kiva utensils — excavated by the Days largely from the numerous cliff dwellings in Cañon de Chelly.[22] Curiously, about two weeks after the sale, Charles L. Day was appointed custodian of the Cañon, with duties of preventing any further unauthorized excavations or depredations.[23]

In another blinding sandstorm the next day, Anselm Weber and Culin struck out for Round Rock. Even though they tacked cautiously back and forth across the trail, they occasionally lost it completely. Eyes bloodshot and themselves thoroughly sand-blown, the exhausted horsemen finally reached Fathers Berard and Dumarest at Round Rock Store in time for a quick rinsing before dinner.[24] Here Culin spent two days writing up the history of Round Rock.[25]

As the mountains to the eastward were crossed only by trails, the party left the buggy at Round Rock and headed on horseback for the Lukachukai foothills, fifteen miles to the east. Frank Walker led the way to a narrow pass that led them into an enclosed valley. High above on the face of the shelving cliff hung terraces of cliff dwellings, dwarfed by the height to toy dimensions. Gripping by fingers and toes they scaled the wall to the first tier of prehistoric penthouses — all but Culin. Frank Walker, Father Berard, Father Mike Dumarest literally dragged him up the cliff to the first shelf. Here he sat, pale and queasy, a pathetic victim of acrophobia, while Berard took a series of photographs. There on the rock floor the forty-five-year-old ethnologist remained while the others explored the terraces, the first white men to enter the tomblike city plastered against the canyon wall. Later on when safely back on the canyon

[20] S. Culin to A. Weber, January 20, 1902, P.A., AR. His work, published by the United States Bureau of Ethnology, was entitled *Games of the North American Indians,* which appeared in the *Twenty-Fourth Annual Report to the Secretary of the Smithsonian Institution,* 1902–1903, pp. 3–809.

[21] A. Weber to Mrs. L. W. Drexel, copy, n.d. (July, 1903), P.A., SJ.

[22] A. Weber, *Sendbote,* 31:226, March, 1904.

[23] Official appointment, Department of Interior to Supervisor R. Perry, June 1, 1903, W.R.C., Letter Book.

[24] A. Weber, *Sendbote,* 31:226–228, March, 1904.

[25] A. Weber to Mrs. L. W. Drexel, n.d. (July, 1903), P.A., SJ.

floor Culin blandly remarked that if he returned to carry on excavations it would be by proxy.[26]

By nightfall the explorers made Black Horse's camp in the Carrizos where they bought and roasted a sheep before retiring in a deserted medicine hogan.[27] By dusk of the next day they had ridden across the eastern desert to Sandovals on the south bank of the San Juan, where Mr. Shoemaker received them warmly and put them up at his construction camp. With justifiable pride the irrigation expert drove them next morning along the freshly cut, four-and-one-half-mile-long ditch. It was the first of two deep lateral canals to be completed. On the following evening the missionaries, Culin and Walker crowded around the head gate as Mr. Shoemaker opened the floodgate and the first San Juan water tumbled into the twelve-foot deep canal. Spontaneously a war whoop shrilled out across the quiet desert as a hundred of Sandoval's outfit hungrily watched the flood pour across the arid flat, water which meant maize, wheat, melons, beans, and fruit.[28] The padres had witnessed the true beginnings of the Shiprock Indian Agency.

Through Headman Sandoval's aid Culin located a half-starved singer who was willing to sell his religious paraphernalia, masks included. At the $50 bid made by Culin the old shaman evinced small interest; nor did $60, or finally $75, draw much response from the poor Navaho. Asked for his price the singer blankly stated his figure: 800 sheep! Angry and disappointed, Culin struck out almost immediately across the desert for Gallup, New Mexico.[29] Later Father Anselm helped Culin to purchase a complete chanter's outfit, including nineteen masks, fox skins, baskets, and other sacred instruments.[30]

To Anselm, the missionary, there lay a curious, if not ominous, dichotomy in the incident of the Navaho jubilation over their newly engineered irrigation works in contrast to the poor, starving medicine man who clung so tenaciously to his ceremonial heirlooms which were woven inextricably into the dim and mysterious past of the *Diné*.[31] As yet, utilitarian innovation had not dented noticeably the inner core of the life, the culture complex, of the Navaho. Father Anselm nonetheless within the next two weeks advanced his own rather hopeful

26 *Ibid.;* A. Weber, *Sendbote,* 31:228–229, March, 1904.
27 A. Weber, *Sendbote,* 31:318, April, 1904.
28 A. Weber, *Sendbote, ibid.,* p. 319.
29 *Ibid.;* A. Weber to Mrs. L. W. Drexel (July, 1903), P.A., SJ.
30 S. Culin to A. Weber, July 20, 1903, P.A., SC.
31 A. Weber, *Sendbote,* 31:319, April, 1904.

suggestions for weaning the Christianized students away from their pagan culture:[32]

> I am convinced that lasting results can only be obtained by gathering as far as practicable the roaming Navajos into permanent settlements with day schools and missions. [This] is especially true with regard to such as leave our school: if they are turned adrift, and the salutary influence upon them is not continued after they 'graduate,' experience seems to teach that it is love and money lost to educate them.
>
> On that account I have for the last four years never lost sight of the San Juan River with its vast possibilities for irrigation and permanent settlements.

After Headman Sandoval assured the friars that he and his band would gladly endorse a land selection for mission and day school, the three priests and Frank Walker mounted their rested horses and struck upstream on the south bank of the San Juan. Beyond the Hogback they passed the Jewett mission on the opposite bank[33] where the Presbyterians had taken over the earlier Methodist foundations of Mrs. Eldridge and Miss Tripp.[34] Eight miles above the Hogback they lunched on the cottonwood flats where the Indians, without government aid, had scooped out their own shallow irrigation ditches. Three miles farther, opposite Fruitland, they skirted Mr. Shoemaker's home, climbed over the rocky knob east of Shoemaker's little place, and entered the beautiful bottom lands where for two years Shoemaker had directed the Indians in laying out ditches and floodgates. Midway along this strip that ran from Fruitland to King's Crossing they hoped to procure a mission site, some three miles down river from Farmington.[35]

At King's Crossing the missionaries examined with much interest Miss Tripp's new Methodist school which was nearing completion. Opposite the Las Animas they left their horses with an Hispano *ranchero* who ferried them across the river. Renting a buggy at Farmington the group drove up the La Plata to Fort Lewis Indian School in Colorado where one hundred and thirty-four Navaho students

[32] A. Weber to Mrs. L. W. Drexel (July, 1903), P.A., SJ.

[33] A. Weber, *Sendbote,* 31:319–320, April, 1904.

[34] P. G. Malehorn, *The Tender Plant,* pp. 22–23. In 1902 this original establishment of the National Indian Association, later developed by the Methodist-Episcopal Board, was sold to the Presbyterians for $1,000. *Ibid.* In 1914 the hospital and school facilities were transferred to Ganado, where Reverend Bierkemper and his wife had opened the day school in 1901. Organized medical and hospital work began at the Presbyterian Ganado Mission about 1912, according to C. B. Salsbury, *Forty Years in the Desert,* pp. 20–22; see Malehorn, *The Tender Plant,* p. 89.

[35] A. Weber, *Sendbote,* 31:320, April, 1904.

were being trained under the principal, Dr. Thomas Breen.[36] After a night and a morning with Dr. Breen, they rode over to Durango and stayed the night with Father J. Duffy and Muños, the latter an *émigré* from Guatemala. The sixty-three miles of beautiful country along the Las Animas to Farmington they clocked in exactly twelve hours on their return trip.[37]

In trying to catch their horses the next morning at the *rancho* across the San Juan, Father Anselm was thrown heavily to the ground by Berard's horse, "Diablo," which reared and plunged after the priest had caught him by the halter. Father Berard and an Hispano lad mounted and finally brought in the other frisky ponies, after which the three priests and Walker rode down river to make the land selection. Dumarest and Berard rode ahead to bring back Headman Sandoval, while Frank and "Adobe," the local Navaho policeman, made for Red Rock for Headman Naakai Dinae. Meanwhile Anselm Weber marked off with his pocket compass the site they hoped the Indians would grant them.[38] Feeling decidedly ill and feverish by this time, Anselm then took a stiff drink of *Tqodilqil* and fell asleep on a sheepskin under Adobe's summer brush shelter. Few Indians had responded to the policeman's invitation to the council, and as neither Sandoval nor Naakai Dinae had been located, Father Weber thanked the Indians, asking them to make a selection themselves at their next council. He promised to return later for their answer and signatures.[39]

Quite sick by this time, the missionary and his party rode west to Sandoval's camp where Mrs. Eldridge treated him expertly with digitalis and quinine. With the intention of spending the night at Red Rock with Naakai Dinae's outfit, they set off from Sandoval's almost immediately. Long after nightfall they were still searching. Hoping to find wood and water, and resigned to sleeping out of doors, the four men spread out and separately combed the darkness, but still no sign of Indians, water, or wood. It was beginning to look serious until Indian camp dogs off in the distance happily raised an alarm. The commotion led them to a camp of Indian friends who soon had roasted mutton ribs and coffee prepared. About midnight, as they were rolling up in their blankets in the crowded hogan, young

[36] A. Weber, *Sendbote,* 31:412, May, 1904. Dr. Breen was forced to resign within a short time after this visit because of alleged charges preferred by *The Denver Post* in a lurid exposé, July 29, 1903. Dr. Breen, who had promised to send all Fort Lewis Navaho pupils to the projected mission school of the friars, died a victim of malicious slander less than a year later, according to A. Weber, *Sendbote, ibid.*

[37] A. Weber, *Sendbote,* 31:413, May, 1904.

[38] *Ibid.,* p. 414.

[39] *Ibid.,* p. 416.

Padre Mike Dumarest in mock seriousness posed the question as to how Anselm could reconcile Canon Law and the mixed company in their sheepskin dormitory. With a snort the older man retorted that the Roman lawyers had no jurisdiction within the Navaho reservation.[40]

The next morning they visited Hosteen Black who was pitifully run down and burning with fever; after leaving what remained of Mrs. Eldridge's quinine, Father Anselm and the others left money for supplies at the trading post, and then left the trail to strike out across the Lukachukai range. At Round Rock Store Father Berard and Mike Dumarest hitched up the buckboard and left for St. Michaels while Anselm and Frank Walker stayed behind to instruct two Navaho girls who were preparing to marry the two young American clerks at the Round Rock Store.[41]

Back at St. Michaels the friars' new adobe mission residence, then under construction, demanded much attention. There were also reports to prepare for the Visitor General, Hugolin Storff, who interviewed the friars on July 19 in preparation for the triennial provincial election and chapter to be held in September.[42] The Visitor was quite blunt in questioning the synthetic environment created for Navaho children at St. Michaels School; he criticized the boarding-school atmosphere as an unrealistic conditioning for equipping young Indians to return as lay apostles to Navaho camp life.[43] Obviously he failed to grasp the full autonomy exercised by the sisters in conducting St. Michaels School.

Chrysostom Theobald was elected provincial at the September, 1903, chapter, and Bernard Nurre, Anselm's close friend, again sat on the definers' board. To St. Michaels were assigned Father Urban Freundt, Frater Norbert Gottbrath, an ailing cleric student, and the cabinet-

[40] *Ibid.*

[41] *Ibid.*, p. 417. Not until later, in 1905, did A. Weber realize for the first time that he had been performing invalid marriages between whites and Indians — according to Arizona law. Several such marriages he reperformed, and all subsequent "interracial" marriages took place across the state line, in New Mexico, usually *sub divo* at the Cow's Head near the Hay Stacks. A. Weber to Provincial Theobald, July 13, 1905, P.A., CL.; see A. Weber, *Sendbote,* 1032–1034, December, 1904; interview with Dr. Wigglesworth, October 30, 1951. This Arizona antimiscegenation law existed as early as 1877 in the territory, and rendered null and void attempted marriages of Caucasians with Negroes, Hindus, Mongolians, Malayans, Indians, and their descendants. In 1942 Indians were eliminated from this proscribed list, and all such previously contracted white-Indian marriages were validated *ab initio* in all respects. 63-107 Ariz. Code, 1939 (1951 Supp.).

[42] *House Chronicle,* p. 54, S.M.C.; the chapter was held late, on September 9 at Mt. Airy, Ohio. *The Provincial Chronicle,* January, 1948, reprint, p. 4.

[43] B. Nurre to A. Weber, August 28, 1903, P.A., BN.

maker, Brother Arnold Holtmann. Brother Arnold was to build altars, benches, and confessional for the new chapel in the friars' mission house.[44] Because of an ailment, however, the young priest, Father Urban, whom Father Anselm impatiently awaited, never left the Gymnasium in Cincinnati where he was teaching.[45]

The same chapter brought many other changes in the West: at Peña Blanca Father Albert Daeger, who arrived the previous summer from Lincoln, Nebraska, was made superior — the fifth friar to hold the position in three years. To Jémez went Juvenal Schnorbus, the cofounder of St. Michaels, as assistant with Florentin Meyers to Barnabas Meyer.[46]

The widening influence of the Navaho mission saw a new expression in Southwestern mission activity when in 1903 the Cincinnati Franciscans accepted the missions of southern New Mexico. Official appointment of Fathers Herbert Brockmann, Eligius Kunkel, and Brother Libor Springob to the Roswell-Carlsbad mission was announced at the chapter. In the previous February Anselm Weber had amazed the Cincinnati friars by forwarding the news of the acceptance of the parish, and of the various appointments to Roswell. Archbishop Bourgade frequently consulted Anselm and enlisted his aid with the Provincial. Such premature divulging of information regarding missions taken over, and of appointments to such missions, was frowned upon by provincial headquarters as serious lese majesty.[47] The Roswell-Carlsbad news was not to have come out until Custos Raphael Hesse on April 21, 1903, accompanied Fathers Herbert, Eligius, and Brother Libor to Roswell. There they found scarcely a handful of Anglos who were Catholics, though Chihuahuita and the Berrendos area were heavily populated by poor Mexican immigrants.[48] Because the Anglo-imposed segregation policy had already fixed the housing pattern, the

[44] *Tabula Definitionis,* 1903, P.A.; A. Weber to Provincial Haverbeck, prechapter requests, September 2, 1903, P.A., HA.; A. Weber to Provincial C. Theobald, July 13, 1904, P.A., SJ. *House Chronicle,* p. 54, S.M.C.

[45] A. Weber to Mother Katharine, September 22, 1903, P.A., SJ.; B. Nurre to A. Weber, September 21, 1903, P.A., BN.

[46] *Tabula Definitionis,* 1903, P.A. On the occasion of the fourth change in superiors at Peña Blanca, Bernard Nurre wondered at the queer impression created in people and Archbishop at the curiously consistent choice of inept rectors and superiors. B. Nurre to A. Weber, July 29, 1902, P.A., BN. Albert Daeger, future Archbishop of Santa Fe, broke the spell; he remained until transferred as superior to Farmington when that parish was taken over in 1910. *Tabula Definitionis,* 1902–1910, P.A.

[47] A. Weber to B. Nurre, February 18, 1903, as recounted in B. Nurre to A. Weber, February 26, 1903, P.A., BN.; also Benedict Haupt to A. Weber, March 24, 1903, P.A., BH.

[48] R. Hesse to A. Weber, May 25, 1903, P.A., RH.

missionaries unthinkingly fell in line and abetted the uneconomic and thoroughly un-Christian institution of racial segregation by founding two separate parishes, one for a dozen Anglos and the other to serve the several hundred Mexican families. Archbishop Bourgade contributed $250 toward this new Franciscan mission.[49]

Father Herbert, the Roswell superior, took charge of the dozen Anglos, offering Mass in the flimsy, false-front bottling works, which looked like a stage prop for a Western movie. He likewise attended the parish at Carlsbad which Bishop Granjon of Tucson had turned over to the new parish as soon as he heard of Archbishop Bourgade's action in Roswell.[50] Previously, since 1898, Fathers Migeon and Giraud had visited the Roswell section of the Tucson Diocese from their parish in Lincoln County.[51]

Father Eligius Kunkel built St. John the Baptist Church close to Chihuahuita, the Mexican quarter. Missions attaching to Roswell and Carlsbad included Hagerman, Elida, Portales, Clovis, and Melrose.[52] Father Raphael Hesse, the custos, tried unsuccessfully in May to interest the Lafayette Franciscan Sisters to accept charges of a Roswell hospital and the contemplated mission school for Mexicans.[53]

Back in the Navaho country it was likewise a problem of new missions. Before definitely asking for another Navaho missionary to substitute for Urban Freundt, who was unable to go West, Father Anselm again visited the San Juan to assure a land site for the long-projected mission along the river. As Frank Walker was spending a few weeks in jail at the time, the friar took along Tom Morgan as interpreter. Charley Mitchell, Chee Dodge, and Naakai Dinae were on the move when Anselm dropped by to invite along one of these headmen, all of whom were highly regarded even outside their regions.[54] Headman Sandoval, Navahowise, was also on the move when the friar reached the river. With only Shoemaker's aid, accordingly, Anselm convened a council on August 21 under the giant cottonwood tree that shaded Adobe's camp.[55]

Shoemaker suggested as a mission site a semi-island, a cottonwood flat of approximately one hundred acres that lay on the south bank

[49] B. Nurre to A. Weber, April 21, 1903, P.A., BN.

[50] Turibius Christman, O.F.M., *F.M.S.*, 1914, p. 11, which contains various photos of the early temporary homes and chapels used for services. See B. Nurre to A. Weber, March 12, 1903, P.A., BN., re Bishop Granjon.

[51] Will Robinson, *F.M.S.*, 1914, p. 4.

[52] T. Christman, *F.M.S.*, 1914, pp. 13, 15.

[53] B. Nurre to A. Weber, May 28, 1903, P.A., BN.

[54] A. Weber, *Sendbote*, 31:502, June, 1904.

[55] A. Weber to Provincial Theobald, July 13, 1904, P.A., SJ.

of the river some three miles above Fruitland, and about seven and a half miles below Farmington.[56] This "island" had formed when the river cut a new north channel some years before; only in high water did the old south channel carry water and create a real island.[57] Shoemaker himself had intended it as his own agency site until he learned that a new man, Shelton, had been appointed as superintendent of the San Juan government agency, a post Shoemaker had confidently expected to receive.[58] Continuing merely as irrigation foreman under the new appointee, Shoemaker insisted that the mission should have the location before all others since the missionary had been trying for a location since 1899.[59]

In accepted Navaho-white procedure, the Indians chaffered quite suspiciously over the whole affair introduced by Father Anselm at the council — mission, school, loss of firewood and corral stakes — but finally edged around to a favorable view.[60] They admitted that they did want a mission and school, and really did want the *e'nishodi* to help them. When it came to their holding Anselm Weber's hand as he signed their names, they were as delighted as children over making "paper names," and left in fine humor.[61] Tom Morgan, the interpreter, testified that each of the twenty Indians who signed the petition knew clearly what land the paper requested. Back at Shoemaker's house the necessary papers were drawn up, including the Indians request, along with Anselm's application and Shoemaker's endorsement for the west half of the southwest quarter of section 17, township 29 north, range 14, west of the New Mexico Meridian.[62] In his endorsement Shoemaker called attention to the fact that the Navaho "were more cordial and gracious in granting this land and their good will than it has been my portion to witness."[63] In a subsequent letter to the Commissioner

56 A. Weber to Mrs. L. W. Drexel, pencil draft, n.d. (October, 1903), P.A., SJ.; A. Weber to W. Ketcham, August 21, 1903, P.A., SJ.

57 Survey plat of sections 17 and 18, township 29 north, range 14 west, P.A., SJ.; sketch of San Juan Island, 10051, 1903, B.I.A., SC 143.

58 A. Weber to W. Ketcham, August 21, 1903, P.A., SJ.

59 A. Weber to L. Haverbeck, September 2, 1903; H.A.C.; S.E. Shoemaker to A. Weber, October 7, 1903, H.A.C.

60 A. Weber, *Sendbote,* 31:502, June, 1904.

61 *Ibid.*

62 A. Weber, Thomas Morgan, and Julian Badaani, in Land Application, August 21, 1903, 55498, 1903, Enclosure, 2, B.I.A., SC 143. The original application erroneously described the site on township 29 north, range 15, as misnumbered on George Butler's irrigation map. This was corrected by Mr. Lusk at the request of A. Weber. A. Weber to Chas. Lusk, August 1, 1904, H.A.C.

63 S. Shoemaker to Commissioner of Indian Affairs, August 22, 1903, 84419, 1903, Enclosure 3, B.I.A., SC 143.

of Indian Affairs, Mr. Shoemaker lauded Father Anselm's unceasing labor for the welfare of the Navaho, and of their close friendship with him.[64] After approval by the Department of the Interior, Mr. Shoemaker officially set aside the island for mission purposes, December 1, 1903.[65]

Father Berard Haile who had been seeking direct missionary work, and who had volunteered in 1903 to begin a Navaho-Hispano mission at Nacimiento, was chosen to take over the San Juan Mission. When Father Berard rode to the island to begin work in April of 1904, Mr. Shelton, the new bonded Superintendent of the northern Navaho agency, challenged the priest's authority to use the approved island mission site.[66] Berard was forced to make the long ride back to St. Michaels to procure the official document of approval. Shelton was still not satisfied; he contested now the right of Mr. Shoemaker to endorse the land selection. After Berard telegraphed his curious stalemate to authorities in Washington, the Indian Commissioner quickly set matters right by directing Shelton to cease his interference.[67]

Father Berard and Frank Walker began immediately to direct operations on a brush and stone revetment to block off the old dry southern channel.[68] This was laid down in an effort to stave off a return of the river to its old channel.

The missionary had rented an Indian hut near Kirtland for $1.50 per month, and planned to begin direct missionary work, and teach day school as well, after erecting a few rooms on the island. Eventually Sisters were to take over the teaching.[69]

After a time the Indians grew disgruntled over the idea of a day school, and were complaining over the absence of free food and clothes. More than complain, one of the Mormon settlers on the opposite bank threw up a diversion dam which completely washed out Berard's revetment and levee.[70] Returning toward the end of May to St.

[64] October 4, 1903, 65787, 1903, Enclosure, B.I.A., SC 143.

[65] S. E. Shoemaker, land transfer, copy, December 1, 1903, H.A.C.; land approval, November 4, 1903, Land, 84419, 1903, copy, P.A., SJ.

[66] A. Weber to Provincial C. Theobald, July 13, 1904, H.A.C.; A. Weber to Mrs. J. W. Drexel, April 25, 1904, H.A.C.

[67] B. Haile to A. Weber, April 21 and 23, 1904, P.A., BH.; A. Weber, *Sendbote,* 31:589–590, July, 1904.

[68] B. Haile to A. Weber, April 27, May 1, 1904, P.A., BH.

[69] A. Weber to Mrs. J. W. Drexel, March 31, 1904, and A. Weber to Mother Katharine, April 25, 1904, H.A.C.; B. Haile to A. Weber, May 1 and 6, 1904, P.A., BH.; A. Weber, *Sendbote,* 31:590–591, July, 1904.

[70] B. Haile to A. Weber, August 3, 1904, P.A., BH.; B. Haile, interview, September 7, 1949.

Michaels, the San Juan missionary explained the difficulties and expressed chagrin that he could have no sizable fund to begin building operations in earnest on a new and safer site.[71] Mother Katharine, it was true, had offered $500,[72] and her aunt, Mrs. Joseph Whorton Drexel, had pledged $600 annually on condition the mission would operate a day school "so pupils can still be with the parents whom God has given them."[73]

With the San Juan Indians, however, objections to a "mere" day school proved serious at the subsequent council held on the river. Father Anselm, who was also present, agreed with Berard that building of a mission and some kind of a small school would have to begin immediately if the land site was to be held.[74] At this point in the developments several settlers on the north bank brought out claims showing that their homestead entries and deeds embraced part of the "mission" land before the river channel had changed and formed the island.[75] By law the entries based on the original 1882 surveys held. The executive order of April 24, 1886, returning to the reservation an eighteen-mile strip along the south bank of the river, was based on the survey maps of 1882. Since the 1882 lines followed the old river channel, before the island was formed, the mission site belonged to the settlers north of the river and was obviously not on reservation land.[76] Nothing remained but to abandon the San Juan site for the present. Financial stringencies, a constant condition at St. Michaels, would allow no realistic thought of purchasing a mission location,

71 A. Weber to Provincial C. Theobald, July 13, 1904; H.A.C.; B. Haile to A. Weber, May 1, 1904, P.A., BH.

72 Mother Katharine to A. Weber, May 14, 1904, H.A.C.

73 Mrs. J. W. Drexel to A. Weber, July 1, 1903, P.A., SJ.; see also *Annals,* 6:83–84, C.H.A.

74 B. Haile to A. Weber, August 3, 1904, P.A., SJ.; A. Weber to Provincial C. Theobald, July 13, 1904, H.A.C.

75 *Ibid.*

76 Acting Commissioner A. C. Tonner to Chas. Lusk, October 10, 1904, P.A., SJ. The San Juan Mission site belonged to the much controverted south-bank river strip running through township 29 north, ranges 14, 15, and 16 west of the New Mexico Meridian. These excellent bottoms had been restored to the reservation January 6, 1880, reopened again to public entry May 17, 1884, and after a near Navaho outbreak had been returned again to the Navaho on April 24, 1886. After removal by troops of the William P. Hendrickson family in 1887, he had moved to section 17 of the next township west, namely to township 29 north, range 14. Part of his pre-emption claim, canceled by the Land Office in 1888, overlapped the mission claim. Fred Miller, Land Office, Santa Fe, to A. Weber, November 18, 1904, and including copy of official plat, P.A., SJ.; A. Weber to Chas. Lusk, August 1, 15, and October 16, 1904, H.A.C. For the details of the Navaho-white land struggle along the San Juan, and the facts on the Hendrickson case, see Frank D. Reeve, "A Navaho Struggle for Land," *N.M.H.R.,* 21:1–21, January, 1946.

although for a time outright purchase of an irrigated site, and the construction of a small day school, hovered as a dream.

Old Melania Dulzo, however, again changed her mind regarding the $6,000 she had agreed to turn over as a trust fund to the Indian missions. Melania Dulzo, Father Tilik's former housekeeper, and close friend of Anselm, had accepted the invitation to set up a trust fund for a day school at Jémez, a project dear to Anselm, Barnabas Meyer, and Archbishop Bourgade.[77] With the failure of the San Juan Island Mission, Anselm had hoped to induce Miss Dulzo to transfer the $6,000 trust to the San Juan project where he as her personal friend would be enabled to purchase land and erect buildings which would come directly under his supervision. However, she wished to retain her principal as security against illness and old age so Father Anselm, in order to compensate Barnabas Meyer for his disappointment in not obtaining the trust fund for Jémez, generously turned over the $600 annuity of Mrs. Drexel to advance the Jémez day school.[78]

As a result no funds were available for the San Juan. Subsequent offers of the Office of Indian Affairs, relayed through Mr. Shoemaker, to allow selection of a new San Juan site on reservation land, could not be acted upon.[79] The San Juan Mission was to remain a simple hope until 1910.

Anselm had counted so heavily on the success of the San Juan Mission that both his health and his morale were at a low ebb when he returned unsuccessful and frustrated from the island venture. Stymied at every turn by finances in his mission and day-school efforts at Chin Lee and on the San Juan, with Indian parents grumbling ominously over the six pupils who had died during the school term at St. Michaels, and with some of the good brethren calling the

[77] B. Meyer to A. Weber, July 29, August 23, 1902; June 8, 1903; February 17, August 4, 1905; May 20, 1906, P.A., BM.; M. Dulzo to A. Weber, with three undated enclosures, in Archbishop Bourgade to A. Weber, February 14, 1904, P.A., HA.

[78] A. Weber to B. Haile, February 14, 1904, P.A., SJ.; A. Weber to W. Ketcham, February 2, 1905, C.I.B.A.

[79] S. E. Shoemaker to A. Weber, November 5, 1904, and January 11, 1905, P.A., SJ. History added a striking commentary on the disappointing efforts of Anselm Weber to obtain either the mission site selected by the Methodists opposite the King Ranch, or the "island" opposite Kirtland. Both suffered disaster in the San Juan flood of October 6, 1911, which washed away all buildings of the Methodist mission and school. The new mission was built on high ground on the north bank, some two miles below Farmington. *Farmington Enterprise,* October 13, 1911, cited in P. G. Malehorn, *The Tender Plant,* pp. 34–39, 125–128. The island above Fruitland disappeared completely in the flood. B. Haile, in B.C.I.M., *The Indian Sentinel,* 1:27, April, 1918.

Navaho mission a farce — Anselm needed sorely the sound priestly advice and warm encouragement lent him at this crisis by his good friend, Father Bernard Nurre.[80] After six strenuous years he had reached the trying stage in the growth of a missionary personality where adolescent missionary idealism and immediacy must compromise and adjust focus to reality and to long-term, almost indefinite, mission planning.

Within the next two or three years he had analyzed the metamorphosis in the missionary personality, and could then objectively express his own and Father Leopold's personal experience:[81]

> Enthusiastic reformers . . . and such as expect recognition and visible results, have long since quit this field in chagrin. As I see it, one needs here not so much an ardent enthusiasm as intelligent and enduring interest, patience, and faith in God's watchful care and all-powerful grace. . . . If one can judge the worthwhileness of a cause by its difficulties and its enemies' persistence, then surely the conversion of the Indians to our Faith is in the forefront.

On graduation day at St. Michaels, August 25, 1904, while still hoping to prove the validity of his San Juan Island claim, Anselm exacted a promise from the Indian parents to bring back their children fifty-four days later. Mounted behind their parents, or on spare mounts or crowded into wagons, the children were squealing with joy to be off home to the mountains and the mesa grazing lands, to the summer camps and the fresh roasting ears and melons. Fifty-four days later, on October 18, only fifty of the seventy-six pupils returned; within the following weeks, however, the stragglers filled out the previous enrollment.[82]

By the time classes were again running smoothly at St. Michaels in late autumn, what Anselm needed most was a change of scene.

[80] B. Nurre to A. Weber, June 17, 1904, P.A., BN.; A. Weber to C. Theobald, July 13, 1904, H.A.C.; C. Theobald to A. Weber, September 13, 1904, P.A., CT. At the end of 1903 already wild rumors were abroad that St. Michaels School was losing its enrollment. See J. G. Walker to A. Weber, December 31, 1903, P.A., WA.

[81] A. Weber, in B.C.I.M., *Indianer Wache,* 1908, p. 25. This is one of his rare commentaries, indirect though it is, on his own personal growth as a missioner. Father Leopold went through a similar period of soul searching and dejection, and would have welcomed a transfer back East at the end of 1905. L. Ostermann to A. Weber, November 9, 1905, P.A., LO.

[82] A. Weber, *Sendbote,* 31:855, October, 1904; *House Chronicle,* pp. 55, 57, S.M.C. Bishop Byrne of Nashville, who had been in Santa Fe for his health, was at St. Michaels for the opening of school in 1904. He came to win support of Mother Katharine for a Negro school in Nashville, and succeeded. Father Juillard also succeeded in inducing Mother Katharine on this occasion to repair and reface Ácoma's fortress church. A. Weber, *Sendbote,* 32:24, January, 1905.

He left in November for an extended "missionary vacation" that took him first to Albuquerque for a conference with Barnabas Meyer concerning the Jémez day school and a discussion with Father Mandalari, S.J., concerning religious instructions at the Albuquerque Indian School. At Peña Blanca he conducted the annual retreat for the friars, repeating this in Kansas City, Missouri. En route there he stopped off at Topeka for a long visit with Howell Jones, Land Commissioner for the Atchison, Topeka, and Santa Fe Railway, a visit which initiated a lifelong friendship and established a working basis for Anselm's future extensive land transactions on behalf of the Indians.[83]

While Berard and Leopold were to find "missionary hobbies" in ethnology and linguistic studies, and Marcellus Troester in developing a Navaho census, Anselm centered his energies over and beyond direct spiritual administration into socio-economic channels, particularly the land problem of the Navaho. In such secular activities which directly aided the Indians or the missions they were to find the immediate compensations needed to answer vicariously their need for visible achievement and success throughout the frustrations of a long-term mission objective.

At Lafayette, Indiana, Father Anselm induced the superioress of the Franciscan Sisters to send teachers to take over the district public schools around Peña Blanca and the projected mission day school at Jémez.[84] After visiting a few days in Cincinnati and in Hamilton, Ohio, where he saw again his sister Gertrude and her growing family, as well as Father Leopold's relatives, he continued on to Washington, D. C. It was his first of more than a dozen future visits to the capital in behalf of the Navaho.

While there in late January and early February, 1905, he met Indian Commissioner Francis E. Leupp and President Theodore Roosevelt, for whom as a stanch Republican he had great regard. Territorial Representative Rodey of New Mexico introduced Father Anselm to the President who charmed the missioner by commending him for his well-known work among the Navaho.[85] Another strong administration man, J. L. Hubbell, had forearmed Anselm with a letter of introduction to Leupp, which, together with Father William Ketcham's personal introduction, proved to be an "Open Sesame" to the various executive departments.[86]

[83] A. Weber, *Sendbote,* 32:229, March, 1905.
[84] A. Weber, *Sendbote,* 32:230, March, 1905.
[85] *Ibid.,* p. 498.
[86] Dated January, n.d., 1905, B.I.A.L.R., 49710, 1905; A. Weber, *Sendbote,* 32:498–499, June, 1905.

Leupp willingly gave his consent for religious instructions to be given in government schools in the Navaho language, a procedure contrary to departmental regulations. He also encouraged Anselm's hopes for a strong Navaho farming community — not on the distant San Juan, but just across the ridge from St. Michaels, in Black Creek Valley, where the department planned a broad irrigation dam. Moreover, Leupp definitely decided the missioner on building a mission day school at Chin Lee since the commissioner gave assurance that there would be no government boarding school there; his new policy was to keep parents, teachers, and children together in their native environment.[87] Mr. Hinton, who headed the irrigation works division in the Office of Indian Affairs, Father Anselm also visited, promoting Navaho irrigation developments on the reservation. Estelle Reel, superintendent of Indian Education, was an old acquaintance; she had met the missioner previously while visiting St. Michaels School.[88]

At the Bureau of Ethnology Anselm Weber met Washington Matthews, Stewart Culin, and Charles F. Lummis, who was editor of *Out West* and promotor of California, its missions, and all things Indian. Lummis created quite a sensation when the group went out to dinner. He was dressed as a frontiersman, in brown corduroy with a Spanish don's wide red sash. In lighting the after-dinner cigars he insisted on using his Indian flint and tinder.[89]

From Washington Anselm made side trips to Baltimore to visit Cardinal Gibbons, president of the Bureau of Catholic Indian Missions, and Father Dyer, the treasurer; in Philadelphia he met with Archbishop Ryan, a member of the Board of Indian Commissioners, and a stanch friend of Mother Katharine and the Indian missions.[90] While in Philadelphia on February 1, he and Josephine Drexel Emmet, the former Miss Josephine, easily prevailed on Mrs. Joseph Whorton Drexel to transfer her $600 annuity from the San Juan to the Jémez day school.[91]

It was during his stay in Washington, only a day or two after visiting at the White House, that President Roosevelt and Commissioner Leupp were accused of surreptitiously reintroducing contract schools in favor of Catholic Indian missions. Senator Bard of California and S. M. Brosius of the Indian Rights Association testified before the Senate Committee on Indian Affairs against the Roosevelt-

87 *Ibid.*, p. 500.
88 *Ibid.*
89 *Ibid.*, pp. 502–504.
90 A. Weber, *ibid.*, 32:325–326, April, 1905.
91 A. Weber to W. Ketcham, February 2, 1905, C.I.B.A.

approved practice of conducting nine Catholic and one Lutheran mission schools with Indian treaty funds which were under government administration.[92] Under the aegis of the Indian Rights Association which opposed such tribal and trust fund contract schools, the case was eventually brought before the Supreme Court in an effort to enjoin the practice.[93]

In *Quick Bear vs. Leupp*, 1908, the use of such funds was vindicated on the score that both Indian treaty and trust funds, while administered by the Treasury Department, belong to, and could be applied by, Indian parents for education of their children in the schools of their choice.[94]

From Washington and the debate over trust and treaty funds, Anselm on February 8 left for New York and a meeting with the director of the newly founded Marquette League.[95] The year before, in April, 1904, Reverend H. G. Ganss had organized this lay organization for Indian missions under the auspices of the New York St. Vincent de Paul Society, with the aim of broadening the effectiveness of the Bureau of Catholic Indian Missions.[96] The circular of the new organization had stressed aid to missionaries in the field, especially in founding schools and missions for Indians. After quoting one of their expansively worded circulars, Anselm continues in the *Sendbote*:[97] "I rushed to New York hoping to get funds for at least the one chapel at Chin Lee." Somewhat ruefully, and yet with a twinkle, he added slyly that he drew a blank, although he was given a small donation and did enjoy the close attention paid to his analysis of Navaho mission planning:[98]

> To civilize and Christianize a nomadic people is in its very nature an extremely hard task. It is simply impossible to reach all Navajos from our one mission. If we are to do justice to our mission to the Navajos we need at a minimum four central missions with resident priests, chapels, and schools with mission stations thrown out wherever the

[92] *New York Times,* February 1, 2, 1905; *The Washington Post,* February 2, 1905. See I.R.A., *Annual Report,* 1905, which gives the pertinent texts covering the entire mission school contract controversy, with stress on the 1905 issue, pp. 6–21 and 48–53.

[93] A. Weber, *Sendbote,* 32:502–504, June, 1905; 33:1084–1088, December, 1906; 35:886–892, October, 1908.

[94] 210 U. S., 80–81 (1908); Schmeckebier, *The Office of Indian Affairs,* p. 213.

[95] A. Weber to W. Ketcham, February 8, 1905, C.I.B.A.

[96] W. H. Ketcham, *Report of the Director of the Bureau of Catholic Indian Missions* for 1904–1905, Washington, n.d.; Marquette League, *Constitution and By-Laws* (New York, 1904), pp. 4–5.

[97] 32:793, September, 1905.

[98] *Ibid.*, p. 794.

government opens any sizable irrigation project. I intend erecting a second mission in the Chin Lee valley . . . because of its central location. and because the government is planning there a huge irrigation system sufficient to provide good land for about 400 Navajo families. . . . We already have a site in this locality and have readied an old stone and log trading post to serve as chapel and residence. . . . Without doubt the Catholic Indian school must serve as the foundation for Christianizing the Indian; if this beginning is to broaden and continue, however, the apostolate must spread afield. We labor among the American Bedouin, a people of strange tongue, moving in a vast country.

If the Catholic missionary effort is to beget radical, lasting change (as the government schools have not) we must help the graduates of our schools to secure decent homes on irrigated lands where in community life they may have an opportunity themselves to live the Christian life and aid us in Christianizing and civilizing their relatives and clansmen.

From New York City he traveled on to St. Bonaventure College, and on to Buffalo, Chatham, Ontario, and Detroit, where he visited Melania Dulzo and discussed the $6,000 trust fund which never materialized. A final visit of several days with his brothers and relatives at New Salem and Byron Center, Michigan, his first since 1898, completed his itinerary.[99]

En route back to the Southwest Anselm paid a special visit to Haskell Indian Institute at Lawrence, Kansas, at the request of Father Ketcham. Here he thoroughly investigated the charges of anti-Catholicism as preferred by the chaplain and town pastor, reporting that tactlessness was as much a factor in the antagonism as anything else. Anselm later gave Ketcham hope that the Cincinnati friars would accept the parish and chaplaincy. The friars, however, did not accept the Haskell charge.[100]

With a renewed spirit and with a deep new conviction that home was now St. Michaels, Anselm Weber returned to carry on the mission plan to which distance, intent lecture audiences, and thoughtful discussion had lent new perspective and significance. The mission treasury was in better condition by $900 as a result of his vacation and the series of stereopticon lectures he had given on the missions.[101]

While Anselm was away from St. Michaels, Father Herculan Zeug, who had been assigned to the mission only the previous summer, and

[99] Itinerary mentioned in A. Weber to W. Ketcham, February 8, 1905, C.I.B.A.; A. Weber, *Sendbote,* 32:990–991, October, 1905.

[100] A. Weber to W. Ketcham, May 27, December 7, 1905, C.I.B.A.; W. Ketcham to A. Weber, November 21, 1905, C.I.B.A.

[101] See p. 113.

Frater Norbert Gottbrath had been transferred, the former to Kansas City, Missouri, and the cleric to complete his studies for the priesthood at Oldenburg, Indiana.[102]

Owing largely to Father Anselm's visit in the East, the Jémez day school, as well as the Chin Lee Mission, was shortly under way. In point both of time and financial sequence, the Jémez day school was the fulfillment of a plan that focused successively on Ganado, Chin Lee, the San Juan, and finally centered in the pueblo of the Jémez Indians on the eastern border of the Navaho country. Vicariously at least, Anselm would have an Indian day school, and the $600 annual grant of Mrs. Joseph Drexel would not go by the board. Typical of his mission outlook — poor though St. Michaels was — Anselm channeled his one secure expansion asset to a closely organized community such as Jémez, where a day school could best succeed.

Archbishop Bourgade selected at Jémez a location for the school opposite the friars' *convento,* with the intention of eventually transferring the pueblo church to the same vicinity along the Jémez River.[103] A few days after the Archbishop's visit Father Barnabas Meyer, on the first Monday in August, began excavations for the two-story adobe school and Sisters' convent. This was completed the next summer with the assistance of $400 from Mrs. Joseph Drexel, and with practically all labor done by the Brothers and priests.[104]

Three Lafayette Franciscan Sisters arrived in Bernalillo on September 22 and left by mule team on the jolting, eleven-hour trip to Jémez.[105] Classes began on October 1, 1906, with twenty-five pupils, about the same number as were enrolled in the government school, originally a Presbyterian contract school dating from 1879.[106] Over and above the $350 he had donated to the building of the Jémez day school, Archbishop Bourgade turned over an additional $400 toward the support of the Sisters. He planned a second day school at Santo Domingo Pueblo which consistently had refused to send any children to the Catholic boarding schools at Bernalillo or Santa Fe.[107] Addi-

[102] *House Chronicle,* p. 56, S.M.C.

[103] B. Meyer to A. Weber, August 4, 1905, P.A., BM.

[104] B. Meyer to A. Weber, May 20, June 27, 1906, P.A., BM.

[105] Fridolin Schuster, O.F.M., *F.M.S.,* 1913, p. 25; A. Weber to W. Ketcham, September 23, 1906, C.I.B.A.

[106] B. Meyer, *per* Florentin Meyers, to W. Ketcham, August 12, 1907, C.I.B.A.; Dr. Dorchester, Superintendent of Indian Schools, Report, May 23, 1893, C.I.B.A.

[107] Archbishop Bourgade to W. Ketcham, October 14, 1906, C.I.B.A.; Sister M. Mathia, Principal at Jémez, to W. Ketcham, Annual Report to the Bureau of Catholic Indian Missions, 1907. The Bernalillo Indian School was conducted by the Loretto Sisters and was supported after federal contracts ended (1901) by the Bureau which

tional support for Jémez school derived from the dollar per month tuition for each Hispano pupil whom the Sisters taught in classes separate from the Indian children.[108]

Father Anselm while at Lafayette, Indiana, in September of 1907 obtained permission from the Franciscan Sister Superior to allow the Jémez Sisters to take civil service examinations as a prelude to having the mission school named the official government Indian school.[109] Although Sisters Mathia and Ursulina failed to pass the teachers' civil service examination, it was possible nonetheless to have the Sisters "covered into" the Indian Service as classified teachers, and placed on federal salary for the school term 1908–1909 and thereafter.[110] As a result religious instructions were given in chapel every morning before classes took up. With the teachers' support now provided by federal salaries, there was considerable easing of the mission's financial burden in feeding and clothing the Indian pupils.[111] In 1910 the cook Sister, too, was placed on government salary under the title of "housekeeper."[112]

This situation, somewhat anomalous in view of the 1897 legislation, which purported to terminate all federal aid to sectarian schools, led in part to Commissioner Robert G. Valentine's "Religious Garb Order" of January 12, 1912, which denied further federal employment to persons wearing distinctive religious garb, and banned all religious symbols from government Indian schools. President Taft by executive order, September 23, 1912, stayed action on Valentine's order, and permitted those already "covered into" the federal Indian Service to remain; no new members of religious communities, however, could be added in the future.[113]

---

donated $756 per quarter for some sixty-three pupils. W. Ketcham to Sister Margaret Mary, January 26, 1901, C.I.B.A.; Report of Sister Margaret Mary to Bureau, May 4, 1901, C.I.B.A. Archbishop Bourgade would have preferred to use these Bureau funds for mission day schools instead of boarding schools. W. Ketcham to Mother Katharine, March 9, 1906, C.I.B.A.

108 B. Meyer to W. Ketcham, December 16, 1907, C.I.B.A.

109 A. Weber to W. Ketcham, September 18, 1907, C.I.B.A.

110 B. Meyer to W. Ketcham, October 19, December 6, 16, 1907, C.I.B.A.

111 W. Ketcham to B. Meyer, December 12, 1907, C.I.B.A.

112 B. Meyer to W. Ketcham, September 16, 1907, C.I.B.A., explaining the cost of the daily lunch and the two suits of clothes given the pupils yearly; W. Ketcham to B. Meyer, February 5, 1910, C.I.B.A.; F. Schuster, *F.M.S.*, 1913, pp. 26–27.

113 Commissioner of Indian Affairs, Circular No. 601, *Religious Insignia*, Washington, January 27, 1912. Complete texts of Valentine's order, its countermand by Secretary of the Interior Walter L. Fisher, and the decision of President Taft, all in *The Catholic Telegraph*, Cincinnati, October 10, 1912. The matter of federal funds for Indian education in sectarian schools was definitely prohibited by law, March 2, 1917. 39 U. S. Stats., 988.

Though in an altered version, the Jémez day school represented Anselm Weber's early and continuous effort to establish a Navaho mission in the Jémez country. Already in the eighteenth century the early friar missionaries stationed at Jémez had followed the trail westward from Jémez Canyon, throwing out their mission outposts in the "province of Navajoo" in the Cabezon-Torreon region.[114] Anselm, likewise, in 1902 and earlier had laid his plans for stationing a friar at the Jémez *convento* with the avowed purpose of an eventual mission home near Cabezon. Father Berard had personally inspected the eastern Navaho mission project in 1903, and had preferred Nacimiento (Cuba), to the north, as the likelier location.[115]

Nacimiento by 1902 had become a regular mission station in the Jémez circuit, but never a center for Navaho expansion. When Anselm Weber accompanied Father Barnabas to aid the Nacimiento Hispano farmers in securing land allotments in 1903, he had his opportunity to check the Catholicity of the Navaho in that area who had been baptized earlier under Archbishop Salpointe. A few questions convinced him of the futility of giving the Sacrament of Baptism with no future organized program of instructions.[116]

Nacimiento, to round out the story, became an autonomous parish under Camillus Fangmann, O.F.M., in 1916, the same year in which the Lafayette Sisters took over the district public school. The "convento," as the natives called the huge, boxlike adobe school and Sisters' home, was begun in 1912, one year after the dedication by Father Barnabas of the adobe Nacimiento Immaculate Conception Church. With an $800 donation from St. John the Baptist Province, and with months of backbreaking work on the part of priests and Brothers, the school still remained unfinished in 1920.[117]

The other leg of the projected St. Michaels-Jémez-San Juan tripod of Navaho missions did finally materialize in 1910 when Archbishop J. B. Pitaval turned over the Las Animas-San Juan parish to the friars.[118] Here again, while Navaho and Jicarilla Indian missions were

[114] Fathers Delgado, Yrigoyen, and Toledo to Commissary Fogueras, July 11, 1746, in Hackett, *op. cit.*, Vol. 3, pp. 421–422.

[115] Barnabas Meyer, answer to questionnaire on the Cabezon-Nacimiento Navaho mission plan, May 14, 1951, P.A., CP. Father Barnabas had carried on considerable correspondence with A. Weber on this project in 1902–1904. Letters of A. Weber were destroyed. *Ibid.*

[116] A. Weber, *Sendbote,* 31:125–126, February, 1904.

[117] "Editorial Review," *F.M.S.,* 1918, pp. 50–51; *ibid.,* 1920, pp. 11–13; Camillus Fangmann to A. Weber, January 23, 1916, P.A., PB.

[118] Archbishop Bourgade to A. Weber, December 31, 1901, H.A.C. The transfer of the San Juan parish was cleared through Anselm Weber. Archbishop Pitaval to A.

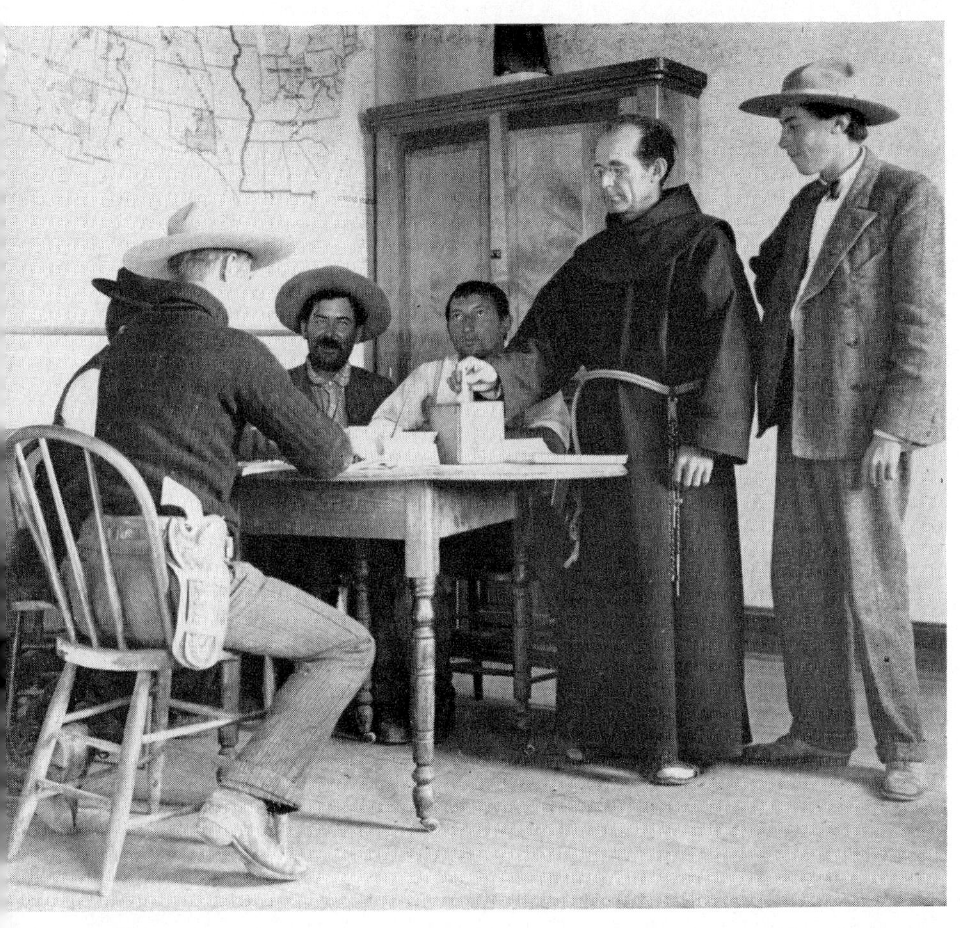

The township went dry. Sammy Day with Colt, Frank Walker, Brother Simeon, Father Anselm, and Dan Mitchell introducing an old United States tradition

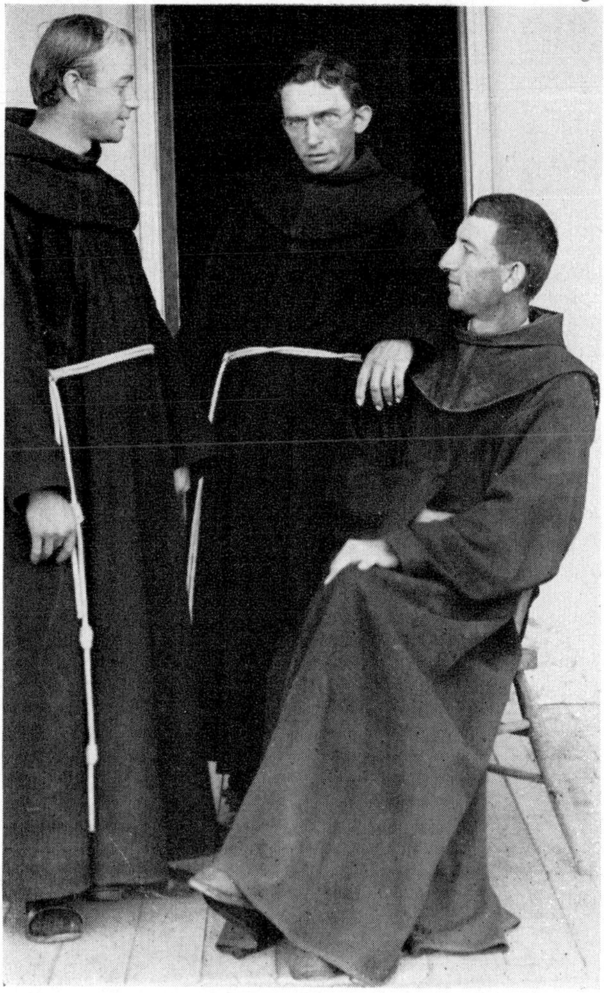

Fathers Egbert Fischer, Berard Haile, and Marcellus Troester, 1911

Old Silversmith

essentially the motive in the transfer, no organized mission work for Indians was initiated from the new headquarters erected at Farmington.[119] The Archbishop had advisedly asked that Father Berard Haile take charge of the Indian phase of the parish work, and Provincial Eugene Buttermann intended to send Marcellus Troester as assistant to Berard.[120] Father Marcellus with four years of active Navaho experience was appointed to Farmington, but difficulties in replacing him at Chin Lee led to the substitution of Fintan Zumbahlen.[121] Father Fintan had also been in Navaho work at St. Michaels School since 1905, but both circumstances and temperament led him to undertake the establishment of a Farmington parish school, which he taught, rather than attempt mission work with the Navaho of the San Juan country.[122]

Albert Daeger, who had become seriously ill at Peña Blanca and needed a change of climate, was elected instead of Berard Haile to take charge of the Farmington parish. He personally preferred to care for the twelve missions attached to the parish rather than to remain at Farmington headquarters. By narrow-gauge rail, but mostly on foot, he traveled constantly, visiting and ministering to the Hispano, Anglo, and Slavic missions that stretched from Largo to Monero.[123]

Along with the Lumberton missions, which were separated from the Farmington parish in 1915, were included the Jicarilla Apache Indians whose reservation headquarters adjoined Lumberton.[124] Albert Daeger had baptized some Jicarillas while on his frequent visits through their territory, and after the division of Lumberton from Farmington, Felician Sandford and Egbert Fischer had tried to start a mission among the Jicarillas. Effective work, however, was hampered by conditions at the Dulce Indian Agency, where another denomination was already in charge. Nothing of permanent consequence in the way

---

Weber, February 14, March 5, 1910; E. Buttermann to J. B. Pitaval, March 2, 1910, and E. Buttermann to A. Weber, March 2, 1910; these and other pertinent letters, P.A., FP.

[119] A. Weber to W. Ketcham, February 14, 1910, P.A., LM.; F. Zumbahlen to A. Weber, September 26, December 12, 1910, P.A., FP.

[120] J. B. Pitaval to A. Weber, February 14, 1910, and E. Buttermann to A. Weber, March 2, 1910, P.A., FP.

[121] *Tabula Definitionis,* 1910, P.A.; A. Weber to E. Buttermann, August 9, 1910, P.A., CI.

[122] F. Zumbahlen to A. Weber, September 26, 1910, P.A., FP.

[123] E. Buttermann to A. Weber, September 23, 1910, P.A., CL.; *F.M.S.,* 1913, pp. 35–36.

[124] J. B. Pitaval to A. Weber, January 31, 1912, and A. Weber to E. Buttermann, August 27, 1910, P.A., FP.

of a Jicarilla foundation was accomplished here, though for a time infants and several adults were baptized.[125]

From Lumberton the friars extended their pastoral charge over the deeply religious parish of Park View, New Mexico. Father Turibius Christman was called in March of 1916 to administer the Last Sacraments to Father Cazals at Durango where the Park View pastor had been visiting. Father Turibius continued to administer the Park View parish of San José until January, 1917, when he was appointed pastor.[126]

Until 1883 when Michael Rolly had been appointed pastor of Park View, this parish along the Chama River had been attended by Father Courbon out of El Rito. Rolly had remained but one year, and was succeeded by Ignatius M. Grom who stayed until 1890 when Joseph Gourcy had been appointed. From 1894 until 1906 Padre Antonio Jouvenceau cared for the huge parish which at that time included practically all of Rio Arriba and San Juan Counties in New Mexico, and a part of Archuleta County, Colorado. When the Franciscans had turned down the proposed San Juan parish in 1900, Padre Antonio Jouvenceau had enlisted the help of Father Garnier who in 1902 made Blanco his headquarters for a San Juan parish.[127]

In many ways it was significantly symbolic of the difficulties of Navaho mission work that — when the cycle had run full turn, and the Franciscans had officially taken over the "old Navaho country" extending roughly from Largo Cañon to the Chama River[128] — no single Indian mission had been planted in that vast territory which Father Anselm and Padre Antonio Jouvenceau had underscored as "the Navaho country."[129]

[125] See A. Daeger to A. Weber, 1910–1914; F. Sandford to A. Weber, 1914–1916; E. Fischer to A. Weber, 1916–1917, all in P.A., FP.

[126] T. Christman to Celestin Matz, November 25, 1918, P.A., FP.; *F.M.S.,* 1918, p. 53; Ubald Schwetchenau, O.F.M., *F.M.S.,* 1919, pp. 30–31; Father Turibius Christman succeeded in bringing in the Oldenburg, Indiana, Franciscan Sisters who came to take over the district schools in 1918 as salaried public school teachers. Introduction of the Sisters was accomplished without dissent at a time when the local male teachers were being drafted into the army. Turibius Christman, interview, February 27, 1951.

[127] Parish Records of St. Joseph Church, Park View, New Mexico; Ubald Schwetchenau, *ibid.* See pp. 56–57.

[128] A. Weber to E. Buttermann, August 27, 1910, P.A., FP.

[129] A. Weber to C. Theobald, July 13, 1904, P.A., SJ.

Chapter X

Attempted Hopi Mission

On the occasion of Bishop Granjon's first visit to St. Michaels Mission in 1904, he spent twelve days from August 12 to 24 visiting the Hopi villages. Since Father Leopold was on his Chin Lee mission circuit at the time, and Father Berard was still on the San Juan, Anselm Weber arranged for Frater Norbert Gottbrath, the tubercular theological student, to accompany the Bishop of Tucson. On his return the Bishop suggested that the pueblo-dwelling Hopi would offer a more responsive mission field than the free-roaming Navaho. Father Anselm argued against the view, since he felt convinced from previous exploratory trips that the Hopi were atavistic in their militant paganism.[1]

This resistance to Christian missionaries grew from social, rather than religious, roots. Chauvinistic to an almost fantastic degree, the Hopis simply wanted no communication with whites — missionaries, government agents, teachers, or anyone else who might interfere with the tight native culture pattern of the Hopi community. Force as in early Spanish days had been resorted to in 1899 by the federal government to enforce sanitary measures and school attendance.[2]

[1] *House Chronicle,* p. 55; A. Weber, *Sendbote,* 31:856, October, 1904. The Hopi Indians from early Spanish days had been hostile to Christian missionaries. They killed Friar Martin de Arvide in 1632 and Francisco de San Buenaventura in 1633; in 1680 during the great Pueblo Indian revolt four other Franciscan missionaries were murdered on August 10: José de Figueroa of Aguatuvi, José Trujillo of Jongopabi, and José de Espeleta at Oraibi by a Hopi, and Augustin de Santa Maria en route to Zuñi by a Zuñi Indian. No permanent Catholic missions were re-established among the Hopi after the revolt of 1680, though at various times Franciscans from New Mexico visited among the villages and attempted to reopen the missions. Distance complicated the Hopi mission problem. Maynard Geiger, *The Kingdom of St. Francis in Arizona* (Santa Barbara, Calif., 1939), pp. 10–12; Bonaventure Oblasser, "The Franciscans in the Spanish Southwest," *The Franciscan Educational Conference,* 18:107, December, 1936; Marian Habig, "The Franciscan Martyrs of North America," *ibid.,* 18:286–289, 297.

[2] See pp. 52–53.

Through the intervening years until 1905 the passive resistance technique of the Hopi had met with continuous governmental pressure to induce Hopi parents to send their children to school.[3]

Hence Father Anselm was thoroughly skeptical as to possible missionary success among these Arizona Pueblo Indians when he received the surprise information that the Franciscans of Cincinnati had accepted the Hopi mission.[4] An earlier request from Bishop Granjon as to possible costs to support a "small beginning among the Moqui" Anselm had interpreted as a preliminary survey and canvass, preparatory to a request for missionaries from the St. Louis Province of Franciscans who were already at work among the Papago and Pima of southern Arizona.[5]

Provincial Chrysostom Theobald suggested to Anselm that he try to educate a few Hopi children at St. Michaels School as an opening wedge. Mother Katharine approved the plan so long as Father Anselm did not fear open antagonism from the Navaho children, who shared a traditional contempt for the sedentary, peaceful Hopi.[6] To expect anything approaching a Hopi invitation, or even tolerance, to the opening of a mission Father Anselm knew to be folly.[7] The Provincial had informed the Bishop that during 1905 the friars would occasionally visit the Hopi villages, and meanwhile secure a mission site in preparation for the two Fathers who would be missioned at Hopi in 1906.[8]

Bishop Granjon was known to be highly enthusiastic over the project, as he similarly was over the restoration of San Xavier del Bac.[9] Within two months after St. John the Baptist Province had accepted the Hopi mission, the Bishop could report pledges of $4,000 toward its opening: $2,000 for the building and $1,000 toward the first year's support of the friars; the Marquette League added $1,000 on condition that the chapel be named after the Blessed Virgin's Annunciation.[10] Without doubt the Hopi mission had surer financial backing than any of the other missions under consideration at St. Michaels.

[3] Belle Axtell Kolp, in *Out West,* 19:47–55, July, 1903.

[4] A. Weber to C. Theobald, July 25, 1905, P.A., MM.

[5] Bishop Granjon to A. Weber, July 1, 1905, P.A., MM.; A. Weber to Mother Katharine, July 25, 1905, P.A., MM.

[6] A. Weber to Mother Katharine, July 25, 1905, P.A., MM.; Mother Katharine to A. Weber, August 7, 1905, P.A., MS.

[7] A. Weber to C. Theobald, July 25, 1905, P.A., MM.

[8] Bishop Granjon to A. Weber, July 23, 1905, copy in *House Chronicle,* p. 56, S.M.C.

[9] Novatus Benzing, O.F.M., Phoenix, to A. Weber, March 25, 1906, P.A., MM.

[10] Bishop Granjon to A. Weber, September 5 and October 15, 1905, copies in *House Chronicle,* pp. 57–58, S.M.C.

William Ketcham of the Bureau of Catholic Indian Missions traveled with Anselm to the Hopi villages after they had chosen the Chin Lee mission location in August, 1905. After witnessing the famed snake dance of the Hopi the two priests checked over possible mission sites on or near the three mesas.[11] Father Anselm on October 20, 1905, forwarded a request through Father Ketcham in Washington for a selection of forty acres near one of the mesas, and another half acre for the mission buildings on top of one of the mesas. These two plots were requested as a lieu selection for the 160 acres around Wipo Spring which had been granted in 1889 to the Bureau of Catholic Indian Missions but never used.[12] Unfortunately the letter of approval from the Office of Indian Affairs, which had been forwarded on November 3 to Superintendent Lemmon at Keams Canyon, could not be acted upon, since the Superintendent left on sick leave at the very time when Father Anselm planned to make his selection.[13] On his return Mr. Lemmon was of the opinion that any site would require the consent of the Hopi. What with the unruly, antigovernment spirit which had only heightened during Lemmon's absence, Anselm realized that such consent was likely out of the question. A definite "no" at the time would possibly write off the whole Hopi mission prospect.[14]

Circumstances soon conspired to jeopardize indefinitely any mission prospects: the constant effort of the government to enforce compulsory education had crystallized the growing split among the Hopis into two antagonistic camps of conservatives and liberals, called Hostiles and Friendlies. Through the whole fabric of community life the friction was real and active; to the Hostiles conformity with government regulations as to education, sanitation, economic controls, or even the acceptance of government aid, meant an end to their independence and traditional way of life. The Friendlies were less disinclined to accept white civilization. What doubly infuriated the Hostiles was the agent's use of Navaho police to enforce school attendance — when the Navaho themselves scoffed at the idea of school and scorned the Hopi who would send their boys and girls to the agency school.[15]

This intratribal feud reached its climax the day after the 1906

[11] A. Weber to Chas. Lusk, September 7, 1905, C.I.B.A.; Theodore G. Lemmon, Visiting Permit, August 20, 1905, C.I.B.A.

[12] *House Chronicle,* pp. 57–58, S.M.C., quoting pertinent letters.

[13] W. Ketcham to A. Weber, November 3, 1905, copy in *House Chronicle,* p. 58, S.M.C.

[14] A. Weber to Bishop Granjon, May 19, 1906, referred to in Bishop Granjon to A. Weber, May 30, 1906, P.A., MM., and reproduced in full, *House Chronicle,* p. 60, S.M.C.

[15] A. Weber, *Sendbote,* 33:991–994, November, 1906; *ibid.,* 34:28–35, January, 1907.

snake dance when on September 7 the combined Friendlies or Oraibi and the other villages forced from the sky village a group of Hostiles from Second Mesa and Oraibi. These one hundred and thirty-five families of Hostiles camped five miles north of Oraibi, and prepared to equip themselves for an exodus into a new land of plentiful springs and much rain, a land foretold in Hopi legend. Reconciliation between the two groups could be effected only by beheading the chief of the opponents, so each side contended. A less bloody solution was finally reached. A primitive tug of war, which was lost by Yukima and the Hostiles, decisively settled the point for the antigovernment faction: they would abandon Oraibi for all time.[16]

Reuben Perry, superintendent of Fort Defiance Agency at the time, was appointed Supervisor for the Hopi in October, and sent to re-establish harmony among the Hostiles and Friendlies. On October 19 two troops of cavalry under Captain E. H. Holbrook left Fort Wingate to lend weight to Perry's authority. En route they spent two nights at St. Michaels during a snowstorm before proceeding to Oraibi.[17]

Troops notwithstanding, no *rapprochement* could be effected; nor would the Hostiles consent to co-operate in any way with government. As a solution, twenty-eight Hostiles, including two chiefs, were taken prisoners. Eleven younger men were sent to school at Carlisle, and seventeen older men were eventually sentenced to Fort Huachuca at hard labor; eighty-three Hostile children were taken back to the Keams Canyon school.[18]

While imprisoned temporarily at Keams Canyon the Hostile prisoners continued their attitude of passive resistance by going on a hunger strike as a protest against signing government vouchers for army rations and utensils. Anselm had left St. Michaels for Keams Canyon to assist Perry in convincing the old men that passive resistance would avail no more than active. Fifteen miles from Keams, however, he learned that the fast had been abandoned after five days. The missionary's attempt on that occasion to induce the Hostiles to

[16] A. Weber to W. Ketcham, September 15, 1906, C.I.B.A.; Harold S. Colton and Frank C. Baxter, *Days in the Painted Desert and the San Francisco Mountains* (Flagstaff: Museum of Northern Arizona, 1932), pp. 46–47.

[17] Simeon Schwemburger, O.F.M., to C. Theobald, October 22, 1906, P.A., HD.; A. Weber, *Sendbote,* 34:121, February, 1907.

[18] War Department *Annual Report,* 1907, volume 3, p. 175; Secretary of the Interior, May 25, 1908, *Report on Employment of U. S. Soldiers in Arresting By-a-lil-le and Other Navajo Indians,* 60 Cong., 1 sess., Senate Document No. 517 (Washington: Government Printing Office, 1908), p. 5. See *The Albuquerque Morning Journal,* December 21, 1906.

send their children to St. Michaels School failed; it would take their little ones too far from home, they complained: if he would build nearer to Keams, they assured him, however, they would certainly prefer his school to the government's.[19]

Deeply disappointed though he was as he rode back from the Hostile camp north of Oraibi, he could not refrain from laughter when in passing Oraibi he saw the Friendlies' burlesque. Twelve Oraibis painted black were pummeling and jostling a crowd of laughing and squealing men while the rest of the village applauded from their gallery seats along the roofs and pueblo ladders. They were re-enacting the Small Pox Incident of 1899 when Negro troops had forced fumigation and vaccination upon the Hostiles of that day. The drama, along with the uproariously laughing villagers, was an object lesson in the Hopi community sense of humor and its dramatic vehicle for transmitting traditions.[20]

On this same visit Father Anselm happened upon another incident not without its touch of humor. He had occasion to discuss the Oraibi situation with Reverend J. B. Epp, the Mennonite minister of Oraibi. The minister later wrote to Anselm Weber that he feared the friar might have misconstrued his missionary remarks concerning the Hostile migrants. Reverend Epp insisted that he had not meant to imply by his conversation that the Mennonite Church would connive at any Catholic mission work among the Hostiles. He rather felt that his church would frown on any such concessions to the Catholics; the Mennonites considered "all Oraibis," Hostiles or Friendlies, as "our field."[21] Anselm replied: "I have no objection in the world to considering Hopies as 'your field.' It is a bad rule that does not work both ways." Having referred to Protestants entering "Catholic fields" along the Rio Grande, in the Philippines, Cuba, Puerto Rico, etc., he concluded: "it would seem to me bad grace on their part to speak about unoccupied fields. . . . In deciding as to a Moqui mission we shall take the wishes of our Protestant friends just as much into consideration as they would ours."[22]

The timing of the Hopi fracas disrupted utterly the Hopi mission plan. Fathers Juvenal Schnorbus and Marcellus Troester had been appointed to St. Michaels, July 25, in answer to Anselm's plea to Visitor General Theodore Arentz for two additional men for the Hopi

[19] A. Weber, *Sendbote,* 34:223, March, 1907; A. Weber to Bishop Granjon, n.d., 1906, copy in *House Chronicle,* p. 62, S.M.C.

[20] A. Weber, *Sendbote,* 34:411, April, 1907.

[21] J. B. Epp to A. Weber, January 24, 1907, P.A., MM.

[22] A. Weber to J. B. Epp, January 30, 1907, copy in P.A., MM.

and Chin Lee missions. Juvenal had been most anxious to enter upon the Hopi work.[23] Instead, however, of opening the building program among the Hopi, as was planned, the first superior of St. Michaels spent a dejected year giving one hour of daily religious instructions at St. Michaels School. At the summer chapter, 1907, Juvenal was chosen as assistant novice master at Mt. Airy, Ohio.[24]

It was at this annual chapter meeting of 1907 that Anselm Weber exercised for the first time his consultive office as a definer of the province of St. John the Baptist. Though elected in the previous summer's chapter for a three-year term, distance had prevented his attendance in July of 1906.[25]

The Hopi mission project lay dormant during the two years following the Hostile-Friendly feud of 1906 and the general antagonism incident to the use of federal troops. Young Lorenzo Hubbell at Keams[26] and a Catholic teacher at Polacca Indian School kept the missionary informed on trends among the Hopi.[27]

Returning to St. Michaels late in October, 1908, after spending five weeks in saddle and Indian camp while surveying and aiding in the allotting of Indians off the reservation, Father Anselm found a notice waiting him from the government allotting agent near Keams.[28] Matthew Murphy wished to settle the unfinished business of the Hopi mission site, and requested the missioner to visit his camp.[29] Arrived there Anselm decided against attempting a selection since he "did not care to risk a refusal on the part of the Indians. I have had several experiences which have cured me absolutely of over-confidence."[30]

In reporting the incident to Bishop Granjon, Father Anselm admitted that he saw no immediate future for a Hopi mission, both from conditions of unrest among the Indians, and because he felt that the St. Michaels missionaries could more effectively spend their efforts

[23] A. Weber to Visitor (Theodore Arentz, O.F.M.), July 19, 1906, P.A., MM. J. Schnorbus pleaded with the chapter for assignment "unter den Moquis oder Navajos." J. Schnorbus to the chapter, July 20, 1906, P.A., JS.; also J. Schnorbus to A. Weber, December 12, 1905, P.A., JS.

[24] C. Theobald to A. Weber, February 14, 1907, P.A., JS.; *Tabula Definitionis,* 1907, P.A.

[25] Father Louis Haverbeck was chosen to serve in A. Weber's absence. B. Nurre to A. Weber, July 25, 1906. P.A., BN.

[26] Lorenzo Hubbell to A. Weber, April 8, 1907, P.A., MM.

[27] Mary E. Haskett to A. Weber, November 12, 1908, P.A., MM.

[28] A. Weber to Chas. Lusk, October 25, 1908, C.I.B.A.

[29] Letter of October 23, 1908, cited in A. Weber to Bishop Granjon, November 23, 1908, P.A., MM.

[30] A. Weber to Bishop Granjon, November 23, 1908, P.A., MM.

among the Navaho with whom they were now after ten years finally gaining status. As superior of the Navaho mission Father Anselm wished that the Bishop might try to find some other order of missionaries for the Hopi. If any new mission should be opened, he felt it should be at Tuba City, or among the northern Navaho beyond the Black Mountains.[31]

Back at Provincial headquarters Provincial Chrysostom Theobald applauded Anselm's decision, and cautioned against taking steps apropos Hopi which would run counter to the missionary's own judgment.[32] Father Ketcham could not quite coincide with the Provincial's view, figuring that the consent of the Indians in 1889 should hold good for the contemplated lieu selection.[33] Bishop Granjon, however, would not hear of the Franciscans bypassing Hopi, adding with sly innuendo that it was only seemly that the friars should continue where their predecessors had left off in the seventeenth and eighteenth centuries — so gloriously — as martyrs.[34] *Touché!*

An invitation in March, 1909, from a group of Tewa-Hopi to found a mission among them could not be honored at the time.[35] Nor could the offer of Miss Mary Haskett, a month later, to use a small private home as a chapel and mission headquarters be accepted.[36] There were simply no men to be sent on the hundred-mile trip to the sky villages.

What with endless work in the field, surveying for Indian allotments beyond the reservation limits, and arranging Indian leases of railroad sections, Anselm Weber himself was unable to visit Hopiland. Nervous exhaustion forced him to spend Lent of 1909 at St. Joseph's Sanatorium in San Diego, California. On his return to Arizona he visited Banning, the Sherman Indian Institute, and took Father Hahn's place at Yuma over a short period. There he greatly admired the lay cathechetical work being carried on by an old friend, Anna Egan.[37]

[31] *Ibid.* Three requests by non-Catholics urging the Franciscans to establish a mission at Tuba had been received in 1903; Berard Haile had requested permission to undertake the mission work there. Finances again thwarted any such attempt. E. A. Brown to A. Weber, March 21, 1903; C. H. Algert to M. J. Riordan, August 21, 1903; B. Haile to A. Weber, July 26, n.d., all in P.A., TM.

[32] C. Theobald to A. Weber, November 30, 1908, P.A., MM.

[33] W. Ketcham to A. Weber, December 19, 1908, P.A., MM.

[34] Bishop Granjon to A. Weber, January 13, 1909, P.A., MM.

[35] Tom Polacca (per H. Polacca) to A. Weber, March 4, 1909, P.A., MM.

[36] M. E. Haskett to A. Weber, April 21 and 28, 1909, P.A., MM.

[37] L. Ostermann to A. Weber, April 12, 1909, P.A., FD.; Mother Katharine to A. Weber, April, n.d., 1909, P.A., MS.; A. Weber to W. Ketcham, June 1, 1909, C.I.B.A.

In the first week of December, 1909, shortly after several Protestant missioners were forced to leave their Hopi missions, Father Anselm made a final attempt to secure a mission site.[38] His request for forty acres at the foot of First Mesa for a mission residence and farm, plus a half acre on the mesa between Sichomovi and Walpi, was approved contingently on his receiving permission from the Indians.[39] To obtain such written permission from Indians who flatly refused to sign any official government document seemed obviously impossible.[40] Both the allotting agent, Matthew Murphy, and Hopi Agent Burton Miller had only strengthened his convictions that all missionaries were unwelcome: when Miller had objected to the Hopis' move in 1909 to oust the Protestant missionaries from Second Mesa, the chief brought out the tongue of an ancient bell used by the early friars, and warned that "this tongue is all of their talk that remains."[41]

Bishop Granjon found it difficult to reconcile himself to the realities of the Hopi situation as faced by Anselm Weber. The Marquette League, on its part wishing that its 1905 donation of $1,000 for the Annunciation Chapel should go to work, requested that this sum be transferred for a mission among the Mescaleros who were also partly under the Tucson Diocese. The Bishop, however, objected, and asked Anselm to bear him out; he wanted Anselm to reassure the League that in the very near future the Annunciation Chapel would be established among the Hopi.[42]

The friar could not conscientiously give the assurance so he hinted to Father Ketcham of the Bureau that it might be of advantage to the Marquette League if they recognized the dim view which the

[38] A. Weber to W. Ketcham, November 24, 1909, C.I.B.A.

[39] A. Weber to Commissioner of Indian Affairs, December 2, 1909, copy in P.A., MM.

[40] Chas. Lusk to A. Weber, December 18, 1909, P.A., MM.

[41] A. Weber to W. Ketcham, May 22 and June 17, 1910, C.I.B.A. Protestant missionaries among the Hopi in 1909, according to George F. Kengott who visited the reservation at this time, were the Reverend Thayer, Baptist, who cared for Keams and Oraibi; Miss A. E. Johnson who was finishing her Baptist church at Polacca; and Miss Mary McLean, Baptist, of the "Sunlight Mission" at Toreva on Second Mesa. *Report of a Special Committee on Appropriations* (Society for Propagating the Gospel Among the Indians and Others in North America, 1911), pp. 70–75. Reverend Kengott had taken the White Steamer driven by Charley Day from Gallup to St. Michaels on August 19, 1910. He recommended the mission for financial aid in establishing a hospital which Anselm Weber was hoping to found. Kengott noted that it took the mail steamer six hours from Gallup to St. Michaels, 27 miles, and only four hours by buckboard to cover the 40 miles farther west to Hubbell's. *Ibid.*, p. 79.

[42] Bishop Granjon to Marquette League, May 10, 1910, copy in P.A., MM.; Bishop Granjon to A. Weber, May 15, 1910, C.I.B.A.; A. Weber to W. Ketcham, May 22, 1910, C.I.B.A.; A. Weber to E. A. Philbin, September 18, 1910. C.I.B.A.

friars took respecting a mission foundation among the Hopi.[43] Obviously Father Ketcham had himself intuitively gauged the situation, for already in March he had suggested to the Marquette League that the $1,000 gift for the "Moqui chapel" should well serve the Mescaleros of southern New Mexico. If and when the Hopi situation cleared, the League and the Bureau between them could raise another thousand dollars for the Franciscans.[44]

Moreover Ketcham had induced Bishop Granjon a month earlier to send Father L. Migeon of Tulerosa for three or four days each month to work among the Mescaleros, a suggestion which the Bishop approved. His only condition respected the providing of chapel and a room for the poor missionary.[45] Accordingly, working on the presumption of the transfer of the Hopi fund, Father Ketcham completed negotiations through Father Migeon and Major J. A. Carroll, superintendent at Mescalero, to begin construction of a log chapel with an enlarged sacristy to accommodate the priest on his overnight visits.[46] To get immediate action Ketcham advanced $825 with a promise of more to come.[47]

The well-laid plan went utterly awry at this point when the Bishop of Tucson put out a call to Berard Haile at St. Michaels for the Hopi chapel fund which had long since been diverted to complete other mission projects. As Anselm Weber was in Europe at the time as companion to Archbishop Pitaval of Santa Fe, Father Berard found himself holding an embarrassingly empty bag. Unhappily he eyed the $1,000 fund frozen solidly in Chin Lee and Lukachukai stone buildings. With no liquid assets at hand there was nothing left for Berard to do but to arrange for a one-thousand dollar short-term loan at 8 per cent interest, and forward it to Tucson.[48]

Everyone was vastly surprised, some happily, others with a shade of chagrin, when the irked Bishop shunted the whole sum — not to the Marquette League, the Bureau, or to the Mescalero mission — to

[43] A. Weber to W. Ketcham, May 22 and June 17, 1910, C.I.B.A.

[44] W. Ketcham to Ellen Rose Byrne, Marquette League secretary, March 10, 1910, C.I.B.A.

[45] W. Ketcham to Bishop Granjon, February 25, 1910, C.I.B.A.; Bishop Granjon to W. Ketcham, March 4, 1910, C.I.B.A. The Santa Fe Chancery was happy to have its section of the Mescalero reservation serviced from Tulerosa. Antonio Fourchegu to W. Ketcham, December 14, 1910, C.I.B.A.

[46] L. Migeon to W. Ketcham, September 3, 1910, C.I.B.A.; W. Ketcham to J. A. Carroll, May 12, 1910, and J. A. Carroll to W. Ketcham, May 24, 1910, C.I.B.A.

[47] W. Ketcham to L. Migeon, November 26, 1910, C.I.B.A.

[48] E. R. Byrne to W. Ketcham, May 22, 1911, C.I.B.A.; B. Haile to Provincial E. Buttermann, July 15, 1911, P.A., BH.

Father Mathias Rechsteiner of the St. Louis Franciscans for extension of the Papago mission field.[49]

Though bilked by this unexpected display of episcopal financial legerdemain, the Marquette League appreciated the deeper embarrassment of the St. Michaels friars and their 8 per cent note.[50] When Father Anselm arrived in New York on his return from Europe, and sought their aid, the League generously found ways and means to contribute $1,000 for Chin Lee.[51] Considered in its aftereffects, the original $1,000 donation for Hopi had paid off handsome dividends: St. Michaels had received an equivalent donation from the League, the Mescalero mission had received close to a thousand dollars; and the province had, with some exasperation, it is true, covered Father Berard's 8 per cent note; in southern Arizona the Papago missions were thoroughly rejuvenated.[52] It had been one of those cases, foreshadowing later Keynesian Economics, where one had brought four for the missions.

To complete the cycle of the Hopi donation, it is noteworthy that Anselm Weber and Barnabas Meyer preached a mission to the Mescalero and Fort Sill Apache beginning on Passion Sunday, 1914, and lasting until Palm Sunday.[53] William Ketcham had requested the friars to give hard-working Father Migeon assistance. Father Barnabas preached in Spanish and English, and after services Anselm mingled with the Indians to ascertain the status of their land-and-water controversy with Senator Fall. Frank Walker knew Naiche, the Fort Sill chief, and was revered by the sons of Victorio and Chihuahua because Frank told them stories of his friendship with the old Apaches before they and their people were exiled.[54] On Palm Sunday the log chapel, which Father Migeon had built on the prospect of the Hopi-fund transfer in 1911, was overcrowded.[55]

A year later Anselm Weber was again among the Mescalero and Fort Sill Indians to organize protest meetings to offset Senator Fall's

[49] M. Rechsteiner, O.F.M., to W. Ketcham, June 7, 1911, C.I.B.A.

[50] E. R. Byrne to W. Ketcham, May 22, 1911, C.I.B.A.

[51] E. R. Byrne to W. Kecham, November 22, 1911, and W. Ketcham to A. Weber, November 25, 1911; see pp. 116–117.

[52] E. Buttermann to B. Haile, August 7, 1911, P.A., BH.; B. Haile to E. Buttermann, September, n.d., 1911, Letter Book-1, S.M.C.

[53] One hundred and eighty-three of Geronimo's people had returned from their Fort Sill exile on April 2, 1913, to share the Mescalero reservation. C.I.A., *Annual Report,* 1913, p. 34. See W. Ketcham to A. Weber, February 28, 1914, C.I.B.A.; A. Weber to D. Engelhard, March 23, 1914, P.A., PI.; A. Weber to W. Ketcham, April 14, 1914, C.I.B.A.

[54] *Ibid.*

[55] Barnabas Meyer to R. Wilken, February 9, 1951, P.A., CP.

attempt to have their reservation opened, ostensibly for a national park, but primarily to open the mountain pastures to large cattle ranchers.[56] Fall had previously gained control by court action, Anselm learned, of certain water rights at Three Rivers, over which the Indians would have turned to violence but for the persuasion of Father Migeon. Nonetheless the Senator tried through Ketcham to have the ailing but zealous old pastor removed on the score of imprudence.[57]

After his first mission visit with Barnabas Meyer among the Mescalero and Fort Sill Apache, Father Anselm urged Father Ketcham to approach the St. Louis Franciscan Provincial in the matter of taking over the reservation. Father Migeon, old and failing, was no longer fitted for the strenuous traveling involved. Within a year this transpired, neatly concluding the circuitous route of the thousand dollar Hopi donation which had gone to the St. Louis Franciscans among the Papagos instead of to the Mescaleros as intended by Father Ketcham. Indirectly, though the Hopi mission project itself misfired, it did occasion new mission fronts among the Papago and Apache.[58]

As to the Hopi mission itself, another attempt was planned under Father Egbert Fischer in 1916, but again it proved abortive.[59] Eight years later, in 1924, final steps were taken by Father Jerome Hesse, Emmanuel Trockur, and Matthias Heile to establish the Keams Canyon Franciscan Mission. As soon as the Navaho headmen of the vicinity comprehended that the friars were friends of the *e'nishodi* called Chischilli, they readily signed the petition for the mission site. Eventually, it was hoped, the friars would be able to expand Navaho work at Keams to include direct mission effort among the Hopi.[60]

[56] *Ibid.;* Ferdinand Ortiz, O.F.M., to A. Weber, January 29 and February 19, 1916, P.A., MM.

[57] A. Weber to W. Ketcham, March 17, 1915, C.I.B.A.; W. Ketcham to A. Weber, March 25, 1915, C.I.B.A.; Barnabas Meyer to R. Wilken, February 9, 1951, P.A., CP.

[58] W. Ketcham to A. Weber, February 28 and May 14, 1914, P.A., MM.

[59] Mother Katharine to A. Weber, June 6, 1916, P.A., MM.

[60] Matthias Heile, O.F.M., in *The Provincial Chronicle,* 11:59–64, 110–116, Winter, Spring, 1939; 12:34–38, 91–97, 165–167, Fall, Winter, Spring, 1940; Jerome Hesse to R. Wilken, February 9, 1951, and E. Trockur to R. Wilken, December 30, 1951, P.A., CP.

Chapter XI

Gallup via Zuñi

Reverend G. J. Juillard began to visit the gaunt, straggling coal-mining town of Gallup in late 1892 when he relieved ailing J. B. Brun as pastor of San Rafael, New Mexico.[1] For several months Juillard resided at Cebolleta, the original parish seat which Reverend Brun had changed to San Rafael. In 1893 he permanently transferred parish headquarters to the railroad town of Gallup.[2]

Cebolleta and Laguna formed the northeastern mission outposts and Zuñi-Atarque the southwestern bounds of this Gallup parish.[3] The Zuñis' curious amalgam of Catholicism and paganism, not uncommon among the southwestern Pueblo Indians, Archbishop Bourgade would not countenance. Notwithstanding Catholic forms — the *fiestas*, the *santos*, and even the traditional colorful welcome to the archbishop, with its blanket-spreading and lavish Spanish pageantry — the Archbishop forbade Juillard to baptize any Zuñi infants. He feared they would not be raised and educated as Catholics.[4] Accordingly Juillard refused to offer Mass at Zuñi until the Indians should symbolize their determination to practice the Faith as part of their community life by rebuilding their ruined pueblo church.[5]

When Berard Haile made the Gallup missions south to Atarque with Father "Mike" Dumarest in 1903 they were mistaken for Protestant ministers at Ojo Caliente because of the camp togs they wore, and the Indians refused absolutely to have anything to do with them. When undeceived the Zuñi in the outlying villages urgently prevailed

[1] *Libro de Bautismos*, Ceboyetta (sic), in Sacred Heart Cathedral Parish Records, Gallup, New Mexico. Anthony Kroger, O.F.M., of Gallup, interview with Mrs. F. J. Allison at whose boarding house Father Juillard took his meals for seven years, beginning in 1892. A. Kroger to R. Wilken, March 20, 1951, P.A., CP.

[2] *Hoffmanns' Catholic Directory*, 1893, p. 182; A. Weber, *F.M.S.*, 1913, p. 44.

[3] *Hoffmanns' Catholic Directory, ibid.*

[4] G. J. Juillard to W. Ketcham, October 10, 1905, C.I.B.A.

[5] W. Ketcham to Provincial C. Theobald, November 24, 1905, P.A., ZU.

on them to baptize their babies.[6] This, however, was not the practice at Zuñi Pueblo.[7]

In 1905, after visiting Chin Lee and the Hopi villages with Anselm Weber, the director of the Bureau of Catholic Missions, at Juillard's request, inspected conditions at Zuñi.[8] Having been deprived of priestly ministrations for several years by that time, the Zuñis pleaded with Father Ketcham to send priests to baptize their children and to dwell among them.[9] Put to the question by Ketcham, Juillard insisted that only a religious community with its organic continuity, and with members able and determined to learn the native language perfectly — as the Franciscans at St. Michaels — could hope for success.[10]

After receiving the hearty endorsement of Archbishop Peter Bourgade,[11] Father Ketcham sent his official request to Provincial Chrysostom Theobald that the Cincinnati Franciscans accept the Zuñi mission. Unwittingly, with adverse effect, Ketcham had thought to strengthen his appeal by having the Apostolic Delegate, D. Falconio, subscribe the petition.[12]

Unlike the case of the Hopi mission, which was taken over without his knowledge, Anselm Weber was not only aware of the request made to the province; he himself promoted the project for the Bureau of Catholic Indian Missions.[13] His warning against enlisting the prestige of the Apostolic Delegate who was "persona non grata in the province" reached Ketcham too late.[14] Not that this incidental point carried decisive weight, but apparently it did not sit well.[15] Heavy demands for friars on the missions to be opened on the San Juan, at Hopi and Chin Lee, the Provincial explained, placed Zuñi out of the provincial picture for years to come.[16] Through Father Bede Oldegeering, a Cincinnati Franciscan then assigned to the Commissariate of the Holy

6 Yazhe (Berard Haile, O.F.M.), "In Zuñiland," *St. Franziskus Bote,* 12:150–153, November, 1903, and 13:402–403, June, 1904. Father Leopold on a similar trip with Dumarest in June, 1902, had visited the Hispano and Indian missions from Gallup to Laguna, and had the privilege of offering Mass at Ácoma on July 3, the first Franciscan to do so since 1847. L. Ostermann, in *St. Anthony Messenger,* 11:262, January, 1904.

7 G. J. Juillard to W. Ketcham, October 10, 1905, C.I.B.A.

8 W. Ketcham to A. Weber, October 3, 1905, H.A.C.

9 W. Ketcham to C. Theobald, November 24, 1905, P.A., ZU.

10 G. J. Juillard to W. Ketcham, October 10, 1905, C.I.B.A.

11 Archbishop P. Bourgade to W. Ketcham, October 30, 1905, copy in P.A., ZU.

12 W. Ketcham to C. Theobald, November 24, 1905, P.A., ZU.

13 A. Weber to W. Ketcham, October 20, 1905, C.I.B.A.

14 Same to same, December 7, 1905, H.A.C.

15 C. Theobald to A. Weber, January 14, 1906, P.A., ZU.

16 C. Theobald to W. Ketcham, December 5, 1905, P.A., ZU.

Land in Washington, Father Chrysostom passed on the suggestion to Ketcham that a centrally located parish on the railroad, like Bernalillo or Gallup, would go far toward inclining the province to take over additional missions such as Zuñi.[17]

Nothing daunted, and politically wise in the workings of ecclesiastical machinery, the Bureau Director wrote Anselm, kindly requesting him to throw his weight in favor of Zuñi, and observing, as an aside, that he disliked the notion of trying to persuade another religious congregation — he had the Canadian Oblates on his list — to come into a territory which was traditionally Franciscan.[18] To the Provincial in Cincinnati, in another letter, he hastened to explain that Hopi man-power needs were limited and perhaps distant, whereas the traditionally Catholic Zuñis were being proselytized by the Protestant minister and his charming and kindly wife, and needed immediate aid. Moreover, he felt certain that he could assure financial assistance for the Zuñi mission, should it be accepted.[19]

During his interview with Theodore Arentz, O.F.M., the general visitor, in the early summer of 1906, Father Anselm pleaded the cause of Zuñi. The Visitor counseled him to take up the issue directly with the members of the definitorium, since the Provincial himself had already determined against new missions. Previously both Juillard and Archbishop Bourgade had pleaded the cause of Zuñi in preference to Hopi. Having first, therefore, instructed Archbishop Bourgade, who was at the time in New York on a collecting tour for the missions, as to the most vulnerable quarter, Anselm himself directed his own appeal to the chapter through the highly respected hands of Visitor Arentz.[20]

Archbishop Bourgade's succinct appeal, with its sincere, postscribed praise and esteem that he and his diocesan priests felt for the friars,[21] balanced nicely against the factual presentation of the Zuñi status quo as given in Anselm's recommendation.[22] Anselm's exposition clearly fixed the problem: the Archbishop, Father Juillard, and Father Ketcham of the Bureau, all preferred the Franciscans for Zuñi; if

[17] C. Theobald to A. Weber, January 14, 1906, P.A., ZU.

[18] W. Ketcham to A. Weber, December 15, 1905, C.I.B.A.

[19] W. Ketcham to C. Theobald, February 9, 1906, P.A., ZU., referring to Ketcham's previous letter to C. Theobald of November 24, 1905, P.A., ZU.

[20] A. Weber to W. Ketcham, July 4, 1906, C.I.B.A.; P. Bourgade to A. Weber, July 20, 1906, P.A., ZU., referring to Anselm's letter to him at Dunwoodie, New York, July 4, 1906.

[21] Archbishop Bourgade to Theodore Arentz, July 20, 1906, P.A., ZU.

[22] A. Weber to Theodore Arentz, July 19, 1906, P.A., MM.

the Canadian Oblates were to take over, it would mean, no doubt, that they would also take over eventually the parishes at Gallup, New Mexico, and at St. Johns, Arizona. If no missionary group were to accept Zuñi, it would mean *carte blanche* for the Christian Reformed Church which would take over completely the semiweekly non-sectarian instructions and the community religious services at the new Zuñi boarding school.[23]

The chapter held in the summer of 1906 was altogether a strongly "mission" chapter. In the *praescrutinium* the Visitor had insisted that one of the southwestern missionaries be elected as a definer, and Anselm was elected on the first ballot. With Bernard Nurre as custos, and ex-Provincial Louis Haverbeck, a stanch friend of the missions, voting as proxy for Anselm, the cause of the mission at Zuñi was assured.[24] The well-timed barrage of letters had not been ineffective. Without definitely accepting the Zuñi mission, the chapter agreed tentatively to have one of the Fathers look after the Zuñi mission needs. Meanwhile the chapter Fathers hoped that the Archbishop might see his way clear to offering the province a mission center along the railroad.[25]

While in the East, Archbishop Bourgade on Ketcham's advice appealed to the prelates who composed the Board of the Bureau of Catholic Indian Missions for additional funds to assist the new Franciscan mission at Zuñi. His appeal was granted and his annual allotment for the archdiocese was increased from $750 to $1,500. Of this additional amount $500 went to St. Michaels for support of the Zuñi missioner, and the remainder was channeled to the Jémez day school.[26]

During the autumn days while Anselm Weber was in the saddle riding from camp to camp to round up the St. Michaels school children, his confrere, Berard Haile, undertook to visit the Zuñi villages, and to give instructions at the Black Rock School. On the feast of St. Francis, October 4, 1906, Anselm wrote of planning a formal council with the Indians, and with Juillard and Berard in attendance, of reopening the ancient Franciscan mission "with a little éclat" late in December.[27]

23 *Ibid.*

24 B. Nurre to A. Weber, July 25, 1906, P.A., BN.

25 *Acta Capituli Provincialis,* September 24, 1906, pp. 31–32, P.A.

26 P. Bourgade to W. Ketcham, November 8, 1906, C.I.B.A.; P. Bourgade to A. Weber, November 23, 1906, P.A., ZU. The same amount was sent for Zuñi in 1907. See P. Bourgade to A. Weber, December 7, 1907, P.A., ZU.

27 A. Weber to W. Ketcham, October 4 and 10, 1906, C.I.B.A.

The "éclat" fell disappointingly flat. Fathers Berard and Juillard made the official trip to open the mission in early December with the avowed purpose of introducing Father Berard.[28] Although at the first council the *principales* said they were Catholics and expressed sadness over the lack of baptism for their children "who were growing up like burros," there was a complete change of attitude during the second council meeting held the next morning. Both Juillard and Berard realized that a cooling and stiffening reaction had come over the Indians during the night; little of what was being said was translated for them by the official interpreter, Lorenzo Chavez. After another period of what appeared to be wrangling, interrupted by the leaving and re-entry of Indian messengers, the padres, were simply informed by Chavez that the Zuñis had voted unanimously against accepting a mission in their midst.[29] The Zuñi mission seemed a lost cause.

In the early part of January, 1907, Father Anselm hastened to Zuñi with Frank Walker to investigate the curiously altered situation there.[30] With tact and friendliness on this occasion and on a subsequent visit,[31] he managed to piece together what had transpired to induce the Zuñis to change their friendly attitude toward the missionaries; Teniente Delgarito, a lieutenant governor, and Jesús Eracho, ex-governor and onetime Sonoran Mexican who was sold to the Zuñis by the Apaches, were the informants.

Their stories both identified Mrs. Matilda Coxe Stevenson,[32] the ethnologist working at Zuñi, as the party responsible for introducing antagonism against the friars. On the occasion of the first council with Juillard and Berard the majority of the fifty Zuñis in attendance favored the mission; at the next morning's council in the plaza it was the same — until an emissary of Mrs. Stevenson, named Cantina, arrived to warn the Indians that the ethnologist had told them to inform the council that if the friars were permitted to reopen the

[28] A. Weber to Supervisor R. Perry, April 5, 1907, P.A., ZU.

[29] A. Weber to W. Ketcham, February 11, 1907, P.A., ZU.

[30] Same to same, January 1, 1907, C.I.B.A.

[31] February 3, 1907, as detailed in A. Weber to W. Ketcham, February 11, 1907, P.A., ZU.

[32] Author of "The Zuñi Indians: Their Mythology, Esoteric Societies, and Ceremonies," *Twenty-Third Annual Report of the Bureau of American Ethnology,* 1901–1902 (Washington, D. C.: Government Printing Office, 1904), pp. 1–634. In this work she writes: "It has been said that the Pueblo Indians are attached to the Catholic Faith; but this is not the case, at least with the Zuñis. For a time their ancestors were compelled to worship in that church, but their pagan belief was not seriously affected thereby." P. 15. Other works of Mrs. Matilda Coxe Stevenson on the Zuñi Indians are listed in the bibliography.

mission it would mean the old Spanish system of *primicias*, or tithing, and the use of the whip to force the Indians to Mass on Sunday. Two more messengers, Ernest and Nina, a Hopi, had next spoken for Mrs. Stevenson, with Nina telling of the ancient interference by the friars in the life of the Hopi people. Both messengers urged the council to prevent the mission as it would mean interference in Zuñi community ritual and dance; it would involve special fees for burial and baptism and marriage, and whippings for nonattendance at Mass even when the people would be busy in the distant fields.[33]

None of this had been interpreted by the official interpreter at the earlier meeting with Berard and Juillard, nor had Juillard's explanation of the real purpose and extent of the mission. While the Zuñis were discussing these new developments, Lorenzo Chavez, Ernest and Nina, the only Indians present who understood English, had told the Fathers with finality that the Zuñis had their own religion and wanted no other.[34]

Anselm Weber and Frank Walker on the night of February 4 held a caucus at the home of a lieutenant governor with the Governor and *principales*. This served as an introduction for the main council on the following day, when over two hundred Zuñis assembled. Anselm explained that the friars would not come among them unless welcome to a large segment of the community. He next debunked the charges of Mrs. Stevenson seriatim as they had previously been relayed to him. He further explained that if they would bring the lady to the meeting he would be happy to answer all her objections.[35]

In the event that the principal officers of the pueblo decided against the re-establishment of the old mission, Anselm explained that he would be satisfied merely to open a small mission in one of the houses, the same as the Protestant minister, in order to care for the religious needs of those Zuñis who had asked for the priest's return.[36] Without asking for any final vote on the question he had then left the meeting.

Upon his return to St. Michaels he had written up the entire proceedings and sent the notes to Ketcham with advice that the Bureau Director use them with the Bureau of Ethnology directors

[33] A. Weber to W. Ketcham, January 24, 1907, C.I.B.A.; A. Weber, *F.M.S.*, 1916, pp. 17–18.

[34] *Ibid.*; A. Weber, *Sendbote*, 34:896, October, 1907. The detailed and highly colorful narrative of the effort to found the Zuñi mission in 1906–1907 is given by Anselm Weber, *Sendbote*, 34:802–807, 892–898, 998–1003, 1089–1093, September-December, 1907.

[35] A. Weber to W. Ketcham, January 24, 1907, C.I.B.A.

[36] A. Weber to Supervisor R. Perry, April 5, 1907, P.A., ZU.

in the matter of Mrs. Stevenson.[37] In a letter to F. W. Hodge, his friend who was in charge of the Bureau of Ethnology, Anselm balanced the values and possible dangers of an ethnology which tried to throw a "Chinese wall around the different pueblos with the inscription: 'Ethnologists' Paradise.' "[38]

> The indirect encouragement consequent to the importance ethnologists necessarily attach to Indian mythology, Indian beliefs and customs is certainly by far outbalanced by the valuable results from such scientific researches. But, is the Bureau of Ethnology prepared to sustain its workers in *directly* encouraging the Indians in their heathenism — in opposing the progress and civilization and Christianization of the Indians? Does it approve . . . trying to keep the Indians in the same state for its [Bureau of Ethnology] special benefit?

To Anselm both Holmes and Hodge expressed their appreciation of his direct approach to their office, assuring him that there would be no more cases of such interference with the missionaries by workers bent on freezing Indian culture for museum and laboratory exhibition.[39] Father Ketcham in his interview with W. H. Holmes, head curator of anthropology in the Washington Bureau of Ethnology, learned that Mrs. Stevenson was scheduled to leave Zuñi within two weeks, a transfer that had been planned even before Anselm's letter arrived.[40]

After Mrs. Stevenson's departure, an investigation into the re-establishment of the Zuñi mission was launched pursuant to charges of the woman ethnologist that the "friars were trying to thrust their mission upon the Zuñis against their will."[41] Reuben Perry, former superintendent at Fort Defiance, was appointed by the Bureau of Indian Affairs to look into the matter. Anselm Weber presented his side of the case to Perry, stressing the points that he wanted no exclusive advantages over Protestants — that he wished no cajoling of the Zuñis in his favor, nor ever desired any internal pueblo political pressure in favor of Catholics. His stand was logical: "There are a number of Zuñis who are Catholic and who desire the ministrations of a Catholic priest; has the Governor, or even the Governor and the majority of the Pueblo, the right to prevent this? I hardly think

[37] A. Weber to W. Ketcham, February 11, 1907, P.A., ZU.

[38] A. Weber to F. W. Hodge, February 11, 1907, copy in C.I.B.A.; A. Weber to R. Perry, April 5, 1907, P.A., ZU.

[39] W. H. Holmes to A. Weber, February 19, 1907; F. W. Hodge to A. Weber, February 19, 1907, both in P.A., ZU.

[40] W. Ketcham to A. Weber, February 19, 1907, P.A., ZU.

[41] A. Weber to W. Ketcham, April 18, 1907, C.I.B.A.

the Pueblos are exempt from the provisions of the Constitution guaranteeing religious liberty."[42]

Having sifted the evidence Supervisor Perry reported that Matilda Coxe Stevenson had influenced the Indians, particularly by warning them against church influence and interference with Zuñi dances and religious ritual, and by stressing the ogre of compulsion and tithing. Perry found that except for the Governor and several of his relatives the majority of *officiales* and older Indians, including the sun priest, were in favor of the mission. Accordingly he recomended Indian Office approval of a mission, but cautioned both the priest and the Christian Reformed minister against beginning school instructions until the next autumn, after the community friction would have worn down.[43] In line with Perry's recommendations, Commissioner Leupp advised that permission to reopen the Catholic mission at Zuñi should be granted contingent on the "cooperation of the Zuñis."[44]

What with the episodes at Hopi and Zuñi, along with his appraisal of mission work among the *Rio Abajo* and Jémez pueblos, the friar had reached a thoroughly realistic conclusion regarding pueblo mission work:[45]

> It is my candid opinion that practically nothing can be done with these ultra-conservative, stubborn, obtuse and dense Pueblo Indians till their village government is broken up. In saying 'nothing could be done' I mean not only by way of christianizing (sic) them, but also by way of civilizing them.
>
> If the Government does not do anything in that line, the Pueblos will be still the same as they are now 'when Gabriel blows his horn.'

Anselm was specifically referring to the political autonomy and quasi-national independent status demanded for the pueblos by the chauvinistic *officiales* and *caciques*. These civil and religious leaders in the pueblos were citing the 1848 Guadalupe Hidalgo Treaty as confirming the former rights and independence as exercised under the Mexican Government. Government Superintendent C. J. Crandall of Santa Fe notwithstanding, the Pueblo *Officiales* continued to administer corporal punishments, such as whipping and imprisonment, to sanction their laws and directives, especially to enforce compliance

[42] A. Weber to R. Perry, April 5, 1907, P.A., ZU.

[43] Commissioner of Indian Affairs, Francis E. Leupp, to Bureau of Catholic Indian Missions, April 25, 1907, C.I.B.A. Leupp quotes the Perry Report in full.

[44] F. E. Leupp to Superintendent Oliver, April 26, 1907, copy in P.A., ZU.; same to W. H. Ketcham, April 26, 1907, copy in P.A., ZU.

[45] A. Weber to W. Ketcham, April 8, 1907, C.I.B.A.

with the demands of community religious ceremonial.[46] Anselm was fully convinced that "the conversion of the Navaho would be far less difficult than the complete conversion of the Pueblo Indians," simply because of the pueblo sacrifice of individual freedom in favor of community control and cultural solidarity.[47] With the Navaho there were fewer social controls and wider opportunity for individualism.

During the three years from 1907 through 1909 when Anselm Weber visited Zuñi, offering Mass and baptizing in the home of the sacristan, he became more acutely aware of the amazing degree of social control exercised by the pueblo Governor: Catholic Indians, even *principales,* if they attended at all, skulked most warily to the sacristan's home for services; many were too timid to brave the official techniques for enforcing conformity, methods that included, besides corporal sanctions, derision, whispering campaigns, forms of community ostracism against those white-loving upstarts who would break down the good old life of their forefathers.[48] Anselm and Father Ketcham seriously wondered whether the Catholic policy of tolerating paganism, while hoping and trying to unsnarl the pueblo religious dichotomy, half pagan, half Christian, would net any long-term results; or whether the Protestant approach in demanding of its converts a complete cultural rupture with pueblo life was not sounder policy.[49]

They hoped to win approval and acceptance from the old, tradition-bound *principales* by repairing the massive ancient pueblo church when the time should arrive for building a mission. To link Catholicism with the ancient pueblo church would be more effective propaganda, they thought, than erecting something new and foreign to the pueblo architecture.[50]

[46] Same to same, April 5, 1907, C.I.B.A. A. Weber also referred to the January 16, 1907, New Mexico Supreme Court decision as handed down by Associate Justice Pope which declared the Pueblo Indians to be nonwards of the government, and hence not subject to the federal statute of January 30, 1897, penalizing liquor transactions with allotted or reservation Indians. See *United States* vs. *Benito Mares and Anastacio Santistevan,* 14 New Mexico, 1; *Albuquerque Evening Citizen,* January 17, 1907. Six years later this decision was reversed in *United States* vs. *Felipe Sandoval,* 231 U. S., 28; C.I.A., *Annual Report,* 1914, p. 71.

[47] Barnabas Meyer, O.F.M., to R. Wilken, February 9, 1951, P.A., CP.

[48] A. Weber to W. Ketcham, February 9, 1909, C.I.B.A. The sacristan proudly showed Father Anselm the old vestments, chalice, paten, missals, the two hide paintings, the two church bells, as well as the venerated *Santo Niño de Zuñi,* all dating back to the seventeenth-century mission days. A. Weber, *F.M.S.,* 1916, p. 20.

[49] A. Weber to W. Ketcham, February 14, 1910, and W. Ketcham to A. Weber, February 22, 1910, C.I.B.A. Both letters are lengthy documents on Indian missionology.

[50] *Ibid.;* Director of the Bureau of Catholic Indian Missions (Ketcham), *Report of Catholic Indian Mission,* 1907, C.I.B.A.

Even after the coldly hostile Governor was replaced in the Christmas elections of 1909, the unfriendly judge continued in office to carry on the internal political antagonism against the Christian missions.[51] The antagonism was directed not merely to the Catholic and Franciscan effort, but toward all non-Zuñi religions.

The Christian Reformed Church had experienced similar opposition. Doctor and Mrs. H. K. Palmer of the Presbyterian Church had originally opened a school and mission in the heart of Zuñi village in 1877. This mission they had turned over in 1897 to the Christian Reformed Church, which sent Mr. and Mrs. A. Van der Wagen to take over the mission. The Van der Wagens had arrived at Fort Defiance in company with Reverend and Mrs. Herman Fryling on October 10, 1896, one year before they occupied the Zuñi Presbyterian mission on October 9, 1897.[52] Mr. Van der Wagen had explained to Juillard and Superintendent Oliver in 1907 that Mrs. Stevenson and the officials had also consistently thwarted his efforts. By the end of 1907 he had abandoned the mission completely in favor of full-time trading with the Indians at Black Rock; somewhat later he leased a township from the Santa Fe Railroad in order to broaden his livestock business.[53] Reverend Herman Fryling, after turning over his Fort Defiance Christian Reformed Mission to the Presbyterians in 1904, had gone back to Minnesota until called back to take over Zuñi from his old friend, Van der Wagen.[54]

Franciscan charge of the Zuñi Catholic mission was transferred from St. Michaels to Gallup in late 1909 when the friars took over Sacred Heart parish in that town. From the time that Father Godfrey Schilling had broached the subject of the Navaho mission in 1897, the Franciscans had hoped at some future date to assume charge of the neighboring town of Gallup on the Santa Fe Railway line.

Off and on there had been tentative offers to transfer the parish to Franciscan care — as in 1903 when George J. Juillard had hoped to receive a prelacy in the Caribbean or Philippine areas through the aid of Archbishop Chapelle and Visitor General Peter Baptist Englert,

51 A. Weber to W. Ketcham, February 9, 1909, C.I.B.A.

52 Reverend J. Dolfin, *Bringing the Gospel in Hogan and Pueblo, 1896–1921* ([Christian Reformed Church] Grand Rapids, Mich., 1921), p. 312; C. Kuipers, *Zuñi Also Prays,* pp. 104–109.

53 A. Weber to R. Perry, April 5, 1907, C.I.B.A.; A. Weber to W. Ketcham, February 11, 1907, P.A., ZU.; A. Weber to Chas. Lusk, December 27, 1909, P.A., LA.

54 J. Dolfin, *op. cit.,* p. 312. Reverend Dolfin was highly skeptical of the "Friars": "They may be willing to let us alone at present . . . but we doubt not the day will come when we will have them to contend with." *Ibid.,* p. 310.

O.F.M.[55] Again in 1907, shortly after the chapter had expressed a willingness to accept Zuñi and its missions — with the prospect of receiving Gallup — Archbishop Bourgade had taken final canonical steps with his board of consultors.[56] He had offered the Gallup parish, and the friars had planned to take over January, 1908.[57] No conclusive steps were taken, however, until early 1909 when Juillard was offered, and refused, the rectorship of the Santa Fe Cathedral.[58] The rectorship was refused because steps had already been taken in the East to have Juillard appointed head of the Society of the Propagation of the Faith, with headquarters in New York, and his friends were hopeful that he would "receive his well-deserved promotion" even though the American hierarchy no longer favored episcopal appointments channeled through this traditionally French missionary society.[59]

On September 20 Juillard received official permission from Archbishop Pitaval to accept the position as assistant director of the Propagation of the Faith in New York, and asked Father Anselm to have his two Franciscan successors appointed by the Provincial.[60] Again in November Archbishop Pitaval wrote to Anselm inquiring whether the Province of St. John the Baptist had accepted Gallup parish or not, and whether parochial appointments had been made.[61]

Anselm immediately urged Provincial Eugene Buttermann to acknowledge the acceptance of Gallup, further suggesting that Fathers Eligius Kunkel and Arbogast Reissler would make a good team as pastor and assistant for the new parish.[62] Later he informed the Provincial that the Archbishop would prefer Fathers Eligius and Robert Kalt; hesitantly he suggested as second choices Camillus Fangmann as pastor with Eligius as assistant. Certainly no newly ordained priest, he explained, should be sent into such a cosmopolitan and disorganized railroad town as Gallup.[63] Nevertheless Provincial Eugene Buttermann, a tough-minded, Prussian-drillmaster type of superior, held with the tentative appointments made at the summer

[55] B. Nurre to A. Weber, February 26 and May 6, 1903, P.A., BN.; Provincial L. Haverbeck to A. Weber, March 21, 1903, P.A., LH.

[56] Provincial C. Theobald to A. Weber, October 10, 1907, P.A., GA.; see G. J. Juillard to A. Weber, September 20, 1909, P.A., GA.

[57] A. Weber to W. Ketcham, September 18, 1907, C.I.B.A.

[58] Same to same, February 9, 1909, C.I.B.A.

[59] W. Ketcham to A. Weber, March 1, 1909, P.A., RI., and November 29, 1909, H.A.C.

[60] G. J. Juillard to A. Weber, September 20, 1909, P.A., GA.

[61] Archbishop J. B. Pitaval to A. Weber, November 15, 1909, P.A., GA.

[62] A. Weber to Provincial E. Buttermann, November 21, 1909, P.A., GA.

[63] Same to same, December 6, 1909, P.A., GA.

chapter; no archbishop could countermand orders of exempt religious superiors, such as Eugene Buttermann! Father Florentin Meyers would be pastor with Father Ephrem Lieftucher, ordained in 1908, as assistant.[64] However, Ephrem begged off, and Father Robert Kalt was assigned in his stead as assistant to Florentin.[65]

Both friars arrived before Christmas to spend a month with Father Juillard, who wished to introduce them to the running of the parish before he left. At Juillard's invitation Anselm accompanied the retiring pastor and Father Robert on a circuit of the missions east of Gallup, a trip which lasted from December 30 until January 12.[66] Father Juillard and Archbishop Pitaval had suggested a geographical division of the Gallup parish so that two missionaries might reside near Paraje, and from there minister to the Indians and Hispanos in the eastern end of the vast parish.[67] This plan was gradually realized: in July, 1913, Anselm spent several weeks with Father Robert Kalt among the Laguna and Ácoma Indians, assisting in organizing a mission plan for that broad area of scattered missions.[68] Eventually in 1920 San Fidel was designated as the central mission headquarters and erected into a parish separate from Gallup.[69]

On Sunday evening, January 23, 1910, the day before Father Juillard's pastorate was officially to end, the people of Gallup held a farewell for their beloved padre, and in the course of the celebration presented him with a watch. Having graciously acknowledged his thanks for the beautiful keepsake, Father Juillard held up his old watch before the audience: "Here I have my old watch; the exterior is not showy but it runs quietly and perfectly. It is like my dear friend, Father Weber." As he handed the timepiece to Anselm with an affectionate French embrace the crowd applauded heartily.[70]

64 E. Buttermann to A. Weber, December 3, 1909, P.A., GA.

65 Same to same, December 7, 1909, P.A., GA.; Archbishop Pitaval to A. Weber, December 18, 1909, P.A., GA.

66 A. Weber to Dennis Engelhard, editor of *Sendbote,* January 3, 1910, P.A., LA.; A. Weber to Chas. Lusk, January 17, 1910, C.I.B.A.; (A. Weber), *F.M.S.,* 1913, pp. 44–46.

67 A. Weber to W. Ketcham, February 14, 1910, P.A., LM.

68 A. Weber to E. Buttermann, July 31, 1913, P.A., LM.

69 *Tabula Definitionis,* 1920, P.A.

70 Barnabas Meyer, O.F.M., to R. Wilken, February 9, 1951, P.A., CP.; Archbishop Pitaval to A. Weber, December 18, 1909, P.A., GA., fixed January 24, 1910, as the term for G. J. Juillard's pastorate. Juillard and his close friend, Anselm Weber, remained in contact through the years of Juillard's connection with the New York branch of the Society for the Propagation of the Faith, and after his retirement in 1915. He did not realize his ambition to wear the purple. See P.A., GJ., especially G. J. Juillard to A. Weber, May 7, 1914, April 15, 1916, November 12 and December 5, 1919; also W. Ketcham to A. Weber, April 15, 1915, C.I.B.A.

With the taking over of the Gallup parish by the Franciscans, regular, organized care of the Indian missions of Laguna, Ácoma, and Zuñi was provided for. As in the case of Peña Blanca, Farmington, Gallup, Lumberton-Park View, and in 1920, Santa Fe, the friars entered the towns of New Mexico as pastors by the missionary route of Indian and Hispano pueblos and hamlets. To care for these missions a centralized town location was advisable. Financially the town parishes helped to support the missionary and his program. With Gallup it was the same need for Indian missionaries that helped the Franciscans realize their hope of 1898 for a parish situated on the railroad near St. Michaels. The Laguna and Ácoma missions, but particularly the difficult Zuñi mission, made place for the Franciscans at Gallup.

In concluding the treatment of the Zuñi mission it is significant to note the similarity of pattern that obtained with these Indians as well as with the Hopi and the San Juan Navaho. In analyzing the indifferent success, if not relative failure, of Father Anselm Weber in his attempts to found missions among these three groups, it seems pertinent to underline the absence of any direct support from local headmen in all three ventures. Neither Sandoval, the local headman, nor Naakai Dinae, Charley Mitchell, or Chee Dodge, outside headmen with wide prestige, could be located to lend their help on the San Juan River when the two councils were held there. At both Hopi and Zuñi the tribal leaders were definitely antagonistic to mission and school.

Neither should it be overlooked that in these three places Protestant missions were already established for over ten years. Barring the contingency of possible direct intersectarian opposition, the implied divergence and competition among Christian denominations was not lost upon the Indians. Untrained in Church history or dogmatic variance, the Indians regarded church duplication as thoroughly uneconomic, confusing, and not without ironical overtones on the disparity between peace-and-love doctrines as preached and as practiced.[71]

[71] A. Weber to Chas. Lusk, September 17, 1916, P.A., PM.; A. Weber to Commissioner Cato Sells, July 27, 1916, copy in P.A., PM.; Peshlakai, speaking in general council held at Fort Defiance, November 8, 1913, copy of general council minutes in P.A., PM.

Chapter XII

Peacemaker

NAVAHO social control respects the individual; uniform collective behavior is achieved not by authoritarian directive imposed from above but rather by creating a favorable public opinion within a region. Discussion, sometimes all but endless, is consequently the normal device socially acceptable for creating unanimity. To the headman of a region or of an outfit belongs the role of the wise leader: he directs councils and meetings concerned with government or tribal policy, with questions of right and justice, and counsels wisely for the group welfare. Reputation for good judgment and rhetorical ability to persuade account largely for his effectiveness as a headman.[1]

Frequently government officials working among The People and trying to get action and results quickly by personal authority would resort to orders and sometimes force — with disastrous outcome. Anselm Weber on several occasions came into the picture as conciliator and peacemaker between government officials and The People. For this service he was admirably equipped by his own peace-loving nature, by his training in patience both as subject and superior in a Franciscan community, and by his intimate understanding of Navaho culture.

In November, 1905, Navaho Superintendent Reuben Perry was seized by a group of fifteen angry Navaho at Chin Lee and was forced to pardon a Navaho accused of rape.[2] The accused Indian, Linni by name, had been charged with lassoing the girl while she was away from camp herding sheep. Through her family the girl had brought charges against Linni. In line with Navaho procedure in such cases, the local Navaho policeman had acted as referee between the accused and the girl's family; the restitution fee, or crime price, was fixed at one white horse. Linni had agreed to this, and had turned over the

[1] *An Ethnologic Dictionary*, pp. 422–423; Kluckhohn and Leighton, *The Navaho*, pp. 69–71.
[2] C.I.A., *Annual Report*, 1906, pp. 115, 121.

white horse to the family of the girl. When news of the affair reached Fort Defiance, Mr. Perry would not recognize the intratribal form of justice, but insisted that Linni come to Fort Defiance to stand trial before himself, the superintendent. This had brought on the riot by the obstreperous Navaho of the Chin Lee and Black Mountain areas.[3]

At Tseili Father Anselm had heard the grumbling over what the Navaho considered the arbitrary flouting of Navaho juridical procedure on this occasion, as well as Perry's customary forceful and direct methods in handling all offenses personally. The missionary had told Chee Dodge of his fears that the Indians were seriously worked up, but had cautioned Chee not to alarm Mr. Perry. He wished personally to discuss the problem with the Superintendent and to suggest that Perry work more from within Navaho political organization. Four days after speaking to Chee Dodge, however, and before the friar could talk matters over with Perry, the riot had occurred at Chin Lee.[4]

Shortly after returning from his harrowing experience at Chin Lee, Mr. Perry called at St. Michaels to discuss the whole affair with Father Anselm and Chee Dodge. They agreed that the mistake had already been made, stressing the point, however, that the agent could not permit the example of successful violence against the government to stand. Either he should apprehend those guilty of violence, Father Anselm suggested, or he should resign.[5]

Perry immediately called for help from Fort Wingate. As a result Lieutenant Lewis and twelve soldiers rode to Fort Defiance. This was shortly before the Yeibichai Dance was to take place near St. Michaels. If trouble were in the air the interaction of widely separated groups at the Yeibichai would likely focus it and give substance to rumor, it was agreed. Lieutenant Lewis after discussing the Chin Lee incident and the approaching "sing" rode off to Gallup; from there he kept in contact by Indian courier and phone with St. Michaels.

Obviously to the friars, the officer expected trouble and possible bloodshed at the dance, but preferred personally not to be on hand to prevent any such disturbances. Once trouble began he could lead

[3] A. Weber, *Sendbote,* 33:510–514, June, 1906; *The Albuquerque Morning Journal,* November 21, 1905.

[4] A. Weber, *Sendbote,* 33:225–226, 412–415, March and May, 1906.

[5] A. Weber, "The Navaho Indian Trouble of 1905," dated March 15, 1907, P.A., ID. This manuscript copy was sent to Father Ketcham to be used before the Commissioner of Indian Affairs in defense of Mr. Perry. For charges of arbitrary, extra-legal penalties in the Chin Lee affair see Secretary of the Interior, May 25, 1908, *Report on Employment of United States Soldiers in Arresting By-a-lil-le and other Navajo Indians,* p. 4.

a full-scale punitive expedition. So, at least, it seemed to those who were trying to avoid trouble. Accordingly Mr. Perry ground the magneto crank on the telephone until he made contact with Fort Wingate. Strong, direct language from the Superintendent brought swift results. Lieutenant Colonel George H. Paddock immediately dispatched K Troop, Fifth Cavalry, from the fort east of Gallup. Fortunately or not, they arrived on November 16, the day after the Yeibichai, with Captain Willard and Lieutenant Cooly in command.[6]

At the "sing" some two thousand Indians had congregated; the headmen moving from outfit to outfit sensed overtones of discontent. Before the dance these leaders had met at St. Michaels to plan their talks to the Indians. Father Weber and Chee Dodge had also brought headmen Black Horse and Tqayoni to Fort Defiance where the headmen chided the Superintendent for bypassing the headmen in government relations with The People. They had told him that he should trust them, the chosen representatives of the Navaho, and that he should consult with them; then he would not be blamed for everything, even for the tiny penalties which he personally had been handing out. If he worked through the headmen, they assured Mr. Perry, he would be cushioned against criticism from the Navaho, and he would find a readier response among the Indians to government policy.[7]

At the Yeibichai itself on November 15, according to the plan arranged at St. Michaels, various headmen spoke to the assembled Indians: Black Horse, Charley Mitchell, Tqayoni, Qastin Yazhe, and Chee Dodge. All stressed the need for peace with the government, and pleaded against the use of whisky at the dance. Chee told for the first time how Manuelito before he died had exacted a promise from young Dodge to lead the people along the right way, and to keep them from destroying themselves again by trying to fight the government. Manuelito had been the last of the Navaho tribal war chiefs, and his words had always made a deep impression. Addressing those who lived off the reservation, Chee Dodge continued:[8]

> The President has given you a long rope so you may graze wherever you please. If a man has a good horse and pickets him out he gives him a long rope in good grass and lets him graze as far as he can; but if he has a mean horse he gives him a short rope with his head tied close to a post so he can get but little feed. The President has

[6] A. Weber, *Sendbote,* 33:596–600, 704–709, July and August, 1906; War Department, *Annual Reports,* 1906, p. 160.

[7] A. Weber, *Sendbote,* 33:601, July, 1906.

[8] Entire speech translated by A. Weber is given in *The McKinley County Republican,* December 16, 1905.

given you a long rope. Some of you have a very long rope; you live very far from the Reservation; others who live nearer the Reservation have a shorter rope; and those who live on the Reservation have a still shorter rope; but the President has a rope on every one of you, and if you do not appreciate the good treatment you are given, if you try to make trouble, he will pull on all the ropes and draw you fellows all together to a tight place. . . . You will lose your stock, you will be afoot, you will be nothing, you will be wiped out, and will be guarded by troops, and everybody will laugh at you and say: 'See what a large tribe this was, and this is all that is left of them.'

During the course of the night-long dance and chant ceremony another Fort Wingate Indian scout brought a message from Colonel Paddock, the officer in charge at the army post. He asked that Father Weber would send the courier back with a message "upon the situation at your mission as regards danger of Indian outbreak."[9] Anselm told the Indian to enjoy the dance and the next morning chuckled as he wrote out an answer to the officer to the effect that the dance had been most peaceful and that "as to your two scouts, I must say they ought to receive the golden medal as the best dancers in the U.S.A. No doubt, their good dancing had a tranquilizing effect, since they pleased the Navajos and appeased the wrath of the angry war-gods."[10]

On the sixteenth of November the missionary accompanied headmen Peshlakai, Attsi Yazhe ni' Biye, Belo, and Chee Dodge to Fort Defiance, where a council was held with Perry and Captain Willard. The headmen agreed to report the situation to the Chin Lee Indians and to tell them that the culprits who had led the riot against Superintendent Perry would have to give themselves up. Peshlakai in his hard, direct way spoke for the headmen before Perry.[11]

Peshlakai was always a good choice as spokesman for the Navaho since they loved to hear the Silversmith "tell off" the government people in his bluff, laconic way. Many times had the Silversmith from Crystal made the white government officials wince and The People laugh. He sensed the bitter hatred of the Navaho against the government practice of sending the children off the reservation to boarding schools, and he caught the Indians' mood in his concrete and devastating criticism: "You drive all over our land in your yellow wagons to take away our healthy children; then you drop them off at Gallup as bags of skin and bones when you are through with

[9] Geo. H. Paddock, Lieut. Col., Fifth Cavalry, to A. Weber, November 15, 1905, P.A., ID.

[10] A. Weber to Lieut. Col. Geo. H. Paddock, November 16, 1905, copy in P.A., ID.

[11] A. Weber, *Sendbote,* 33:804–805, September, 1906.

them."[12] His disdain for soldiers was almost as low: "You say our horses no good; you bring in your stallions. You say our sheep no good; you bring in your rams. You say our children no good; you bring in your soldiers."[13]

However, on November 16 when Peshlakai spoke for the headmen at Fort Defiance, he was less abusive — and with reason. As head of the Tqachini clan, to which most of the Chin Lee culprits belonged, his personal prestige was at stake. His was the task of convincing and bringing in the culprits involved in threatening and roughing up Perry. Glumly he agreed to act as leader of the group of regional headmen whose mission was to represent the whole tribe in seeking out the guilty parties.[14]

The sight of the headmen, and their fully armed followers, was too much for the individuals around Chin Lee who were involved. Winslow, who had grabbed the bridle of Perry's team, and Linni, accused of inciting to violence, meekly surrendered to Belo, and were brought in to Fort Defiance on November 19, 1905. Dlad, the muscular brave who had pinioned Perry's arms when he tried to draw a Colt, and his brothers, Tsossi ni' Biye, and Dinelgai, went into hiding.

Captain Willard who was in charge of apprehending the rioters next called in a second contingent of headmen from the general Chin Lee region, reminding them that they were bound by the 1868 treaty to aid their agent in apprehending criminals. In red ink the headmen made their crosses to a compact that within fifty days they would bring in the hiding culprits, or, failing, would substitute themselves to stand trial. Peshlakai, Belo, and Attside Yazhe ni' Biye promised to back them to the full.[15]

Early in December while Willard, Cooly, and Perry were spending the night at St. Michaels a rider came in from Crystal with news that Dlad and his brothers had fled from their hideout in Cañon de Chelly and had surrendered to their clan headman, Peshlakai. On December 7 they rode in together to Fort Defiance. Doyaltqihi, the Black Mountain headman, who had egged on the rioters, was later brought in by the Chin Lee-area headmen.[16]

All seven accused were arrested and without any semblance of court trial were sent to the federal penitentiary at Alcatraz at from

[12] A. Weber, *Sendbote,* 35:36–37, January, 1908.

[13] Dr. Wigglesworth, interview, October 31, 1950.

[14] A. Weber, *Sendbote,* 33:805, September, 1906.

[15] *The McKinley County Republican,* December 16, 1905. This lengthy article was written by Anselm Weber. See A. Weber to W. Ketcham, March 15, 1907, P.A., ID.

[16] *Ibid.;* A. Weber, *Sendbote,* 33:806–808, September, 1906.

one to two years' hard labor. The sentence was urged by Perry and imposed by the Secretary of the Interior. Because of waning health at Alcatraz the prisoners were later removed to Fort Huachuca, Arizona, in 1906.[17]

This practice of punishment and imprisonment of Indians without trial involved the same Captain Willard in the Byalille case two years later. The Captain while ostensibly on training maneuvers with seventy-five mounted man had aided Superintendent W. T. Shelton of the Northern Navaho Agency at Shiprock to arrest Byalille.[18] Byalille, a somewhat obstreperous old singer of the Black Mountain region, had consistently opposed government interference with the Navaho way of life. He openly spoke against compulsory education and against sheep dipping, and made a point to let it be known rather widely that he would generally oppose the dictatorial methods employed by Mr. Shelton. In building up his Shiprock School, and in successfully pushing irrigation, the Superintendent had depended on his Navaho police rather generally to enforce compliance instead of trying to win over the Indians to his projects.[19]

Fearing trouble in any attempt to arrest Byalille, Shelton enlisted the services of Troops I and K under Willard to bring in the outspoken and thoroughly individualistic singer. After an all-night ride from Shiprock to the vicinity of Aneth, Utah, Willard had surprised old Byalille and Polly, along with their outfit. The scuffle and arrest took place before dawn on the twenty-ninth of October, 1907, near McElmo Canyon. The camp had been completely encircled by Indian police and troops before the arrest was attempted. Informants had previously described the hogan where the old singer would be sleeping off the exhausting effects of a long ceremony he had performed in the neighborhood.

The old man had awakened as the police entered the hogan, and had put up a reputable scuffle and outcry before he was overpowered. Several members of Byalille's outfit had grabbed their rifles at the sound of the uproar, and in the dim half-light fired on the attackers, killing a sergeant's horse but otherwise inflicting no damage on policemen or soldiers. With the first shot the Indian police and the soldiers had opened fire, killing two Navaho.[20]

Possibly to dramatize the situation and to set an example of what

[17] C.I.A., *Annual Report,* 1906, p. 118; *ibid.,* 1907, pp. 91–92.
[18] C.I.A., *Annual Report,* 1908, pp. 89–94.
[19] A. Weber, *Sendbote,* 36:13–17, January, 1909.
[20] I.R.A., *Annual Report,* 1908, pp. 32–33; C.I.A., *Annual Report,* 1908, p. 90.

Smiling daughters of *The People* at the entrance of adobe-covered hogan

Diné Tsossi: Slim Navaho

comes to those who passively resist government policy, Shelton and Willard recommended ten years at hard labor for Byalille and Polly, and when the penitentiary term was finished, perpetual banishment from the reservation. They recommended two-year terms for seven other Navaho. Commissioner Leupp had endorsed the sentence, and the Indians were taken to Fort Huachuca to serve their terms.[21]

Three weeks later Commissioner Leupp spoke to Father Ketcham about the case and asked him to contact Anselm Weber for a report on the situation on the reservation. Were the Indians angered and in arms? The Indian Rights Association and Reverend Andrew Antes of Aneth, Utah, were publicizing the affair, and criticism of the government's unnecessary violence and kangaroo court methods in sentencing the Indians was mounting.[22]

After checking with Captain Willard at Fort Wingate on Thanksgiving Day, and after reading his reports, Father Anselm called a meeting with other Navaho spokesmen in and about Fort Defiance. After sifting the various stories, checking thoroughly for facts in the situation, Anselm Weber sent in his report and recommendations to the Bureau of Catholic Indian Missions, which in turn relayed them to the Commissioner of Indian Affairs. Customarily such business was handled verbally between the Commissioner and Father Ketcham or his secretary, Mr. Charles Lusk, thus avoiding official records and the contingency of compromising situations involving missionaries and the local Indian officials.[23]

In his lengthy communication to Father Ketcham, the Navaho missioner detailed the facts in the case, exonerating Captain Willard on the score that once fired upon he had no recourse but to return the fire. His criticism he directed at the San Juan Superintendent who had unnecessarily brought on the incident by his "arbitrary and autocratic" methods. Father Anselm pointed out how the government agent had dispensed with the headmen in his area and had turned all law enforcement over to his Navaho policemen, who were generally a meddlesome lot at the Shiprock agency, men who frequently used their office to antagonize their personal enemies. The friar further excoriated the inspector whom Leupp had sent out to investigate the

[21] C.I.A., *ibid.*, p. 92.

[22] W. Ketcham to A. Weber, November 20, 1907, C.I.B.A.; see C.I.A., *Annual Report*, 1908, pp. 32–35.

[23] A. Weber to Chas. Lusk, November 26, 1907, C.I.B.A.; A. Weber to W. Ketcham, December 1, 1907, C.I.B.A. Many letters in the archives of the Bureau of Catholic Indian Missions bear annotations giving the date when the communication was discussed with the government officials involved.

Aneth incident. This inspector had apparently been still dreaming of his Rough Rider days under Roosevelt, as he had raced around the reservation with a spirited team, firing his revolver constantly to force on his jaded horses. To the Navaho the man was an utter fool.[24]

As to Captain Willard's current plan to move strong concentrations of troops through the Black Mountains in an effort to impress the grumbling Indians, Anselm thought it sounded positively weird.[25]

> Submit to whom and to what? I know some of the Black Mountain Indians and I assure you that such a course would be preposterous, not to say criminal. If such a course is pursued, I shall join the Black Mountain Indians and 'howl' with them so that the whole United States will hear us. . . . All those Indians need is a good competent, reasonable superintendent. . . . The Navahos are men who resent mere coercion.

On April 14, and again on April 19, 1908, Brigadier General Hugh Scott, head of West Point, called on Anselm Weber at St. Michaels for further investigation of the Byalille incident. He did so at the instruction of Commissioner Leupp whose connivance with the extra-judicial mode of sentencing Indians without benefit of trial was being publicly assailed.[26] The Indian Rights Association had continued their agitation, and the government wished to quash and hush once and for all the Aneth affair.

In his discussion with Scott the missioner again stressed the fact that though Superintendent Shelton was an excellent agriculturist he was not the administrator type suited to handle Indians, nor could he be generally upheld in the Aneth fracas. The friar admitted that there was widespread discontent among the Indians of Shelton's jurisdiction. For the good of Government-Indian relations, Father Anselm believed, Mr. Shelton should be replaced.[27]

General Scott apparently disregarded much of Anselm's testimony; his favorable report upholding the government's conduct in the Aneth arrests and imprisonment did not, however, quiet the public protests.[28] Through the insistence of the Indian Rights Association the case went to the Arizona Supreme Court which handed down the decision that "Indians are not wards of the executive officers, but wards of the United States, acting through executive officers, it is true, but expressing its fostering will by legislation. . . . Our attention has not been directed to legislation expressly authorizing such

[24] A. Weber to W. Ketcham, December 1, 1907, C.I.B.A.
[25] *Ibid.;* A. Weber, *Sendbote,* 35:1083, December, 1908.
[26] A. Weber to W. Ketcham, April 15, 1908, C.I.B.A. [27] *Ibid.*
[28] Secretary of the Interior, May 25, 1908, *op. cit.,* pp. 2–3.

summary methods."[29] The Arizona Supreme Court ruled the imprisonment unlawful, and granted the writ of Habeas Corpus. Since the newly elected Taft administration decided against appealing the decision to the Supreme Court of the United States, the Indians were released March 20, 1909.[30]

Prior to the outcome of the Arizona Supreme Court case Mr. Shelton and Captain Willard had been successful in carrying through their earlier plans for overawing the Black Mountain Navaho. Four hundred and fifty troops converged on Fort Defiance from Forts Huachuca, Apache, and Wingate during July, 1908.[31] With journalese abandon the press informed the public that the Indians were again "on the verge of an uprising."[32] By chance, passing through Albuquerque at the time, Father Anselm warned the editor half seriously that his paper's scare lines might turn a few hot and thirsty soldiers trigger happy at sight of the bloodthirsty Navaho tending their sheep or hoeing a gully corn patch.[33] Outside the fact that interpreter Frank Walker was earning $25 weekly as guide, the friar thought the whole pacifying campaign "ridiculous."[34]

It was in 1913, fifteen years after Father Anselm had come to live among the Navaho, that he had an opportunity to act directly as a conciliator and possibly to prevent actual bloodshed between government troops and Navaho Indians. On this occasion, according to local newspapers, fifteen hundred Navaho braves were dug in on the high mesa on top of Beautiful Mountain, an impregnable fortress, where they meant to defy the United States Army.[35] Accurate, on-the-spot note taking by Anselm Weber recounts a far less bloodcurdling set of facts, and, incidently, portrays his deep concern for peace.[36]

[29] 12 Arizona, 153–154, as cited in Schmeckebier, *The Indian Office,* p. 259; complete texts on the trial are contained in S. M. Brosius, *Decision rendered by the Arizona Supreme Court in the Proceedings Instituted by the Indian Rights Association for a Writ of Habeas Corpus in the case of certain Indians Imprisoned without trial, with accompanying papers,* 61 Cong., 1 sess., Senate document No. 118, pp. 1–6.

[30] I.R.A., *Annual Report,* 1909, pp. 5–10; F. E. Leupp, *The Indian and His Problem,* p. 266; see Walter Dyk, *A Navaho Autobiography* (Viking Fund Publication in Anthropology, No. 8; New York: Viking Press, 1947), pp. 130–134, 163–165, for a Navaho's memories of Byalille. [31] A. Weber, *Sendbote,* 36:220–223, March, 1909.

[32] *The Albuquerque Morning Journal,* July 12, 1908.

[33] A. Weber, *Sendbote,* 36:223, March, 1909.

[34] A. Weber to Chas. Lusk, August 30, 1908, C.I.B.A.

[35] *Albuquerque Evening Herald,* November 19 and 20, 1913; *The Albuquerque Morning Journal,* November 20, 1913.

[36] A detailed account of the entire incident is continued in a manuscript journal of sixteen ledger pages written by A. Weber over the five-week period involved, and entitled "Beautiful Mountain Journal, January, 1914," P.A., ID.

Superintendent Shelton of Shiprock had sent his Navaho policemen to arrest Hatali Yazhe on charges of polygamy, and to investigate Indian charges of witchcraft. Hatali was the son of Bizhoshi, an old and highly respected singer, or medicine man, of the Beautiful Mountain country. Hatali was away on a deer hunt when the police arrived to place him under arrest, so to insure his coming in to the Shiprock agency they arrested his three wives instead. Returning home to find his wives "stolen," as he put it, Hatali had turned to his father, old Bizhoshi, for advice. The old man after discussing the wife-stealing with members of his outfit decided to talk Mr. Shelton out of his determination to have Hatali hailed before a federal court. With his son Hatali and ten other men of his outfit, all armed, Bizhoshi rode into Shiprock. Shelton was away so the clansmen decided for the present to take home the "stolen" wives of Hatali who were living in a hogan on the agency grounds. A Navaho policeman who tried to block the mounted men was disarmed and roughed up.[37]

Superintendent Paquette of Fort Defiance met with Father Anselm and Chee Dodge on October 18, after Mr. Shelton had called on United States Marshal Hudspeth at Santa Fe and had sworn out warrants for the twelve "renegades."[38] As a result of the conference at St. Michaels, Anselm Weber, Chee, Peshlakai, Charley Mitchell, and Black Horse, all headmen of esteem, sought out Hatali Yazhe and his followers at a great squaw dance held in the Lukachukai Mountains. Hatali's group agreed to meet at St. Michaels for a general talk on the matter, but they insistently refused to surrender; over and over they repeated the issue basic to their stand: they had only taken back the three women who belonged to their clan.[39]

On the appointed day Marshal Hudspeth, Shelton, Paquette, Chee, and Father Anselm waited in vain at St. Michaels for the Indians to appear.[40] Another trip by Peshlakai and Charley Mitchell induced Bizhoshi, who had by this time assumed the leadership for the accused, to show up at St. Michaels with his party for a parley. After much discussion at the mission and at Fort Defiance they agreed to surrender to the federal marshal on November 13.[41] Subse-

[37] Testimony of hearing held at St. Michaels, November 1, 1913; shorthand notes and typed transcription, H.A.C.

[38] Fort Defiance Office Diary, October 18, 19, 1913, W.R.C.; *The Albuquerque Morning Journal,* November 21, 1913.

[39] Fort Defiance Office Diary, October 19, 1913, W.R.C.; A. Weber to W. Ketcham, November 17, 1913, P.A., ID.

[40] Fort Defiance Office Diary, October 26, 1913, W.R.C.

[41] *Ibid.,* October 31–November 3.

quently, however, they became frightened at the prospect of going to Santa Fe "where it always costs so much money" (in fines), and withdrew again into the security of their vast and inaccessible homeland on the mountain.[42]

After word reached St. Michaels from the Bureau of Catholic Indian Missions that Commissioner Sells wished Anselm to enter the case personally and try for a peaceful settlement, the missionary set out across the Chuska range on November 29 with a medicine man and Frank Walker.[43] After an evening conference with Bizhoshi Biye and his people at Noel's Store, Anselm was invited to visit and continue the talks on top of Beautiful Mountain where Hatali Yazhe was crippled up with rheumatism. Taking along the singer, Frank Walker, and three other respected Navaho of the vicinity, the friar climbed up the narrow defile to beyond the rimrock of Beautiful Mountain where he met with Bizhoshi and six of his people in their large hogan.[44]

There as at St. Michaels the Indians begged Anselm to settle the affair out of hand, since they would not leave the reservation, nor would they surrender to Mr. Shelton, who had been mean to them, they explained, ever since he had taken over on the San Juan. They insisted that the Shiprock agent was always picking on them and that his policemen only wanted to get Navaho into trouble. They said that Navaho were always in jail at Shiprock because Shelton needed men to farm the school gardens and wanted women of The People on hand to weave blankets for the Indian Agency and for other things which were bad. Life under Shelton was not good like the old days, they said; they were "like little birds in the rocks, unprotected, and the agent was picking them off, and if he had his way he would next castrate them so they could have no more sons." No, they insisted, they would not go to jail for Mr. Shelton; what they did want was peace and to be let alone. If Mr. Shelton wanted to see them he could come to visit them, but they would never leave or be put off the reservation which was their old home.[45]

Father Anselm reported to Shiprock and brought back from there Major McLaughlin who had been sent from Devil's Lake, Minnesota, to help settle the Navaho trouble. At Noel's Store more conferences were held, but the Indians would not agree to surrender and be

[42] "Beautiful Mountain Journal, January, 1914," P.A., ID.

[43] Telegram from W. Ketcham to A. Weber, November 8, 1913, H.A.C.; Fort Defiance Office Diary, November 9, 1913, W.R.C.

[44] "Beautiful Mountain Journal, January, 1914," P.A., ID.

[45] *Ibid., The Albuquerque Morning Journal,* November 18, 1913.

punished. They said they were sure that the Inspector would tell the President at Washington that they had not *stolen* the women, and that they were good Navaho who wanted no trouble, and only wished to be let alone by the white people at Shiprock, especially Mr. Shelton. A whispered remark by one Navaho at this juncture that several of them should embrace Chischilli and beg him to settle the business at once was distorted by one of the Indians present as a threat to grab Father Anselm and hold him as a prisoner and hostage. This led to the false rumor the next day that even the missionary's life would not be respected by the renegades. All that Inspector McLaughlin could promise Bizhoshi in the matter of settling the controversy was his assurance that he would "make a paper" in which he would report the interview to the Secretary of the Interior.[46]

On November 16, when back again at St. Michaels, Father Anselm learned that troops were arriving at Gallup from Nebraska, and that General Hugh Scott, his old friend, was being sent to Navaho country from El Paso, where he had recently been sent to patrol the border during the Mexican revolutionary turmoil.[47]

Peter Paquette, superintendent at Fort Defiance, Chee Dodge, Doctor Norbert Gottbrath, and Anselm Weber hurried to Gallup as soon as the General had set up quarters in the local hotel. They stressed the implications involved in bringing armed troops onto the reservation during such a period of tension. General Scott reassured them that he had no intention of bringing on an Indian war, but counted on deploying his troops to overawe and impress the Navaho with the seriousness of the situation in the mind of the government.[48] The General suggested that Father Anselm and Chee Dodge contact Bizhoshi and his outfit to request a peaceful conference with the General at Noel's Store three days hence.[49]

It was raining and snowing when the party of four left the General's hotel room on Sunday night. Mr. Paquette's automobile bogged down incessantly in the mucky gumbo clay so that they did not reach Fort Defiance until four o'clock the next afternoon. Chee

[46] "Beautiful Mountain Journal," *ibid.*

[47] *The Albuquerque Morning Journal,* November 19, 20, 1913; Fort Defiance Office Diary, November 16, 1913, W.R.C.

[48] Fort Defiance Office Diary, November 23, 1913, W.R.C.; H. L. Scott to John Forest McGee, O.F.M., April 3, 1933, P.A., ID.

[49] For General Scott's narrative on the Beautiful Mountain disturbance see H. L. Scott, *Some Memories of a Soldier* (New York: Appleton-Century Company, 1929), pp. 491–495.

Dodge accompanied Father Anselm and Doctor Gottbrath on horseback across the Chuskas from Crystal in deep snow which prolonged to two days the trip to Noel's Store. General Scott and his son, Lieutenant D. H. Scott, United States Deputy Marshal, J. R. Galusha, and Frank Walker were already there, having mucked their way from Gallup with a troop of soldiers who literally pushed the General's auto as far as Tohatchi. There the soldiers themselves became mired in. Mr. Shelton with his whole police force had shortly thereafter met Scott en route, to urge an immediate assault on Beautiful Mountain "before the outlaws should escape." The General refused, and even forbade Shelton or his police to accompany him to the store.[50]

Runners who belonged to the same clan as Bizhoshi were dispatched by Chee Dodge and Father Anselm to request the old singer's presence at another council, this time with General Scott and the St. Michaels group. With an eye to the high status enjoyed by women in the Navaho social structure, the missionary had relayed the information that Bizhoshi's young wife should by all means attend the conference with General Scott. One of the messengers, named John Brown, had also played dramatically on the old Navaho's love of family to win his consent to another council; if the singer would not meet the General and go to see the judge in Santa Fe, he had urged, it would be "like putting his wife in one pocket and his children in the other, and then jumping off the cliff."[51]

At the store the next day seventy-five to one hundred armed Navaho assembled from their winter homes in the surrounding mountains. They did not mean to fight, but if Bizhoshi would not surrender they would be willing, they said, to substitute themselves in order to save their communities and their flocks from bloodshed and misery at the hands of the soldiers. Kit Carson and his scorched-earth warfare of the 1860's was a living memory.

In the afternoon Bizhoshi, Attside Naez Biye, his wife and two daughters, and three others from Beautiful Mountain arrived for the council; Hatali Yazhe and two others had been off in the mountains hunting, and could not be reached immediately. It was Thanksgiving Day, November 27, 1913, and in good American tradition General Scott put on a grand dinner for all the assembled

[50] "Beautiful Mountain Journal, January, 1914," P.A., ID.; *The Albuquerque Morning Journal,* November 28, 1913. Frank Walker, interpreter for General Scott, supplied A. Weber with details not witnessed by the priest. RW.

[51] A. Weber to W. Ketcham, February 15, 1914, P.A., ID.; "Beautiful Mountain Journal, January, 1914," P.A., ID.

Indians. The council took place in Noel's Store after the mutton had been finished off.[52]

Chee at the General's left did the interpreting while Anselm Weber sat on the right; in front squatted the half-dozen accused men. The General had been heralded in the newspaper for his ability with the Indian sign language, but since the Navaho do not use that mode of Indian communication, he had to rely on the interpreter.[53]

Over the period of two days during which the other offenders gradually wandered in, General Scott listened to their story repeatedly and tried to make clear his reasons for bringing in the soldiers. Even if Mr. Shelton were in the wrong, he insisted, the Navaho must learn to use the United States law and its courts of enforcement; they could not throw the officers and headmen of the United States to one side and judge their own acts. He explained the laws and the courts, and the relationship of Mr. Shelton to the United States Government. They had brushed Mr. Shelton aside without going to the courts, and now he, a general with three thousand men under him in Texas, had been sent to bring them to the court at Santa Fe. He would at any cost, moreover, bring them to court! If they would not come peaceably he would have to use force and soldiers. This would be bad, he said, because the soldiers could not tell friend from enemy, nor Navaho men from Navaho women at a distance. To fight would bring much blood and much trouble.[54]

Bizhoshi later in the evening walked apart with Chee, and Chee advised him strongly to think not only of himself but also of his family and of all the Navaho people who would suffer. Bizhoshi said that he was willing but that his son, Attside Naez Biye, refused. Moreover he was afraid that the big, dark, silent son would influence his other son, Hatali Yazhe. Chee next invited Attside for a talk in the General's tent, and again stressed what his defiance would mean to his wife, family, and to all of The People in that part of the country. After an hour Attside Naez Biye broke down. All was ready for the Friday afternoon council during the course of which one after the other of the Indians involved agreed to surrender. As they came up to hold the General's hand the seventy-five Indians who had been watching silently and worriedly outside the store began to cheer and clasp hands all around, with the accused men, with the General, with Anselm and the other headmen.[55]

[52] *Ibid.;* H. L. Scott, *Some Memories of a Soldier,* pp. 493–494.

[53] H. L. Scott to J. F. McGee, O.F.M., April 3, 1933, P.A., ID.

[54] "Beautiful Mountain Journal, January, 1914," P.A., ID.; see H. L. Scott, *Some Memories of a Soldier,* p. 494.

[55] *Ibid.*

The General agreed to give them two days to return to their homes on Beautiful Mountain to put their affairs in order, and to find the two other men who were still missing. The accused also won a promise from Chee Dodge and Father Anselm that these two good friends would accompany them to the judge at Santa Fe.[56]

At Santa Fe on December 3, the day after Bizhoshi and his seven companions had embraced the General in farewell, Judge William H. Pope opened the hearing on the case in the Federal District Court.[57] General Scott had sent a special appeal addressed to Judge Pope, and Father Anselm was called to testify along with Chee Dodge as to the facts in the case, and especially with respect to the total misconception of United States law on the part of the Navaho. Attorney Francis C. Wilson, appointed to defend the eight prisoners, scored the Indian policemen of Shiprock for their rumor mongering and misrepresentations of the case. Others, too, had ballooned the incident out of all proportion, he explained, so that public opinion had become hysterical.[58]

On December 4 Judge Pope, after lecturing the Indians on respect for the law of the country, imposed nominal sentences for rioting on seven of the accused. Jail sentences ranged from ten to thirty days at the Gallup county jail, purposely chosen because it was closest to Navaho country. In effect the light terms amounted to a vindication of the Indians in the light of the tremendous furore raised over the episode.[59]

An Albuquerque paper which on November 18 had headlined the defiance of 1500 Navaho on Beautiful Mountain now declared patronizingly that "the Indians are a different and an inferior race to the Caucasian," and that Indian polygamy should be viewed in that tolerant light.[60]

Back at Shiprock there was much indignation over the light sentences, and, with the indignation, reported efforts to keep Father Weber, Chee Dodge, Peshlakai, Black Horse, and Charley Mitchell, the best-known headmen, from coddling and spoiling the obstreperous elements among the Indians.[61] Mr. Shelton, who sometime after the

[56] A. Weber, *F.M.S.*, 1919, p. 16; *The Albuquerque Morning Journal*, December 4, 1913.

[57] *The Santa Fe New Mexican*, December 3, 1913.

[58] *Ibid.;* General Scott to J. F. McGee, O.F.M., April 3, 1933, P.A., ID.

[59] *The Albuquerque Morning Journal*, December 5, 1913; A. Weber to D. Engelhard, telegram, December 4, 1913, P.A., ID.; A. Weber, *F.M.S.*, 1919, p. 17.

[60] *The Albuquerque Morning Journal*, November 18 and 20, 1913; December 5, 1913.

[61] Mrs. M. L. Eldridge to Chee Dodge, December 23, 1913, P.A., IA.; same to A. Weber, December 22, 1913, February 9 and 11, 1914, H.A.C.

conclusion of the incident had reportedly decided to resign his post as superintendent because of the illness of his wife, swiftly disclaimed any intent to resign after a Farmington, New Mexico, newspaper printed lurid and unfounded charges against him.[62]

Something of a cynical note, stridently reminiscent of the official Navaho Government Service indifference to missions and missionaries among the Navaho,[63] attaches to the selfless effort of Father Anselm in the Beautiful Mountain affair. "The great department of the Government that had so urgently demanded his help, never at any time made public acknowledgement of . . . services," was Father Ketcham's summing up of the "execrable treatment accorded you [Anselm] in the Shiprock matter."[64] For all his strenuous physical effort in crossing and recrossing the Chuskas in deep snow, his tireless and successful efforts to induce the accused Indians to sit at repeated councils at St. Michaels and at Noel's Store, his expenses in feeding his Indian companions, as well as the accused, and providing horse fodder — for his entire effort — not one official word of gratitude or approval was tendered to Father Anselm Weber by the Washington officials. William Ketcham reimbursed the poor missionary from Catholic Indian Bureau funds, since he had relayed the Commissioner's request that Anselm try to negotiate a peaceful settlement.[65]

General Scott, it is true, personally thanked the missioner and did recommend Father Anselm's good work to the Secretary of the Interior.[66] In September, ten months after the incident, the Office of Indian Affairs did reluctantly approve and pay a claim of $46.20 which covered only the expenses for the first trip to Beautiful Mountain.[67]

It would be a distortion to imply that by and large Anselm Weber's work for peace and good will between government and Indians went

[62] Fintan Zumbahlen, O.F.M., to A. Weber, February 28, 1914, P.A., ID.; *Farmington Enterprise,* Special Edition, January 22, 1916.

[63] "In view of the long-time services of missionaries among the Navajos as indeed among all American Indians, the Inquiry was much surprised to note the indifference of the Navajo Government Service and also of many of the Indian people to the Mission Centers on the Reservation." Phelps-Stokes Fund, *The Navajo Indian Problem — An Inquiry,* p. 115.

[64] W. Ketcham, in B.C.I.M., *The Indian Sentinel,* 1:315, July, 1921; A. Weber to W. Ketcham, May 3, 1914, C.I.B.A.; W. Ketcham to A. Weber, May 14, 1914, P.A., MO.

[65] W. Ketcham to A. Weber, April 25, 1914, C.I.B.A.

[66] H. L. Scott to A. Weber, December 11, 1913, H.A.C.; H. L. Scott to Secretary of the Interior, December 13, 1913, copy in P.A., ID.

[67] C. F. Hauke to Auditor of the Interior Department, July 31, 1914, Treasury Claim 255892, copy in P.A., ID.; R. W. Woolley to A. Weber, September 12, 1914, Treasury Claim 255892, H.A.C.

unthanked. Individual government officials did appreciate deeply, and did acknowledge his constant and effective efforts for harmony on the reservation. Superintendent Reuben Perry, who had figured in the quelling of the Navaho disturbances of 1905 and the Hopi rioting of 1906 expressed simply and quietly his official thanks to his good friend: "Father Anselm Weber has been helpful in many ways."[68]

Later on he translated this more fully: In 1917 Anselm Weber lay sick in Washington, D. C., on the occasion when a joint representation of Navaho and Laguna Indians had moved on the capitol with Father Anselm to lobby for settlement of land problems.[69] In a warm personal note, testifying to fifteen years of mutual co-operation and deep friendship, Perry affectionately characterized the friar's life as peacemaker and missionary: "The Navahos claim that you belong to them. . . . I desire to say that you belong to all the Indians, and the Catholic and Protestant peoples of the Southwest."[70]

The Navaho themselves were little given to any formal expressing of thanks to Anselm Weber for his peacemaking work. He and his tireless labors for the good of The People were more or less taken for granted, as if such service for the Indians were the expected function of a missionary. Perhaps the finest expression of their appreciation for the friars' work in their behalf was to be found in the Navaho's increasing demand for the priest's time and help in solving their personal and tribal problems. One or the other written expression of their esteem for Anselm Weber remains for the record — and definitely not effusive in any instance: Chee Dodge who worked closely with the friar, and for whom the missionary was lawyer, investment broker, and friend above all, summed up briefly and concretely what the Indians thought of Father Anselm: "The Navajos are very anxious. . . . If you left them they would feel like they had lost . . . their main teeth."[71] Years before, Peshlakai, the old Silversmith, had told Commissioner Leupp in one of the three English phrases he knew that Chischilli was "pretty good all right," using the idiomatic superlative of Southwestern Hispano-English.[72]

Happily Father Anselm Weber had not entered the Navaho mission field with any design on recognition or status to be achieved; neither would his efforts toward maintaining peace on the reservation alter in the least because of any man's thanks, or the lack of it.

[68] C.I.A., *Annual Report,* 1906, p. 183; see *ibid.,* 1907, pp. 84–92.
[69] Celestin Matz, O.F.M., to B. Haile, February 6, 1917, P.A., IL.
[70] R. Perry to A. Weber, February 18, 1917, P.A., MI.
[71] Chee Dodge to A. Weber, February 19, 1921, P.A., IL.
[72] Mentioned in A. Weber, *Sendbote,* 35:132, February, 1908.

Chapter XIII

Missionary Approach to Navaho Culture

"With reference to the adult portion of the tribe," wrote Anselm Weber in 1909, "we are trying to uplift them morally and economically, instead of beginning with preaching the Gospel to yet unprepared and unwilling ears."[1] Conversion of the Navaho tribe he and his confreres viewed as a long-term process that would proceed from a previous winning of hearts and minds through "tangible signs of the whites' good will."[2] His "great influence with the Navajos," wrote ex-President Theodore Roosevelt on a trip through the Navaho country, "Father Weber has attained because of his work for their practical betterment. He doesn't try to convert the adults . . ." — by direct evangelizing, he should have added.[3] Others have stated that Father Anselm himself maintained he would "abandon the Navaho field at once . . . if he [had] thought there was no hope of converting an adult Navajo."[4]

Baptisms as a numerical criterion of successful apostolic work, he was certainly aware, could not apply to the Navaho field: "Here among the American Bedouin we face practically unsurmountable obstacles," he admitted in 1908.[5] Five years later he spelled this out more in detail when he explained: "To civilize and Christianize a nomadic people is obviously a difficult task. Scarcity of water, and

[1] A. Weber to Howell Jones, Land Commissioner for the Santa Fe Railroad, March 10, 1909, P.A., MI.

[2] *Catholic Standard and Times,* Philadelphia, February 22, 1913; Fridolin Schuster, O.F.M., to A. Weber, May 29, 1918, P.A., LA.

[3] *Outlook,* 105:365, October 18, 1913.

[4] W. Ketcham, in B.C.I.M., *The Indian Sentinel,* 2:313, July, 1921.

[5] In B.C.I.M., *Indianer Wache,* 1908, p. 25. The terms "Bedouin" and "nomad" are used in the popular, nontechnical sense of "pastoral," and imply simply the rather common custom of the Navaho use of two or three hogans to facilitate regional grazing. In this regard see Kluckhohn and Leighton, *The Navaho,* pp. 7–8.

the general topography of a country which is fit for grazing purposes only, force the Navaho to live scattered."[6]

He dismissed as irrelevant many government and denominational programs which aimed at Americanizing the Navaho through certain physical symbols, such as by unblanketing, hair shearing, routing the Navaho out of hogans and into houses, or by forcing them to speak English. This was only the outer shell enclosing the inner life of The People. The heart of the matter for the friar rested in a new form of stable home and community life.[7] How to achieve such cultural change would admit of no pat solution, experience was to prove to Father Anselm, as it has since been proved to others. His mission approach became experimental and many-faceted.

In the modern period of Navaho history the military commander in New Mexico, Brigadier General James H. Carleton, had insisted in 1864 that by concentration at Bosque Redondo under the military control of Fort Sumner the Navaho would, "like the Pueblos, become an agricultural people, and cease to be nomads. This should be a *sine qua non,*" he insisted, in any civilizing program adopted for the Navaho.[8] Accordingly the concentration program to wholly agrarianize the Navaho was organized and carried through at great expense by the federal government. Region, drought, and general lack of planning, however, conspired to defeat this experiment in controlled culture reform. Four years later, in 1868, the Navaho won permission to return to their own country of desert and mountains that lay to the west and north.[9] Bosque Redondo stands as a symbol of a disastrous experiment at enforced cultural reconstruction of an entire Indian nation; it likewise underscores the tough resistance and inner resilience of the tight culture core of the Navaho. They have consistently resisted planned and predicted revampings of their customary ways and institutions, a truth that experience was to teach government as well as church agencies.

With the breakdown of the old order, wrote the authors of a thorough study of United States Indian missions,[10] "except among Pueblos and Navahos of the Southwest, it was almost inevitable that the Christian mission . . . should become the center of a new com-

[6] A. Weber, *F.M.S.,* 1913, p. 22.

[7] A. Weber, *Sendbote,* 32:28, January, 1905.

[8] *To the People of New Mexico,* address given at Las Cruces, New Mexico, December 16, 1864, printed, n.d., Library of Congress.

[9] Frank D. Reeve, "The Federal Indian Policy," *N.M.H.R.,* 13:25, January, 1937; Edward E. Dale, *The Indians of the Southwest,* p. 57.

[10] Meriam and Hinman, *Facing the Future in Indian Missions,* p. 187.

munity." Definitely except the Navaho! Indicative of their unusually strong cultural integration, the Navaho have been able to assimilate easily and rapidly a wide variety of technological innovations respecting their industrial life without losing noticeably the complex of values composing their unique native way of life.[11]

Most of the varied expedients attempted by Father Anselm Weber in his mission plan to Christianize The People were directed along three avenues of approach to the Navaho: education, the land problem, and Navaho ceremonial.

Education

Following the accepted pattern as laid down by the Catholic Church in the United States, and as practiced by the Bureau of Catholic Indian Missions, Anselm Weber placed Catholic schools as a primary factor in his mission policy. "Catholic schools," he wrote after ten years in the field, "are the groundwork for the conversion of the Indian — but schools followed up with a continuous, supporting missionary program. Decent homes with a Christian environment, and Indian lay apostles, capable of strenuous missionary action, are essential."[12]

Like Francis M. Neel of the Fort Defiance government school,[13] Father Anselm foresaw the need for setting up school-colony combinations. On such parochial settlements St. Michaels graduates could farm on irrigated land, live in village communities, marry, and they and their families remain under the influence of a closed Christian community.[14] This policy underlay much of the extensive land acquisitions at St. Michaels, the efforts on the San Juan River, at Chin Lee, and to a modified extent at Lukachukai with its planned substations.

After the miscarriage of the San Juan day-school scheme, owing primarily to land and financial difficulties, and after his observation of the indifferent success encountered by Reverend Bierkemper's day school at Ganado,[15] Anselm Weber declared definitely against the idea

[11] Kluckhohn and Leighton, *The Navaho,* p. 28.

[12] A. Weber, in B.C.I.M., *Indianer Wache,* 1908, p. 25.

[13] Neel advised: ". . . pupils of this school [Fort Defiance] and returned students from other schools might be colonized on irrigated tracts, homes built, and more tangible evidence given of the good done by the schools. But now the discharged student goes where he . . . must herd sheep, plant corn in some desolate wash, do some other kind of labor, marry and make his squaw and children support him, sponge or steal." C.I.A., *Annual Report,* 1899, Part 1, p. 160.

[14] A. Weber, *Sendbote,* 31:126, February, 1904.

[15] Agent Peter Paquette disparaged the day-school idea partly because of the meager attendance off and on of thirteen pupils at Ganado. Report, March 22, 1910, Letter Book, W.R.C.

of day schools except for populous areas like Lukachukai; from this time on he declared in favor of boarding schools.[16]

While acknowledging the sentiment which favored educating Navaho children in their local communities, and the advantage to both pupil and teacher in learning together in the midst of the Navaho scene,[17] Anselm attacked the ecological absurdity of day schools. He summed up his thinking in the matter in a classical sociological exposé addressed to Senator Charles Curtis of Kansas:[18]

> Lately a Supervisor remarked [that] the Navajos should be forced to abandon stock raising to make a living by farming. Well, if our Lord had consulted him in creating this part of the globe, it might have become an agricultural country.
>
> With the exception of a few favored places where irrigation is practicable . . . the Navajo Reservation is good for grazing *only.* On account of the character of the country the Navajos can never be turned into an exclusively agricultural people. Neither do I see why an attempt should be made to force a people inhabiting a country good for grazing only to turn farmers; unless it be to fit facts to theory and build day schools instead of boarding schools. It really seems 'stubborn facts are mere babes beside a stubborn theory.'

His own dreams and theories of Catholic colonies gradually faded under the grind of realistic experience and the frustrations imposed by inadequate mission support.

On the question of religious instruction at Fort Defiance government school, the "staid and composed . . . professor [who] was considered a better student and lover of books than a practical man for a virgin missionary field"[19] quickly cut his polemical eyeteeth. Shortly before meeting Commissioner of Indian Affairs, William J. Jones, at Fort Defiance, "a fine old gentleman" and the first commissioner to visit the Navaho reservation,[20] Anselm had fought for and won permission to give nondenominational instructions at the agency school.[21] A year later the friar reported to Ketcham that nonsectarian instructions were a poor makeshift, and that his or Father Leopold's role at the Fort

16 A. Weber to Bishop Granjon, November 23, 1908, P.A., MM.; A. Weber, *Sendbote,* 36:410–413, May, 1909.

17 See Francis E. Leupp, *In Red Man's Land,* pp. 77–79; Davida Woerner, *Education Among the Navajo,* pp. 48–58; Edward E. Dale, *The Indians of the Southwest,* pp. 186–187.

18 A. Weber to Hon. Charles Curtis, February 3, 1912, P.A., LP.

19 B. Haile, *F.M.S.,* 1922, p. 9.

20 On July 31, 1902, as given in A. Weber to Provincial L. Haverbeck, August 1, 1902, P.A., CI.

21 See p. 87.

school was merely that of assistant to the Protestant minister.[22] Proselytizing was strictly forbidden.[23] Yet to teach an anemic, bloodless Christianity, Anselm maintained, was to promote vague doctrinal indifferentism, to foster Protestantism, and to prepare pagans to enter any Protestant denomination they should choose after leaving school. Why could not pagan children be taught Catholic doctrine if they and their parents so wished?[24]

When this matter was brought up to Commissioner Leupp in 1907 he took the question under advisement[25] — and kept it there until after President Taft's inauguration, and the appointment of Commissioner R. G. Valentine on June 15, 1909. On September 25, the same year, after Anselm Weber had spent several hours with Valentine at his Washington office explaining the situation, Valentine signed a set of new regulations covering religious worship and instructions in government schools. These rules granted completely Anselm's request to instruct pagan children in denominational religion.[26] Signed petitions of parents or guardians of children under eighteen were deemed sufficient to "class a child as belonging to a certain denomination."[27] Even though a Protestant committee representing seventeen denominations, objecting to the use of the government school system to enforce denominational instructions, held up official promulgation of the rules,[28] Valentine sent an *ad interim* permission, advising the missionary to submit the written petitions of the parents to the superintendent in charge "who will give the necessary facilities for carrying out the wishes of the parents."[29]

[22] (William Ketcham), *Report of the Director of the Bureau of Catholic Indian Missions,* 1903–1904, p. 62.

[23] Commissioner W. A. Jones to United States Indian Agents and Bonded Superintendents, December 20, 1902, circular 87, copy in S.M.C., CH.

[24] A. Weber, *Sendbote,* 37:21–24, January, 1910; A. Weber to W. Ketcham, March 25, 1907, P.A., CI. The "Rules" covering religious services and instructions to which A. Weber referred are to be found in: United States Office of Indian Affairs, *Rules of the Indian School Service* (Washington, D. C.: Government Printing Office, 1900).

[25] Commissioner F. E. Leupp to Bureau of Catholic Indian Missions, April 25, 1907, copy in P.A., ZU.; Acting Commissioner C. F. Larrabee to W. Ketcham, May 10, 1907, P.A., CI.

[26] W. Ketcham to A. Weber, March 1, 1909, P.A., CI.; A. Weber, *Sendbote,* 37:108–111, February, 1910.

[27] R. G. Valentine, *General Regulations for Religious Worship and Instructions of Pupils in Government Indian Schools* (Carlisle, Pa.: Carlisle Indian Press, 1909), pt. 1, art. 2, c.

[28] W. Ketcham to Chas. Lusk, November 23, 1909, C.I.B.A.; A. Weber, *Sendbote,* 37:398, May, 1910.

[29] R. Valentine to Chas. Lusk, October 15, 1909, Ed. Adm. 55404, 1909, P.C., copy in P.A., CI. On March 10, 1910, the *General Rules for Religious Worship* were finally

Getting the parents' signatures now became the big problem. The missionary purposely attended the July Fourth celebration held belatedly at Hubbell's on August 12, 1910, in honor of a host of Republican politicians. Assistant Secretary of War Oliver with a coterie of army officers, along with the Arizona Territorial Delegate, Ralph Cameron, stopped off for several days at Ganado while en route to the Hopi Snake Dance. Over two thousand Navaho from all over the reservation, and beyond, assembled for the two days of horse racing, *nahoqai,* the Mexican chicken pull, and for free feasting.[30]

In their official talks to the congregated Indians at Hubbell's, and a week later at Chin Lee, the headmen explained that *Chischilli* and *Tseijini Tso,* Big Chin Lee Tribesman, as Father Leopold was called by Silversmith, both needed help. The speakers made it clear that the *e'nishodi* needed the fathers' and mothers' "signs" in order to give their instructions and say their prayers at the government schools.[31] From mid-July to early September Anselm Weber was in the saddle and on the move continuously from camp to camp, seeking out families with children attending the Fort Defiance school. He was more than content to take his chances with camp fare, and truly grateful to the Indians for the extra sheepskins on which he slept under the summer brush hogans. Within six weeks he had covered well over seven hundred miles within the Fort Defiance superintendency, and had received 198 fingerprints from pagan parents who gave him permission to give Catholic instructions to their children at the government schools.[32] While welcoming the headmen's support, Anselm made sure personally to explain to each parent the purpose of the "paper" he signed.[33]

After delays entailed by the construction of the new Fort Defiance assembly hall, and the quieting of protests entered by the local Protestant minister, distinctly Catholic instructions began on Tuesday evening, February 7, 1911. Slightly over two hundred pupils received catechism instructions on Tuesday and Thursday evening, the younger children in Navaho, the older in English.[34] Mass was offered on the

---

released by the Office of Indian Affairs. See A. Weber, in B.C.I.M., *The Indian Sentinel,* 1:18, April, 1918.

[30] A. Weber, *Sendbote,* 37:987–990, November, 1910; A. Weber to Chas. Lusk, June 22, 1910, C.I.B.A.; same to W. Ketcham, August 6, 1910, C.I.B.A.

[31] *Ibid.;* A. Weber, *Sendbote,* 37:1069–1072, December, 1910; A. Weber to W. Ketcham, March 20, 1911, C.I.B.A.

[32] (A. Weber), *F.M.S.,* 1915, p. 9. The early practice of marking an "X" had been supplanted by the accurate fingerprint identification.

[33] A. Weber to W. Ketcham, March 20, 1911, C.I.B.A.

[34] *Ibid.;* (A. Weber), *F.M.S.,* 1915, p. 9.

first and third Sundays as previously arranged with Reverend Black and Superintendent P. Paquette.[35]

At the close of 1910 the Superior at St. Michaels had reported in his official statistics of the mission that of two hundred and sixty pupils at Fort Defiance none was Catholic, and Mass had been offered three times at the Fort.[36] With the new denominational instructions in effect, however, a tremendous buzz of religious activity soon began. Father Egbert Fischer was appointed to St. Michaels at the summer chapter of 1911, arriving while Father Anselm was in Europe as companion and secretary to Archbishop Pitaval.[37]

As chaplain at Fort Defiance Father Egbert took over organized instructions on Tuesday and Thursday evenings from 6:30–8:00 p.m., and on the first and third Sundays after Mass; one hundred and seventy pupils attended.[38] Five months later, on February 25, he baptized at St. Michaels the first group of government school pupils. Two other groups he baptized on April 28 and May 19, both groups having spent Friday evening until Sunday in retreats held at St. Michaels School in preparation for Baptism and First Communion.[39]

Using the accepted parochial approach current in urban areas of the period, Father Egbert had the children memorize the English Penny Catechism throughout, as well as the standard prayers, as a condition for entrance into the new life of the Church.[40]

On June 16, 1912, Bishop Henry Granjon of Tuscon confirmed eighty-nine Catholic Navaho at Fort Defiance where Superintendent Paquette gave a dinner after services for the clergy and Catholic employees in honor of His Grace.[41] Three years later, on November 25, 1915, after having confirmed at Chin Lee and St. Michaels, Bishop Granjon returned to Fort Defiance to dedicate the new chapel of Our Lady of the Blessed Sacrament which had been built, and almost entirely paid off through the efforts of hard-working Father Egbert.[42]

[35] Letter Book, January 31, 1911, W.R.C.; Peter Paquette was an unmarried half-blood Winnebago Indian, baptized but not a practicing Catholic. A. Weber to W. Ketcham, March 21, 1911, C.I.B.A.

[36] Annual Report to the Bureau of Catholic Indian Missions, 1910, C.I.B.A.

[37] E. Fischer to A. Weber, October 2, 1911, P.A., EF.; *Tabula Definitionis,* 1911, P.A. Besides Anselm Weber and Barard Haile, Fathers Edward Leary and Romuald Helmig and Brothers Felix Bruening and Ewald Boehler were stationed at St. Michaels in 1911.

[38] Egbert Fischer, quoted in *F.M.S.,* 1915, pp. 9–11.

[39] Fort Defiance Office Diary, February 25, April 26, May 17, 1912, and Miscellaneous Letters, April 14, 1912, W.R.C.

[40] E. Fischer, quoted in *F.M.S.,* 1915, *op. cit.,* p. 11.

[41] *Ibid.,* p. 15; Fort Defiance Office Diary, June 16, 1912, W.R.C.

[42] A. Weber, in B.C.I.M., *The Indian Sentinel,* 1:19, April, 1918; A. Weber to B. Haile, November 6, 24, 1915, P.A., BH.; E. Fischer to A. Weber, December 21, 1914,

Stanchly maintaining "*Sacramenta propter homines*," the ancient theological adage which favored a liberal, rather than strict, administration of sacraments, Father Egbert continued to run up a record for baptisms throughout his five years at St. Michaels.[43]

Mission policy at St. Michaels until around 1915 had definitely discountenanced conversion drives or anything smacking of competition with Protestant missioners.[44] Church law moreover prohibited baptism for children of pagan parents if any serious danger of subsequent loss of faith were present.

After 1915 the competitive element heightened noticeably, brought on in large measure through denominational efforts to win parental signatures and the accompanying struggle to give instructions in schools which previously had been vaguely regarded as pre-empted territories belonging to Catholic or Protestant churches.

Extension of Catholic instructions to government schools at Fort Defiance, Chin Lee, Tohatchi, and Lukachukai — all in this period from 1911 to 1916 — led to needless competition between missionaries and, contrary to accepted procedure, to pirating of parental signatures in order to gain numerical advantage in pupils under religious instruction.[45] Mild and peace-loving Father Anselm was loathe to scandalize the Indians with "an eternal wrangle to the edification (?) of the heathen Navajos. Life is too short to spend it in such warfare," he wrote.[46] But if the troublemakers continued their agitation, he added, "I shall drop all my other work and visit every Navajo who has signed for the Protestants (I except the Episcopalians) to induce them to 'change' over to us. That would be a fine spectacle, but I can't help it."[47]

---

and Provincial E. Buttermann to E. Fischer, January 17, 1914, P.A., EF.; Mother Katharine to A. Weber, June 6, 1916, P.A., MM.

[43] A. Weber, *F.M.S.*, 1913, p. 19, 1914, p. 37; E. Fischer, quoted in *F.M.S.*, 1915, p. 21; *Tabula Definitionis*, 1916, P.A.; Ermin Schneider, O.F.M., interview, January 14, 1951.

[44] A. Weber to Gertrude Golden, June 14, 1916, P.A., MI.; B. Haile to A. Weber, December 23, 1915, P.A., LU.; same to same, December 12, 1915, P.A., MI.

[45] See Woerner, *Education Among the Navajo*, pp. 85–87. Gertrude Golden, principal teacher at Fort Defiance 1912–1915, to R. Wilken, December 30, 1950, P.A., CP.; proceedings of a council held at Fort Defiance, November 8, 1913, signed by P. Paquette, John Walker, interpreter, and B. H. Dooley, clerk, copy in P.A., PM. Commissioner Cato Sells to P. Paquette, December 4, 1913, copy in P.A., PM.; A. Weber to Inspector S. A. M. Young, March 13, 1916, P.A., CI.; Commissioner Cato Sells to Rev. Howard C. Clark, Presbyterian minister, February 19, 1920, Ed-Emp 97977, 1919, 5689, 1920, copies in P.A., CI. See numerous letters in P.A., folders CI. and PM.; also Rev. J. Dolfin, *Bringing the Gospel in Hogan and Pueblo*, p. 198.

[46] A. Weber to Chas. Lusk, September 17, 1918, P.A., PM.

[47] *Ibid.*; for accounts of constant campaigns for signatures and for pupils for St.

Anselm Weber had "as one of his chief characteristics common sense and a willingness to obey the rules . . . a tact and fairness not only with the Indians but with government officials and the Protestant Missionaries."[48] As to proselytizing through education or otherwise, Anselm confessed that "I have never asked a Protestant to join our Church and that I have never received a Protestant into our Church during the 27 years of my priesthood."[49] He was not, of course, referring to pagan Indians, many of whom he received into the Catholic Church.

Headmen, and their attitudes toward any mission project advanced by Father Anselm Weber, quite decisively influenced the mission program at St. Michaels. He constantly slotted the mission program of St. Michaels into the political framework of the tribe. His success in procuring pupils for St. Michaels, or signatures for instructing pagan children in government schools, in obtaining mission sites, in serving as peacemaker, or his success as land agent — resulted in large part from his friendship with the leaders of the Navaho: "Especially through the influence of their headmen we have succeeded in leading them into lines of advancement it seemed hopeless, only a decade ago, to attempt," he was able to write after ten years' experience.[50]

No single chief headed the tribe since the death of Manuelito in 1895; in fact no one *ruled*.[51] Headmen freely chosen on merit, especially for renown in oratory and good judgment, were looked to by The People for leadership and wise direction.[52] In the conduct of their internal Navaho community life men and women in family groups and larger outfits determined freely the running of their affairs. Headmen who commanded respect could urge and suggest, and

---

Michaels, see A. Weber, *Sendbote,* 47:124–128; 222–226, February, March, 1920. Anselm Weber in editing *The Franciscan Missions of the Southwest,* which solicited advertising from all and sundry, was most careful to exclude mention of the interdenominational friction. A. Weber to B. Haile, January 23, 1916, P.A., MI.

[48] F. E. Leupp to R. Perry, May 13, 1907, P.A., MI.; G. M. Golden to R. Wilken, December 30, 1950, P.A., CP.

[49] A. Weber to Commissioner Cato Sells, September 11, 1916, Land-Sales 81971, 1916, copy in P.A., MI.

[50] A. Weber to Howell Jones, March 10, 1909, P.A., MI.; J. Dolfin in a somewhat querulous mood complains: "One reason why there is a marked decrease on our side and an increase on the side of Rome, is that Rome [Franciscans] influences the headmen of the Navajoes." *Bringing the Gospel in Hogan and Pueblo,* p. 198.

[51] A. Weber, in B.C.I.M., *The Indian Sentinel,* 1:32, April, 1918; Washington Matthews treats the loose political institutions of the Navaho as correlative to their unusual polytheism. *Navaho Legends,* p. 33.

[52] *An Ethnologic Dictionary,* pp. 422–423.

frequently saw their views prevail; but they could not demand or command.[53]

In technical matters concerning federal policies, court procedure, or legal niceties concerned in land allotment, leasing and homesteading, the Navaho tended to rely heavily on the personality of their spokesman or headman in a way that suggested the passive caudillismo of the New Mexican natives, a group psychology of unquestioning dependence on the leader.[54] In this aspect of personal leadership which grew during twenty-three years of selfless battling for Indian rights and welfare, Father Anselm won their deep trust and affection, and for himself the status and role of *naatani,* the headman.[55]

Land

In fighting land problems for the Navaho Anselm Weber doubtlessly achieved his greatest prestige among the pastoral and farming tribesman. The problem itself was an old one, a demographical equation compounded of biological expansion in people and herds, overspilling and exhausting a restricted land base.

Article 13 in the 1868 Fort Sumner Treaty stipulated that except for hunting excursions no Navaho might trespass beyond the treaty reservation, and this under penalty of forfeiture of tribal "rights, privileges, and annuities."[56] Within this treaty reservation were some 3,500,000 acres of semiarid and mountainous grazing land, set aside for approximately 9000 Navaho and their 35,000 sheep, horses, goats, and cattle.[57] Subsequent extensions had expanded the original treaty reservation to slightly less than 10,000,000 acres by the turn of the century

[53] See Kluckhohn and Leighton, *The Navaho,* pp. 63–65, 70–72, 100–103.

[54] After Father Anselm's death in 1921 Navaho came from all over the reservation, huddling together in groups at St. Michaels, many crying openly, "like children who have lost their mother and don't know where to go or what to do," asking for the new headman (Franciscan Superior) and wondering whether he, too, would save their land and their sheep from the white cattlemen. M. Troester, O.F.M., to Provincial R. Bonner, August 17, 1921, P.A., MI.

[55] A. Weber to Chas. Lusk, February 11, 1916, P.A., PM. A. Weber mentions this deprecatingly to answer a charge that he had assumed the superintendent's office; it was applied not only to Superintendent Paquette, he explained, but to any trusted and loyal friend, headman, or one in charge. See A. Weber to H. Jones, March 10, 1909, P.A., MI., in which he wrote: "singly and in large numbers [they come] to consult with us. Before important councils at Fort Defiance they come here to prepare for them, to advise and consult."

[56] 15 U. S. Stats., 671.

[57] Rough estimates of Captain F. T. Bennett, in C.I.A., *Annual Report,* 1870, p. 612; United States Department of the Interior, *You Asked About the Navajo!* Information About American Indians, Pamphlet V (Washington, D. C.: United States Indian Service, n.d. [1949]), p. 3. See J. A. Krug, *The Navajo: A Long-Range Program for Navajo Rehabilitation,* pp. 1–3.

as the official resource base for some 20,000 Navaho with hugely increased herds — twice as many as the reservation could support according to Major Hayzlett, agent in charge.[58]

County government and homesteaders in southern Utah, northwestern New Mexico, and northeastern Arizona were clamoring for taxes or removal of the Navaho squatters back to the reservation. According to the testimony of the Indians themselves, however, the Navaho had been encouraged in 1868 to return to their old home districts, the same as before their exile in 1864. These off-reservation Indians complained against removal to the reservation since they had never attempted to leave the reservation; they had never lived on it, they maintained.[59]

Principally through ignorance of the law on the part of Indians and Indian agents the extended Homestead Law of 1875 had not been applied to the Navaho.[60] None living off the reservation had filed for homesteads which would have secured their springs and improvements, while allowing them to retain tribal rights.[61]

The much-heralded 1887 Dawes Severalty Act, which aimed to break down tribal cohesion and culture by introducing private property holdings for Indians, permitted the allotting of reservation tracts to individual Indians under twenty-five-year government trust patents. Citizenship rights, according to the philosophy of the Act, would be exchanged for tribal independence and tribal ownership, and citizenship would be identified with Indian private property holding.[62]

Though allotting on the reservation already had been permitted and encouraged by the offer of farming bounties in the 1868 Treaty, no Navaho had been allotted, and no "Land Book" for that purpose

[58] C.I.A., *Annual Report,* 1899, Part 2, pp. 158, 582; *ibid.,* 1900, p. 601. For thorough treatment of Navaho reservation land expansion, H. J. Hagerman, *Navajo Indian Reservation,* Report of Special Commissioner, 72 Cong., 1 sess., Senate document, No. 64 (Washington, D. C.: Government Printing Office, 1932), pp. 3–8.

[59] Agent Hayzlett to Hon. Alfred Ruiz of St. Johns, Arizona, September 7, 1899, Letter Book, W.R.C.; Chee Dodge to Commissioner Cato Sells, November 2, 1920, P.A., NH., describes the trek of the headmen and their outfits from Fort Defiance in 1868 to their old haunts on and off the Treaty Reservation.

[60] L. B. Priest, *Uncle Sam's Stepchildren: The Reformation of United States Indian Policy,* 1865–1887 (New Brunswick, N. J.: Rutgers University Press, 1942), pp. 180–182; Van Valkenburgh, *A Short History of the Navajo People,* pp. 50, 54, 55.

[61] *Ibid.;* A. Weber, *Sendbote,* 28:642, August, 1901.

[62] L. B. Priest, *op. cit.,* pp. 185–197, 249–251; I.R.A., *The Dawes Land in Severalty Bill and Indian Emancipation* (Philadelphia: Indian Rights Association, 1887), pp. 1–7; W.N.I.A., *Annual Report,* 1889, p. 11; I.R.A., *Annual Report,* 1903, pp. 43–44; Francis E. Leupp, *In Red Man's Land* (New York: Revell Company, 1914), p. 55.

had ever existed at Fort Defiance. Throughout his years among the Navaho Anselm Weber strenuously opposed any such private ownership in severalty for the Indians on the Navaho reservation proper which was owned outright by the whole tribe.[63]

An already complicated land problem was curiously overburdened in the case of the Navaho by reason of railroad lands which checkerboarded the southern strip of extended reservation lands. By act of July 27, 1866, the Atlantic and Pacific Railroad Company had been granted a forty-mile primary swath of odd-numbered sections along each side of its right of way through the territories; an additional ten-mile indemnity strip was added to cover possible losses in the primary strip occasioned by existing claims.[64] In 1880 the Atchison, Topeka and Santa Fe bought a half interest in the enterprise, later turning over these land grants to a subsidiary, the Santa Fe Pacific Railroad Company. The Atchison, Topeka and Santa Fe Railroad Company operates the railroad line.[65]

Many Navaho off the reservation had been living for years on land, both surveyed and unsurveyed, which belonged to the federal government, to the railroad, to both, or — after 1912 — to the states and to state school boards. After cattlemen began to move in, and small homesteaders started to take up selections — all seeking the springs and water holes controlling thousands of acres of adjoining waterless grazing lands — the Navaho squatters felt the pinch. Unversed in the law, they fell easy victims to the whites who had immediately filed claims on government land, or had leased or purchased railroad lands. Some did both.[66]

It was to this jumbled land problem of the Navaho that Anselm Weber addressed his talents and energy in a successful effort to aid

63 See 15 U. S. Stats., 668, Article V; A. Weber to C. Curtis, January 21, February 3, 1912, copies in P.A., LP.; H. J. Hagerman, *op. cit.*, p. 11.

64 14 U. S. Stats., 292; Sanford A. Mosk, *Land Tenure Problems in the Sante Fe Railroad Grant Area* (Berkeley and Los Angeles: University of California Press, 1944), pp. 11–13. See résumé of land work carried through by A. Weber, in *Sendbote*, 46:323–328, April, 1919.

65 29 U. S. Stats., 622; 32 U. S. Stats., 405. W. O. Hancock, U. S. Bureau of Land Management, to R. Wilken, May 28, 1951, P.A., PC. For general information and map of this land grant and its gradual adjustment, see Sanford A. Mosk, *op. cit.*, pp. 11–20; United States Department of the Interior, *Transportation, Information Concerning Land Grants for Roads, Canals, River Improvements and Railroads,* Information Bulletin, 1939 Series, No. 5 (Washington, D. C.: Government Printing Office, 1940), p. 6.

66 A. Weber, *The Navajo Indians, A Statement of Facts* (St. Michaels, Ariz., 1914), pp. 18–21.

the distressed Indians. His earliest training in survey work developed out of the St. Michaels Mission land tangle, and from the practical techniques taught him by Sam E. Day. For equipment he used an ancient field compass, rods and tape, for which he had traded an Indian blanket; later he acquired a more serviceable theodolite.[67] His "chain gang" was occasionally made up of Frank Walker, one of the missionaries, and perhaps an Indian or two, but more frequently "he himself ran boundaries and chained until friends had to insist that he allow the beneficiaries to do the chaining, confining his own work to sighting and directing."[68]

From his earliest efforts in 1901 to file claims on public domain, or purchase railroad lands for Navaho living south of the reservation, he met with ready support from the railroad and from the government. The railroad promised to give priority in buying and leasing its sections to Indian settlers. The Washington Land Office supplied special Indian homestead blanks, and procedural information for Indian homesteading off the reservation, a service unknown to the Prescott Land Office, Apache County land officials, or to the Fort Defiance agent.[69]

After passage of the acts of April 21, 1904, and March 4, 1913, it became possible to exchange certain base lands lying within the extended reservation which had been relinquished by the railroad for lieu selections elsewhere on public domain.[70] In selling its lands to Indians south and east of the reservation, the railroad followed a reasonable policy of selling only in whole sections, and leasing generally in whole townships. To deal with both the federal government and the railroad in these involved land dealings, Anselm Weber became for all practical purposes both land agent and lawyer for the *Diné*. By 1912 he personally was handling railroad leases for Navaho groups covering 110,139 acres, and had surveyed, filed, and processed home-

[67] A. Weber, *Sendbote,* 31:947, November, 1904; *ibid.,* 46:323, April, 1919; B. Haile, *F.M.S.,* 1922, p. 10; E. Auweiler, in *St. Anthony Messenger,* 29:453, March, 1922.

[68] B. Haile, *ibid.;* E. Auweiler, *ibid.*

[69] A. Weber, *Sendbote,* 28:722–727, 817–821, September and October, 1901; A. P. Maginnis, Land Department, Santa Fe Pacific Railroad Company, to A. Weber, July 2, 1901, P.A., LP.; Howell Jones, Land Commissioner, Santa Fe, Pacific-Atchison, Topeka and Santa Fe Railroad Company, to A. Weber, September 17, 1901, October 4, 5, 1902, August 20, 1903, April 16, 1904, P.A., HJ.; A. Weber to H. Jones, October 12, 1903, P.A., LP.; same to same, August 20, 1903, H.A.C.; Register, Prescott, Ariz., to A. Weber, June 9, 1902, H.A.C.; Binger Hermann, United States Land Commissioner, to A. Weber, June 13, 1902, 159747, 1902, H.A.C.

[70] Exchange Act, 33 U. S. Stats., 211, and Small Holding Claims Act, 33 U. S. Stats., 556; see also Act of March 4, 1913, 37 U. S. Stats., 1007; C.I.A., *Annual Report,* 1914, p. 49.

stead claims for ninety-nine Indian families off the reservation.[71]

When government allotting agents were sent in to locate Indians on the temporary reservation extensions, Father Anselm accompanied and helped them find old monuments and corners known to him from his private surveys.[72] To congressmen, government and railroad officials he became an advisor on Indian land matters, and for the Navaho a protector and vigilant champion in legislative matters. Almost annually from 1907 until 1921 he made trips to Washington to lobby and plead for enabling legislation to facilitate extending the Navaho reservation, and to push settlement of particular Indian land cases. By 1913 already it was reported that "no missionary in the field keeps the Catholic Indian Bureau so busy with the President, with Congress, with the Interior Department and the Indian Office as does Father Anselm."[73]

Though it is difficult to assess accurately the measure of Father Anselm's direct and indirect responsibility in the matter of reservation extensions, it appears that he initiated or promoted every major move made from 1907 until his death in 1921 to procure more land for the Navaho. It was he who caucused with Navaho headmen, and outlined their arguments, before the important council at Fort Defiance with Commissioner Leupp in June, 1907, relative to reservation extension to the south and east. In July of the same year he hurried to Washington to discuss the matter with President Theodore Roosevelt and members of the Interior Department; in November almost three million acres were withdrawn from settlement east and south of the reservation.[74] White stockmen had begun to close off vast areas from Indian stock by leasing tiers of townships from the railroad, and then excluding Indian outfits from the even-numbered government sections.

[71] A. Weber to Howell Jones, October 12, 1903, H.A.C., and January 6, 1907, March 16, 1908, P.A., LP.; Howell Jones to A. Weber, January 9, 1907, May 14, 31, 1907, P.A., LP.; A. Weber to Commissioner F. E. Leupp, March 16, 1908.

[72] Howell Jones to A. Weber, January 8, September 10, October 28, 1908; August 26, 1909, and June 27, 1913, P.A., LP.; A. Weber to Chas. Lusk, December 27, 1909, C.I.B.A.; A. Weber to W. Ketcham, February 20, 1910; same to B. Haile, December 30, 1915; same to Commissioner Cato Sells, September 6, 1914, P.A., LP.; A. Weber, *Sendbote*, 46:324, April, 1919.

[73] *Catholic Standard and Times*, Philadelphia, February 22, 1913; W. Ketcham, in B.C.I.M., *The Indian Sentinel*, 2:314–315, July, 1921; E. Auweiler, in *St. Anthony Messenger*, 29:453, March, 1922; A. Weber to Honorable Carl Hayden, December 6, 1920, P.A., LP.; Chee Dodge and other Navaho (accompanied by A. Weber), address to Honorable F. K. Lane, January 18, 1917, copy in P.A., LP.

[74] H. J. Hagerman, *op. cit.*, p. 31, C.I.A., *Annual Report*, 1909, p. 38; *ibid.*, 1912, p. 98; *ibid.*, 1919, p. 94; W. Ketcham to Howell Jones, December 17, 1907, C.I.B.A.; A. Weber, *Sendbote*, 35:224–225, March, 1908.

The missioner's well-known brochure of a few years later, *The Navajo Indians, A Statement of Facts,* clarified this issue.[75]

By the Executive Order Withdrawals of November 9, 1907, as amended January 28, 1908, it became possible for the government to allot 325,000 acres to 2064 Navaho, most in New Mexico, within the next ten years. Anselm Weber opposed widespread allotting in Arizona to prevent reopening of the southern extension to settlement by whites, a normal sequel to expect after all Indians squatters would be given their titles.[76] Subsequent Executive Orders of 1908 and 1911 restored 1,600,000 acres to the public domain in New Mexico, a restoration urgently sought by white cattlemen.[77]

As Indians allotted on reservation extensions might also homestead additional quarter sections, the priest pushed this procedure which enabled the herdsmen to augment their holdings of semiarid grazing land.[78] For these Navaho living off the reservation he insisted that not only the husband, but the wife as well — who often predominates the Navaho family organization — should be permitted to homestead in her own name. Realizing also the anomalous position of wives number two (sometimes wives three and four), in the event of the polygynous husband's death, Anselm Weber pleaded their full marital rights to lands and herds in context with native culture.[79] With like acumen he arranged that railroad leases would fall due immediately after sheep shearing and wool sales by the Navaho; when this was impossible he advanced lease money from St. Michaels, a lending agency since its foundation.[80]

Only after continued illness, and repeated visits to the Mayo Clinic

[75] A. Weber, *A Statement of Facts,* pp. 7–14, 24–25; P. Paquette to Commissioner of Indian Affairs, June 22, 1912, Letter Book, W.R.C.; A. Weber to Honorable E. B. Merritt, August 9, 1920, P.A., LP.; same to C. Curtis, December 6, 1920, P.A., LP.; E. B. Merritt to C. Tallman, December 17, 1920, Land Allotments 92410, 1920, HVC, copy in P.A., LP.

[76] A. Weber to C. Curtis, December 31, 1917, P.A., LP.; C.I.A., *Annual Report,* 1917, pp. 86–88; Act of March 4, 1913, 37 U. S. Stats., 1007; H. J. Hagerman, *op. cit.,* p. 31.

[77] Executive Orders of December 30, 1908, and January 16, 1911, 35 U. S. Stats., 457, 787; C.I.A., *Annual Report,* 1912, p. 98.

[78] F. M. Conser to A. Weber, November 21, 1907, Land 91097, 1907, 313, P.A., LP.; S. V. Proudhit, Assistant Commissioner, to Chas. Lusk, May 14, 1909, Land 50834, 1909, copy in P.A., LP. See 23 U. S. Stats., 96; 24 U. S. Stats., 388; 26 U. S. Stats., 794; 34 U. S. Stats., 182; C.I.A., *Annual Report,* 1912, p. 60.

[79] A. Weber to W. Ketcham, January 19, 1912, P.A., IA.; Commissioner Cato Sells to A. Weber, February 14, 1920, with enclosures 7701, P.A., LP.

[80] A. Weber to Malcolm McDowell, May 31, 1919, P.A., LP. Railroad leases cost 1 cent per acre per year, or $115.20 per township; later the fee was doubled. A. Weber to Chas. Lusk, December 27, 1909, C.I.B.A.

in Rochester, Minnesota, did Father Anselm relinquish his role as quasi land agent and conveyor of allotments for Indians unreachable by the postal service or the Fort Defiance superintendent.[81] Illness, and even hospitalization, did not, however, hamper him from carrying on appeals in behalf of Navaho land matters. In the last days before his death on March 7, 1921, he was at work drafting plans for lease, purchase, and for consolidation of railroad sections beyond the extended reservation. On February 14, three weeks before his death, the appropriation for $100,000, ten thousand of which was earmarked for leasing, was approved.[82]

Particularly during the years from 1910 to his death in 1921 the Navaho land problem occupied the major portion of Father Anselm's time and effort.[83] His correspondence on land issues which he carried on with the Office of Indian Affairs, the Land Office, with members of the Board of Indian Commissioner, congressmen, the Santa Fe Railroad, and the Bureau of Catholic Indian Missions — and their replies — fill fifty-five large letter folders carrying a total of over three thousand letters and items.[84] His very effective exposé of Southwestern political skulduggery, which aimed to force the Navaho back on an overcrowded reservation, was a public indictment of Senators Fall and Smith, and, to a lesser extent, of T. B. Catron.[85]

In his ceaseless work to extend the reservation — before statehood for New Mexico and Arizona would endanger further extension — Anselm viewed the large-scale expenses for irrigation, as at Shiprock,

[81] A. Weber to Honorable Francisco Delgado, July 25, 1919, copy in P.A., LP.; D. K. Parrott, Land Office, to A. Weber, August 23, 1919, Santa Fe 011136, "K" LEH, in P.A., LP.; C. M. Bruce, Land Office, to A. Weber, October 3, 1919, Santa Fe 011136, "K" LEH, in P.A., LP.

[82] 41 U. S. Stats., 408, 423; A. Weber to Hugh Scott, January 13, 1921; H. Scott to A. Weber, February 2, 1921; A. Weber to Ludger Oldegeering, O.F.M., January 23, 1921; M. McDowell to A. Weber, January 29, February 4, 1921; C. Curtis to A. Weber, February 7, 1921, originals or copies in P.A., LP. See A. Weber, *Sendbote,* 47:885–889, 946–950, November, December, 1920.

[83] B. Haile, *F.M.S.,* 1922, p. 11.

[84] A detailed study of Anselm's land dealings would provide a base, as well as subject material, for a thorough study of Navaho land and water problems. RW.

[85] In *A Statement of Facts, op. cit.* The original manuscript of this brochure was stripped by Father Ketcham of all direct allusions to personalities. Unexpurgated manuscript is found in P.A., SF. Senator Fall, nothing daunted by the obvious thrusts in *A Statement of Facts,* continued to oppose further extensions of the Navaho reservation, as he likewise argued against pampering the Mescaleros. See *Congressional Record,* January 29, 1917, pp. 2178–2182, and January 30, 1917, p. 2242. Senator Fall also succeeded in pushing through a San Juan bridge for Shiprock, New Mexico, funds for which were appropriated from moneys which were to be reimbursed to the government from future Navaho tribal funds. In 1913, $16,500 was appropriated; in 1919, $4,226. 38 U. S. Stats., 91; 41 U. S. Stats., 18.

untimely, and as a miscarriage of extremely meager Indian Affairs appropriation. Quite differently from his outlook of 1900, he was by 1911 pleading for "small inexpensive irrigation systems where they live and farm at present. In that line the Navaho themselves, of their own initiative," he insisted, "have done more than the government."[86] While piously wishing for extensive farming communities, he believed that he had "sense enough and experience enough to see that . . . stock raising will remain their main industry . . . though the sons of such who have very little stock may locate below Mr. Shelton's expensive irrigation ditch at Shiprock." He saw much of the irrigation projects as a device to force all Navaho back on the reservation, the same plans as were worked out, but failed, in the Dawes Severalty Act of 1887.[87]

Anselm Weber was not unlike old Chief Manuelito, who with a clear conception of the most vital issue, begged constantly of every government official for more land: "Just a little piece more, brother, and when you see the big chief at Washington, let him set aside for us that strip yonder to the east, to the west, or to the south." Manuelito and Anselm Weber will long be linked together in the history of their tribe.[88] Both knew the meaning of more land for a prolific people who depended economically rather entirely on grasslands.

A student of Navaho land problems has stated that Anselm Weber "probably knew more about them [the Navaho] and their affairs than any white man ever has."[89] No more railroad checkerboard sections remained on the reservation after 1918 — all had been exchanged — and Father Anselm could humbly report that he was generally held responsible for gaining 1,439,160 acres within and without the reservation for his people.[90]

Navaho Religious Belief[91]

To the Navaho mind life is a unified pattern in which the natural and the supernatural blend into a colorful whole. Misfortune and

[86] A. Weber to Bascom Johnson, April 10, 1911, C.I.B.A.

[87] A. Weber to Chas. Lusk, April 30, 1911, C.I.B.A.; A. Weber, *Sendbote,* 47:946–947, December, 1920; C.I.A., *Annual Report,* 1887, p. 67.

[88] Cited by B. Haile, *F.M.S.,* 1922, p. 15. Lieutenant Brown blamed Manuelito and the Navaho in general for crying more land while they would not work to clean out and dam the water holes and springs already available. Department of the Interior, *Reports Upon the Conditions of the Navajo Indian Country,* 1893, p. 6. See also Herbert Welsh, *Report of a Visit to the Navajo, Pueblo . . . ,* 1885, p. 15.

[89] H. J. Hagerman, *Navajo Indian Reservation,* p. 31.

[90] A. Weber, *Sendbote,* 46:327, April, 1919.

[91] In trying to analyze Navaho religious belief one presumes to enter a sphere of culture, vague as to precise facts, and extremely uncongenial to easy interpretation,

happiness are personal functions of an animistic cosmic harmony.[92] Men and animals, plants and places, lightning and death and "supernatural" beings all conspire in this balanced mechanism called life. All about men hovers the pressure of "Holy People" whose origins and emergence from lower worlds to the present furnish the map of life for earth-surface people of today. Place names and objects in the Navaho country all remain to bear witness to their fantastic mythical cosmogony.[93]

The mysterious "Holy People" whose history furnishes behavior patterns for earth-dwelling people today are "holy" in the curious sense that they respond automatically to the proper rituals.[94] According to fixed rules in the general economy of order and harmony, these "supernatural" beings, who live in the remote corners of the world, can bring both evil and good to man.[95]

Man is at the core of the whole religious system. Dogma — if one dares to use the term — is anthropomorphic, based on the myths and legends recounting the origins and trek of the "Holy People" from lower worlds to the present. Navaho beliefs are vague, and not yet tightly organized into any genuine system of theology.[96] The medicine man, or singer, having memorized one or more of the chants, usually also knows something of the legends upon which his particular chant or chants are based.[97] There exists no tribal school for singers which might make for uniformity in the interpretation of the legends, and

---

particularly for the layman in the field of anthropology. Regretful that A. Weber's letters and writings offer precious little by way of analysis, the writer wishes to prefix the obvious admission that what is offered here as background for a study of Father Anselm's missionology comprises an attempted brief synthesis of what reputable scholars in the field of Navaho religion have recorded. RW.

92 Gladys A. Reichard, *Navaho Religion, A Study of Symbolism,* 2 vols. (with continuous pagination); Bollingen Series XVIII (New York: Pantheon Books, Inc., 1950), pp. 23–25. Hereafter to be cited as *Navaho Religion.* See also Alexander H. and Dorothea C. Leighton, *The Navaho Door* (Cambridge, Mass.: Harvard University Press, 1944), p. 24. Hereafter to be cited as *The Navaho Door.*

93 Gladys A. Reichard, "Distinctive Features of Navaho Religion," *Southwestern Journal of Anthropology,* 1:202, Summer, 1945; *Navaho Religion,* pp. 21, 58; Kluckhohn and Leighton, *The Navaho,* p. 25.

94 Gladys A. Reichard, *Prayer: The Compulsive Word,* Monographs of the American Ethnological Society, VII (New York, J. J. Augustin Publishers, 1944), p. 6. Hereafter to be cited as *The Compulsive Word.*

95 *An Ethnologic Dictionary,* p. 346; *Navaho Religion,* pp. 49–50.

96 *An Ethnologic Dictionary,* pp. 346, 349–353; *Navaho Religion,* p. 6; *The Navaho,* pp. 134–135.

97 *An Ethnologic Dictionary,* p. 347; Berard Haile, *Origin Legend of the Navaho Enemy Way,* Yale University Publications in Anthropology, No. 17 (New Haven: Yale University Press, 1938), pp. 12–13; hereafter to be cited as *Enemy Way.*

which might create an integrated synthesis tying together, and organizing, the interpretations of the myths and legends into a body of beliefs. What strikes whites as jarringly inconsistent in Navaho lore seems quite acceptable to the Navaho. Variant interpretations by different singers do not apparently disturb The People. All incongruities in belief can be rationalized congenially by "proper" interpretation of the myths surrounding the "Holy People." Moreover, a powerful "god" may seemingly be thwarted quite easily.[98] Ritual would seem to be the key for managing the "gods."

Ritual accurately carried out is the specific for maintaining or restoring harmony within the Navaho universe.[99] Should a baby touch a corpse, an adult burn wood split by lightning, should one go to excess in anything, or be hexed by a human witch, then there is dire need for a specific formula or "sing" to set matters right, and to remove the resultant disease or misfortune.[100] Folkways and mores determine in general the law of reciprocal harmony between earth-surface men and the "Holy People," but devious sources of disharmony are unknown. This knowledge and sense of responsibility to nature is the aim of Navaho upbringing and training.[101]

Rank and file Navaho, however, must normally rely in large measures on the superior knowledge and ritualized controls gathered and learned by the singers. According to their effective knowledge of the esoteric rituals and chants, the singers achieve recognition, status, and good pay for services rendered. Many simple ceremonies, daily blessings, and prayers, nonetheless, are bound up with the everyday life of Navaho families.[102]

Navaho have no clear belief in a Creator, nor in one supreme God, nor do they hold to a belief in a future reward or punishment in a heaven or hell.[103] Along with such an absence of the bases for personal responsibility, their religion understandably omits reference to recognition of a personal immortal soul; they do believe, it must be noted, in "that which stands in one," which is sent by Dawn Woman

[98] *Navaho Religion,* pp. 13, 58; Berard Haile, *Enemy Way,* p. 13.

[99] *The Compulsive Word,* pp. 6, 11.

[100] Gladys A. Reichard, "Distinctive Features of Navaho Religion," *op. cit.,* p. 5; *The Navaho,* p. 132.

[101] Dorothea Leighton and Clyde Kluckhohn, *Children of the People* (Cambridge, Mass.: Harvard University Press, 1947), p. 40; hereafter to be cited as *Children of the People. Navaho Religion,* pp. 35, 38.

[102] *An Ethnologic Dictionary,* pp. 106, 363; *The Navaho Door,* p. 27; Gladys Reichard, "Distinctive Features of Navaho Religion," *op. cit.,* pp. 204–205; *The Compulsive Word,* pp. 13–14; *The Navaho,* pp. 160–161.

[103] Washington Matthews, *Navaho Legends,* p. 33; *An Ethnologic Dictionary,* p. 346.

and which enables one to breathe and to speak. At death "that which stands in one" returns to the lower world.[104] According to another interpretation, death is a fusion with the universe, and the beginning of individual inertia; what remains of a dead person — excepting the stillborn, the very young, and the very old — is an impersonal residue, a potentiality for evil to the living. They call this fearsome residue a *chindi,* crudely translated as "ghost." The Franciscan Fathers, however, point to a Navaho concept of an afterlife of vague happiness with the peoples of the lower world.[105]

Suffering and worry belong to this life, not to the safe and effortless harmony of death. All men and "Holy People" strive toward final perfection, or harmonized control with the universe.[106] What in man fails of achieving this harmony remains as *chindi,* as malignant human aftermath, strictly to be avoided. No such *chindi* lingers behind after the death of a person who had reached a stage of happy old age. Because of this fear of the dead, the Navaho mentality finds profound difficulty in accepting the basic Christian belief in the Resurrection of Christ.[107]

Like their dogma, Navaho "ethics" seem full of inconsistencies to one trained in the concepts of Christian culture. To a Navaho, good can be bad, and bad good, depending again on the degree of ceremonial and the knowledge of these ritual controls, long since decreed by the "Holy People."[108] Socially disapproved conduct if discovered brings a bad name and perhaps ridicule; doing good to others is good, but deceit and stealing under certain rules of the game are also acceptable since the "Holy People" practiced the same.[109] Social and economic considerations, such as the restitution payments involved, render many acts reprovable or bad. Conformity to group standards and controls, not the prospect of future rewards, influence behavior.[110]

Here again ritual becomes the restorative of balance and the remover of fear over the actions that might otherwise have brought down the vengeance of the "deities."[111] Conscience, which Matthews describes as "that standing within me that speaks to me," may be a fear of

[104] *Navaho Religion,* pp. 33, 43. Catholic missioners are trying to adopt the Navaho concept of "that which stands in one" to explain the Judaic concept of "soul." Burcard Fisher, O.F.M., to R. Wilken, January 2, 1952, P.A., CP.

[105] *Ibid.,* pp. 41–42, 48; *An Ethnologic Dictionary,* p. 346.

[106] *Navaho Religion,* p. 45.

[107] *The Navaho,* p. 126; W. W. Hill, interview, Albuquerque, November 22, 1953.

[108] *The Compulsive Word,* p. 5; *Navaho Religion,* p. 49.

[109] *Children of the People,* pp. 171, 240.

[110] *Navaho Religion,* pp. 131–140.

[111] *An Ethnologic Dictionary,* p. 350.

possible "supernatural" retribution, or shame over social disapproval, but conscience in the Christian concept of personal, intelligent, or moral judgment concerning right and wrong appears foreign to Navaho ethics.[112] In some respects, sin for Navaho seems to approximate the Jewish concept of legal defilement, if legal be taken to connote the impersonal cosmic law of order.

Ritual and prayers throw the balance between good and evil; it is compulsive in its magical control of universal and individual security and safety.[113] While ritual does positively seek blessings and the good will of the "Holy People," it is more in demand as a curative and restorative for sickness and misfortune. If illness persists, ritual and dogma are not questioned; proper knowledge and the correct formula with frequent repetition will restore order and normality.[114]

These religious beliefs for the most part were understood within a few years by the friars who had begun immediately in 1898 to study the sources and to win the confidence of the chanters. By 1910 they were able to summmarize these religious concepts of the Navaho in their classical *An Ethnologic Dictionary,* and in the same year to publish in Navaho thought forms the fundamentals of Catholic doctrine. Christian ideas were translated into Navaho conceptual modes and put to native melodies, and later also set to Navaho chant melodies.[115]

From the writings and letters of Anselm Weber it seems rather clear that next to the grace of God he counted on the mission's ability to undermine the function and influence of the chanters — in his plan to infiltrate Navaho religion and supplant it with Christianity.[116] The singers were the carriers of Navaho legend and myth, and the principal source, culturally understood, of tribal cohesion and solidarity. Though they did not dominate politically, nor even form a priestly social caste, they personified the sense of greatness and the oneness and uniqueness of The People. They guarded the legends and held the key to knowledge and power in the dark, mysterious world of the here and the beyond.[117]

[112] Washington Matthews, *Navaho Legends,* p. 59; *Children of the People,* pp. 106, 171. [113] *The Compulsive Word,* p. 6; *Children of the People,* p. 40.

[114] *An Ethnologic Dictionary,* pp. 105–106, 363; Berard Haile, *Enemy Way,* p. 12; *The Navaho Door,* p. 24; *Navaho Religion,* pp. 81–82; *The Navaho,* pp. 132, 224–225.

[115] Emmanuel Trockur, O.F.M., to R. Wilken, July 17, 1951, P.A., CP.; B. Haile, *A Catechism and Guide* (St. Michaels, Ariz.: St. Michaels Press, 1937), pp. 40–45.

[116] See A. Weber, *Sendbote,* 30:303, April, 1903.

[117] *An Ethnologic Dictionary,* pp. 382, 422; *Enemy Way,* pp. 12–13; *The Navaho Door,* p. 30; *The Navaho,* pp. 163, 166, 171; Gladys A. Reichard, "Distinctive Features of Navaho Religion," *op. cit.,* pp. 204–205.

Chee Dodge

Chee Dodge, General Scott, his son, and Anselm Weber, after Beautiful Mountain episode

When in 1902 his personal friends, the headmen Silversmith and Charley Mitchell, dropped all thought of rounding up pupils for the new St. Michaels School, and threw themselves utterly and unquestioningly into the business of procuring hand tremblers, or diviners, for their sick relative; when the diviners diagnosed the malady as the work of a "bone shooter," the two headmen outdid themselves in procuring a rare wizard to supplement the local chanter.[118] This convinced Anselm that breaching the Navaho religious citadel, and eventually Christianizing Navaho culture, would depend on effective medical demonstration. A patient, kind, and tolerant Catholic doctor would serve as a missionary of the highest order. He felt that government doctors had failed to a large extent because up to that time most Indians Service medics had only ridiculed and antagonized the medicine men and The People.[119]

His plan received ready, but not financial, endorsement from the Provincial; nor could Mother Katharine be prevailed upon to subsidize a Catholic physician, though undoubtedly the high mortality at the boarding school definitely warranted such medical care. Her final refusal to support a young Catholic physician from Phoenix — after all preliminary steps had been concluded by Father Anselm — came as a heavy disappointment.[120]

As definer he was able to promote the medical ambitions of the young friar cleric, Norbert Gottbrath, who had lived with the St. Michaels Franciscans for eighteen months, and who had grasped the mission role of a competent doctor. After a brilliant medical career at Georgetown University the young priest-physician arrived at St. Michaels in 1913. Arrangements were in process to have him practice medicine as a government officer until the papal dispensation, allowing a priest to practice medicine, arrived. Permission was granted by Rome on condition that no fees be accepted: *"gratis et titulo caritatis dumtaxat."*[121] This came again as a heavy blow to Father Anselm's missionary plans since the mission was unable to provide even a room, not to mention the bare equipment needed to maintain a clinic of sorts.

118 See pages 75, 104. 119 A. Weber, *Sendbote,* 30:301–306, April, 1903.

120 A. Quetu, pastor of Prescott, Arizona, to A. Weber, May 29, 1903; Novatus Benzing, O.F.M., to A. Weber, June 26, 1903; Severin Westhoff, O.F.M., to A. Weber, July 2, 24, 1903; Chrysostom Theobald to A. Weber, December 22, 1903; Mother Katharine to A. Weber, August 4, 1903; A. Weber to Mother Katharine, December, n.d., 1903; Mother Evangelist to A. Weber, December 22, 1903, all in P.A., MI.

121 Provincial E. Buttermann to A. Weber, September 1, 1913, P.A., NG.; G. J. Juillard to A. Weber, May 7, 1914, P.A., GJ.

All the bright prospects built up in Anselm Weber's mind during the long wait for his dream to come true blacked out utterly when in 1913, after the Beautiful Mountain peacemaking episode, Doctor Norbert abandoned the Navaho field completely and left to join Father Juillard in New York City.[122]

During the remaining eight years of his life Father Anselm was unable to carry through his plan for a professional medical apostolate as part of St. Michaels Mission approach to the Navaho. The friars had to rely on common remedies which they gave to sick Indians in connection with "sick calls" on which occasions they administered Catholic Sacraments, blessings, and prayers. Extreme Unction, known as the Last Sacrament, along with *Viaticum,* the "journey-food," as the Eucharist is called when given to the dangerously ill — all these Last Rites had some superficial resemblance to Navaho ceremonial traditions. On sick calls to Christians the pagan parents were happy to welcome the *e'nishodi* as the new medicine man, especially since the missionary brought "the prayer" along with him. On sick calls to pagans, however, the medicine man, if present, resented the Christian "interference." In the lay viewpoint St. Michaels Mission itself was always by way of being a combination medical dispensary, Navaho inn, council house and legal chambers, loan office and hock shop.[123]

While Protestant missioners frequently tended to antagonize the singers, and stir up competition with them, the Franciscan Fathers managed to avoid open conflict. These singers co-operated quite willingly — also for pay — in the linguistic, and less willingly in the ethnological work at St. Michaels.[124] Outsiders who investigated these relationships between pagan Indians and missionaries seem to agree that the Catholic missionary found it possible to accept a broader and more optimistic attitude toward pagan ceremonial and ethics than was generally acceptable to the Protestant missionaries.[125]

[122] *"Abiit, excessit, evasit, erupit. Nil mirari."* A. Weber to E. Buttermann, December 16, 1913, P.A., ID.

[123] M. Troester, *F.M.S.,* 1915, pp. 30–38; E. Auweiler, in *St. Anthony Messenger,* 29:453, March, 1922; interview with Dr. Wigglesworth, October 30, 1950.

[124] A. Weber to W. Ketcham, February 25, 1914, P.A., NL.; A. Weber, *Sendbote,* 35:131–132, February, 1908; Silversmith's speech at Fort Defiance Council, November 8, 1913, in P.A., PM.; Commissioner Cato Sells to P. Paquette, December 4, 1913, copy in P.A., PM.; *Enemy Way,* p. 13.

[125] Lewis Miriam, director, Institute for Government Research Studies in Administration, *The Problem of Indian Administration* (Baltimore: The Johns Hopkins Press, 1928), pp. 827–829; Coolidge and Coolidge, *The Navajo Indians,* pp. 288–289. See *The Navaho,* pp. 82, 85.

Personally, Anselm Weber was given the accepted status of a singer or medicine man with respect to his supernatural functions. Old Naakai Dinae would permit no other medicine man to hold a ceremony in his house at Red Rock because Chischilli had brought his medicine bag (Mass kit) to his hogan, and no other medicine sack could be tolerated at the same time.[126]

Rarely an old pagan Navaho would ask for Baptism, as was the case, however, with Dine Tsossi, grandson of Narbona and last surviving war chief of the Navaho. Anselm has surveyed and filed homestead claims for the leathery old fighter, and for members of his outfit. He had visited him frequently at his home fifteen miles south of St. Michaels in the valley of Teltschinti. During his last sickness the revered old man dismissed the medicine men and asked for Baptism from Chischilli. After his death, eight days later, Dine Tsossi, Slim Navaho, was buried from St. Michaels Chapel, February 22, 1907.[127] Such cases of adult conversion were the rare exception.

There is little evidence to indicate that Anselm Weber devised any organized system whereby the missionaries might directly attempt to cross-fertilize Navaho ritual with Catholic liturgy, such as blessing corn pollen or otherwise "baptizing" Navaho ceremonial, as an introductory wedge to the substitution of Christian theology.

In the same sphere of culture it is apparent that in the architectural designs for chapels and residences no attempt was made to identify Christian places of worship with Navaho life and environment. Rather the symbols of Christianity remained identified as foreign and white, like boarding schools, near which, incidentally, the early missions sprang up.

To anthropologists in the Navaho field there is general feeling that the concrete and earthy thought forms of the native ideology, along with its hedonistic and pragmatic world view, do not accommodate easily to the deeply spiritual, other-worldly theology of Christianity. They note that relatively few hogan Navaho have converted fully to the Christian Faith.[128]

Anselm Weber neither agreed nor disagreed with Father Berard's conclusion in this matter: "I hope the time is far off when I must preach to these Indians and that for courtesy or some other reason they would willy-nilly listen to me. . . . Such a policy . . . of forcing doctrines upon the people against their desires, against their protests

126 A. Weber to Commissioner Cato Sells, September 11, 1916, P.A., MI.
127 A. Weber, *Sendbote,* 34:516–518, June, 1907; A. Weber, *F.M.S.,* 1915, pp. 45–48.
128 *Children of the People,* pp. 112–113, 239–240; *The Navaho,* pp. 81–82, 85.

. . . and open opposition . . . is against my grain."[129] "Mission work among such," wrote Father Leopold Ostermann in praise of Father Anselm's bravery and utter selflessness, "is not only hard in the extreme, but so very indefinite, painfully slow, and all but disheartening" except to a man of long vision such as "The Apostle of the Navaho."[130]

There seems to be small question but that Father Anselm in his later years, while giving most of his time to identifying himself with the Navaho through his social apostolate, attached his missionary hopes largely in the coming generation of those reared and partly Americanized in boarding schools where the religious instruction program offered a grounding at least in the Christian Religion.[131]

Granted that the first generation of such neophytes might well be marginal men, half Christian and half pagan, yet Father Anselm felt sure of their ultimate conversion to Catholicism.[132] As to justifying a marginal, half-Christian, half-pagan situation, as obtained among many Pueblo Indians, he was not too sure: "If it is theologically wrong to have Catholic heathens, is it practically right? What mode of procedure can be followed? . . . if I followed my instincts I would run away from these perplexing, undefinable questions and hide somewhere in the cañons of Arizona, preferably near Chin Lee."[133]

But Anselm Weber "followed his instincts" here no more than he did in sparing himself while suffering constant illness during his later years. Priestly compensations such as alert, waiting pulpit audiences, long queues of confessional penitents, the swelling voice of a singing congregation, full attendance at Mass and Holy Communion — he had none. His was the daily ministering to poor Navaho with their land problems, to a young couple who needed work, defending a widow and her children, or a criminal, at court. Converts to the Church were few, but many Navaho Father Anselm converted from suspicion to affection and trust for the "long dragging robes."

In something of a defense mechanism against priestly frustration, he had turned his talents and his indefatigable energy to serve the least ones in the ministry of the body, knowing that in God's own

[129] B. Haile to A. Weber, December 12, 1915, and A. Weber to B. Haile, December 19, 1915, P.A., MI.

[130] L. Ostermann, *Sendbote,* 49:165, March, 1922.

[131] E. Trockur to Provincial Urban Freundt, September 7, 1928, P.A., MI.

[132] *Ibid.;* Barnabas Meyer, O.F.M., to R. Wilken, February 9, 1951, P.A., CP.; W. Ketcham, in B.C.I.M., *The Indian Sentinel,* 2:313, July, 1921.

[133] A. Weber to W. Ketcham, February 10, 1910, P.A., MI.

time He would see them safely home. Meanwhile he would plow and sow the seed, watering the land with his sacrifice and prayers.[134]

Among the friars at St. Michaels there later arose a difference of opinion regarding the mission policy of Father Anselm. Father Marcellus Troester, who as second superior of St. Michaels inherited Father Anselm's debts, began to curtail expenses at the mission. Gradually he cut down on the expenditures formerly made to feed and keep the many Indians who looked on St. Michaels as a free inn. The new Superior also gradually cut down on the land work; he aimed at wider and more thorough instructions at the mission and at government schools, and worked constantly to make follow-up work possible through accurate census tabulation. Already in 1909 Visitor Hugolin Storff had misread the social and ethnological work carried on, and had reported with unenviable lack of vision that good politicians and good ethnologists worked among the Navaho, but not missionaries.[135]

Fathers Leopold Ostermann and Berard Haile who had entered Navaho mission work in 1900 held for a continuation of Anselm Weber's broad policy of keeping close to the headmen, of instruction at school, with small hope for accomplishing any considerable work with adult Navaho. Relative to the economies won by curtailing hospitality to visiting Navaho, they feared that notable prestige had been lost to the mission since Anselm Weber's death.[136]

[134] Jerome Hesse, O.F.M., to R. Wilken, February 9, 1951, P.A., CP.

[135] M. Troester to Provincial Edmund Klein, July 19, 1924, P.A., MI. This document is a lengthy, detailed report on Navaho mission policy, 1906–1924.

[136] L. Ostermann to Provincial Edmund Klein, June 17, 1924, P.A., MI.

Chapter XIV

Mission Support and the Preservation Society

During the twenty-three years given to the Navaho mission by Anselm Weber the friar could never free himself from the nagging, thwarting incubus of financial indebtedness. Edwin Auweiler, O.F.M., a close personal friend of Father Anselm who had put in the latter half of 1913 at St. Michaels, bluntly — and with perhaps an overdrawn optimism — stated that the friars would easily have won over the whole second generation of Navaho in the St. Michaels mission shed if the mission had been properly financed.[1]

After twelve years at St. Michaels, ten of these as superior, Father Anselm had to admit that he had been "unable to ascertain just upon whom devolves the support of our mission. No one is willing to 'plead guilty.' "[2] A few months previously in a begging letter to Mother Katharine Drexel, who was the mainstay in supporting the bulk of American Catholic Indian schools,[3] he wrote:

> It is hardly fair to have us . . . enter upon a missionary field and then throw us upon our own resources. The Church Authorities seem supinely indifferent. Whilst personal and individual missionary endeavor is in the forefront, it is my candid opinion that the Church as an organization, neglects its duty. . . . I do not mean the Catholic Indian Bureau.[4]

Doubtlessly the crux of the problem lay in the curious marginal status of the mission: was the Navaho mission under Mother Katharine, under the Province of St. John the Baptist, or under the Bishop? To the provincial authorities St. Michaels apparently stood as an

[1] E. Auweiler, in *St. Anthony Messenger,* 29:454, March, 1922.
[2] A. Weber to W. Ketcham, November 14, 1910, P.A., SM.
[3] H. G. Ganss, in *The Indian Advocate,* 16:131–139, May, 1904.
[4] A. Weber to Mother Katharine, May 22, 1910, P.A., MS.

adjunct to Mother Katharine's boarding school.[5] With obviously a contrary outlook, Provincial Louis Haverbeck had assumed to subsidize the friars among the Navaho to the extent of paying two thirds of the new mission residence in 1902, and had likewise assured Anselm of assistance, upon request, over and beyond the $1,000 annual salary paid to the friars by Mother Katharine.[6]

The next provincial administration under Provincial Chrysostom Theobald (1903–1909), though it assured an additional annual grant of $1,000, seemed, however, less inclined to accept financial responsibility for the mission — at least according to the sad admission of the Provincial.[7] Provincial aid in this period took the shape of coverage for subsistence, with no assured budget for direct mission expansion. This period, it is to be noted, coincided with the growth and spreading out of the Navaho mission.

Gruff Provincial Eugene Buttermann grudgingly admitted that "*Was nichts kostet das taugt auch nichts.*" Indicating his genuine regard for the missions, he and the definitorium had contributed $3,300 in two years to the Navaho mission.[8] During his double term from 1909 to 1915, and during the two terms of his successor, Rudolph Bonner, from 1915 to 1921, comparably more consideration was shown by the definitorium to meet both current expenses at St. Michaels and those incurred in erecting Franciscan residences at Chin Lee and Lukachukai.[9] Father Anselm in 1910 transferred the $1,000 annual subsidy from the province to Father Leopold at Chin Lee, and Father Berard in 1916 was given the same allowance for Lukachukai. In 1918 this annual salary for Lukachukai and Chin Lee was raised to $1,800, and was given directly by the province.[10] Always selfless, Anselm Weber after transferring the provincial subsidy to Chin Lee depended on income from benefactors to run the mother mission at St. Michaels.[11]

Obviously a policy had gradually crystallized which permitted of

[5] A. Weber to Bishop Granjon, October 16, 1911, P.A., SM.

[6] See p. 90; A. Weber to W. Ketcham, November 14, 1910, P.A., SM.

[7] C. Theobald to A. Weber, April 11, 1908, P.A., SM.; A. Weber to C. Theobald, July 13, 1904, H.A.C.

[8] E. Buttermann to B. Haile, August 7, 1911; same to A. Weber, July 25, 1913, both in P.A., BH.

[9] E. Buttermann to A. Weber, January 6, 1911, July 25, 1913; R. Bonner to B. Haile, August 15 and September 11, 1915, July 13 and October 13, 1916, P.A., SM.; E. Buttermann to B. Haile, August 7, 1911, P.A., BH.

[10] A. Weber to L. Ostermann, June 6, 1910; E. Buttermann to A. Weber, July 25, 1913; R. Bonner to A. Weber, July 26, 1915, P.A., SM.; Annual Reports of St. Michaels to Chapter, 1919, P.A.

[11] A. Weber to L. Ostermann, June 6, 1910, P.A., SM.

official provincial aid for the friars themselves and their residences; mission work was to be financed from other sources.[12]

Donations from provincial headquarters to the Navaho missions from October, 1898, through June, 1921, reached the sum of $60,512, averaging out at approximately $2,750 per year. Of this amount $18,476 was earmarked for Chin Lee during the period 1908 through 1921; from 1916 through 1921 Lukachukai received $13,305. Besides the $28,731 intended for St. Michaels itself by the province, the central mission during this period received miscellaneous donations plus the income from the Preservation Society.[13]

Many additional donations for chapels were channeled to St. Michaels through friars of the province who acted as friends of the Indian missions in their roles as pastors, preachers, and teachers. In this way many confreres in the Midwest directly aided the expansion program among the Navaho.[14] As expected, donations for chapels, especially memorial chapels, were far more readily obtainable than was support for missionaries or for their necessary mission projects which did not bear the conventional marks of mission expansion. A new chapel, a new altar, a mission bell, or statue seemed to symbolize "spreading the Faith," whereas paying a missioner's salary for a year, aiding financially in the language studies, or restoring a dilapidated mission house or church apparently did not.[15]

By and large, however, the Navaho mission, the first mission adventure of the province, was regarded by the pastors of St. John the Baptist Province as any new parish undertaking: once founded, St. Michaels should manage to provide for itself, the same as any other parish. By 1902 the novelty had worn off and the pastors around Cincinnati were complaining that parochial aid diverted to the Navaho mission would cut too deeply into their parochial income.[16]

Provincial Louis Haverbeck while visiting St. Michaels in November, 1902, had agreed to urge the Franciscan pastors to establish the national Society for the Preservation of the Faith in their parishes. This society had been formed in 1901 under the stimulus of Bishop Horstmann of Cleveland, a personal friend of Mother Katharine. He

[12] A. Weber to Mother Katharine, May 22, 1910; same to W. Ketcham, November 14, 1910; same to Bishop Granjon, October 15, 1911, P.A., SM.

[13] Annual Reports of St. Michaels to Chapter, 1899–1921, P.A.

[14] See Lucas Gottbehoede, O.F.M., to A. Weber, March 29, 1909; C. Theobald to A. Weber, February 8, 1912; R. Bonner to B. Haile, September 30, 1915, February 10, 1916, P.A., SM.

[15] See W. Ketcham to A. Weber, October 3, 1905, H.A.C.

[16] Vincent Trost, O.F.M., to A. Weber, October 8, 1902, P.A., SM.

realized that some organization was essential to maintain the Catholic Indian schools which had been left without federal contract aid since 1900.[17] This society Anselm Weber saw as the long-term solution to the problem of Indian mission support, and he had strongly endorsed the society in the *Sendbote*.[18] "If all Archbishops and Bishops showed as much interest in Indian schools as Archbishop Ryan of Philadelphia and Bishop Horstmann of Cleveland," he wrote in all frankness, "the problem would be solved."[19]

His appeal that the society be promoted in Franciscan parishes was officially turned down, however, by the definitorium. Father Vincent Trost in reporting the refusal, sympathized with his old faculty friend, Anselm, over what he emotionally called the

> extreme selfishness [of the province] to have accepted those places 'out West' and then refuse to give assistance. . . . It is folly and short-sightedness to imagine that the parish loses when the parishioners of their own free will give to a deserving charitable purpose as is the case with you.[20]

With diocesan pastors it was frequently the same fear of losing parish support in favor of Indian missions that led several of them so far as to threaten to refuse the Sacraments to promoters and solicitors of the Preservation Society. If the bishops and pastors would not help, Father Anselm was forced to admit, the faithful could not be reached.[21]

Through constant appeal in his monthly *Sendbote* articles Anselm Weber realized some "meager donations," and certain parishes did put on drives to furnish vestments and liturgical equipment — several parishes collected 9000 Floradora tags to procure an Este melodeon for St. Michaels Mission in 1904.[22] Expectedly, such support was superficial and sporadic, and of no proportion to warrant and secure an organized mission expansion program.

Accordingly in 1906 Anselm Weber enlisted the backing of Visitor

[17] Bishop Horstmann to Mother Katharine, February 25, 1902, C.H.A.; W. A. Ketcham, "Bureau of Catholic Indian Missions," *The Catholic Encyclopedia* (New York: The Encyclopedia Press, Inc., 1910), Vol. VII, pp. 745–747.

[18] *Sendbote,* 29:732, September, 1902.

[19] *Ibid.*

[20] V. Trost to A. Weber, January 12, 1903, P.A., SM.

[21] A. Weber, *Sendbote,* 32:894, October, 1905; A. Weber to D. Engelhard, July 11, 1910, P.A., SM.

[22] A. Weber, *Sendbote,* 31:766, September, 1904; Pius Niehaus, O.F.M., to A. Weber, eighteen letters, 1900–1903, P.A., PN.; A. Weber to Mother Katharine, May 22, 1910, P.A., SM.

Theodore Arentz, O.F.M., to begin a Franciscan Mission Society. The Visitor suggested a Franciscan branch of the national Preservation Society, with all returns from Franciscan parishes reimbursable to the friars' missions. A broad membership at small fees of 25 cents annually, he hoped, would assure the regularized support the expanding Navaho mission demanded. Each member according to his plan would automatically belong to the national organization, and would receive a copy of *The Indian Sentinel,* organ of the Preservation Society.[23]

On July 24, 1906, this arrangement was approved by the provincial chapter which was presided over by the Visitor; thereupon all provincial pastors were urged by Provincial Chrysostom Theobald to promote the Franciscan Preservation Society in their parishes.[24] Approval by the prelates on the board of the national Preservation Society was given at their fall meeting in Washington — for a one-year trial period.[25]

According to plans worked out by Anselm Weber, the Provincial, and Father William Ketcham, promoters of the new Franciscan branch of the national society were to be appointed in the various parishes by the respective Franciscan pastors. The pastors of the promoters themselves were to send in returns from the society directly to St. Michaels. The Navaho mission headquarters would supply the membership blanks and copies of *The Indian Sentinel* which were obtainable at Washington, D. C. The mission would also forward returns to the Washington office of the national Preservation Society which after deducting expenses for materials would refund the net returns to St. Michaels. This allowed for a direct check on returns from the Franciscan parishes, and would enable St. Michaels to stimulate interest, or call attention to loss of memberships in the various Franciscan parishes.[26] Provincial Theobald generously printed Anselm's appeal to the pastors, and himself addressed an urgent endorsement of the society to all Franciscans of the Cincinnati Province.[27]

To strengthen the annual appeal of the United States hierarchy for spread of the national society, Anselm Weber sought and obtained

[23] A. Weber to W. Ketcham, July 4, 1906, C.I.B.A.; A. Weber to T. Arentz, July 19, 1906, P.A., MO.

[24] *Acta Capituli Provincialis,* 1906, p. 30, P.A.

[25] W. Ketcham to A. Weber, October 3, 1906, C.I.B.A.

[26] C. Theobald to A. Weber, November 16, 1906; A. Weber to W. Ketcham, December 4, 1906; A. Weber to "Reverend dear Father," a form letter sent to all Franciscan pastors, January 4, 1907; A. Weber to "Reverend dear Father," a form letter, August 27, 1907, P.A., SM.

[27] C. Theobald to "Reverend Father," a form letter, January 10, 1907; C. Theobald to A. Weber, January 9, 23, 1907, P.A., SM.

through Minister General Denis Schuler at Rome a fervent papal appeal to American Catholics for more generous support of the society.[28] Pope Pius X directed his letter of April 3, 1908, through Cardinal Gibbons, and the General of the Friars Minor personally sent a donation of $200 to St. Michaels — through the provincial office for hopeful exemplary effect.[29]

Net returns from the Preservation Society amounted to $426 in 1908; for 1909, $661; for 1910, $745.[30] By 1912 the society had an enrollment of 5000 patrons whose 25-cent annual pittance netted $800 after expenses.[31] The average income after postage and office expenses were deducted reached slightly more than $600 annually during the years from 1908–1912. Totally inadequate to cover St. Michaels current expenses, such a return could never be counted on to bolster any continued mission expansion program.[32]

Father Anselm's next move was to send promoters from Franciscan parishes into non-Franciscan areas where the national society had not been solicited or established. If bishops or pastors should have attempted to block his desperate tries at increasing membership in this manner, he had decisively resolved to "make a tour East, collect the necessary money to pay my debts, and resign. If the Church as such, as an organization," he flatly insisted, "does not feel obliged to support missionary endeavor, individual responsibility ceases to exist."[33]

He was $1,700 in debt earlier that same year of 1910.[34] Time "frittered away" in trying to wrangle support through the Preservation Society, or by secular pursuits, such as running post offices, was simply stultifying mission work.[35]

By spending three months on a begging tour in the East, after returning from Europe with Archbishop Pitaval in the autumn of 1911, he was able to clear off most of his debts — almost. The funds raised on that begging tour included a generous donation from Mother

[28] By personal appeal to Minister General Schuler at Washington in September, 1907. *Sendbote*, 35:803, April, 1908, and by follow-up letter, A. Weber to Minister General D. Schuler, March 13, 1908, P.A., SM.

[29] Amadeus Lubboech, O.F.M., Secretary General, to A. Weber, March 28, 1908, P.A., SM.

[30] C. Lusk to A. Weber, September 5, 1908; A. Weber to W. Ketcham, January 13, 1909; W. Ketcham to A. Weber, December 13, 1909; A. Weber to E. Buttermann, February 18, 1910; W. Ketcham to A. Weber, January 17, 1911, P.A., SM.

[31] A. Weber, *F.M.S.*, 1913, pp. 2–3.

[32] A. Weber to W. Ketcham, November 14, 1910, P.A., SM.

[33] *Ibid.*

[34] A. Weber to Mother Katharine, May 22, 1910, P.A., SM.

[35] See *ibid.*

Katharine.[36] Four months later, in April of 1912, he received a curt dun from a large Gallup wholesaler for immediate payment on a five-month-overdue balance of $795. Again he was forced to beg Mother Katharine to "bail him out."[37]

Bishop Granjon of Tucson over a period of fifteen years had been unable to aid the Navaho missioners with more than $125 since the bulk of his $2,000 average annual allowance from the Bureau of Catholic Indian Missions was applied to the restoration of San Xavier del Bac Mission.[38]

Archbishop Bourgade of Santa Fe had found it possible to aid in the Zuñi work, and his successor, J. B. Pitaval, helped both the Navaho missions and Father Anselm personally with substantial donations.[39] On his part, it should be noted, Father Anselm had responded readily to all calls of Archbishop Pitaval for literary and other assistance: Anselm Weber and Leopold Ostermann had drafted the speeches of the Archbishop before the 1908 and 1913 national American Catholic Missionary Congresses held at Chicago and Boston.[40] Father Anselm had also drawn up a masterful defense for the Santa Fe prelate in his successful efforts to prevent the archdiocesan see from being transferred to Denver.[41] Anselm had likewise preached in behalf of the Archbishop in New York for several weeks after they returned together from their European pilgrimage in September, 1911.[42] During the greater part of the trip abroad the

[36] A. Weber to D. Engelhard, October 7, 1911; same to Mother Katharine, January 28, 1912, P.A., SM.

[37] C. N. Cotton to A. Weber, April 22, 1912; A. Weber to Mother Katharine, May 2, 1912, P.A., SM.

[38] A. Weber to E. Buttermann, November 19, 1913, P.A., SM.; Annual Records, 1907–1913, C.I.B.A. In 1911 Cardinal Gibbons and the Apostolic Delegate prevailed on Bishop Granjon to turn over San Xavier del Bac and the Papago Missions to the St. Louis Franciscans who were ready to undertake organized mission work in this new field. Cardinal Gibbons to Bishop Henry Granjon, May 22, 1911, copy in C.I.B.A.

[39] See p. 163; A. Weber to E. Buttermann, February 18, 1910, P.A., SM.; J. B. Pitaval to A. Weber, June 30, 1909, P.A., CSF.; same to same, January 31, 1912, P.A., FP.; A. Weber to D. Engelhard, March 24, 1919, P.A., AC.

[40] C. Theobald to A. Weber, November 30, 1908, P.A., CT.; J. B. Pitaval to A. Weber, and A. Weber to Archbishop J. B. Pitaval, six letters, February to August, 1913, and typed speeches, P.A., CSF.; see Francis C. Kelly, editor, *The First American Catholic Missionary Congress, Official Proceedings* (Chicago: J. S. Hyland and Company, 1909), pp. 85–95.

[41] J. B. Pitaval to A. Weber, July 22, 30, 1918, with five-page typed enclosure in defense of Santa Fe as metropolitan see, P.A., CSF.

[42] A. Weber to B. Haile, July 13, 1911, P.A., ET.

Navaho missioner had also served as secretary to his close friend, the Archbishop, and had conducted one section of the pilgrimage through Germany.[43]

It was during his prolonged stay in Germany where he attended the Catholic Congress at Breslau and met directors of various German missionary societies, that Anselm Weber conceived the idea of an annual Navaho mission publication.[44] His trip to Germany was the occasion for contacts with the Saxon Franciscan Mission Society, the *Ludwig-Mission-Verein,* and the *Leopoldinen Stiftung,* all of which contributed generously to the support of the Navaho missions until the outbreak of World War I curtailed further exchange export by European mission societies.[45]

With the advice of Father Berard Haile, Anselm Weber requested permission shortly after his return from Europe to publish a mission magazine. Such a magazine originating from the center of Navaho mission work would focus exclusive attention on Franciscan missions of the Southwest, it was planned; the new publication would replace *The Indian Sentinel,* which gave coverage for all Indian missions throughout the United States.[46]

The definitorium at the July 17, 1912, provincial chapter acceded to Father Anselm's request to publish a provincial mission journal, but only on condition that it be an annual.[47] For the first four years from 1913–1916, the attractive magazine, *The Franciscan Missions of the Southwest,* highly praised by the Minister-General at Rome, was printed at the St. Michaels Mission Press. Anselm Weber edited both the English and German publications until his death.[48]

By 1915 the periodical, which sold for 25 cents and was given to every member of the Franciscan Preservation Society, grossed approxi-

[43] W. A. T. Smith to M. McGrane, n.d., 1911, P.A., ET. Archbishop Pitaval had broached the subject of Father Anselm serving as auxiliary bishop of Santa Fe but the friar had decisively refused to accept any such appointment that would take him from the Navaho mission. A. Weber to D. Engelhard, March 24, 1919, P.A., AC.

[44] A. Weber, *F.M.S.,* 1914, p. 40.

[45] A. Weber to B. Haile, August 21, September 25, 1911, P.A., ET.; E. Buttermann to A. Weber, May 20, 1912; G. Brueckl to A. Weber, December 29, 1913; Dr. Fred Wimmer to A. Weber, April 20, 1914, P.A., SM.; A. Weber to D. Engelhard, May 13, 1914, P.A., MA.

[46] E. Buttermann to A. Weber, July 27, 1912, P.A., WR.; A. Weber to D. Engelhard, November 26, 1920, P.A., SM.

[47] Minutes of the Chapter, cited in E. Buttermann to A. Weber, July 27, 1912, P.A., WR.

[48] Fr. Pacificus, *Min. Glis.,* to *Reverende Pater* (A. Weber), May 29, 1913; Peter Begley, O.F.M., to A. Weber, June 10, 1913; B. Haile to A. Weber, December 19, 1915, P.A., BH.; L. Ostermann, "Rev. Anselm Weber, O.F.M.," *F.M.S.,* 1922, p. 7.

mately $1,200 yearly with a net slightly over $800.[49] In 1917, the year when Rosenthal of Cincinnati printed the issue for $774, the magazine grossed $2,146; printing costs increased to $925 in 1918, reflecting wartime inflation. Father Celestin Matz, then in charge of the Preservation Society and bookkeeper at St. Michaels, scoured the Rocky Mountain region for advertising to meet the printing and postage bills.[50]

While he succeeded at great effort to defray this heavy outlay, the financial returns from the unique mission and anthropological journal never reached a figure that warranted the effort and time taken from active mission work to publish.[51] In 1922, the year after Father Anselm's death, and the tenth issue of the magazine, *The Franciscan Missions of the Southwest* was discontinued.[52] As a fund-raising vehicle the mission magazine, as well as the Preservation Society, had not succeeded in meeting Father Anselm's expectations.[53]

When Father Anselm Weber died in 1921 there remained a total indebtedness of $7,500 outstanding against the Navaho mission.[54] On leaving for Rochester, Minnesota, for the last of his many operations at the Mayo Clinic, he drew up a final statement explaining various debts. There were several notes drawn on Gallup banks at 12 per cent interest which he had cosigned for needy Indians. Other loans for current expenses and mission expansion had been made through provincial channels, and others had been taken against funds in trust for future mission chapels, or from the Lynch estate over which Anselm Weber had been appointed administrator.[55]

Had he lived longer he had planned to liquidate part of this mission debt through the exchange of lands on the section of land near St.

[49] C. Matz to Provincial Rudolph Bonner, March 30, 1916, with enclosure itemizing returns of Preservation Society and magazine by parishes, P.A., IS.

[50] C. Matz to A. Weber, October 14, 1917, P.A., CM.; Annual Reports of St. Michaels to Chapter, 1917–1918, P.A.

[51] A. Weber to D. Engelhard, November 26, 1920, P.A., SM.

[52] J. Forest McGee, memorandum, n.d., P.A., IS.; same, in *The Provincial Chronicle,* 28:147, Spring, 1936. John Forest McGee, O.F.M., editor of the *St. Anthony Messenger,* agreed at a provincial editing conference to assume the task of editing eight pages of mission news monthly, and of dedicating the entire March issue of the *Messenger* as a yearly mission number. He was transferred from the magazine in July, 1923, and since that time the annual March mission number has been dropped. RW.

[53] The work of the Preservation Society was centralized in 1922 in the organizing of the Franciscan Indian Mission Aid Society under Claude Mindorff, O.F.M. See *F.M.S.,* 1922, pp. 38–39.

[54] M. Troester to R. Bonner, August 24, 1921, P.A., SM.

[55] A. Weber to L. Oldegeering, O.F.M., January 23, 1921, P.A., SM.

Michaels which had been donated to Father Anselm by the Santa Fe Railroad in 1909.[56]

His principal collateral, however, over and above the substantial mission buildings at Chin Lee, Lukachukai, Fort Defiance, Tohatchi, and St. Michaels, consisted in the priceless assets of trust and love lavishly given him by the Navaho people. Though financially intangible and frozen, these real values for effective mission work were assets that would be sorely missed by the St. Michaels friars for decades to come.[57]

[56] *Ibid.;* Howell Jones to A. Weber, April 9, 1909; A. Weber to Howell Jones, October 23, 1912, P.A., HA.

[57] L. Ostermann, *F.M.S.,* 1922, p. 1.

Chapter XV

Illness and Death

In January, 1917, when unrestricted German submarine warfare was rapidly leading the United States toward war with Germany, Anselm Weber led a representation of Navaho and Laguna Indians to Washington to plead land extensions for the Indians.[1] The Navaho were seeking withdrawal of public lands from entry in the vicinity of Crown Point, New Mexico, leasing of railroad sections in the Leupp area, and extension of the reservation south of the Little Colorado River in Coconino County, Arizona.[2]

Father Anselm worked an average of eighteen to twenty hours daily during this period while he prepared data at night and accompanied Indian delegations by day through the intricacies of effective lobbying and buttonholing of war-distracted politicians.[3] Largely as a result of this dramatizing of the Indian land problem, the Navaho reservation was increased May 17, 1917, by 94,000 acres in the Coconino County, Arizona, region,[4] and some 60,000 acres were withdrawn from public entry in the Crown Point area of New Mexico for Navaho allotment.[5] The Lagunas received an addition to their reservation of approximately 150,000 acres; this extension, along with various other requests of the Lagunas, were won, as Father Schuster admitted, "mainly through his [Anselm Weber's] efforts and hard work. . . . It was during this visit at the National Capital that we realized the wonderful prestige

[1] F. Schuster, *F.M.S.,* 1922, p. 18.

[2] Navaho Indians to Secretary of the Interior F. K. Lane, address, January 18, 1917, P.A., LP. This statement of land conditions, judged by contents, style, typing, and interlinear notes, is obviously the composition of Anselm Weber. RW.

[3] Dr. Northrup, medical history and diagnosis, Grand Rapids, Michigan, March 8, 1917, copy in Mayo Clinic, file number 212016; F. Schuster, *F.M.S.,* 1922, p. 18. Hereafter the Mayo Clinic file on A. Weber will be cited as M.C.F., 212016.

[4] H. J. Hagerman, *Navaho Indian Reservation,* pp. 7–8.

[5] *Congressional Record,* January 29, 1917, pp. 2178–2179. See C.I.A., *Annual Report,* 1917, pp. 3–5; 1918, p. 23.

Rites of initiation

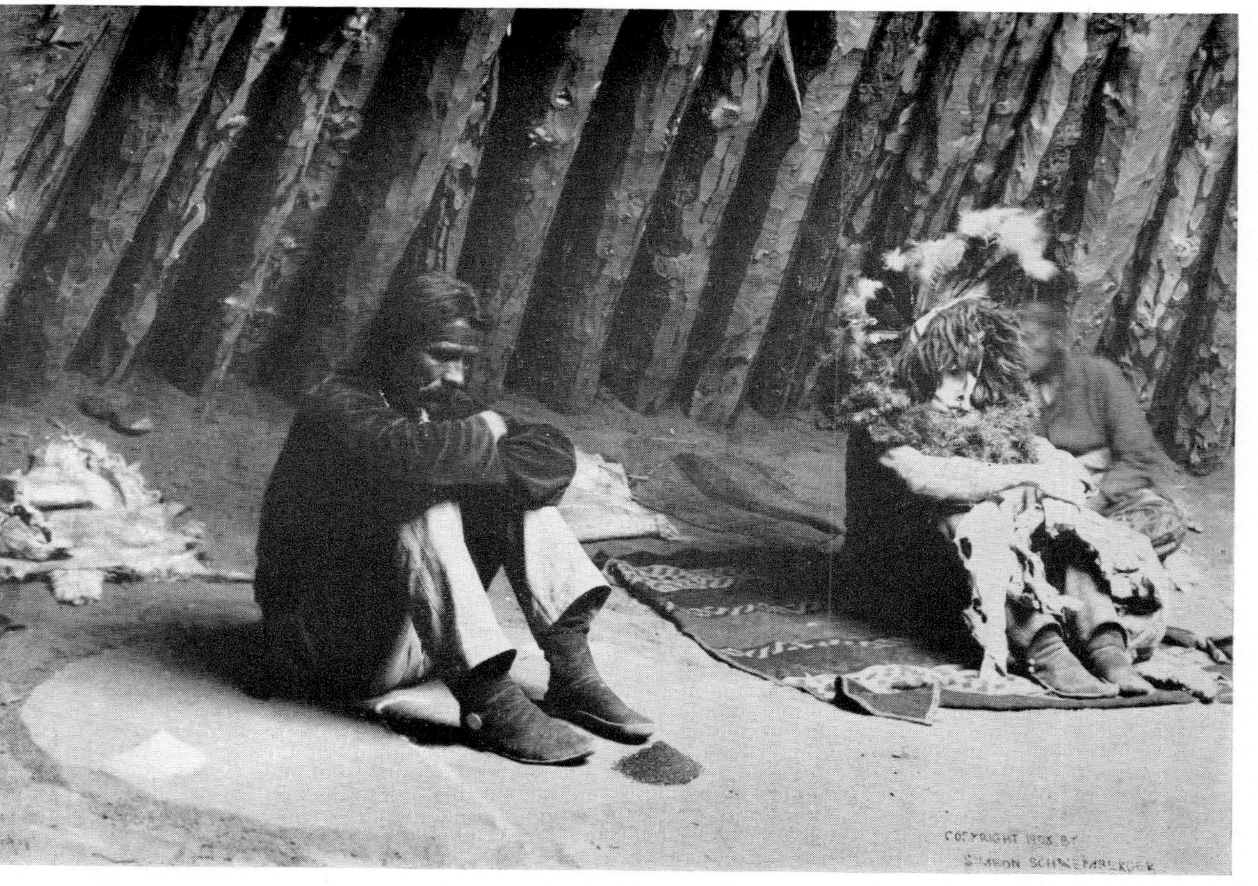

Patient and chanter: restoring harmony

which Father Anselm enjoyed among senators, congressmen, and other government employees."[6]

After the Indian Affairs business was finished Father Anselm stayed on in Washington at the bedside of the singer, Hatali, a Navaho delegate from the Castle Butte country who had contracted pneumonia. Hatali chose Providence Hospital because, as he remarked on seeing the Sisters in charge, he "would not be among strangers." Daily the other Navaho visited their brother who begged to be taken home as his condition grew worse. Unable to remove the dying medicine man, Chee Dodge led his countrymen home while Anselm Weber remained in Washington to comfort and to instruct the dying chanter. Hatali was baptized "Anselm" and received Extreme Unction on January 25 while fully conscious and able to understand and answer emphatically the questions in the ritual with the distinctive four affirmative nods of the Navaho way. He died the next day, and was buried at Mount Olivet Cemetery by Father Anselm. A few Chippewa and Winnebago Indians, along with several Indian Office employees, attended the burial.[7]

After caring for Hatali, Father Anselm himself was ordered to bed for two weeks of rest, and was put on a diabetic's diet.[8] Since January 10 he had been voiding blood and had felt generally weak and run down.[9] Somewhat recovered after this rest he traveled from Washington to New Salem, Michigan, to visit his married brother Joe, his sister Mary, and other relatives. At Grand Rapids he underwent a thorough clinical examination after which Dr. Northrup advised him to undergo a kidney operation at Mayo Brothers in Rochester, Minnesota.[10] Provincial Rudolph Bonner had advised Mayo's already in February.[11]

Previous to this time Anselm had suffered off and on from his chronic nervous spasms, from neuralgia and headache, but his life among the Navaho had been strenuous and tireless nonetheless; his friends had frequently chided him for his ceaseless, driving pace.[12]

[6] F. Schuster, *F.M.S.*, 1922, p. 18.

[7] A. Weber to G. Rausch, January 26, 30, 1917; C. Matz to B. Haile, February 6, 1917, P.A., IL.; news item in B.C.I.M., *The Indian Sentinel,* 1:28–29, April, 1917.

[8] A. Weber to D. Engelhard, February 2, 1917, P.A., DE.

[9] Dr. Northrup, medical history and diagnosis, March 8, 1917, M.C.F., 212016.

[10] A. Weber, medical history of case, presented at Mayo Clinic, October 25, 1917, M.C.F., 212016.

[11] R. Bonner to B. Haile, November 28, 1917, P.A., IL.

[12] A. Weber to E. Buttermann, July 31, 1913, P.A., MM.; same to B. Haile, December 30, 1915, P.A., BH.; W. Ketcham, in B.C.I.M., *The Indian Sentinel,* 2:314, July, 1921.

Hence Anselm Weber felt that all he needed was a good rest to clear up his troubles. Accordingly, he spent three months at the Kneipp Sanatorium, Rome City, Indiana, taking the Kneipp cure and simply resting. When he returned to Arizona in late June he was still passing blood, but felt noticeably stronger.[13] To Father Berard's intense exasperation Father Anselm cajoled himself into believing that his Manitou nostrum and his Kneipp Kidney Tea were healing the lesions in his kidneys and stopping the blood flow.[14] After resting for two weeks at Gallup Anselm entered into his wonted round of missionary activity: Indian councils at Manuelito and Chin Lee in July, land transactions, pupils to line up for St. Michaels, and parents' signatures for Catholic instruction of children who would enter government schools in fall.[15] In early October he went to St. Anthony's Hospital in Denver for further diagnosis; here through probable misreading of the X-ray plates, the specialists located the source of trouble in the right kidney and in the prostate gland. Upon advice of Provincial Bonner and others, however, he left for Mayo's in late October, 1917.[16]

The clinical examination at Mayo's beginning on October 25 proved the Denver diagnosis "altogether wrong."[17] On November 7, Dr. William Mayo removed the left kidney which was seriously impaired by cancer.[18] In early December he was able to leave Rochester for St. Michaels where he rushed through the delayed editing of the 1918 copy of *The Franciscan Missions of the Southwest,* some articles of which he had written while at Rochester, Minnesota.[19]

By May of 1918 the friar was able to ride horseback again for the first time in eighteen months, and was feeling in good fettle.[20] Short-lived the respite proved to be, however. Renewed appearance of the malignancy required repeated visits to Mayo's during 1918, 1919, and

[13] A. Weber, medical history of case, presented at Mayo Clinic, October 25, 1917, M.C.F., 212016; A. Weber to G. Rausch, April 4, 1917, P.A., IL.; F. X. Stacher to D. Engelhard, June 29, 1917, P.A., DE.

[14] B. Haile to A. Weber, August 27, November 4, 1917; A. Weber to R. Bonner, September 4, 1917, P.A., IL.

[15] A. Weber to R. Bonner, *ibid.*

[16] R. Bonner to W. Weber, October 19, 1917; A. Weber to D. Engelhard, October 17, 1917, P.A., IL.; A. Weber, medical history of case, October 25, 1917, M.C.F., 212016.

[17] A. Weber to G. Rausch, October 31, 1917, P.A.; see Sisters of St. Francis (Denver), Findings of X-Ray Examinations, October 23, 1917, M.C.F., 212016.

[18] W. Mayo to W. Northrup, November 7, 1917, M.C.F., 212016.

[19] A. Weber to G. Rausch, December 2, 1917, P.A., IL.; Mayo Clinic to W. Northrup, memo, December 4, 1917, M.C.F., 212016.

[20] A. Weber to R. Bonner, May 26, 1918, P.A., HA.

1920 for more operations, radium treatment, and cauterization.[21] Other X-ray treatments and cauterizing were administered at Los Angeles, Gallup, and Albuquerque.[22] Final surgery to eradicate the source of his trouble was performed under local anesthesia on February 4, 1921, by Dr. Braasch of the Mayo Clinic. To all appearances the patient recovered rapidly and left the hospital ten days later to convalesce. He was optimistic about returning to St. Michaels in two weeks "perfectly well."[23]

Throughout his last days he carried on his usual heavy correspondence on Navaho land matters[24] and with relatives and personal friends.[25] After a sudden relapse an emergency operation was performed by Dr. Judd, February 28, on Father Anselm's remaining right kidney. He had received the Last Sacraments from the hospital chaplain on February 26. During the next few days he seemed to rally, but on March 4 he took a serious turn for the worse.[26] Telegrams went out to provincial headquarters in Cincinnati, to St. Michaels, and to his relatives at New Salem, Michigan, regarding his critical condition.[27]

From Michigan Joseph Weber, Anselm's brother, started immediately for Rochester where he arrived on March 7, reaching his brother's bedside at 9 p.m. Anselm pressed his brother's hand and smiled his gratitude; he was in extreme pain and misery, and could not carry on any conversation. He held on to Joe's hand and occasionally with

[21] December 5, 1918; January 3, October 30, 1919; February 24, July 6, September 21, 1920, M.C.F., 212016.

[22] A. Weber to Dr. H. Bowing, Mayo Clinic, December 4, 1919; January 15, 1920; Dr. A. Peterson, Los Angeles, to W. F. Braasch, December 16, 1920; A. Weber to W. Braasch, January 10, 1921, M.C.F., 212016.

[23] A. Weber to Ade Rausch, a niece, February 6, 16, 1921, P.A., IL.

[24] A. Weber to General H. L. Scott, January 13, 1921; H. L. Scott to A. Weber, February 2, 1921; A. Weber to Senator C. Curtis, January 22, 1921; C. Curtis to A. Weber, February 7, 1921; Malcolm McDowell, Secretary of the Board of Indian Commissioners, to A. Weber, January 29, February 4, 1921; Chee Dodge to A. Weber, February 19, 1921, P.A., LP.

[25] A. Weber to D. Engelhard, January 31, February 1, 1921; A. Weber to Mother Katharine, February 6, 1921; Mother Katharine to A. Weber, February 10, 1921; L. Ostermann to A. Weber, February 22, 1921; E. Auweiler to A. Weber, February 22, 1921; Anna Day and S. E. Day to A. Weber, February 21, 1921; E. M. Wigglesworth to A. Weber, February 23, 1921; Mary Weber, sister, to A. Weber, February 20, 1921; R. Bonner to A. Weber, February 28, 1921; G. Rausch, sister, to A. Weber, February 28, 1921; Joe Weber, brother, to A. Weber, February 21, 1921; A. Brockhuis to A. Weber, March 2, 1921; Ade Rausch to A. Weber, February 25, 1921; E. B. Lincoln to A. Weber, March 1, 1921, P.A., IL.

[26] Autopsy report, March 8, 1921, M.C.F., 212016; see *Sendbote*, 48:209, April, 1921.

[27] Custos Flavian Larbes, O.F.M., to A. Rausch, March 5, 1921; L. Oldegeering to Edmund Klein, O.F.M., March 3, 1921, P.A., IL.

great effort whispered, "My God, Joe." At midnight the nurse tried to persuade the visitor to return to a hotel for rest, and asked Father Anselm if he did not wish him to retire. Anselm shook his head and managed to say: "No, Joe should stay with me." In a coma he uttered a long sentence, probably in Navaho, while his brother and the attending nurse prayed the rosary and litany of the Blessed Virgin. At 1:10 a.m., March 8, he breathed his last.[28]

His brother, who sent the telegram to Cincinnati announcing Anselm's death, was surprised and grieved that none of Anselm Weber's confreres had visited him during his last five weeks of sickness and suffering, not even after the recent telegram had warned of the critical condition. He immediately had the body prepared for transfer and burial at New Salem, Michigan, and was entrusted with the papers and effects belonging to his deceased brother.[29] The autopsy had been performed which disclosed that the recent surgery had removed all traces of cancer; uremia and cardiac insufficiency were listed as causes of death.[30]

Father James Archinger, O.F.M., a classmate of Anselm Weber, arrived at Rochester to assume charge of affairs at about the time Joseph Weber was prepared to leave early in the afternoon of March 8. Mr. Weber turned over a full box of papers and correspondence to Father James, who in turn gave him Father Anselm's watch, pocketknife, and two small notebooks as souvenirs. A shabby overcoat, a cap, black suit decidedly worn, bathrobe and sleeping tunic, and several changes of patched underwear comprised the dead friar's wardrobe.[31]

On Friday, March 11, 1921, a solemn funeral Mass was offered at St. Francis Seraph Church in Cincinnati for the repose of the beloved Franciscan missionary. As Provincial Bonner had left a week earlier for the general chapter in Rome, Custos Flavian Larbes officiated, with confreres Stephan Hoffmann and Francis Xavier Buschle as deacon and subdeacon. Monsignor William Ketcham conducted interment services at St. Mary's Cemetery, St. Bernard, Ohio. Around the open grave the friars present sang the plaintive, lovely song-prayer of the Tyrolese Franciscans, the *Ultima,* the traditional German,

[28] Joseph Weber to Mary Weber, sister of Anselm Weber, March 21, 1921; same to L. Oldegeering, June 13, 1921, P.A., PM.

[29] *Ibid.*

[30] Autopsy report, March 8, 1921, M.C.F., 212016.

[31] Mrs. Joseph Weber to G. Rausch, March 10, 1921; Joe Weber to Mary Weber, March 21, 1921; Lena Funk to L. Oldegeering, June 12, 1921, P.A., PM.

and distinctively Franciscan, folk song which pleaded with the Mother of God for a happy death.[32]

Condolences poured in from the prominent and from many others who were little known. From the Indian Commissioner, Cato Sells, went a message of sincere sympathy to Father Ludger and the friars at St. Michaels.[33]

> I share with you and your associates at St. Michaels deep sorrow because of the passing of Father Weber. He wielded a large Christian influence and was a tried and true friend of the Navajo Indian. His many protestations and accomplishments in their behalf should cause him to be revered by them throughout the years to come.

Charles S. Lusk, secretary of the Bureau of Catholic Indian Missions since its inception under General Ewing in 1874, declared that Father Weber "did more and greater constructive work than any Indian missionary that I know of during . . . the last fifty years."[34]

"The Apostle of the Navajos, and the pillar of our missionary work in this part of the country is gone," wrote the Jesuit, Father Mandalari of Albuquerque. "The Church lost an apostolic missionary, and we priests and religious a comfort, a leader, a real friend. . . . I cannot forget a Franciscan Father, whose friendship has done me so much spiritual good."[35]

Lengthy eulogies and life sketches appeared in the Cincinnati *Catholic Telegraph*,[36] the Dubuque *Daily American Tribune*,[37] the Gallup *Carbon City News*,[38] *The Gallup Independent*,[39] *Sendbote*,[40] *The Indian Sentinel*,[41] *The St. Anthony Messenger*,[42] and the final number of the *Franciscan Missions of the Southwest*, 1922, was entirely dedicated to the life and works of Anselm Weber as reviewed by his confreres of the Navaho Mission.

Formal letters of condolence and simple notes of sorrow, which told very simply that Father Anselm had been their closest friend,

[32] Editorial, "Der hochw. P. Anselm Weber, O.F.M.," *Sendbote*, 48:209, April, 1921.

[33] Cato Sells to L. Oldegeering, telegram, March 9, 1921, P.A., PM.

[34] Chas. Lusk to L. Oldegeering, March 11, 1921, P.A., PM.

[35] A. M. Mandalari, S.J., to Archbishop A. T. Daeger, O.F.M., n.d., 1921, P.A., PM.

[36] March 10, 1921.

[37] March 15, 1921.

[38] March 19, 1921.

[39] Alva C. Shinn, "Reservation News Notes," April 7, 1921.

[40] Editorial, *Sendbote*, 48:209–211, April, 1921; L. Ostermann, *Sendbote*, 49:163–166, March, 1922.

[41] William H. Ketcham, in B.C.I.M., *The Indian Sentinel*, 2:312–315, July, 1921.

[42] E. Auweiler, in *St. Anthony Messenger*, 29:451–454, March, 1922.

came to St. Michaels from everyday folk, Indian Service officials and teachers, from priests, and from the Indians themselves.[43] Excerpts from several representative letters spell out simply but grandly the meaning of Anselm Weber's life: from Pablo Abeita of Isleta Pueblo, well-known spokesman for the Pueblo Indians, came a profound bit of Indian philosophy:[44]

> We, the Indians of the West, have lost a friend, a friend whom one and all liked and loved. It is a loss that will take years to fill, if it is ever filled, and if it is ever filled it will be on our Lord's side, because it will never be filled on the Indian side. Others may take his place and do what Father Weber did and more, but it will take years and years to open the Indians' confidence in their hearts, same as they had for Father Weber. . . . We were made to work, but not to finish our work. If we were to finish our work there would be no world. . . .

From an Indian Service inspector, S. A. M. Young, came the simple message, "my best friend is gone. I never had a more faithful friend,"[45] Howell Jones, Land Commissioner for the Santa Fe Railroad, wrote: "In the death of Father Weber, New Mexico and Arizona have lost a valuable citizen and the Indians their best friend. I will mourn his death and miss him more than words can tell, for I not only admired him, but loved him."[46]

Agnes Chester, a niece of Chee Dodge, and a former student at St. Michaels School, revealed the degree to which Father Anselm had won his way into the personal affections of the Navaho:[47]

> . . . My father was away for a long time at Keams Canyon with Mr. Dodge and some other fellows. When my father came back, he told us that Rev. Anselm Weber died two days ago. Oh, dear me, my heart is broken. We all wept at once. Still we will never forget him . . . now the white people can do what they please with us because our Father is gone. Now, too, the white people can do everything they please with our lands, because our dear Father looked after everything. . . . We just worry like poor dogs. Nothing doing for us. No more like him. Poor Mr. Dodge, he wept like everything for his friend, and Frank Walker also. . . . I am nearly dying for Father Anselm. My heart got so weak from worrying. I wish I could see him how he looks now. . . .

Possibly few knew and loved Father Anselm more than his co-

[43] See folders PM. and IL. in P.A.

[44] B.C.I.M., *The Indian Sentinel,* 2:316, July, 1921.

[45] S. A. M. Young to L. Oldegeering, March 17, 1921, P.A., PM.

[46] Howell Jones to Eligius Kunkel, O.F.M., March 10, 1921, P.A., PM.

[47] Agnes Chester to Sister Honora, March 13, 1921, in *The Indian Sentinel,* 2:316, July, 1921.

missioner, confrere, and intimate friend, Father Leopold, who suffered a deep personal loss in Anselm's death. Two months had almost slipped by since his *carissime's* death when he confided: "His death does not look real to me yet. If an auto stopped here [Chin Lee] today and Father Anselm stepped out and walked into the house, I do not think I would be a bit surprised or think it extraordinary."[48]

Both Leopold Ostermann and Berard Haile asked to remain at their missions at Chin Lee and Lukachukai rather than attempt to take the place of the dead *Naatani Chischilli* at St. Michaels. Realizing the need for continued residence among the Navaho people at their own missions, they hoped to accomplish far more by "slow, kind, patient, and optimistic work [and to hold] their trust, confidence, and good will."[49] Both realized that they could "not do much good with the old Indians, yet we need their good will and cooperation . . . very much."[50] Their request, however, that Father Fridolin Schuster be appointed successor to Anselm Weber, who had served as superior at St. Michaels for twenty-one years, was not honored. Rather, Anselm's petition, written shortly before his death, was acted on, and Father Marcellus Troester, prior to the chapter of August 30, 1921, was appointed to take charge of the Navaho mission. He was instructed to carry on the policies of Father Anselm in dealing with the Navaho.[51]

One of Marcellus Troester's first tasks, assigned to him by Howell Jones in all devotion and enthusiasm for Father Anselm's humanitarian work among the Navaho, was to sound out the influential Navaho on the prospect of erecting a statue to perpetuate the memory of the Apostle of the Navaho.[52]

Almost too pat Mr. Jones's project symbolized the utter incomprehension of typical white Americans toward the mission problem presented by the Navaho way of life. Father Marcellus who had fifteen years of experience with the Navaho to back his judgment dismissed the idea of a monument to Father Anselm as a thoroughly dubious enterprise, precocious by at least a century. Likely most of the Indians would fear a statue of their old friend whose "ghost"

[48] L. Ostermann to J. F. McGee, O.F.M., May 1, 1921, P.A., PM.

[49] L. Ostermann to Custos F. Larbes, March 11, 1921, subscribed to by B. Haile, P.A., PM.

[50] L. Ostermann to Provincial Edmund Klein, June 17, 1924, P.A., PM.

[51] A. Weber to (Provincial R. Bonner), first page missing, n.d. (February, 1921); M. Troester to R. Bonner, August 17, 1921, P.A., PM.; M. Troester to R. Bonner, August 24, 27, 1921, P.A., MS.

[52] Howell Jones to E. Kunkel, March 10, 1921; same to L. Oldegeering, March 24. April 1, 12, 1921, P.A., PM.

might bother them. Second, Father Marcellus had realistically asked the wealthiest headman among the Navaho, a close friend of Father Anselm, to what extent he would be financially willing to show his appreciation of the dead missionary. The Indian, who according to Father Marcellus had made approximately $500 on an automobile deal with Anselm Weber shortly before his death, replied bemusedly that he might be able later on to give $100.[53]

The new Superior of St. Michaels concluded that to attempt any such collection for a statue of Father Anselm "would undo, with one fell blow, all the work it has taken Father Weber years to build up."[54] Navaho were accustomed to honor a man's memory as they squatted around a campfire, by swapping lively stories of his prowess and shrewdness — but never by a statue.[55]

Could Father Anselm's tastes have been consulted on the monument business it is not unlikely he would have chuckled exuberantly, but quietly, and turning to a typewriter, would have suggested that his good friend, Howell Jones, work rather for a decent irrigation dam on Black Creek, or possibly turn over to the Navaho an extra dozen railroad townships south of the tracks. A statue would have bothered the unassuming missionary far more than it would the Navaho.

[53] M. Troester to Howell Jones, November 5, 1921, P.A., MI.

[54] *Ibid.*

[55] Gladys Reichard, *Navaho Religion, op. cit.,* pp. 43–45.

Bibliography

Primary Sources

Archival

Bureau of Catholic Indian Missions Archives. Letters and documents filed chronologically by states and missions, 1873 to date; scrapbooks with news clippings, 1870–1900; miscellaneous pamphlets published by the Bureau. Search covered 1880–1921. Bureau of Catholic Indian Missions, Washington, D. C. These archives are extremely valuable for mission studies since the Bureau acted as clearinghouse and representative for both missions and government. Archives contain government documents, memos on conversations with government officials relative to government-mission relations.

Bureau of Indian Affairs. Special Cases 143, Miscellaneous Navajo, 1880–1905; letters received and outgoing correspondence, 1895–1906. The National Archives, Washington, D. C.

——— Navajo Indian Service Records. Letter books, 1880–1912; miscellaneous office diaries, 1902–1917; record books, 1898–1919. Navajo Indian Service, Window Rock, Arizona.

Cornwells Heights Archives. Sisters of the Blessed Sacrament, *Annals,* 36 volumes of typed letters with annotations, 1891–1945; original letters chronologically filed. Search covered 1895–1921. Motherhouse of the Sisters of the Blessed Sacrament for Indians and Colored People, Cornwells Heights, Pennsylvania.

Day, Anna Burbridge, *Diary,* 1869–1933. Personal day journal of an early settler in Arizona, the wife of Sam E. Day. This diary which is written in notebooks, loose papers, and on the rear of calendars is in the possession of Jewell Adams, Shawnee, Oklahoma.

Franciscan Fathers, *Papers*. Letter books, letters, record books, news clippings, chronicle; unorganized in great part. Franciscan Fathers, St. Michaels, Arizona.

Parish Records:

Annunciation Church, Chin Lee, Arizona.

Immaculate Conception Church, Tohatchi, New Mexico.

Our Lady of Guadalupe Church, Peña Blanca, New Mexico.

Sacred Heart Cathedral, Gallup, New Mexico.

St. Isabel Mission, Lukachukai, Arizona.

St. Joseph Church, Parkview, New Mexico.

St. Michaels Mission, St. Michaels, Arizona.

Provincial Archives of St. John the Baptist Province. Materials arranged by person and/or subject, and filed in four drawers under name of Anselm Weber. Other diaries, letters, and records are filed outside the Anselm Weber Collection by receiver or subject. Search covered 1890–1930. St. Francis Monastery, Cincinnati, Ohio.

Trockur, Fr. Emmanuel, O.F.M., *Papers*. Letter folders and boxes of materials collected by Fr. Emmanuel Trockur, O.F.M., Tegakwitha Indian Mission, Houck, Arizona. Most of this material has since been transferred to St. Michaels Mission.

Documents

Abel, Annie Heloise, editor, *The Official Correspondence of James S. Calhoun while Indian Agent at Santa Fe and Superintendent of Indian Affairs in New Mexico*. Washington, D. C.: Government Printing Office, 1915.

Annals of the Propagation of the Faith, Volumes, 16–36, 1855–1875. London: C. Dolman; Baltimore: Kelly and Piet. Translations of the *Annales de la Propagation de la Foi;* contains mission reports from Bishops Lamy, Machebeuf, Salpointe.

Armstrong, Samuel Chapman, *Report of a Trip Made in Behalf of The Indian Rights Association to Some Indian Reservations of the Southwest*. Philadelphia: Indian Rights Association, 1884. Armstrong was principal of Hampton School and traveled through Navaho, Pima, Papago, Apache reservations, giving detailed reports on each.

Board of Indian Commissioners, *Annual Report,* 1900–1915. Washington, D. C.: Government Printing Office, 1901–1916.

Bureau of Catholic Indian Missions, *Annals of the Catholic Indian Missions of America,* 1877–1878. Vols. 1–2. Washington, D. C.

——— Brouillet, J. B. A., editor, *The Work of the Decade;* ending December 31, 1883. Washington, D. C., 1883.

——— Brouillet, J. B. A., *Management of the Catholic Indian Bureau at Washington*. Washington, D. C., 1878. Apologia for the Bureau after an attack by *Freeman's Journal,* January 19, 1878.

——— *Bureau of Catholic Indian Missions, 1874–1895*. Washington, D. C.: The Church News Publishing Company, 1895.

——— Ewing, General Charles, editor, *Petition of the Catholic Church in Behalf of the Pueblos and Other Indians of New Mexico*. Washington, D. C.: S. and R. O. Polkinhorn, printers, 1874. Concerns the contracting of Presbyterian schools for the Pueblo Indians of New Mexico.

——— Ewing, General Charles, *Circular of the Catholic Commissioner for Indian Missions to the Catholics of the U. S.* Baltimore: John Murphy and Co., 1874.

——— *Official Construction of President Grant's Indian Peace Policy*. Washington, D. C., n.d.

——— *Report of Rev. J. A. Stephan for the year 1891–1892*. Washington, D. C.: Gedney and Roberts Press, 1892.

——— *Reports,* 1898–1910. Washington, D. C., 1898–1910.

Carleton, James H., *To the People of New Mexico,* address given at Las Cruces, New Mexico, December 16, 1864. Printed, n.d., Library of Congress.

Catalogus Fratrum Provinciae Cincinnatensis S. Joannis Baptistae, O.F.M. Cincinnati, Ohio, 1933.

Catholic Clergy of the Province of Oregon, The, *Address to the Catholics of the*

United States on President Grant's Indian Policy, in its Bearing upon Catholic Interests at Large. Portland, Oregon: The Catholic Sentinel Publishing Company, 1874.

Cohen, Felix S., *Handbook of Federal Indian Law.* Washington, D. C.: Government Printing Office, 1942.

Commissioner of Indian Affairs, *Annual Report,* 1870–1921. Washington, D. C.: Government Printing Office, 1870–1921.

——— *Report on substituting government for contract schools.* 53 Congress, 3 session, House executive document, No. 107. Washington, D. C.: Government Printing Office, 1894. Advocates' abandonment of contract school policy.

Congressional Record, 46:2178–2182, January 29, 1917, and 46:2242, January 30, 1917. Senator Fall argues against extending Navaho reservation at the expense of the public domain.

Connelley, William Elsey, *Doniphan's Expedition And the Conquest of New Mexico and California.* Topeka, Kansas, 1907. This carries the Hughes Reprint.

Davis, William Watts H., *Private Journal At a Treaty with the Navajo Indians,* New Mexico, July, 1855. Manuscript in the Library of Congress at Washington which the Territorial Governor of New Mexico used for Chapters 17 and 18 of *El Gringo.*

Dyk, Walter, *A Navaho Autobiography.* Viking Fund Publication in Anthropology, No. 8. New York: Viking, 1947. Memories of a Navaho; several references to "Andy" (Rev. Andres of Aneth, Utah), Superintendent Shelton and the Byalille affair.

Executive Orders Relating to Indian Reservations. Volume I, from May 14, 1855, to July 1, 1912; Volume II, from July 1, 1912, to July 1, 1922. Washington, D. C.: Government Printing Office, 1912, 1922.

Hackett, Charles Wilson, editor, *Historical Documents relating to New Mexico, Nueva Vizcaya, and Approaches Thereto, to 1773.* Collected by Adolph F. A. Bandelier and Fanny R. Bandelier. Volume 3. Washington, D. C.: Carnegie Institution of Washington, 1937.

Hagerman, H. J., *Navajo Indian Reservation.* Report of Special Commissioner to negotiate with Indians on the status of Navajo Indian Reservation Land Acquisitions. 72 Congress, 1 session, Sen. Doc., no. 64. Washington, D. C.: Government Printing Office, 1932.

Hodge, Frederick Webb, Hammond, George P., and Rey, Agapito, *Fray Alonzo de Benavides' Revised Memorial of 1634, with Numerous Supplementary Documents Elaborately Annotated.* Albuquerque: The University of New Mexico Press, 1945.

Indian Rights Association, *Annual Reports,* 1884–1929. Philadelphia, 1885–1930.

——— *Annual Reports of the Executive Committee,* 1897–1929. Philadelphia, 1898–1930.

Joint Special Committee, Report of the, *Condition of the Indian Tribes.* 39 Congress, 2 session, Report no. 156. Committee appointed under Joint Resolution of March 3, 1865. Washington, D. C.: Government Printing Office, 1867.

Kappler, Charles J., compiler and editor, *Indian Affairs. Laws and Treaties.* Laws compiled to December 1, 1913. Washington, D. C.: Government Printing Office, 1913.

Kenngott, Rev. George F., *Report of a Special Committee on Appropriations.* New York: Society for Propagating the Gospel Among the Indians and Others of North America, 1911. Objective report on all missions.

Lake Mohonk Conference of Friends of the Indian, *Proceedings of Annual Meetings,* 1895–1916. Philadelphia, 1895–1916. Many items are inflated success stories.

Leupp, Francis E., *Notes of a Summer Tour Among the Indians of the Southwest.* Philadelphia: Indian Rights Association, 1897. Tour included Navaho, Apache, Jicarilla, and Hopi country.

Message from the President of the United States Transmitting Certain Reports Upon the Condition of the Navajo Indian Country. Report of water and irrigation surveys carried out September and October, 1892, by Lieutenants Brown, Suplee, and Gurovits. Washington, D. C.: Government Printing Office, 1893. Geophysical maps included.

Office of Indian Affairs, *Rules for the Indian School Service.* Washington, D. C.: Government Printing Office, 1900.

Owens, M. Lilliana, S. L. Goñi, Gregory, S.J., and Gonzales, J. M., S.J., *Jesuit Beginnings in New Mexico 1867–1882.* Jesuit Studies — Southwest, Number One. El Paso, Texas: Revista Catolica Press, 1950. Translated documents with some editing.

Rencher, A., *Indian Disturbances in the Territory of New Mexico.* 36 Congress, 2 session, House executive document, No. 24. Washington, D. C., 1861. Contains letters regarding Navaho of Governor of New Mexico Territory to General Cass, Secretary of State, 1858–1860, and Special Message to Legislative Assembly, December 17, 1858.

Secretary of the Interior, May 25, 1908, *Report on Employment of U. S. Soldiers in Arresting By-a-lil-le and Other Navajo Indians.* 60 Congress, 1 session. Senate Document no. 517. Washington, D. C.: Government Printing Office, 1908.

Shaw, Clarence H., *The Snake Dance of the Moqui Indians.* Phoenix, Arizona, 1902. Photographs.

Simpson, Lieutenant J. H., *Report of an expedition into the Navajo Country in 1849.* 31 Congress, 1 session, Senate executive document, No. 64, Report of the Secretary of War. Washington, D. C.: Union Office, 1850. Treats events leading up to the Treaty of September 9, 1849, including the killing by United States soldiers of Chief Narbona; an eyewitness and graphic account; refers to encampment at Cienega.

Tabula Definitionis Congregationis Capitularis. Archives of St. John the Baptist Province, Cincinnati, Ohio. 1889–1921. For assignments and locations of the friars.

Testimony taken by Colonel H. L. Scott regarding Trouble on Navajo Reservation. 60 Congress, 2 session, Senate document, No. 757. Washington, D. C.: Government Printing Office, 1909. Investigation of the killing of Navaho near Aneth, Utah, by federal troops, including visit with Anselm Weber.

United States Bureau of Indian Affairs, *Report relating to care of Indians in Sectarian and denomination schools.* 58 Congress, 3 session, Senate document, No. 179. Washington, D. C.: Government Printing Office, 1905.

United States Office of Indian Affairs, *Rules of the Indian School Service.* Washington, D. C.: Government Printing Office, 1900.

United States Statutes at Large and Recent Treaties, Conventions, and Executive Proclamations.

Valentine, R. G., *General Regulations for Religious Worship and Instructions of Pupils in Government Indian Schools.* Carlisle, Pennsylvania: Carlisle Indian Press, 1909.

War Department, *Annual Reports,* 1906–1914. Washington, D. C.: Government Printing Office, 1906–1914.

Welsh, Herbert, *Report of a Visit to the Navajo, Pueblo, and Hualpais Indians of New Mexico and Arizona.* Philadelphia, 1885.

Whipple, A. W., and Humphreys, A. A., *Report of Explorations and Surveys, 1853–1854.* Volume 3. 33 Congress, 2 session, House executive document, No. 91, Washington, D. C.: A. O. P. Nicholson, Printer, 1856.

Women's National Indian Association, The, *Annual Reports,* 1883–1908. Name changed to The National Indian Association in 1901. Philadelphia, 1883–1908. Reports of the organization which planned and opened many of the Navaho missions which were later turned over to the government or to Protestant denominations. A source book for Navaho missions.

Books

Barnes, Lemuel Call, *Missions to the Heathen.* The American Baptist Home Mission Society, New York, n.d. (1910?). Description of some mission work of Rev. Lee I. Thayer, Baptist, at Two Grey Hills. Refers to other Protestant missions; no mention of St. Michaels.

Davis, William Watts H., *El Gringo; or, New Mexico and Her People.* New York: Harper and Brothers, 1857. Gives details on the resignation of Sarcillo Largo in favor of Manuelito.

Dolfin, Rev. J., *Bringing the Gospel in Hogan and Pueblo,* 1896–1921. Grand Rapids, Michigan: Christian Reformed Church, 1921. Chapter 7, "A Pioneer Missionary to the Navahos," is by Rev. J. W. Brink, a Dutch Reformed minister contemporary of Anselm Weber.

Eickemeyer, Carl, *Over the Great Navajo Trail.* New York, 1900. Travelogue: a trip from Santa Fe in 1896 west through San Mateo, Gallup, and on to Round Rock.

Haile, Berard, *A Catechism and Guide, Navaho-English.* St. Michaels, Arizona: St. Michaels Press, 1937,

——— editor and translator, *The Holy Gospels for Sundays and Holy Days.* St. Michaels, Arizona: St. Michaels Press, 1938.

——— *Preparation for the Sacrament of Penance.* St. Michaels, Arizona: St. Michaels Press, 1940.

——— *The Way of the Cross.* St. Michaels, Arizona: St. Michaels Press, 1944.

Hoffmanns' Catholic Directory, Almanac and Clergy List. Milwaukee: M. H. Wiltzius Co., 1895–1900.

Kenedy, P. J., Company, compiler, *The Official Catholic Directory, 1950.* New York: P. J. Kenedy, 1950. For the period 1864–1895, *Sadlier's Catholic Almanac;* 1895–1900, *Hoffmanns' Catholic Directory, Almanac and Clergy List.* Sadlier's for the period 1864–1895 is not altogether accurate as regards New Mexico.

Kluckhohn, Clyde, *Navaho Witchcraft.* Papers of the Peabody Museum of

American Archaeology and Ethnology, Harvard University, Volume XXII, No. 2. Cambridge, Massachusetts: Peabody Museum, 1944. A psychosociological study of Navaho ritual against evil spirits based on interviews by an expert and original anthropologist.

Kneale, Albert H., *Indian Agent.* Caldwell, Idaho: The Caxton Printers, Ltd., 1950. Autobiographical, by a retired United States Indian agent who was superintendent at Shiprock, 1923–1929.

Kuipers, C., *Zuñi Also Prays.* (Grand Rapids) Christian Reformed Board of Missions, 1946. Mission story of the Dutch Reformed Church among the Navaho, especially at Zuñi.

New Mexico Supreme Court Reports. Volume 14, 1907–1908. Santa Fe, New Mexico: New Mexican Printing Company, 1909.

Parisot, Pierre Fourier, O.M.I., *The Reminiscences of a Texas Missionary.* San Antonio, Texas, 1899. Purely reminiscence with some good description; some travel in Arizona and New Mexico, 1887.

Sadlier's Catholic Directory, New York: D. and J. Sadlier Co., 1864–1895.

Scott, General Hugh, *Some Memories of a Soldier.* New York: Appleton-Century Company, 1929. Several pages on the Beautiful Mountain Navaho disturbance.

Segale, Sister Blandina, *At the End of the Santa Fe Trail.* Milwaukee: Bruce Publishing Company, 1948.

Thomas, Alfred Barnaby, *The Plains Indians and New Mexico, 1751–1778: A Collection of Documents Illustrative of the History of the Eastern Frontier of New Mexico.* Albuquerque: The University of New Mexico Press, 1940.

(Weber, Anselm, editor) *A Navaho-English Catechism of Christian Doctrine for the Use of Navaho Children.* St. Michaels, Arizona: The Franciscan Fathers, 1910.

——— *The Navajo Indians, A Statement of Facts.* St. Michaels, Arizona, 1914.

Articles

Anonymous, "Reminiscences of Fort Defiance, New Mexico, 1860," *Journal of the Military Service Institution of the U. S.,* 4:90–92, 1883.

Bureau of Catholic Indian Missions, *The Indian Sentinel,* 1902–1916, an annual; from July, 1916, a quarterly. *Indianer Wache* is the German edition of this annual to which Anselm Weber contributed several articles, letters, and reports. *Indianer Wache,* 1902–1915; *The Indian Sentinel,* Volumes 1–2, 1916–1922. Good factual material for this dissertation.

Franciscan Missions of the Southwest, The. Annual, 1913–1922. St. Michaels, Arizona. Historical, ethnological, and descriptive materials; by the missionaries at St. Michaels.

Roosevelt, Theodore, "Across the Navajo Desert," *Outlook,* 105:309–317, October 12, 1913.

——— "The Hopi Snake Dance," *Outlook,* 105:365–372, October 18, 1913.

St. Anthony Messenger. 1897–1950. This Franciscan magazine contains many news items and articles on the Southwest missions. Of special significance for the Navaho mission is the excellent series of articles by Fr. Leopold Ostermann, O.F.M., under the title, "Franciscans in the Wilds and Wastes of the Navajo Country," running from Volume 8, February, 1901, through Volume 17, October, 1909.

Weber, Anselm, Hartung, Frederick, and Fischer, Egbert, *et al.,* O.F.M., "Die Franziskaner-Mission unter den Navajo-Indianern," *Der Sendbote des Göttlichen Herzens Jesu.* Under this title Anselm Weber wrote a series of monthly unsigned accounts of mission activity in the Southwest, 1899–1921. Fr. Frederick Hartung, O.F.M., filled in from July through November, 1900; Fr. Egbert Fischer, O.F.M., for several issues during 1912, 1913, 1915. Discounting certain errors and occasional romanticizing of mission life, this magazine offers the best printed source material on the Navaho mission.

"Yazhe" and "Y" (Berard Haile, O.F.M.), and Juvenal Schnorbus, O.F.M., many unsigned news articles and features in *St. Franziskus Bote,* 1898–1905. Berard Haile ran a translation of Benavides in German from 11:8 to 12:41, July, 1902, through August, 1903, and a narrative of a mission trip with Fr. Michael Dumarest, 12:78 through 12:400, September, 1903, through June, 1904.

Interviews

Allison, Mrs. F. J., March 20, 1951, at Gallup, New Mexico, *per* Father Anthony Kroger, O.F.M.

Christman, Father Turibius, O.F.M., February 27, 1951, at Batesville, Indiana.

Day, Sam, Jr., April 13, 1951, at St. Michaels, Arizona, *per* Father Silver Meyer, O.F.M.; November 5, 1951, *per* Mrs. Jewell Adams.

Goodman, Mrs. Barbara Hubbell, and Hubbell, Romano, July 16, 1950, at Holbrook, Arizona.

Haile, Father Berard, O.F.M., September 2, 1949, and June 20–23, 1950, at St. Michaels, Arizona.

McGee, Father John Forest, O.F.M., September 5, 1951, at Detroit, Michigan.

Neri, Mother Philip, S.B.S., November 8, 1950, Cornwells Heights, Pennsylvania.

Rauch, Adeline, niece of Anselm Weber, O.F.M., February 16, 1951, at Hamilton, Ohio.

Ripperger, Father Maurice, O.F.M., January 14, 1951, at Mt. Healthy, Ohio.

Schneider, Father Ermin, O.F.M., January 14, 1951, at Mt. Healthy, Ohio.

Sisters Angela, Crescentia, and Mary of the Annunciation, first Sisters at St. Michaels School, November 7, 1950, at Cornwells Heights, Pennsylvania.

Wellinghoff, Mrs. Mary, niece of Anselm Weber, O.F.M., February 16, 1951, at Hamilton, Ohio.

Wigglesworth, Dr. A. M., Fort Defiance physician and close friend of Anselm Weber, O.F.M., October 30, 1950, at Washington, D. C.

Secondary Sources

Books and Pamphlets

Bancroft, Hubert Howe, *Arizona and New Mexico,* 1530–1888. Volume 17 of Works. San Francisco: The History Company, 1888.

Brain, Belle M., *The Redemption of the Red Man.* New York City: The Board of Home Missions of the Presbyterian Church in the U.S.A., 1904. Includes material on the Navaho missions.

Coolidge, Dane, *Lorenzo the Magnificent.* New York: E. P. Dutton, 1924. On John Lawrence Hubbell.

Coolidge, Dane, and Roberts, Mary, *The Navajo Indians.* New York: Houghton Mifflin Company, 1930. General popular treatment.

Culin, Stewart, "Games of the North American Indian." Smithsonian Institution, Bureau of American Ethnology, *Twenty-Fourth Annual Report,* 1902–1903, pp. 3–809. Washington, D. C.: Government Printing Office, 1907.

Dale, Edward Everett, *The Indians of the Southwest: A Century of Development under the United States.* Norman, Oklahoma: University of Oklahoma Press, 1949. A scholarly survey of government relations, 1848–1948.

Defouri, Very Rev. James H., *Historical Sketch of the Catholic Church in New Mexico.* San Francisco: McCormick Bros., 1887. A companion volume to Salpointe's *Soldiers of the Cross* for nineteenth-century Church history of New Mexico. Uses diaries and memoirs, such as Coudert's on Lamy's 1864 trip through war-desolated Navaho country.

Department of the Interior, *Transportation: Information Concerning Land Grants for Roads, Canals, River Improvements and Railroads.* Information Bulletin, 1939 Series, No. 5. Washington, D. C.: Government Printing Office, 1940.

Dykhuizen, Dorothy, *Go Quickly and Tell.* Grand Rapids, Michigan: Wm. B. Eerdmans Co., 1946. Light, inspirational, and descriptive account by a teacher of beginner pupils at Rehoboth.

Engelhardt, Zephyrin, O.F.M., *The Franciscans in Arizona.* Harbor Springs, Michigan, 1899. Leans heavily on Bancroft; Anselm Weber wrote pages 208–211, the sketch of St. Michaels, Arizona.

Farish, Thomas Edwin, *History of Arizona.* 8 volumes. Phoenix, Arizona, 1918. Especially good for place history: relies considerably on memoirs and accounts of old-timers.

Faust, Harold S., *The American Indian in Tragedy and Triumph.* Presbyterian Historical Studies, No. 1. Philadelphia: Presbyterian Historical Society, 1945. A study of Presbyterian missions from the sources.

Federal Writers' Project, *The Navaho.* Sponsored and published by Arizona State Teachers College at Flagstaff. Flagstaff, 1938.

Forrest, Earle Robert, *Missions and Pueblos of the Old Southwest.* Cleveland: A. H. Clarke, 1929.

Franciscan Educational Conference, *Franciscan History of North America.* Santa Barbara, California, 1936.

Franciscan Fathers, The, *An Ethnological Dictionary of the Navaho Language.* St. Michaels, Arizona: The Franciscan Fathers, 1910. A primer for students of the Navaho.

Garraghan, Gilbert J., S.J., *The Jesuits of the Middle United States.* 3 volumes. New York: American Press, 1938. Critical work with excellent index; good for reference on Jesuits who served in Southwest.

Geiger, Maynard, O.F.M., *The Kingdom of St. Francis in Arizona* (1539–1939). Santa Barbara, California, 1938. A brief but good survey.

Gillmor, Frances, and Wetherill, Louisa Wade, *Traders to the Navajos* (John Wetherill's of Kayenta). Boston: Houghton Mifflin, 1934.

[Haile, Berard, editor in chief] *An Ethnologic Dictionary of the Navaho Language.* St. Michaels, Arizona: The Franciscan Fathers, 1910.

[Haile, Berard, editor] *A Vocabulary of the Navaho Language.* St. Michaels, Arizona: The Franciscan Fathers, 1912.

Haile, Berard, editor, *A Manual of Navaho Grammar*. St. Michaels, Arizona: The Franciscan Fathers, 1926.

——— *Origin Legend of the Navaho Enemy Way*. Yale University Publications in Anthropology, No. 17. New Haven: Yale University Press, 1938.

——— *Learning Navaho*. St. Michaels, Arizona: St. Michaels Press, 1941–1948.

——— *Origin Legend of the Navaho Flintway; Text and Translation*. The University of Chicago Publications in Anthropology: Linguistic Series. Chicago: The University of Chicago Press, 1943.

——— *The Navaho War Dance, A Brief Narrative of Its Meaning and Practice*. St. Michaels, Arizona: St. Michaels Press, 1946.

——— *The Navaho Fire Dance, or Corral Dance; a Brief Account of Its Practice and Meaning*, St. Michaels, Arizona: St. Michaels Press, 1946.

——— *Navaho Sacrificial Figurines*. Chicago: University of Chicago Press, 1947.

——— *Starlore Among the Navaho*. Santa Fe, New Mexico: Museum of Navajo Ceremonial Art, 1947.

——— *Head and Face Masks in Navaho Ceremonialism*. St. Michaels, Arizona: St. Michaels Press, 1947.

——— *Prayer Stick Cutting in a Five Night Navaho Ceremonial of the Male Branch of Shootingway*. Chicago: The University of Chicago Press, 1948.

——— *Legend of the Ghostway Ritual in the Male Branch of the Shootingway, Part One: Suckingway Its Legend and Practice, Part Two*. St. Michaels, Arizona: St. Michaels Press, 1950.

Harmon, George Dewey, *Sixty Years of Indian Affairs: Political, Economic, and Diplomatic*, 1789–1850. Chapel Hill: The University of North Carolina Press, 1941. Southwest Indians mentioned; strong on government's financial treatment of the Indians. Good periodical bibliography except for Southwest.

Hewett, Edgar L., and Fisher, Reginald G., *Mission Monuments of New Mexico*. Handbooks of Archaeological History, editor, Edgar L. Hewett, No. 5. Albuquerque: The University of New Mexico and the School of American Research, 1943.

Hill, W. W., *The Agricultural and Hunting Methods of the Navaho Indians*. Yale University Publication in Anthropology, No. 18. New Haven: Yale University Press, 1938.

——— *Navajo Salt Gathering*. The University of New Mexico Bulletin 349, February 1, 1940. Albuquerque: The University of New Mexico Press, 1940.

Hinman, George Warren, D.D., *The American Indian and Christian Missions*. New York: Fleming H. Revell Company, 1933.

Institute for Government Research Studies in Administration. Lewis Meriam, director, *The Problem of Indian Administration*. Baltimore: The Johns Hopkins Press, 1928. Broad yet scientific, with statistical studies and excellent interpretation. Contains sound Indian missionology.

Kelsey, Rayner Wickersham, *Friends and the Indians*, 1655–1917. Philadelphia: The Associated Executive Committee of Friends on Indian Affairs, 1917. Scholarly, on Quaker missionary efforts; nothing on New Mexico or Arizona.

Kinney, J. P., *A Continent Lost — A Civilization Won: Indian Land Tenure in America*. Baltimore: The Johns Hopkins Press, 1937. An intricate topic thoroughly treated; up to date.

Kluckhohn, Clyde, and Leighton, Dorothea, *The Navaho.* Cambridge, Massachusetts: Harvard University Press, 1947. An excellent summary of the social life of "The People" with good introductory history.

Kluckhohn, Clyde, and Spencer, Katherine, *A Bibliography of the Navaho Indians.* New York: J. J. Augustin Publisher, 1940.

Krug, J. A., Secretary of the Interior, Report of, *The Navajo: A Long-Range Program for Navajo Rehabilitation.* Washington, D. C.: Government Printing Office, 1948.

Landis, Paul H., *Population Problems: A Cultural Interpretation;* third edition. New York: American Book Company, 1943.

Leighton, Alexander Hamilton, and Dorothea C., *The Navaho Door.* Cambridge: Harvard University Press, 1944. An insight into Navaho culture via personality: Navaho society and social controls approached sociologically by anthropologists using interviews.

Leighton, Dorothea C., and Kluckhohn, Clyde, *Children of the People.* Cambridge, Massachusetts: Harvard University Press, 1947.

Lemmens, Leonard, O.F.M., *Geschichte der Franziskanermissionen.* Münster, Westfalen, 1929.

Leupp, Francis Ellington, *Civilization's Lesson to Barbarism.* Leaflet. Philadelphia: Indian Rights Association, 1897.

——— *The Indian and His Problem.* New York: Charles Scribner's Sons, 1910. Viewpoints of an understanding ex-Commissioner of Indian Affairs.

Lindquist, G. E. E., *The Red Man in the United States.* An intimate study of the social, economic, and religious life of the American Indian. New York: George H. Doran Company, 1923. Speaks of "Monsignor Webber"; map of missions among Navaho and Hopi.

Luomala, Katherine, *Navaho Life of Yesterday and Today.* U. S. Department of the Interior, U. S. National Park Service. Berkeley, California, mimeograph, 1938. Contains an extensive bibliography in the field of anthropology, along with a good selection in history.

Malehorn, Pauline G., *The History of the Navajo Methodist Mission, Farmington, New Mexico, 1891–1948.* Mimeograph (Farmington, 1948). A mission story with some documentation, especially first three chapters, written by the mission librarian.

Matthews, Washington, *Navaho Legends.* Memoirs of the American Folk-Lore Society, Volume 5, 1897. Boston: Houghton Mifflin and Company, 1897.

McCombe, Leonard, Vogt, Evon Z., and Kluckhohn, Clyde, *Navaho Means People.* Cambridge: Harvard University Press, 1951. A photographic document study of the Navaho with a brief text based on Kluckhohn and Leighton, *The Navaho.*

McDowell, Malcolm, *Christian Missions Among the American Indians.* Board of Indian Commissioner, Bulletin No. 280; mimeograph. Washington, D. C.: Department of the Interior, 1927. Has a chronology of Christian missions among the Indians to 1921. Wrongly ascribes the *Ethnological Dictionary* to Anselm Weber.

Meriam, Lewis, and Hinman, George W., *Facing the Future in Indian Missions.* New York: New York City Council of Women for Home Missions and Missionary Education Movement, 1932. A good study of the missions.

Moffett, Thomas C., *The American Indian on the New Trail. The Red Man of the United States and the Christian Gospel.* New York: Missionary Education Movement of the United States and Canada, 1914.

Moore, J. B., *The Navajo.* Crystal, Navajo Reservation, New Mexico, 1911. Really a Navaho blanket advertisement; valuable for the excellent photographs by Simeon Schwemberger, lay Brother for several years at St. Michaels.

Moorehead, Warren K., *The American Indians in the United States: Period 1850–1914.* Andover, Massachusetts: The Andover Press, 1914. Quotes Anselm Weber to answer charges of white cattlemen and congressmen against Indians.

Morrison, William Brown, *The Red Man's Trail.* Richmond, Virginia: Presbyterian Committee of Publication, 1932.

Mosk, Sanford A., *Land Tenure Problems in the Santa Fe Railroad Grant Area.* Publications of the Bureau of Business and Economic Research University of California. Berkeley and Los Angeles: University of California Press: 1944.

Newlin, James W. M., *Proposed Indian Policy.* Philadelphia, 1881. On allotting the Indians.

Office of Indian Affairs, *Subject Index of Indian Office Circulars, numbers 160 to 1000, from July 8, 1907, to June 25, 1915.* Washington, D. C.: Government Printing Office, 1916.

Page, Elizabeth M., *In Camp and Tepee . . . An Indian Mission Story.* New York: Fleming H. Revell Company, 1915. Story of Dutch Reformed Church in the United States.

Phelps-Stokes Fund (Inquiry Staff: Thomas Jesse Jones, Charles Loran, Harold B. Allen, Ella Deloria), *The Navajo Indian Problem.* New York, 1939. Chapter 7, pp. 94–110, is a penetrating analysis of missionary work among the Navaho.

Piolet, J. B., S.J., *Les Missions au XIX Siècle.* 6 volumes. Paris: Armond Colin, 1901–1903. "Les Etats Unis," 6:165–295, by M. Alexandre Guasco, gives especially thorough treatment of the French bishops of New Mexico and Arizona.

Priest, Loring Benson, *Uncle Sam's Stepchildren: The Reformation of United States Indian Policy,* 1865–1887. New Brunswick, New Jersey: Rutgers University Press, 1942. Fine broad and thorough coverage.

Reichard, Gladys A., *Spider Woman, A Story of Navajo Weavers and Chanters.* New York: The Macmillan Company, 1934. Popular descriptive anthropology; excellent for Navaho atmosphere and landscape.

——— *Prayer: The Compulsive Word.* Monographs of the American Ethnological Society, VII. New York: J. J. Augustin Publisher, 1944.

——— *Navaho Religion, A Study of Symbolism.* 2 volumes. Bollingen Series XVIII. New York: Pantheon Books, Inc., 1950.

Riverside, California, Public Library, *Indians.* 1916. Bulletin 136.

Salpointe, Jean Baptiste, *Soldiers of the Cross.* Banning, California: St. Boniface Indian Trade School (printers), 1898. Not critical but most useful; drew on the lost Lamy Diary.

Salsbury, Cora B., *Forty Years in the Desert, A History of Ganado Missions, 1901–1941.* Ganado, Arizona, n.d. A popular history by the wife of the well-known Dr. C. G. Salsbury, former superintendent of Ganado Presbyterian Mission, and including memoirs of Mrs. Barbara Goodman, daughter of J. L. Hubbell.

Sanchez, George I., *"The People": A Study of the Navajos.* United States Department of the Interior, United States Indian Service. Lawrence, Kansas: Haskell Institute Print Shop, 1948. One of many analyses covering the requirements of the education system currently functioning on the Navaho reservation.

Saunders, Lyle, compiler, *A Guide to Materials Bearing on Cultural Relations in New Mexico.* Albuquerque: The University of New Mexico Press, 1944.

Schmeckebier, Laurence F., *The Office of Indian Affairs: Its History, Activities and Organization.* Baltimore: The Johns Hopkins Press, 1927. Excellent bibliography, especially of government documents; a thorough, broad study for the Institute for Government Research Service Monographs of the United States Government, of which this is No. 48.

Schoolcraft, Henry R., *Historical and Statistical information respecting the history, condition, and prospects of the Indian tribes of the United States.* 6 volumes. Philadelphia, 1851–1860. Part I, 1851, pp. 242–246, Charles Bent, "Indian Tribes of New Mexico."

Shiya, Thomas S., editor, *Navaho Saga: Franciscan Golden Jubilee.* St. Michaels, Arizona: Franciscan Fathers, 1949. Graphic popular sketch of Navaho life and the Franciscan mission.

Twitchell, Ralph Emerson, *The Leading Facts of New Mexican History.* 5 volumes. Cedar Rapids, Iowa: The Torch Press, 1911–1917.

United States Indian Service, *You Asked About the Navajo!* Pamphlet 5. Information Pamphlets About American Indians. Washington, D. C.: United States Indian Service, n.d. (1949). General popular survey.

United States Superintendent of Documents, *Indians.* Washington, D. C.: Government Printing Office, 1927.

Van Valkenburgh, Richard F., *A Short History of the Navajo People.* Radio Series — Station KTGM, U. S. Department of Interior, Navajo Service, Window Rock, Arizona, 1938. Excellent survey up to 1900 from good sources which are not, however, cited when used.

Watkins, Frances E., *The Navaho.* Southwest Museum Leaflets, No. 16. Los Angeles, 1943. Introductory history to a cultural study of Navaho weaving.

Webb, Walter Prescott, *The Great Plains,* New York: Ginn and Company, 1931. Pages 85–139 offer an interesting interpretation of "The Spanish Approach to the Great Plains."

Woerner, Davida, *Education Among the Navajo . . . An Historical Study.* Privately printed doctoral dissertation submitted at Columbia University, New York, 1941.

Works Progress Administration, *Arizona, A State Guide.* American Guide Series. New York: Hastings House, 1941.

——— *New Mexico. A Guide to the Colorful State.* American Guide Series. New York: Hastings House, 1940.

Articles

Coxe Stevenson, Matilda, "The Religious Life of the Zuni Child." Smithsonian Institution, Bureau of American Ethnology, *Fifth Annual Report,* 1883–1884, pp. 533–564. Washington, D. C.: Government Printing Office, 1887.

——— "The Zuni Indians: Their Mythology, Esoteric Societies, and Ceremonies." Smithsonian Institution, Bureau of American Ethnology, *Twenty-*

Third Annual Report, 1901–1902, pp. 1–634. Washington, D. C.: Government Printing Office, 1904.

——— "Ethnobotany of the Zuni Indians." Smithsonian Institution, *Thirtieth Annual Report,* 1908–1909, pp. 31–102. Washington, D. C.: Government Printing Office. 1915.

Eckel, Mrs. Le Charles Goodman, "History of Ganado, Arizona." *Museum Notes,* 6:47–50, April, 1934. Life story of John Lawrence Hubbell by his granddaughter.

Editorial, "Religious Garb and the Constitution," *America,* 6:446, February 17, 1912.

——— "Monsignor William H. Ketcham," *Franciscan Herald,* 10:5, January, 1922.

Habig, Marion, "The Franciscan Martyrs of North America," *The Franciscan Educational Conference,* 18:274–330, December, 1936.

Haile, Berard, "Racial Mentality and the Missionary," *Primitive Man,* 2:18–19, 1929.

——— "Navaho or Navajo?" *The Americas,* 6:85–90, July, 1949.

Hall, Edward Twitchell, Jr., "Recent Clues to Athapascan Prehistory in the Southwest," *American Anthropologist,* 46:98–105, January-March, 1944.

Hodge, Frederick Webb, "The Early Navajo and Apache," *The American Anthropologist,* 8:223–240, July, 1895.

Hoopes, Alban W., "The Indian Rights Association and the Navajo, 1890–1895," *New Mexico Historical Review,* 21:22–46, January, 1946.

Hurt, Wesley R., Jr., "Eighteenth Century Navaho Hogans From Canyon de Chelly National Monument," *American Antiquity,* 8:89–104, July, 1942.

Huscher, Betty H. and Harold A., "Athapascan Migration Via the Intermontane Region," *American Antiquity,* 8:80–88, July, 1942.

Indian Advocate, The, Volumes 15–20, January, 1903–December, 1908.

Ketcham, William H., "Bureau of Catholic Indian Missions," *The Catholic Encyclopedia,* 7:745–747. New York: Robert Appleton Company, 1910.

Land of Sunshine, The, Volumes 3–25, 1895–1906. Title changed to *Out West* with Volume 16, January, 1902, and continues with semiannual volumes.

Letherman, Jonathan, "Sketch of the Navajo Tribe of Indians, Territory of New Mexico." Smithsonian Institution, Bureau of American Ethnology, *Tenth Annual Report,* 1855. Washington, D. C.: A. O. P. Nicholson, printer, 1856. Good socioanthropological survey.

Lutomski, Ammian E., O.F.M., "A Padre of the Trail," *Arizona Highways,* 23:11–15, July, 1947.

(Manion, Gene) "The First American — The Apaches of Navajo," *St. Anthony Messenger,* Volumes 43–44, August, 1935–October, 1936.

Matthews, Washington, M.D., LL.D., "The Gentile System of the Navajo Indians," *The Journal of American Folk-Lore,* 3:89–110, April–June, 1890.

——— "Navaho," in Frederick Webb Hodge, editor, *Handbook of American Indians, North of Mexico,* Part 2, pp. 41–45; Smithsonian Institution, Bureau of American Ethnology, Bulletin No. 30. Washington, D. C.: Government Printing Office, 1912.

Mindeleff, Cosmos, "Navaho Houses." Smithsonian Institution, Bureau of American Ethnology, *Seventeenth Annual Report,* 1895–1896, Part 2, pp. 475–517. Washington, D. C.: Government Printing Office, 1898.

Oblasser, Bonaventure, "The Franciscans in the Spanish Southwest," *The Franciscan Educational Conference,* 18:98–121, December, 1936.

Ostermann, Leopold, "The Navajo Indians of New Mexico and Arizona," *Anthropos,* 3:857–869, 1908.

Pitaval, Archbishop J. B., "The Religious Conditions in New Mexico," in Francis C. Kelley, editor, *Official Proceedings, The First American Catholic Missionary Congress,* pp. 85–95. Chicago: J. S. Hyland and Company, 1909.

Provincial Chronicle of St. John Baptist Province, The, 1927–1950. Cincinnati, Ohio, 1927–1950. Contains much of historical value on the parishes and missions of the Cincinnati Franciscans.

Reeve, Frank D., "The Federal Indian Policy in New Mexico, 1858–1880." *New Mexico Historical Review,* 12:218–269; 13:14–62, 146–191, 261–313, 1937–1938.

——— "A Navaho Struggle for Land," *New Mexico Historical Review,* 21:1–22, January, 1946.

Reichard, Gladys A., "Distinctive Features of Navaho Religion," *Southwestern Journal of Anthropology,* 1:199–220, Summer, 1945.

Stephan, A. M., "The Navajo," *The American Anthropologist,* 6:345–362, October, 1893.

Weber, Anselm, "Navajo Indians," *The Catholic Encyclopedia,* 10:720–721. New York: Robert Appleton Company, 1911.

Newspapers

Albuquerque Evening Citizen, January 17, 1907.

The Albuquerque Evening Herald, November 19, 20, 1913.

The Albuquerque Morning Journal, November 21, 1905; December 21, 1906; November 15, 1909; September 23, 1912; November 12, 17, 18, 19, 20, 21, 24, 25, 27, 28, 29, 1913; December 4, 5, 1913; March 9, 1914.

The Carbon City News (Gallup, New Mexico), July 3, 1920; March 19, 1921.

Catholic Standard and Times (Philadelphia), February 22, 1913.

The Catholic Telegraph (Cincinnati), October 10, 1912; March 10, 1921.

The Catholic Transcript (Hartford, Connecticut), November 27, 1913.

The Coconino Sun (Flagstaff, Arizona), March 9, 1917.

The Daily American Tribune (Dubuque, Iowa), March 15, 1921.

The Denver Post, June 25, 1904.

The Gallup Independent, April 7, 1921.

The McKinley County Republican (Gallup, New Mexico), December 16, 1905.

The Michigan Catholic (Detroit), March 16, 1921.

New Mexico Union (Santa Fe), January 9, 1873.

New York Times, February 1, 2, 1905.

Ohio Waisenfreund, October 2, 1912.

The San Juan Times (Farmington, New Mexico), November 10, 17, 1899.

The Santa Fe New Mexican, December 3, 1913.

Washington Daily Morning Chronicle, November 10, 1872.

The Washington Post, February 2, 1905.

Index

Abeita, Pablo, 232
Ácoma, repaired by Mother Katharine, 139 *n*
Aldrich, S. E., 78
American Protective Association, 20
Antes, Rev. Howard R., 19, 179
Anthropology, "bone shooting," 104; ethnology and paganism, 166; inept cultural approach, 124; Navaho concepts of, 45; polytheism and social structure, 198 *n;* wizards, 75
Apaches, Jicarilla, 147
Archinger, Fr. James, 230
Architecture, 213
Arentz, Fr. Theodore, 153, 162, 220
Atlantic and Pacific Railroad, 201
Auweiler, Fr. Edwin, 216

Bierkemper, Rev., 109–110
Bizhoshi, chanter, 182
Black Horse, and anti school riot, 101
Bonner, Fr. Rudolph, 227
Bosque Redondo, 11; school at, 15
Bourgade, Archbishop Peter, 26, 56, 70–71, 125, 133, 170; accepts friars, 32; financial support from, 144; and land survey, 30; requests friars, 66
Bradley, Roy, 116
Breen, Dr., Indian school, 65
Brockmann, Fr. Herbert, 133
Brooklyn Museum, 127–128
Brown, Lieut. H. C., quells riot, 102
Browning Ruling, 80
Brun, Fr. J. B., 160
Buerger, Bro. Placid, 31, 34, 52, 70, 87; at Chin Lee, 113; death, 114
Bureau of Catholic Indian Missions, 144 *n,* 163, 179, 203
Buttermann, Fr. Eugene, 147, 170
Byalille, 178; Arizona Supreme Court decision on, 180–181

Cameron, Ralph, 195
Cañon de Chelly, 13; Sisters' excursion to, 97
Carleton, Brig. General, and Navaho campaign, 11
Carlisle Indian School, 76
Carson, Kit, 11
Cebolleta, baptisms at, 14; Navaho colonizing, 7–8; parish, 160
Chants, Mountain, 81–82
Chapelle, Archbishop, 17, 23
Chin Lee, Episcopal Mission site, 1889, 19; mission construction, 113–114; water supply of, 114
Christman, Fr. Turibius, 148
Christmas, first at St. Michaels, 40
Cienega Ranch, purchased for Navaho Mission, 23–26
Cliff dwellings, 128
Cole, Henrietta, 58, 111
Condon, James J., benefactor, 121
Connolly, George, printer, 117, 118
Conversions, 108
Cooke, Capt. George B., 31
Culin, Stewart, 127–128
Curtis, Senator Charles, 193

Dabb, Edith, 60
Daeger, Fr. Albert, 114, 147
Damon, Anson Chandler, 45
Dawes Severalty Act, 200, 206
Day, Anna Burbridge, 43
Day, Charley, guide, 58; interpreter, 42
Day, Sam E., 24, 107, 110–111; clerk at Ft. Defiance 67; ethnological collection of, 127–128
Delgado, Fr. Carlos, on early Navaho conversions, 7
De Smet, 14
Dictionary, English-Navaho, 44–45
Dine Tsossi, 213
Dodge, Chee, 227, 232; address to Navaho, 175; aids in translations, 68–69; tribute to Fr. Anselm, 189

Dolfin, Rev. J., 106
Drexel, Mother Katharine, 17 *n*, 22, 29, 66, 80, 82, 90, 113, 141; language studies, 118; and mission expenses, 37; physician, 211
Dulzo, Melania, 70, 138
Dumarest, Fr. Michael, 72, 127, 132, 160

Education, boarding *vs.* day schools, 115; Christian, 192–199; nondenominational, 194; religious, in government schools, 87–88; religious, by vote, 196; Sisters in public schools, 145–146
Egan, Anna, 155
Eldridge, Mary, 59–60
Englert, Fr. Peter Baptist, 51
Epp, Rev. J. B., 153
Ethnologic Dictionary of the Navaho Language, 118, 119
Ethnology, Bureau of, 44; encouraging paganism, 166
Everest, Blind Luke, 51

Fall, Senator Albert G., 157–158, 205 *n*
Fangmann, Fr. Camillus, 146
Farmington, Indian colony project, 65; parish, 146–147
Federal aid, 145
Fischer, Fr. Egbert, 147; and group baptisms, 196–197
Fleurant, Rev., mission at Fort Sumner, 15
Foley, John, 26, 79, 80
Fort Defiance, 28, 44; chapel at, 196; founded, 10; mission site, 1887, 17; religious instructions at, 87–88; school, 1883, 76
Fort Lewis, Indian school, 130
Fort Sill, 158 *n*
Fort Wingate, 31
Franciscans, accept Navaho Mission, 29; accepted for Navaho Mission, 32; build Cuba school, 146; chapter leaks, 133; chapter politics, 73–74; and conversion drives, 197; Hispano missions, 66; and language studies, 39; martyrs at Hopi, 149 *n;* provincial politics, 133, 161–162; of St. Louis Province, 150; 1744 mission to Navaho, 7–10; to southern New Mexico, 133; visitation, 1900, 57; visitation of, 73–74
Fryling, Rev. Herman, 45, 169

Gallup, extent of parish, 1898, 28; friars accept parish at, 169; New Mexico, parish, 160–161; New Mexico, parish prospect, 57
Ganado, mission planned, 110; Presbyterian mission, 110, 130 *n*
Ganss, Fr. H. G., 142
Gasparri, Fr., 16
Gaston, Charity A., 105 *n;* teacher, 16
Gelting, Fr. Samuel, 86
Geography, Lukachukai, 120
Gibbons, Cardinal, 23
Gietl, Fr. Andrew, 26
Gottbrath, Fr. Norbert, 144, 149, 184, 211; priest physician, 211
Government, arbitrary punishment of Indians, 177–178; Hopi passive resistance to, 149–150; and religious instructions, 117, 141; *re* transporting pupils, 79–80; treatment of Indians by, 175, 179
Granjon, Bishop Henry, 134; at Fort Defiance, 196; and Hopi project, 150; and Hopis, 155; and mission aid, 222
Grom, Fr. I. M., 148
Guadalupe Hidalgo treaty, 1848, 167

Haile, Fr. Berard, 84, 164, 215, 233; appointed to St. Michaels, 74; chaplain at school, 103; and Ethnologic Dictionary, 117–119; and the Hopi fund, 157; and Jémez plan, 146; and Lukachukai, 119–122; and San Juan mission, 136
Hartung, Fr. Frederick, 71
Harwood, Rev. Thomas, 19
Haskell Indian Institute, 143
Haskett, Mary, 155
Haverbeck, Fr. Louis, 88, 163, 217; elected provincial, 74
Hayzlett, Major, 87
Headmen friends of friars, 159, 173
Heinrichs, Fr. Leo, 73
Hesse, Fr. Jerome, 159
Hesse, Fr. Raphael, 29, 73
Hildebrand, W. E., contractor, 116
Hispanos, discrimination, 133–134; segregation, 133–134
Hodge, F. W., 166
Holbrook, Captain E. H., 152
Holmes, W. H., 166
Holtmann, Bro. Arnold, 87
Homestead law, 1875, 200
Hopi, exodus, 152; mission site, 151–152; mission site, 1889, 17; Navaho antagonism to, 150; passive resistance of, 53, 149–150, 152
Horstmann, Bishop, 218

Hubbell, J. L., 88, 107, 110, 154; politics, 140; trade, 97; Trading Post of, 53–54
Hudspeth, Marshal, 182
Huelshorst, Bro. Vital, 87
Hyde Expedition, 62–63

Indian Assn., Women's National, 239
Indian Missions, Bureau of Catholic, 17
Indian Rights Assn., 141–142, 179, 180
Indians, and liquor, 168 *n;* religious freedom for, 166
Indian Sentinel, The, 220
Indian *vs.* white cattlemen, 203–205
Industrial School, Methodist, 127
Irrigation, Black Creek, 141; McHenry project, 65; at San Juan, 126

Jémez, day school, 138; day school and convent, 144; financial aid to, 163
Jémez Pueblo, friars return to, 1900, 126
Jones, Commissioner W. A., 48
Jones, Howell, 140, 232, and statue to A. Weber, 233
Jouvenceau, Fr. Antonio, 17, 27, 62, 64, 148; San Juan missions, 56
Juillard, Fr. George J., 28; and Cienega ranch, 26; Gallup parish, 160, 169, 212; leave-taking, 171

Kalt, Fr. Robert, 171
Kendrick, Episcopal Bishop, 19
Kengott, George F., report on St. Michaels, 156
Ketcham, Fr. William, 87, 156–157; and Hopi mission, 151, 162, 188, 220, 230
King's Crossing, Methodist school, 130
Kreke, Fr. Markus, 44
Kunkel, Fr. Eligius, 133

Ladd, Horatio O., 18
Lamport, J. A., surveyor, 50
Lamy, Bishop, 14; opens Navaho mission, 15; government, 16
Land, Indian, homesteading on, 24; railroad, 30
Land base, increase of Navaho, 12–13
Law, *re* transporting pupils, 79 *n*
Leavengood, Superintendent, 106
Lemmon, Superintendent, 151
Leupp, Francis E., 140, 179; opposed to boarding schools, 115; and religious instruction, 194
Lezaún, Fr. Juan, 8
Ludwig Mission Verein, 223
Lukachukai, meaning, 120 *n*
Lummis, Charles F., 141
Lusk, Charles S., 30, 231
Lynch estate, 224

Mandalari, Fr. A. M., 231
Manuelito, headman, 198; last war chief, 175
Marquette League, 142; aids Chin Lee, 116; and the Hopi fund, 157–158
Martin, Fr. A. A., 26–27
Mass, first Christmas, at St. Michaels, 40–41
Matthews, Dr. Washington, 38
Matz, Bishop, 126 *n*
Matz, Fr. Celestin, 224
McJunkins, Bert, 84
Medicine men, paraphernalia of, 129
Menaul, Rev. John, 16
Mennonites, the, 153
Methodist-Episcopal Church, Womens' Home Missionary Society of, 59
Methodist mission, and San Juan flood, 1911, 138 *n*
Mexico, secularization laws of, 14
Meyer, Fr. Barnabas, 126, 138; and Apaches, 158
Meyers, Fr. Florentin, 126, 171
Migeon, Fr. L., Mescalero, 157
Military, overawing Navaho, 181
Missionary, hobbies, 140; long vision needed by, 214; non-Catholic among Navaho, 1902, 88; tolerance of pagan rites by, 212; use of Navaho ritual, 213
Mission Methodist Episcopal, 18, 19
Missionology, accommodation to native ritual, 213; acculturation, 72; acculturation mission, 130; anthropology, 38; architecture, 124, 168; central parish for missions, 161–162; Christianity and Navaho, 45; Christianity and pagan culture, 9; communal approach, 65; contract schools, 18, 19; co-operation with government, 198; cultural antagonism, 150; cultural block, 13; delayed baptism, 108; education, 192; effects of isolation, 66; ethnology and paganism, 166; financing, 216–224; geography, 143; hothouse religion, 124; Indian co-operation needed, 165–167; lack of educational carry-over, 123; lack of policy, 110; language, Catechism and hymns, 68; language frustration, 38; language study, 118–119; lay apos-

tles, 192; mission life, 73–74; Navaho project, 71; nondenominational instructions, 88; patronizing, 77; polygamy, 204; priestly frustration, 115, 138–139; priests as medicine men, 83; pro-mission chapter, 163; respect for corpse taboo, 107–108; San Juan mission project, 56–66; sectarianism and Indians, 172; social work, 214; socioeconomic approach, 215; Spanish and Navaho, 7 ff; Spanish proselytizing, 7; surveying Indians' lands, 50; tight culture complex, 129; vicarious compensations, 140

Missions, and agriculture, 109–110; approach to family, 192; Bureau of Catholic Indian, 30, 87, 231; Catholic, Protestants in, 153; Chin Lee, 109 ff, 173–175, 217; Dutch Reformed, 169; episcopal aid to, 222; farming colonies, 130; finances, 116, 216–224; Franciscan Society, 220; Fruitland, New Mexico, 125; geography, 143, 190–191; government aid to, 59; government indifference to, 188; Jémez, 146; Jewett, 130; Keams Canyon, 159; Lukachukai, 119 ff, 217; Lumberton, New Mexico, 147; and medical aid, 211; Mescalero, 157; Navaho opposition to, 19; Papago, 158; Peña Blanca, 70; Presbyterian for Zuñi Indians, 169; Protestant, at Hopi, 156; Protestant Navaho, 18–20; Protestant *vs.* Catholic, 172; San Juan, 125 ff; San Juan River, 64; Spanish among Navaho, 7–10; Spanish political pressure upon, 9; Zuñi, 164

Mitchell, Charley, 75, 77, 80, 211

Mormon, missionaries to Navaho, 18

Morrell, General 125

Naakai Dinae, 213; headman, 131

Nation, Carey, 49

Navaho, adult education, 59; agriculture, 5; antagonism to whites, 101; backgrounds, 3 ff; "bone shooting," 75–76; Catechism, 68; Christian, 28; community outlook, 78; country, extent of, 6; culture, 129; culture, effects of horses on, 5; and democracy, 198; democratic councils of, 82; dictionary, 68; dislike for Hopi, 52; economics of, 4, 6; English-speaking, 38; enlisting missionaries for, 26, 28; establishment of Reservation, 1868, 11; face painting, 48; farming, 198; food, 82; at Fort Lewis, 130; function of headmen, 173; geography of the, 4–6; government compulsion of 178; handcrafts of, 6; herding, 193; 199–205; history, 3–21; homesteading by, 85; Hopi antagonism to, 150; independence of, 82, 100; irrigation by, 60, 65; land area, 199; land base, 199–200; and land problems, 195–206; language, 38, 43–44, 50–51, 68, 141, 175–176; language, Christian hymns, 68; language used for religious teaching, 105; leader control, 177; livestock statistics of, 104; medicine men, 75–76; migration, 4 ff; mobility, 134; music of the, 45; name, 3 *n;* origin myth, 78; police, 178, 187; political freedom of, 168; political organization, 173; polygamy, 50, 182–184; population of tribe, 12–13; poverty of, 104; pragmatic outlook of, 78; pragmatic religion of, 112–113; prestige and control of headmen, 176–177; religious concepts of, 13, 47, 68, 129, 206–215; resistance to Christianity, 191; seasonal migration of, 123; and slavery, 10; social controls among, 168; social status of women, 185; sociology, 9 ff; and the Spanish, 6; thought patterns of, vii, 186, 187; tribal ownership of land, 201; tribe solidarity, 186; view of U. S. law, 182–183; women, 41; women, and land allotment, 204

Nurre, Fr. Bernard, 43, 57, 139

Oberly, Commissioner Indian Affairs, 18

Oraibi, 152

Osborne, Tom, 41, ranchman at St. Michaels, 27

Ostermann, Fr. Leopold, 57–58, 66, 86, 115, 215, 233; to St. Michaels, 74; study of Navaho by, 117; Tseijini Tso, 195

Overton, George, 27, 39, 41, 84, 107

Paddock, Col. G. H., 175

Palmer, H. K., 169

Paquette, Peter, 182

Peace Policy, U. S. Indian, 15

Peach Treaty: 1868, between U. S. and Navaho, 11; stipulations, 15

Peña Blanca, 87; cemetery, 114; New

Mexico, mission, 70–72; Sisters arrive, 140; superiors, 133
Perry, Reubin, 152, 166, 173–174, 189
Pinart, M. Alphonse, ethnologist, 51
Pitaval, Archbishop J. B., 170; and Anselm Weber, 222; and San Juan mission, 146
Pius X, Pope, 221
Polygamy, 204
Pope, Judge W. H., 187
Population, Navaho, 12–13
Presbyterians, 109–110; given Navaho mission, 16
Priests, Navaho, 42; number in Southwest, 1866, 15
Propagation of the Faith, Society for, 170
Proselytizing, Protestant, 162
Protestant mission, government subsidy for, 111
Protestants, opposition to denominational instructions, 194
Public schools, religious instruction in, 141
Pueblo Indians, Fr. Anselm's aid of, 189; marginal Christianity of, 168; political autonomy of, 167; Protestant approach to, 168

Quick Bear vs. Leupp, 142

Railroads, and Indian land, 201-206; land exchange, 202; land policy of, 30
Rainfall, Lukachukai, 120
Rechsteiner, Fr. Mathias, 158
Reductiones, 109; attempted Navaho, 191
Reel, Estelle, 141
Rehoboth, Dutch Reformed Mission, 106 *n*
Riggin, Rev. F. A., 19
Riordan, Dennis M., 76
Roberts, Rev. J. M., 16
Rolly, Fr. Michael, 148
Roosevelt, Pres. Theodore, 140; on Anselm Weber, 190; and Indian treaty funds, 141–142
Roswell, New Mexico, 133–134
Ryan, Archbishop, 219

Sacraments, Baptism of adults, 213; first Baptisms, 70; *propter homines,* 197
St. Anthony Messenger, Mission issue, 224
St. Catherine's School, 57, 80; Navaho pupils, 76–81
St. John Baptist, Franciscans Province of, 73–74
St. Michaels, accepted by friars, 29; almost abandoned, 67; *beneplacitum,* 88–89; buildings, 35; cavalry encamped at, 152; change in policy at, 215; conversions at, 213; converted trading post, 31; description of, 1902, 91–95; finances, 113, 137; financial support of, 216–224; first Indian school, 1899, 46–48, 68; first Mass, 36, 40–41; first sermons at, 44; founding of, 22–31; founding of boarding school, 73 ff; friars arrive, 1898, 33; friars' house at, 89–90; headmen consult at, 175; housewarming, 42; inn and pawn shop, 212; land, problems of, 84; land, purchased, 25; mission house, 217; mission press, 223; Navaho mission plan, 146; plan of first building, 31; post office, 1902, 88; printing press, 118–119; winter rations, 40
St. Michaels School, 85; construction of, 86; enrollment figures, 108; First Communion Class, 108; first Sisters, 96–97; founding, 82–86; Hopi pupils in, 150; illness of pupils at, 107–108; impact on Indian culture, 123; industrial training at, 106; objectives, 83; opening, 103
Salpointe, Bishop J. B., 16–18; made archbishop, 64
Sandford, Fr. Felician, 147
Sandoval, headmen, 129–130
San Juan, land problems of, 137; mission attempt, 126–138; mission site, 134–137
San Juan River, debated Navaho mission, 27; offer of mission on, 56
San Juan Times, 63
Santa Fe, transfer of see, 222; trial of Navaho, 183, 187
Santa Fe Railroad, 30, 140; land gift by, 225
San Xavier del Bac, 222
Schell, Fr. Leander, 87
Schilling, Fr. Godfrey, 28–29
Schnorbus, Fr. Juvenal, 31, 34, 73, 77, 133, 154; leaves St. Michaels, 74
Schools, boarding, 193; day, failure of, 192–193; government contract, 18; St. Catherine's, 22 ff
Schuler, Fr. Denis, 73
Schuler, Minister General, 221
Schuster, Fr. Fridolin, 226, 233
Schwemberger, Bro. Simeon, 87, 103

Scott, General Hugh, 180, 184–187; and Anselm Weber, 188
Sectarianism, effect on Indians, 172; Protestant, 106
Sells, Commissioner Cato, 231
Sendbote, 142–143, 219
Shelton, Navaho agent, 135, 136
Shelton, W. T., 178, 182, 185, 186
Shipley, Dana, 100 ff
Shiprock, irrigation at, 1903, 129
Shoemaker, Samuel, 125, 129, 135
"Signatures," 195
Simpson, Dick, trading post of, 61
Simpson, Lieut. J. H., 1849 expedition of, 13
Singers, Hatali, death, 227
Sisters, status in government schools, 145
Sisters of the Blessed Sacrament, 84
Slaves, Navaho, 14
Society for Preservation of the Faith, 218–219
Springob, Bro. Libor, 133
Squatters rights, 25–26, 84–85
Staud, Fr. Hugh, 44 *n*
Stephan, Msgr. J. A., 22, 23, 26, 28, 87 *n*
Stevenson, Matilda Coxe, ethnologist 164
Storff Fr. Hugolin, criticism of mission, 215
Stuerenberg, Fr. Francis, 72
Survey, of mission land, 30, 84, 121

Thacker, George, 45
Theobald, Fr. Chrysostom, 161
Thuemmel, Bro. Gervase, 112 *n;* builder, 122
Tilik, Fr. W. A., 34, 70
Trading posts, mission at Chin Lee, 111; Moore's, 79; Noel's, 64; Round Rock, 78; Samson's, 107; Wyant's, 84–85
Treaty, 1868, 199
Tree-ring dating, 4
Trigo, Fr. Manuel, 8
Tripp, Mary, 59–60, 127
Trockur, Fr. Emmanuel, 159
Troester, Fr. Marcellus, 115, 153, 215; made superior at St. Michaels, 233; Tohatchi, 122
Two Grey Hills, Methodist mission, 58

Utes, 4–5

Valentine, R. G., on religion in public schools, 194
Van der Wagen, A., 169
Verwyst, Fr. Chrysostom, 68

Walker, Frank, 28, 68–69, 181, 232; Beautiful Mountain, 185
Warfare, Navaho, 10 ff; United States *vs.* Navaho, 10
Weber, Fr. Anselm, actionist, 193; advises Senator Curtis, 193; against corporal punishment, 105; and Apaches, 158; assigned to St. Michaels, 31; and Byalille Affair, 179; called *Chischilli,* 47; and Carey Nation, 49; chapter requests, 73–74, 113; construction supervisor, 86; on "conversion drives," 197; co-operation with officials, 197–198; correspondence, ix, 205; and Cuba survey, 146; and debts, 221, 224; definer, 163; diary, 46; early life, 34–35; and eclipse of moon, 99; in Europe, 116, 157, 222–223; explores the San Juan, 58 ff; first Navaho pupils of, 46–48; frustration, 138–139; as ghost writer, 222; and headmen, 198; and Hopi mission, 154; as horseman, 195; horse trades, 63; illness, 71; illness and death, 226–234; and Indian land, 206; and Laguna, 226; land lobbyist, 226; and land problems, 199–206; language studies, 118–119; letter on ethnologists, 166; lobbies for Indians, 189; and marginal Christians, 214; meets Mother Katharine, 80; mission outlook, viii; mission reports, 70, 71; mourned by Indians, 232; *The Navajo Indians,* 204, 205 *n;* obituaries, 231; ordination, 34; peacemaker, 173 ff, 189; personal glimpse of, 91–92; poverty of, 230; as preacher, 140; prestige in Washington, 226–227; and provincial politics, 162–163; and public school religious instructions, 194; receives last Sacraments, 229; refused bishopric, 223; relatives, 227; San Juan mission report, 65–66; San Juan trip, 57–65; and severalty, 201; and study of Navaho language, 45 ff; as surveyor, 84, 121, 202; teacher, 34–35; and temperance, 107; thrown by horse, 131; and Ute Indians, 126 *n;* vacation, 1905, 141–143; views on Pueblo Indians, 167; visit to Hopi villages, 53–55; wins status of headman, 199; writings, viii–ix, 40
Welsh, Herbert, Indian Rights Assn., 20
Wetherill, Lynn, 103

Whorton, Josephine, 81
Whorton Drexel, Mrs. Joseph, 141
Wilkin, Joe K., 24, 25, 64, 100, 103
Wilson, Captain, 177, 178
Wilson, Francis C., 187
Women's Natl. Indian Assn., 59
Wyant, J. M., 24, 25

Yazhe, Fr. Berard, 122
Young, S. A. M., 232

Zeug, Fr. Herculan, 143
Zumbahlen, Fr. Fintan, Farmington, 147
Zuñi, friars return to, 163; marginal Christians, 160, 164–165